The
Ethical
Crises
of
Civilization

For my Family and Friends,
who renew my hopes for Humanity

The
Ethical
Crises
of
Civilization

Moral Meltdown
or Advance?

◆

LESLIE LIPSON

SAGE Publications
International Educational and Professional Publisher
Newbury Park   London   New Delhi

For information address:

 SAGE Publications, Inc.
2455 Teller Road
Newbury Park, California 91320

SAGE Publications Ltd.
6 Bonhill Street
London EC2A 4PU
United Kingdom

SAGE Publications India Pvt. Ltd.
M-32 Market
Greater Kailash I
New Delhi 110 048 India

Printed in the United States of America

Library of Congress Cataloging-in-Publication Data

Lipson, Leslie, 1912-
    The ethical crises of civilization: moral meltdown or advance /
Leslie Lipson.
        p.   cm.
    Includes bibliographical references (pp. 320-326) and index.
    ISBN 0-8039-5242-2.–ISBN 0-8039-5243-0 (pbk.)
    1. Civilization, Modern—1950- —Moral and ethical aspects.
    2. Civilization—Moral and ethical aspects. 3. Civilization—
Philosophy. I. Title.
CB430.L56 1993
901'.3—dc20   93-7505
                                                                      CIP

93 94 95 96 10 9 8 7 6 5 4 3 2 1

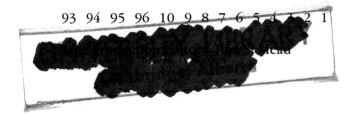

Contents

Movements and Events of Note in Selected Civilizations
(Those of special ethical significance, good or bad, are in boldface.)

Time Period	China — Political and Social	China — Ethical and Cultural	India — Political and Social	India — Ethical and Cultural
Before 1000 B.C.	Shang kingdom Chou kingdom	Sinic culture evolves along Yellow River Bronzes Progress in mathematics, astronomy	Walled cities at Harappa and Mohenjo-daro Aryan invasion **Castes introduced**	Indus culture **The Rig-Veda** **Hindu metaphysics**
1000-500 B.C.	Rival kingdoms (Spring and Autumn period) 722-481	**Lao-tzu ?600-531** **Confucius 551-479** Advances in medicine, astronomy	Kingdom of Magadha	Mahabharata **Bhagavad-Gita** Upanishads **Gautama, the Buddha ?563-483** Mahavira, the Jains, 600-527

Mesopotamia, Egypt, and Persia		The West	
Political and Social	*Ethical and Cultural*	*Political and Social*	*Ethical and Cultural*
Civilizations of Nile Valley, Sumer and Akkad	Developments in mathematics, astronomy, alphabetic writing	Minoans in Crete Mycenaeans on mainland Greece	Art at Knossos
Babylon			
	Code of Hammurabi	Trojan War	
Egypt unified			
Ikhnaton 1385-1358			
Assyrian Empire			
First mention of Arabs in Assyrian inscription, 853 B.C.	Assurbanipal's library, Assyria **Zoroaster, ?630-553**	David & Solomon, Kings of Israel **Solon's reforms in Athens, 594**	Homeric poems **Hebrew prophets**
Cyrus founds Persian Empire, 553-529		Roman Republic, begins in 509	Thales, Greek philosopher, 624-545
		Democracy in Athens, 508	

Time Period	China		India	
	Political and Social	Ethical and Cultural	Political and Social	Ethical and Cultural
500-1 B.C.	Great Wall begun Warring States 453-221 King Cheng of Ch'in unifies China as Emperor Shih Huang-ti 221-210 Han dynasty, from 202 Expansion of empire	**Contending schools of philosophy** Technical inventions Influence of Legalists in Kingdom of Ch'in **Scholars executed, books burned** **Ban on punishment by mutilation,** 167 **Emperor Wu-ti makes Confucianism official doctrine,** 136	Alexander's invasion, 326 Mauryan Empire, 323-185, **reaches peak with Ashoka,** 273-232	The Arthashastra, treatise on political power Advances in mathematics, grammar Buddhism divides into Mahayana and Himayana
1 A.D.- 500	Han dynasty ends, 220 **Rebellion of Yellow Turbans** Period of Three Kingdoms	First census, 2 A.D., population of 58 million Production of paper and steel Invention of wheelbarrow Spread of Buddhism	Guptan Empire, 320-550 Peak in reign of Chandra Gupta II, 375-415	Cultural peak Kalidasa, playwright

Mesopotamia, Egypt, and Persia		- The West	
Political and Social	*Ethical and Cultural*	*Political and Social*	*Ethical and Cultural*
Empires established by Seleucus and Ptolemy in succession to Alexander	Hellenistic Age Library at Alexandria	Persian wars Periclean Age Peloponnesian War, 431-404	History writing, tragedy, and comedy The Parthenon
Parthian Empire		Empire of Macedon Alexander's conquests, end of independent polis Roman Empire expands Emperorship replaces Republic	**Socrates, Plato, and Aristotle** **Stoicism** *Jus gentium* Augustan Age in literature
Sasanids rule in Persia		Age of the Antonines, 96-180 Christianity becomes official religion of Rome Papacy established Roman Empire ends in the West, 476	**Jesus of Nazareth ?4 B.C.-27 A.D.** **Romans persecute Christians** All inhabitants of empire, except slaves, receive Roman citizenship, 212 St. Augustine

Time Period	China		India	
	Political and Social	Ethical and Cultural	Political and Social	Ethical and Cultural
500-1000	China reunified by Sui, 589 Tang Dynasty, 618-909 Administrators recruited by competitive examinations, 669 Chinese defeated by Arabs at River Talas, 751	Cultural peak Buddhism and other foreign religions suppressed 842-845 **Neo-Confucianism** Block printing of books, 868 Inventions in mechanics	Political disintegration	Rock carvings at Ajanta and Ellora Philosopher Shankara 780-820
1000-1400	Sung Dynasty, 960-1279 **Formula for gunpowder, first mentioned, 1044** Mongol conquest, Yuan dynasty 1260-1368	Artistic peak **Foot-binding of women** Su Tung-Po, poet and painter, 1036-1101 Compass used in ships	Muslim invasions from Ghazni in northwest Sultanate of Delhi, 1206-1388 **Tamerlane sacks Delhi, 1398**	Muslims crush Buddhism Ramanuja, philosopher, 1025-1137 **Firuz, 1351-88, abolishes torture**

Islam		The West	
Political and Social	*Ethical and Cultural*	*Political and Social*	*Ethical and Cultural*
Umayyad caliphs at Damascus 661-750	**Mohammed,** 570-632	Byzantine Empire ruled from Constantinople	Justinian's Digest of Roman Law
Abbasid caliphs at Baghdad, from 750	Hegira, 622	Germanic kingdoms in Western Europe	Academy closed at Athens
Moors in Spain	Division between Sunnis, Shiites		The "Dark Ages"
	Spread of Islam	Franks halt Arab advance	Cultural decline
	Arabs learn papermaking from Chinese	Charlemagne, ruled 768-814	
	Cultural peak at Cordoba	Holy Roman Empire, founded 800	
Saladin 1170-1193	Persian poets, Firdawsi, Omar Khayyam, Sa'di	Consolidation of kingdoms	Monastic movement
Mongols sack Baghdad, 1258	Philosophers, Avicenna, Averroës	Feudalism	Universities founded
End of caliphate	Ibn Khaldun, historian, 1332-1406	Holy Roman Empire	**Christians persecute Jews**
Ottoman Empire founded		Papacy at peak	Church sculpture and architecture
		The Inquisition	**Francis of Assisi,** 1182-1226
		The Crusades	
		In England: Magna Carta, 1215	Thomas Aquinas, 1226-1274
		First Parliament 1265	Dante, 1265-1321
			The Black Death, 1347-1351

Time Period	China		India	
	Political and Social	Ethical and Cultural	Political and Social	Ethical and Cultural
1400-1750	Ming dynasty 1368-1644 Naval expeditions to Indian Ocean, Persian Gulf, and Red Sea, 1405-1433 Europeans reach China by sea Ch'ing dynasty (Manchu) begins in 1644	Peaks in arts and scholarship Ku Yen-wu, historian, 1613-1682 Philological criticism, Tai Chen, 1723-1777 Official compilations and encyclopedias	Babur founds Moghul Empire (Muslim), 1526 Akbar, 1556-1605 Penetration by Europeans British Empire supplants rivals	Nanak, 1469-1538 founder of Sikhs Moghul arts The Taj Mahal
1750-1914	Chinese Empire at greatest extent 1789 European penetrations Opium War, 1839-1842 Decline of Manchu dynasty T'ai P'ing Rebellion, 1851-1864 Boxer uprising, 1900 End of Manchu dynasty Sun Yat-sen establishes republic, 1912	Literary Inquisition by Emperor Ch'ien-lung, 1774-1789 Chang Hsüeh-ch'eng, philosopher of history, 1736-1796	British rule India Mutiny of Indian Army, 1857 Indians admitted to Civil Service	Higher education of Indians in English

Islam		The West	
Political and Social	*Ethical and Cultural*	*Political and Social*	*Ethical and Cultural*
Ottomans capture Constantinople, end of Byzantine Empire	Architectural peak	Protestant Reformation **Peasant revolts**	The Renaissance revival of Greco-Roman studies
Ottoman Empire at peak		Columbus crosses Atlantic, 1492	Humanism in Florence
Suleiman I, 1520-1566 Safavid Dynasty in Iran Shah Abbas, 1588-1629		Western Europeans build maritime empires **Wars between Catholics and Protestants** Nation-states organized English revolution Parliament supreme	Leonardo, Michelangelo, Machiavelli, Copernicus, Galileo, Shakespeare, Cervantes, Rembrandt, Descartes, Newton, Leibniz **Age of Toleration**
Ottoman Empire declines Revolution of "Young Turks," 1908	Stagnation of Islam	Absolute monarchies Revolutions: American, French, Industrial Napoleon Smith, Marx **Colonial empires at peak** **Rebirth of democracy** Cities expand **Functions of government expand to control economy, create social justice**	**The Enlightenment** Voltaire, Rousseau Musical peak in Germany, Austria Bach, Mozart, Beethoven **Declarations of Rights** Philosophy at peak **Slavery abolished** **Humanitarian reforms** Emerson, Thoreau, Nightingale **Women's status improves** Darwin, Freud, Einstein Influence of the press **Universal public education**

Time Period	China		India	
	Political and Social	Ethical and Cultural	Political and Social	Ethical and Cultural
1914-1992	Nationalist regime from 1927 under Chiang Kai-shek	Philosopher, Hu Shih, 1891-1962	British power declines	**Mahatma Gandhi leads nonviolent resistance**
	Civil war of Nationalists versus Communists	**Egalitarian ethic**	Movement for independence grows	Rabindranath Tagore, poet
	Japanese invasions and occupation, 1931-1945	Cultural Revolution victimizes intellectuals	**India independent, 1949**	Sectarian conflicts
	Communists win power, 1949	Population explosion	**Leadership of Nehru**	Population explosion
	China governed by Marxists		**Social democracy**	**Mother Theresa**
	Mao Tse-tung dies, 1976		**Disabilities of "Untouchables" removed by law**	
	Peasants and businessmen allowed to produce for profit			
	Tanks crush demonstrators in Beijing, 1989			

Islam		The West	
Political and Social	*Ethical and Cultural*	*Political and Social*	*Ethical and Cultural*
End of Ottoman Empire	Western influences versus anti-Western traditionalism	**World War I**	**Movements for social democracy**
Kemal modernizes Turkey as secular republic	Rise of religious fundamentalism	Russian revolution	Physicists split atom, harness its energy
Arab states established	Shiite theocracy in Iran	**League of Nations**	**Atomic bombs**
Nationalist movements		Economic depression	**Advances in health, welfare, and education**
Oil flows out, wealth flows in		**Fascism, Nazism**	
		Adolf Hitler	**Challenges to racism, sexism**
		World War II	
		United Nations	**Universal Declaration of Human Rights**
		End of European empires	**Ethical leaders: Albert Schweitzer Pope John XXIII Martin Luther King, Jr. Eleanor Roosevelt**
		Separate states multiply	
		European community created	
		United States at peak of power	
		"Cold war" of United States versus Soviet Union	Impact of television
		Proliferation of nuclear weapons and missiles	Technological advances in communication, electronics, genetic engineering
		Dissolution of Soviet Union	

NOTE: Because warfare, slavery, the subjection of women, and inequalities of wealth and status have been co-eval with civilization, they are not listed under particular periods.

Foreword

*I*n the beginning, according to an ancient Chinese myth, there was a creature called P'an-ku. P'an-ku kept growing, ten feet every day, and on its death the various parts of its body were transformed into the world we know. One eye became the sun; the other, the moon. Its voice turned into thunder; its breath, into wind; and so forth. But from which part of P'an-ku would you imagine that we humans evolved? As the Chinese believed, we are all descended from its fleas.

This book is a commentary on the civilizing of P'an-ku's fleas.

Preface

I wrote this book because of a deeply felt conviction that we have arrived at a critical stage in human history. Both the opportunities for improving our current level of civilization and the dangers of self-destruction are far greater than they have ever been. There is, I believe, a growing awareness of the fact that we face unprecedented choices, that it is now realistically possible to create on earth either a paradise or a hell. Hence it is the obligation of a scholar to do what one can, by contributing to the public discussion such knowledge as may be useful, by raising the issues that are crucial, and by stating unequivocally which values would help rather than harm us. While my academic discipline is political science, I do not belong to that school of thought that prides itself on being "value-free." Instead, I consider it one's duty both to express the opinions to which one is led by the evidence and to apply the results of long studies, in Bacon's phrase, "for the relief of Man's estate."

This work has occupied ten years—six of them spent in reading about the world's major civilizations and four in the writing. The genesis of the idea occurred in discussions with my late wife, Elizabeth Monroe Drews, with whom I coauthored *Values and Humanity.* Her values and ideas, had she lived, would have resulted in a book somewhat different than this in content as well as interpretation. My own point of view, derived from extensive reading of history and social thought and reinforced by a lifetime of observation and reflection, is that of the humanist and philosophical rationalist. In politics I am what would be called a liberal in the United States, a social democrat in Europe.

The members of my family and various friends have helped me through these labors, in many more ways than I expect they realize.

I want particularly to thank those who were so generous with their time as to read earlier drafts and to give me their invaluable, constructive criticism: Kenneth E. Boulding, Ernst B. Haas, Lawrence Senesh, Patricia Springborg, and Milton Stern. Also, I express my gratitude to Bonnie Nadel of the Frederick Hill Associates Literary Agency in San Francisco, who read the entire manuscript twice and offered her expert suggestions. To Sara Miller McCune, Publisher and Chairman of Sage Publications, I have a special debt. Not only does she believe that this book is saying something significant and timely to thoughtful members of the reading public, but her good taste and wise experience have strengthened the work editorially. As with my previous books, the typing was superbly done by Sheila Saxby, who both transformed an untidy scrawl into elegant print and appropriately questioned those statements that might need further reflection. During the research and writing, I neither sought nor received any grants from any source, nor did I have the help of any assistants. Hence I take full and sole responsibility for everything in the text. Finally, my abiding thanks are due to my wife, Helen Fruchtman Lipson, who has supported me in every possible way—reading the draft of every chapter and commenting with her sound judgment. Moreover, she has steadfastly tolerated those alternating spells of protracted silence and continuous eloquence that are the occupational disease of writers.

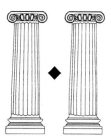

We all know civilization is
in danger. . . . Man's
attitude to the world must
be radically changed.

Havel

1

Prologue

The Paradox of Our Time

*P*romise and peril together, both to a degree unparalleled in the past, confront humanity at this time. The possibilities open to us as we await the advent of a new millennium extend across a range immeasurably greater than ever before in the history of our species. Moreover, the contrast between the options at the two extremes could by no stretch of the imagination be more stark. For human civilization has evolved to the point where either collective annihilation or collective betterment has become a practical choice—a choice that no previous generation has had to face.

By now, we have acquired the knowledge and possess the means to improve the quality of life substantially for far larger numbers than was possible in past ages. If we are so minded, the opportunity is ours to eliminate, once and for all, the ancient evils of hunger, poverty, and ignorance, as well as many forms of disease. Beyond that, we could create a more just and more humane society than has yet been achieved, except in a few very small and relatively uncomplicated communities. The Good Society of the philosophers' theories was once, as Plato said of it, "a model set up in the sky."[1] Tomorrow, it could become the reality on earth.

But while we glimpse those lofty heights, an abyss yawns at our feet. Starting in 1945, after discovering how to release the energy locked inside the atom, the first practical use we made of that knowledge was to manufacture nuclear weapons that we have since stored away in huge numbers and that many countries are now able to produce. So deadly are these that, if employed on a large scale, not only would civilization come to an end, but most forms of life would be extinguished across wide expanses of our planet. But even if no bombs explode, yet another deadly threat endangers our physical survival. Systematically, we are proceeding to destroy the physical environment on which our very lives depend. Not a day passes without our poisoning the air we breathe, the water we drink, the food we eat. Simultaneously, we are using up the Earth's resources, many of them irreplaceable, at a rate that is as reckless as it is ruthless. Hence, if our self-destruction does not come about through the "Big Bang" of nuclear fission or fusion, it could be accomplished through the slow but equally sure death of environmental decay.

The Moral Crisis That We Face

It is this dual potentiality, either for unprecedented good or for unprecedented evil, that marks this point in time as unique in human evolution. Such possibilities as these were never within reach of any previous generation; to us, however, they have presented themselves simultaneously. Consequently, we face not only the opportunity, but also the necessity, to choose. In the fact that such choices exist, as in the nature of our options, lies the paradox of our time.

Self-evidently, this choice is a moral one. By this I mean that, aside from the other factors—political, economic, or technological—that may enter into it, the primary considerations are questions of ethics. For these options are the products of human activity. They are the fruit of our brainwork and our handiwork. They present antithetical values concerning human relationships. Are we not therefore responsible before the bar of history for how we choose? What course of action, we must ask, would now be right or wrong, wise or foolish, under these circumstances that we ourselves created? What is the good way to act or the bad? And most important of all, what is the likelihood that we shall opt for the good and avoid its alternatives?

I wrote "alternatives" in the plural because our lives, whether individual or social, do not consist only of simple, clear-cut dichotomies where we are restricted to two possibilities. A third possibility remains that, because it is intermediate, permits of several gradations. If past experience is a valid guide to the future, does it not seem likely that the coming decades might turn out to be neither the utopia of our dream nor the holocaust of our dread? May not the future, at least in the short run, be a confused continuation of this bizarre blend of opposites that form our contemporary world—a clash of progress and barbarism, a contradictory state that contains elements of peace and war, a perplexed age of aspirations and anxieties? Indeed, the two coming generations, whose strengths will be at their peak during the first half of the next century, may merely reproduce our own ambiguous pattern. They could drift and flounder in a crisscross of tendencies, exactly as we are doing, surviving without significantly advancing. If that should occur, the results, although unsatisfactory, would be preferable to the worse of the alternatives stated above. But they will be greatly inferior to the better. If humanity manages somehow to muddle along in a moral limbo, replete with its conflicting values and contradictory trends, there would be tremendous relief in that we did not perish from bombs or pollution. Yet the relief would be accompanied by the consciousness of failure, because in all honesty we would have to recognize that our achievement could have been so much better. To see the good and to know that it is feasible, but then not to accomplish it, is a confession of shame.[2]

There were other times in the past that resemble ours in one particular respect that, looking back with the advantages of hindsight, we can identify them as turning points. Changes occurred of a kind so fundamental that the ensuing period differed in important features from the preceding. That our age is one of these turning points cannot be doubted. What we do not yet know is the direction in which humanity will turn. Nor can we be at all certain that, however strong the need to change, the better option will in fact be seized. Did not other generations before ours miss the opportunities presented to them? The British historian G. M. Trevelyan wrote thus about the events of 1848, when uprisings against autocratic regimes erupted across Europe: "The year 1848 was the turning-point at which modern history failed to turn. The military despotisms of Central Europe were nearly but not quite transformed by a timely and natural action of domestic forces. It was the appointed hour, but the despotisms just succeeded in surviving it."[3] This is a sobering reminder, and particularly so in the early 1990s when a new attempt is under way to transform the age-old despotisms of central and eastern Europe. But Trevelyan's remark has wider reference than that, and it prompts us to inquire of ourselves: Are we keeping our appointment, or will we too miss it?

Finding ourselves in so extraordinary a situation, it is essential that we consider our prospects of choosing wisely. Which of the various possibilities, we must ask, is the most probable? What is the likelihood that we shall in fact realize the existing potential to improve the quality of life for masses of people? Or are we just as likely to destroy ourselves? Or instead, shall we continue muddling along in this twilight zone between a breakthrough and a breakdown? Is there a right way, and how can we find it?

I am writing this book because of my deep conviction that such a way does exist. Although undeniably difficult, it is certainly possible. That can be stated as a fact because something like it did happen in the past; and what has happened before could occur again. Put succinctly, what the world needs most at the current time is a revolution in our ethical practices—in our practices, I emphasize. The right principles are already well known; indeed, they have been known for two and a half millennia. Our problem is to transform practice to conform with principle. How can that be done? The starting point must be a clearer intellectual comprehension of what is at stake, resulting in a sufficient psychological goad to impel us into collective and individual action. My hope through this book is to contribute to that end.

What We Can Learn From History

To acquire the necessary understanding, a rich source exists from which we can derive enlightenment. That source is our own history. Whenever an ethical argument is presented—to the effect that such and such ought to be done—its plausibility is strengthened by the demonstration that this, or something like it, did happen at some past time and place. At the very least, such an argument cannot then be dismissed on the ground that it is utopian or impractical; and, at the most, if the consequences were beneficial in the past, they inspire some hope for our own future. Much of the content of the following chapters therefore, particularly in the first half of the book, draws heavily on the historical record for comparisons, analysis, and explanation.

But how are we to use that record? Always, the answers elicited from Clio, the Muse of History, are shaped by the framing of the questions. Those who ignore the "lessons" of history, we are constantly reminded, are condemned to repeat its mistakes. How true! And at this stage in our evolution, ignoring the past is no excuse for committing similar errors in the present. But the general statement that we should learn from history must be offered with a necessary reservation. History does not repeat itself, Voltaire observed; historians do. It is impossible for history to repeat itself in the identical form for compelling reasons. No two events can recur in precisely the same context. Also, the later event is influenced to some extent by the memory of the earlier. Hence we should remind ourselves that, whenever we observe a similarity between this epoch and one in the past, we should not overlook the other factors that mark our age as different.

There is, first, the new fact of life that our current problems are global. From this it follows that their solutions must similarly be global. It was in the twentieth century that a world war took place, followed by a world depression, and that in turn by a second world war. In former periods, the effects of a catastrophe in any one civilization or region could be contained, because the rest of humanity was seldom affected. That is not the case today, when interdependence—not independence or isolation or autonomy—constitutes the reality of living on this planet. Terrorism, drugs, AIDS, nuclear fallout, acid rain, and global warming transcend the boundaries of nation-states and mock the jurisdictions of their governments. All of them can affect anyone in the world, anywhere. No one is wholly immune or safe. Of similarly universal scope are famine relief, economic and technical assistance, and a concern for fundamental rights. These are valid not merely for nations but for humanity.

Nay, more than that: Interdependence has now become the precondition for human survival. This is because of the second feature of today's world that marks us off from the past—namely, the options now available. Their character makes it less likely that coming generations will be able to drift along as was done heretofore. Why is this so? Because the current alternatives contain imperatives that we can hardly evade or escape, and their resolution will require a treatment that in the light of tradition is thoroughly radical. The awareness that the knowledge and the mechanisms now exist for ensuring a higher quality of life for all humanity has given rise in this century to what is aptly called "the revolution of rising expectations." The world's underprivileged,[4] who are the great majority in Asia, Africa, and Latin America, will not permanently accept their age-old inequalities, particularly when the contemporary media display continuously the visual evidence of what others enjoy. "A house divided against itself cannot stand."

Nor can a world with a double standard. The demand for more equitable sharing is inexorable; eventually, it will be irresistible.

The opposite alternative—the end of civilization and the extermination of much of our species—is inconceivable to the sane. But we should not on that account dismiss it from a rational calculus. Can one call it sanity that prompted the accumulation of the stockpiles that now exist in the United States and the republics of the former Soviet Union, and to a lesser degree in Britain, China, and France? If heads of governments have been insane enough for more than four decades to think that security can be ensured by hoarding so many weapons of this type, at some time in some place someone will be insane enough to use them. And even if their use is not ultimately sanctioned by a demented person in authority, there is the very high probability that mechanical error—a malfunctioning computer, for example—or human error in interpreting the signals on a radar screen[5] could trigger humanity's holocaust. A solution to this problem has to be found if our species is to endure. No less suicidal is the wanton despoliation of our physical habitat that continues by incremental steps day in and day out. The wealthy and the well educated are doing this from shortsightedness and greed; the poor act thus from a combination of compelling need and desperation. Whatever the motive, the effects are the same. All of us—governments, private corporations, individuals—are together destroying the Earth that sustains us. That being so, paradoxical though it sounds, what would otherwise appear utopian or visionary assumes the guise of urgent practical necessity. "Business as usual" is no longer a realistic formula. If there is to be any world tomorrow, today's idealism must become tomorrow's realism.

Because the choices we face include some that are without precedent, does it not follow that the solutions, to succeed, must involve some fundamental innovations? We should search in our history for the experience of those ages when humanity needed, as we do today, to consummate a significant ethical advance, and then either achieved it or failed. To the extent that such situations offer parallels with our own time, presumably we can learn something from past success or failure. By the same logic, where no parallels are applicable, we must perforce invent, as did our forebears on some critical occasions. Because today's conditions are unique in vital respects, we would be wiser to draw encouragement from the spirit or attitude with which our ancestors approached their problems than to imitate the specifics of their attempted solutions.

The Keys to Understanding

For a discussion of such topics to make sense, the analysis should rest on a few key concepts that form, as it were, the central pillars to support the argument. In this work, they are these three: civilization, values, and ethics. These, as I shall show, are interrelated and mutually reinforcing. It is the use of these concepts that differentiates my treatment and interpretations from other writings in this field.

In the mid-eighteenth century, Rousseau composed an essay on a theme announced by the Academy of Dijon: whether the reestablishment of the arts and sciences had contributed to a moral improvement.[6] The question that I am addressing is related to that, but broader in its terms of reference. I am exploring humanity's ethical development during the course of civilization and am inquiring into where and when we advanced or regressed. If some pattern, some relation of cause and effect, some general conclusion, should emerge, it could offer us hope or warning in our contemporary situation.

The Meanings of Civilization

Why, you will ask, do I select civilization as the basic social grouping for this inquiry? There are good reasons for this choice. The alternatives are either too restrictive, such as states whose function is government, or too formal and abstract, such as society or culture, which are analytical terms employed by sociologists or anthropologists. Civilizations possess the merit of being historical entities with a record. You can write the history of civilization; you cannot write the history of culture or society. Moreover, for purposes of comparison, civilizations are not nearly as numerous as states nor as ephemeral. The total identified thus far ranges between two and three dozen, less than ten being in existence today. Civilizations have not only been the rarest of social phenomena, but they are the most complex of all social works of art.[7] They are indeed our culminating collective creation. Only within civilization, and through the opportunities it provides, can human potentialities unfold to their fullest. That is why, in terms of space and time, the major civilizations have extended over vast areas, even across continents, and a few have endured for more than two millennia. That is why the future of our species on this planet will be whatever kind of civilization we manage to create.

When we speak of civilization, however, what does this mean? To which of its several characteristics do we attribute a special importance? These are necessary questions because previous thinkers have disagreed about where to place the emphasis. There are those, for example, who maintain that technology is the criterion that identifies a civilization and endows it with its character. Thus a modern Chinese philosopher, Hu Shih, who was a disciple of John Dewey, contrasted Eastern and Western civilizations in terms of the tools they used—human labor in Asia, machines in the West.[8] The American historian Charles A. Beard held the same view, affirming that "Western or modern civilization is in reality a technological civilization."[9]

Others prefer a social to a material criterion. Not surprisingly, the etymology of the very term *civilization* has supplied a clue. Kenneth Clark suggested the point in this way, although with some reservations: "Cities, citizen, civilian, civic life: I suppose that all this ought to have a direct bearing on what we mean by civilization."[10] Likewise Lewis Mumford, the social philosopher of *The Culture of Cities*, states emphatically: "The city is the point of maximum concentration for the power and culture of a community. . . . Here in the city the goods of civilization are multiplied and manifolded. . . . Here is where the issues of civilization are focused."[11]

Undeniably there are elements of truth in arguments that emphasize these factors. But the full truth has more to it than that. For surely those interpretations miss the essence. Is this all that we have in mind when we think of civilization? Is it even the most important? Is civilization synonymous with its technology or its urban framework? Take the case of ancient Athens for an example. Is the significance of Athens primarily due to its technology, which extracted silver from the mines at Laurium, or built the triremes for the navy, or fired the kilns for its ceramic industry? Is it even the *acropolis* and *agora* and those long walls that protected the *polis* and joined it to its outlet, the port of Peiraeus? Or is it rather Socrates questioning the Athenians in the *agora* and questing for truth? Is it Pheidias and Ictinus together embodying their concept of the beautiful in the marble that they fashioned into the Parthenon? Is it Pericles speaking for *demokratia* at the funeral of citizen-soldiers who had died that Athens might live? Is it Sophocles probing the drama of human destiny as the *Oedipus* is performed in the theater of Dionysus? For all of these happenings, technology furnishes the means and the city supplies the stage. True, but who supplies the meaning of the play? And just what is that meaning?

The Primacy of Ethical Values

As can be inferred from those queries, the real meaning of civilization lies at another level. To lead us to it, consider this insightful judgment by Ruskin. "Great nations," he said, "write their autobiographies in three manuscripts, the book of their deeds, the book of their words and the book of their art. Not one of these books can be understood unless we read the two others, but of the three the only trustworthy one is the last."[12] Ruskin was on the right track, but I would substitute yet another book: the book of their values. For me, the prime distinguishing feature of a civilization is the values that it espouses. These are what endow a civilization with its significance; these are what mold the lives and shape the behavior of the human beings whom a particular civilization embraces. By their values therefore shall we know them.[13]

A civilization, in this respect, resembles a single person, and the reasons why this is so are rooted in human nature. In the ordinary course of living as individuals, we are continually faced with alternatives. Something has to be done, and we could accomplish it in several ways. Whenever we act, we are preferring one kind of behavior over others, selecting among the various possibilities the one that seems best under the circumstances. These preferences indicate our priorities; the latter express our values; and these mold our character.[14] And it is just the same with those large human groupings that we call civilizations. What character is to an individual, civilization is to humanity. For a civilization is essentially a choice of values. It endows a cluster of people with a recognizable personality. By whatever values it selects, a civilization defines itself and thus resembles or differs from others.

Our values, of course, are of many kinds because they are relevant to varied facets of our lives and to the several spheres that are basic to our being human. These include our image of the universe and of our place in it, our aesthetic appreciation of beauty and ugliness as we perceive them, our intellectual standards involving the quest for truth, and—above all—the social bonds that unite us with others. Among these, the values that hold the primacy are the ethical. This is for the self-evident reason that we are social creatures first and foremost. Ethics consist in the principles by which people behave, or are supposed to behave, in all their relations with one another. They embrace the entire gamut of our transactions, both public and private. They include both our standards and our behavior.

I believe it is necessary to examine the standards and evaluate the practices, even though clear-cut judgments may be impossible. For if human civilization is to continue, let alone advance, self-awareness is essential. How can we formulate long-term goals unless we understand where we are now? And does not such understanding require insight into where we came from and how we arrived here? One recalls that Socrates, when on trial at the age of 70, said that he had not been satisfied to lead "an unexamined life."[15] The meaning of that profound remark could well be applied by us all to the world we inhabit. We, too, cannot function or survive in an unexamined world. In earlier ages, people might be content to resign their future to what they considered to be fate or fortune, or to the arbitrament of deities in whose power they believed. We cannot. In our times, such formulations would be patent evasions. Notions of that sort, employed in this day and age, are childish alibis for our ignorance, our weakness, or our fears. They confess our inability and unwillingness to mobilize the intelligence we possess and summon the necessary willpower to trace a reasoned path to a better future.

Faulkner once wrote that human beings are the only creatures who can both laugh and cry because we are the only ones who can see things as they are and as they ought to be. His comment is apt. What makes a being human is our self-consciousness. As humans, we remember the past; we anticipate a future; we are cognizant both of continuity and of change. Both in speech and in writing we communicate to others whatever we think and how we feel. We can imagine better alternatives to what now exists. We can conceive of programs to be developed in decades ahead whose outcome we shall not live to see. Only one ineluctable necessity governs the human condition—the certainty that each of us must die. Until that day comes, many possibilities are open, among which we possess some freedom to choose.

In each of these respects, the human animal is unique. These are the capacities that distinguish us from other creatures. They explain why we have made so strong an imprint on this planet, why we even succeeded in leaving it to step upon the Moon. That event, first occurring in 1969, was a spectacular demonstration of the power of science and technology when harnessed to efficient social institutions. Yet, as we take pride in that achievement, we also ask ourselves about the wisdom of a policy that allocates scarce resources of highly trained persons, of precious money and materials, to such a goal—before the Earth itself, on which those daring adventurers gazed back from outer space, has rid itself of hunger, ignorance, poverty, disease, and war. The supreme issues of our time, whether phrased in terms of politics or economics or science or technology, are fundamentally ethical in that they concern our treatment of our fellow human beings. That is basic to everything else.

But when I speak of ethics, I do not imply that this is synonymous with good ethics. All values are two sided; every good has its antithesis. The ethical values of Albert Einstein and Albert Schweitzer, of Eleanor Roosevelt and Mother Teresa, of Pope John XXIII, the Reverend Martin Luther King, Jr., and Mahatma Gandhi, were not those of Adolf Hitler or Joseph Stalin. Each of those individuals made a profound difference to civilization in the twentieth century. Our social record consists of the evil as well as the good. Although we sometimes think of civilization as a beneficent process of qualitative improvement, its actual history, as there will be many occasions to note, is marred by endemic ills. Not only are these coeval with it, but they persist alongside the continuing progress. The virtues we admire—all the glorious achievements of mind and imagination, the building of more humane societies, the increased rejection of racism and sexism—are balanced by our vices—the grossly unequal distribution of wealth, the injustices in the relations between social classes, and the wars of organized communities.

Therein lies our fundamental paradox. Whoever inspects the social record of our species on planet Earth confronts a medley of contrasts and contradictions, inextricably intertwined—of good and evil, wisdom and folly, compassion and cruelty. We owe to L. T. Hobhouse the pointed reminder that "there is an evolution of evil as well as of good."[16] Our ethics form a double helix where our higher aspirations and our frequently opposite practices spiral around each other, and where the criterion of what could and should be is the measure of the shortcomings of what is. These inherent conflicts will supply a recurrent motif throughout this work.

Theme and Variations

Such then is the theme that the following pages will explore, drawing on the past to illuminate the present and assessing the present so as to estimate what may be possible or probable in the future. Chapter 2 will examine the highly contrasted values in the long-enduring civilizations of China and India. That will prepare the way for Chapter 3, where I shall discuss the split personality of Western civilization, which has yet to decide definitively between its two conflicting traditions. Because some civilizations died out in the past and disappeared, the circumstances and the reasons for their rise or decline will be explored in Chapter 4. Any general conclusions should help us to assess the standings nowadays of contemporary civilizations. Then comes the topic of Chapter 5, one that is always a stimulus to speculation: Why is it that civilizations have experienced certain periods of peak performance when their achievements were at the highest? When did these occur, and where? These general questions will then be applied in Chapters 6 and 7 to those specific occasions of the past when momentous advances occurred of an ethical character. After that, I shall focus on this incredible century of ours and shall attempt to draw up the balance sheet of its hopes and horrors, its triumphs and tragedies. That will provide the subject of Chapters 8 and 9. Finally, Chapter 10 will look ahead and hazard guesses about our possibilities and probabilities as we enter a new millennium. What are the prospects for our species to inhabit One World in harmony?

In addition to my focus on ethical values as central to the discussion, this work also differs from earlier treatments in the philosophy I hold and in the assumptions that permeate my argument. Because a reader is entitled to know where an author stands in these matters, I should make my position clear at the outset. Philosophically, I write as a rationalist and a humanist. I think that human history, although animated by our passions and replete with irrational happenings, is susceptible to rational understanding and analysis. The faith to which I adhere is a faith in humanity. It is based on the potentialities for good that reside within our species; and, whereas the differences of race and culture, of nationality and civilization, are meaningful and genuine, I think them far less important in the long run than the common humanity that unites us all. The world that we share has become at this time a dangerous place. But amid the dangers, there is hope. For our hopes to be realized, we need clear thinking, the wisdom to choose the right values, and the boldness to dare. The discussion in the following pages is pointed, I trust, in that direction. If my conclusions should require some melting of golden calves, some secularizing of sacred cows, some challenges to conventional thinking, so be it. A humanist does not speak with the professed objectivity of the social scientist or with the dogmatic certainties of the "true believer." The evidence concerning the human condition must be evaluated in the light of humane values and on the scale of human possibilities.

When you do not know
life, how can you know
about death?

Confucius

He who at the time of
death, thinking of Me alone
[Krishna], goes forth,
leaving the body, he attains
unto my Being. There is no
doubt in this.

The Bhagavad-Gita

2

This-Worldly China, Other-Worldly India

$\mathcal{V}$alues, as we conceive them, are abstractions. They acquire their specific content, however, within a particular civilization. It is here that they leave the mind, as it were, and come to life within a social and historical context. Therefore, to understand better what the values signify, we should examine their impact on the civilizations they animate. For this purpose, I am selecting three major examples, all long lasting and all in existence today. This chapter will discuss China and India; the following chapter, the West. Because these three contain at least half the human race, if any valid conclusions emerge, they would tell us much about civilization and about humanity.

This-Worldly or Other-Worldly Values

How does one proceed to compare whole civilizations, these being so complex and all-encompassing? There is a possible way, if one is to avoid a mere recital of separate and unrelated data. The mass of facts must be grouped around some basic criteria that supply human beings with their "operative ideals."[1] In all civilizations these are the values expressed in our conceptions of the universe, of humanity's place therein, and of the ethics that seek to regulate the social system. How then can these be meaningfully sorted out and compared?

In the process of speculating on these large questions, civilizations have generally veered toward one of two polar opposites or have zigzagged between them. The choices are these: The dominant values of a civilization may be either this-worldly or other-worldly. If the former, the focus of concern is what happens to human beings during this life. Not only is humanity the center of any this-worldly system of values, but the world in question is this universe of phenomena that we perceive through the senses and comprehend through the intellect. Such beliefs may properly be labeled rationalist because reason, and reason alone, is the ultimate arbiter of their truth or falseness. They can also be called humanist because the beginning and end of the inquiry is the human condition. This does not imply that there are not forces external to humanity that function in the physical universe and whose operation, when discovered, may be formulated as laws. But these forces are not personified; still less are they thought to be endowed with any will or intention affecting human life in general or rendering judgment on individual conduct. The inference to be drawn from all this, insofar as it has a bearing on human behavior, is very clear: This life is the only one of which we truly know. Therefore we should make the best of it. Our fate is in our hands.

The alternative view rests on opposite beliefs and reverses the priorities. According to this thinking, reality cannot be found in the data of sense perception. Because the images that the senses present are changeable and contradictory, their picture of existence is not truth but illusion. The truth is elsewhere; it underlies, or lies beyond, the appearances. Reality transcends this finite world of the here and now. It can be known only through an intuition that is more mystical than intellectual and that flashes on a true self or soul submerged within the sensate phenomena. Our mortal existence is a preparation for the soul's afterlife in another world of being, the realm of the powers manifesting themselves in the universe. Translated into religious terms, these powers are conceived as gods, culminating in some theologies in the notion of a single omnipotent Supreme Being.

Both of these sets of beliefs, this-worldly and other-worldly, have their variants. In certain movements, indeed, the logic may not be contrasted as sharply as in the summaries just presented. Thus Confucius, whom I shall interpret as a humanist, does not refute the concept of Heaven (*T'ien*); whereas Gautama, although his prescription is to seek the other-worldliness of *nirvana,* excludes deity from his teaching. In actual historical cases, what matters is the emphasis, the priority, the central focus. Are our values directed to this life or an afterlife, to this world or another? Do we think we are in charge of our destiny or the objects of a nonhuman force? And if the latter, is this an impersonal mechanism or some Supreme Judge with a controlling purpose?

In analyzing three of the major civilizations, it will be apparent that each has contained its crosscurrents and countermovements. No historical experience is wholly of one kind or the other. Nevertheless, there is generally a prevailing pattern that sets the tone. As a result of this, and depending on which choice is preferred, the operative ideals will vary and the practical consequences can, literally, be poles apart. One set of values accepts the world around us and tries to improve it; the other prefers to withdraw from this life and seek salvation elsewhere.

That contrast supplies the theme of this chapter and the next. This-worldly values were paramount in the Confucianism that became central to Chinese civilization, whereas an other-worldly vision has permeated India. For its part, the West suffers from a split personality, consisting in a maladjusted fusion of the two contradictory principles. That is why we are so puzzled and confused about our direction.

The Civilization of the Chinese

The unique importance of China in world history is the self-evident justification for treating it first. In addition to being one of the longest-enduring continuous civilizations, it has shaped the lives of more human beings than any other. Even today under a new dynasty, differing from its predecessors in some respects though otherwise resembling them, this civilization continues to mold one-fifth of the human race. There must be an explanation for such a unique accomplishment. Is it possible to discover it? In particular, can someone who is not Chinese, especially a westerner, really comprehend this extraordinary people? Granted the pitfalls, one must nevertheless make the attempt, and I draw encouragement from a comment of Goethe's at a time when the Western world was far less informed about the Chinese than we are nowadays. In one of his conversations with Eckermann, he mentioned that he was reading a Chinese novel. To which his friend responded: "A Chinese novel? That must be rather curious." "Not as curious as one might be tempted to think," said Goethe. "These people think and feel much as we do, and one soon realizes that one is like them."[2] Let us then assess the achievement of the Chinese civilization, with emphasis on the values that it has espoused.

A civilization that has lasted so long and endured so much, which has embraced so many people and covered so huge an area, has faced the problem of maintaining a continuous identity. Crises arose at fairly regular intervals because of internal breakdowns or external threats, crises that compounded the ongoing need to hold together a diversity of peripheral cultures through the potent attraction of a central core. In the history of this people, certain persistent themes emerge with vivid clarity. We read of a distinctive civilization, labeled Sinic, evolving along the midcourse of the Yellow River and its tributaries, and of the surrounding peoples gradually becoming "Sinicized." The same story is repeated of those conquerors from the North and West—Mongol and Manchu alike—who battered down the defenses of a declining dynasty, installed their own regimes, but then eventually succumbed to assimilation by the conquered. We learn of divisions reappearing—how East and West, North and South, would pull apart and then, laboriously, be reunited across a span of centuries. For this to happen, for that same sequence of events to recur in widely separated epochs, there must have been some nuclear force that survived intact despite change and challenge. What was it that possessed enough strength to hold China together? Can it be pinpointed?

Yes, it can. Indeed, there is nowhere you look in China where you will not find it operating. During four millennia the building block of China's civilization has been its family system. The family, not the individual, has always been the nucleus of Chinese society. Combinations of families created larger entities, the villages, which served in turn as the foundations for the still larger urban aggregates ministering to the needs of wider areas. Although basically a kinship group, the family performed functions that were social, economic, and religious, and also, in some respects and at certain periods, even military and governmental. Dynasties could come and go, territories the size of European states could be added or lost, central power might wax or wane, but the family system endured. Through it all, as generation succeeded generation, indestructible China lived on.

Where, then, did the values of Chinese civilization fit into that scheme of things? This is a question that, given the character of the Chinese culture, can admit of only one answer. For values to gain a wide acceptance, they had to be compatible with the fundamental facts of the family system. Viewed in this light, expressions of the ideal were the natural extrapolations of social realities. A clue to this is supplied by the composition of the character that in Chinese writing signifies "what is good."[3] This character consists of two parts. The left side represents a woman; the right, children. What clearer evidence could one seek of the central importance of the family? The dominant values were those that could explain, justify, or sanctify the role that the family performed within society—that is to say, explain to the intellectuals, justify to the moralists, and sanctify to the superstitious. Keeping this in mind, let us examine the basic values and concepts of China's civilization to see whether they were what might be expected.

Metaphysics and Morals

In the conception of life that evolved among the Chinese, the notions that stand out most prominently are those of *yang* and *yin* and the teachings of K'ung Fu-tzu (Master Kung), latinized by westerners as Confucius. If any ideas could be called distinctively Chinese, marking out the thought of this people and molding its behavior, these are the principal ones. What becomes evident on examining them is that they are statements about the importance of the family.

Yang and *yin* are the terms for two forces manifesting themselves in the universe. Although opposites, they are complementary in the sense that neither can take effect without the other.[4] Yang is active, positive, and strong; yin is passive, negative, and weak. Yang is further represented as light and male; yin, as dark and female. The connection between these stereotypes and the patriarchal Chinese family is obvious. This pair of forces was believed to operate on the five basic elements that compose the world and govern it in sequence—namely, water, fire, metal, wood, and earth. Their relation is circular, given that water extinguishes fire, which melts metal, which destroys wood, which subdues earth, which absorbs water.[5] The significance of such notions is what they reveal about the cast of mind that shaped them. Here is an image of a universe in dynamic flux, regulated by complementary principles balancing one another in a rhythmic succession. This is an orderly universe, obedient to its inner laws, knowable and to some extent predictable. Absent from it is the kind of doctrine that has played a major part in some other civilizations— that of the absolute, the transcendent, the supernatural, of an omnipotent will ruling by a mix of command and caprice.[6] The Sinic universe was the macrocosm where the interaction of yang and yin produced a harmony, which male and female reproduced on earth by their own interaction within the family microcosm.

This imaginary cosmology was not, however, the central concern of Confucius, the most revered and far and away the most influential of the Chinese sages. Primarily, he was neither metaphysician nor speculative philosopher but an ethical teacher. Even in the field of ethics, his recorded sayings consist of a medley of moral maxims, which he is content to propound without inquiring, as Socrates would have done, into their logical validity. The focus of his interests is this world, of whose existence we can be certain, not another world about whose possible nature we can only surmise. In this world, it is human behavior that engrosses him. The contrast between how we live and how we ought to live is the theme he reiterates. He sees people around him, high and low alike, leading bad lives. This need not be so, he reflected, for it was not always so. Earlier, in the time of the Chou dynasty, society had been more virtuous. Why could it not be thus again? How could the current corruption be eradicated? By what principles should rulers and ruled govern their conduct?

The Confucian Orthodoxy

Confucian teaching revolves around a few fundamental ideas.[7] These are *jen,* signifying humanity, the common bond that unites our species; *chün-tzu,* the noble or superior person, in the sense of goodness rather than high birth; *li,* which connotes order, propriety, and ritual; and *te,* the power that derives from moral example. Together, these notions constitute the core of his ethics. *Jen* would inspire us with love for our fellow creatures, thus leading the way to altruism. As *chün-tzu,* we would give priority to ethical qualities and not to status, power, or wealth. Observing *li,* we would be conscious of our responsibilities and obligations, rendering their due to all in proper form. *Te* would be the inner strength that radiates outward from those imbued with moral goodness.

Confucius (551-479 B.C.) lived in a time of political turmoil and personal insecurity. He therefore made it his mission—one might call it his obsession—to reform the society around him by restoring what he believed were the higher standards of a past era. This he sought by various means—the personal example of upright conduct, teaching a higher ethic, training a band of disciples, seeking public office, and advising the rulers of kingdoms in a China not yet unified and hence at war within itself. Confucian principles, as is evident, were tailor-made to extend across the social and political structure from the private intimacy of the immediate kin group to the public functions of an emperor. The same rules, and the same style of rule, that governed the family could be applied to governing the empire—for was not the latter, in a metaphorical sense, the great family of the Chinese?[8] Society was constituted as a hierarchy. Those of lower status must show respect to superiors, while the latter reciprocally fulfilled their duties toward inferiors. Within the ideal family, significantly described as "five generations in one hall," filial piety (*hsiao*) should link children to parents and unite the living with the dead, whose spirits were objects of worship. Outside the family, in the great society, ultimate homage was due to the emperor, the "Son of Heaven" entrusted with the "Mandate of Heaven." The lines of obligation flowed in both directions, upward and downward. Also, they extended outward, because "in the four seas all men are brothers." Sincerity, righteousness, moderation, reciprocity, and ceremony—these were the necessary pillars of family, province, and empire.

Confucius died a frustrated man and, as it must have seemed, a failure. Society had not been reformed. The rulers whom he had tried to influence—including those of his own kingdom of Lu—rejected the way of virtue that he prescribed. But something remarkable happened three and a half centuries later during the reign of Wu Ti, the fifth emperor of the Han dynasty. This powerful and long-lived monarch held sway over the China that Shih Huang Ti had finally welded into one. The Hans were centralizers and expansionists, pushing out their dominions in all directions—into Korea, to the southeast and thence overseas, and also westward so as to stop incursions by the troublesome Huns (Hsiung-nu). A vigorous policy, if it is to bear fruit, needs an organized administrative base, and durability demands a stabilizing ethic. The emperor of a unified China could safely do what appeared so unsafe to the kings of the Warring States. He could give official blessing to the morality of Master Kung, exactly as Constantine, in the hour of Rome's political and military need, would convert to the religion of the Christians.[9]

In 136 B.C. the teachings of Confucius were adopted as a state cult. Institutionalization swiftly followed. The dicta of the sage were systematized; Confucianism was born. By Wu Ti's orders a national academy was founded, whose curriculum consisted of studying the ancient classics plus Confucian ethics. Still later, beginning in 606 A.D. under the Sui dynasty, appointment to the highest posts of officialdom depended on a mastery of these subjects, which the candidates displayed in rigorous competitive examinations. Thenceforth, what was originally propounded as reformist ethics was transmuted into the orthodoxy of a conservative establishment, whose influence managed to survive the vicissitudes of 13 centuries. The morality of Confucius became, in practice, the mores of the Mandarins.

This history suggests several queries that invite reflection. How is one to characterize the teachings of Confucius? How did they relate to other Chinese philosophies and to religious beliefs? Why was this the body of doctrine that a powerful emperor would bless with official sanction?

Confucianism, in essentials, is an ethical system whose principles were intended to apply throughout society to both private and public relationships. When you start evaluating this system, the descriptive categories that first suggest themselves to a Western mind are humanist and rationalist. Its thinking and values are primarily of this world, and they are those of an optimist. What the sage observes is a sick society whose distempers he thinks can be cured. Confucius is not one of those theorists, of whom China has had its fair share,[10] who see human nature as bad and recommend a regimen of strong restraints. Nor does he follow the mystical route, proffering salvation in another realm of Being or through some total change of consciousness. There is enough common sense, plus a touch of skepticism, in his outlook to insist on making life more tolerable here and now. What follows, then, is a series of prescriptions for a hierarchy of stable relationships within the family and beyond it, all based upon the mutual observance of duties and ceremonies. Surely, that is the secret of its appeal to the Chinese. Here we have the apotheosis of the family, whose image was projected on the larger screen of kingdom or empire: hence its acceptance by those institutions, hence the reinforcement it supplied to the conservative influences of continuity and tradition.

I have been referring to Confucianism as a body of ethical doctrine. But is this also a religion? Was it so regarded by the

Chinese? These are questions whose answers will further illuminate the values of that civilization. In point of fact, they have engendered no little discussion. Confucianism has been interpreted in one of two ways: as a human-centered ethical system, designed as a model for our conduct during this life on earth, or as ethics that also includes a religious content among its appropriate rites and beliefs. Some scholars have argued, as does Arnold Toynbee, that "religion . . ., in any civilization, is the key to the civilization as a whole."[11] This is a judgment with which, as a humanist, I disagree. Hence it makes a difference to our analysis which of these two views of Confucius is taken as correct.

There are those who consider Confucius an agnostic and compare his thinking with the tradition of European rationalism. A modern Chinese sociologist, Yang Ch'ing-k'un, in a careful essay on this subject, has written as follows:

> In the spectrum of opinions already expressed on the matter, one may discern one leading view, which dwells upon the rationalistic and agnostic nature of Confucianism. This has been maintained by a long line of Western scholars from Voltaire to James Legge, as well as by modern oriental scholars such as Suzuki in Japan and Liang Ch'i-ch'ao and Hu Shih in China. Some modern Chinese have even considered that, because of the dominance of Confucianism over the Chinese social and political order, the rationalism of Confucianism has logically given rise to a rationalistic Chinese society in which religion plays only an unimportant part, if it is admitted to exist at all.[12]

Doubts about this interpretation, however, have been expressed by Herrlee Creel, who attributes it to later influences and does not find it stated earlier than the Sung dynasty. He and others, including Yang himself, point to Confucius' own references to *T'ien* (Heaven) and to his approval of sacrifice and other religious rites.[13]

Where Chinese scholars and Western orientalists disagree among themselves, one who is neither of these is at risk in expressing a judgment. Nevertheless, it appears to me that Confucius' teachings, unsystematic and diffuse as they are, follow a main drift, and it is this that explains in what manner they could subsequently be applied. As an ethical teacher, Confucius is highly pragmatic. When he speaks about right conduct, his patently sincere idealism is mixed with counsels of prudence. While propounding reform, he is the true conservative who advocates what he thinks, fancifully or not, to have been the best of the old, traditional ways.

Because he seeks a close-knit, hierarchical society, he accepts those customs that instill reverence and foster solidarity. Among these, inherited from the past, are certain notions and practices that Confucius simply incorporates under the heading of *li*, the appropriate rites and ceremonies. The Shang dynasty had a concept of *Ti* (God) or *Shang-ti* (High God), and the early Chou had employed the concept of Heaven (*T'ien*). Both Ti and T'ien were supposed to have some influence on human destiny. In addition, there was the traditional belief in the spirits of one's ancestors, which could help you if you showed them respect and might hurt you if you did not. These the sage treats as a cautious conservative would. He says in so many words that he does not know much about them, yet he is not prepared to affirm a disbelief. Indeed, his rationalism comes to the fore in his oft-quoted statement: "When you do not know life, how can you know about death?"[14] If I may express his attitude in contemporary terms, he is prudently paying the premium on an insurance policy. Those beliefs, after all, could be true. Ti and T'ien may exist; there may be spirits. Acting on this assumption does not harm society. On the contrary, it reinforces family unity across the generations while inculcating the proper deference to higher powers in society at large. So, go ahead and worship your ancestors. Offer them sacrifices and give T'ien its due. This is all reasonable, worldly wise, and thoroughly non-metaphysical. And let us recognize that his pragmatism worked after its fashion. For almost two millennia, his ideas functioned as the canonical values of a durable civilization.

The Taoist Alternative

But, having said that, let me now backtrack and pursue the discussion along another line. Thus far I have focused on Confucian values because these, in conjunction with yang and yin and the Five Elements, have been central to China's civilization. But that does not complete the picture. For there was another aspect of China that was not Confucian, that existed concurrently and was sometimes in competition.

What appears the strength of a value system, when seen from one point of view, is its weakness when judged from another. There were Chinese for whom to be rationalist and humanist was not enough, who did not share the caution of the conservative, who wanted more than ceremony and pragmatism. Among the other beliefs that gained a following, two acquired a special significance: Taoism and Buddhism. Why was this? What values did they emphasize that Confucianism did not?

Taoism expresses a strain of China's civilization in marked contrast with the qualities esteemed by the Confucians. The term itself comes from *Tao,* the "Way," in the title of the movement's basic text or Bible, the *Tao-te-ching* (the Way and Its Power). This is the work attributed to Lao-tzu, the "Old Master," of whom many stories are told but nothing has been historically authenticated. The book exists, however, and somebody had to be its author. Moreover, like a flower giving off a scent that is purely its own, the contents of this work exude an individual personality, Chinese but hardly typical. If one follows the Way, one takes leave of Confucius' circumscribed world of pieties and proprieties. Lao-tzu is one of the earliest exponents of a philosophy that has always had an appeal to certain individuals and social groups in Asia as in the West. We humans are conceived as a part, a very small part, of the universe or natural world that obeys the laws of its existence and follows its own rhythms. The right way for us to live is to conform to nature; then we shall spontaneously express ourselves as we truly are. The wrong way is to bow to the constraints that the social structure imposes. For that is something artificial, constructed by human beings and imposing its curbs on what our natures crave. The way of salvation is to withdraw from social activity, discover one's inner essence, and become absorbed in the oneness of the universe that can only be intuited and that words can never define.

This alternative is a far cry from the Confucian ethic. Be done with ritual, it says; abandon *li.* Instead, follow the Tao and set yourself free. That was a message that attracted many—some to the life of quiet contemplation, others, as in the case of the Yellow Turbans,[15] to active revolt against constrictive institutions. Moreover, the appeal of Taoism ranged across several levels. It soared to the enlightenment of the mystic, but it also sank into vulgar superstition. Mysticism, as Huston Smith has well remarked, can become mystification.[16] For the less sophisticated and the more emotional, there are always shamans and charlatans who exploit credulity. So it was with "popular" Taoism, which degenerated into magic and similar rubbish.

Unlike Confucianism as its founder taught it, Taoism possessed many of the attributes of a religion. It had a creed whose content was other-worldliness. Its truths were attainable through nonrational intuitions. It bred both saints and priests. Rejecting conventional ceremony, it nevertheless produced ceremonies of its own. All in all, it holds a special place in Chinese civilization. Liang Ch'i-ch'ao has written: "Since China's indigenous culture contains no religion, the history of Chinese religion is made up mainly of foreign religions introduced into China. . . . Taoism is the only religion indigenous to China."[17] Significantly, this one religion that grew from Chinese soil had a close affinity with the powerful movement that of all the foreign imports most influenced the Sinic culture. That one was Buddhism.

The Buddhist Intrusion

The teachings of Gautama were such as to appeal to the same mentality as would listen to Lao-tzu. Your salvation, the Buddha had said, lies within you; release from pain is yours to grasp. What you must do is to exercise the strongest control over the desires and stimuli of the sensate world. Concentrate your psychic energy on the contemplation of your inner being. If you follow the Eightfold Path (the Tao of the Buddhists), enlightenment awaits you at the end. You will have extinguished (*nirvana*) the finite self. You become one with the infinite.

There was so much in this to which a Taoist could subscribe—notably the rejection of conventional society and the focus on inward redemption—that Buddhism and Taoism developed an ambivalent relationship. They might cooperate and even merge, or they could act as competitors for clientele in the same spiritual market. In the latter case, each had an advantage it could exploit. Taoism could represent itself in truth as indigenously Chinese, while arousing xenophobic prejudice against a foreign rival—which some of its practitioners were not loath to do. But the Buddhists had an advantage on their side, which for half a millennium enabled them to hold their own. They developed the institutions of an organized religion, complete with its priesthood, monasteries, landed property, and financial assets. With good reason, Buddhism in its organized manifestations has been called the Catholicism of Asia. The parallelism is indeed striking. Except that it lacked a pope and a central office to expound and propagate the faith, the Buddhist presence in eastern Asia was remarkably similar to that of the Catholic church in medieval Europe.

Buddhism began spreading in the Middle Kingdom, as the Chinese called themselves, in the first and second centuries A.D., during the later phase of the Han dynasty. When that dynasty finally disintegrated, three and a half centuries elapsed (220-581) during which China lacked a central authority. This was "a time of troubles" analogous to that of the Warring States, which had preceded the first unification under the Ch'in. The Confucianism that had become a pillar of imperial power under the later Han was no longer in a position to resist the inroads of the new doctrine. Amid the persisting insecurity, Buddhist monasteries afforded oases of order, peace, and hope. The faith from the foothills of the Himalayas adapted itself to China, organizing among its adherents entire communities of the faithful.

The consequences that followed anticipated by a few centuries what Europe was to experience under Catholic domination. There was the spiritual life and asceticism for some, the growing wealth of the monasteries and with it their worldliness, an inspired outpouring of architecture and sculpture, and a fervor among the credulous masses who fell prey to the crudest superstitions. All of this came to a climax when political unification was reestablished by the short-lived Sui dynasty and then was continued under the illustrious T'ang. Buddhist power within society had grown to a degree that provoked an understandable reaction. The monasteries were functioning as states within a state. Strong in their economic base and the zealotry of their members, they claimed an autonomy that challenged the empire at its core. Students of Western history will note the parallel between Europe's long travail under the papal doctrine of the Two Swords, which underlay the controversies over the investiture of bishops and the power to tax the clergy, and the earlier arguments over essentially the same issues depicted in Chinese characters, as when the monk Hui-yüan (334-417) proclaimed his separation from the temporal arm in a "Treatise Explaining the Reasons Why Monks Are Not Obliged to Pay Homage to Sovereigns." In 819, when a relic of the Buddha was moved from one site to another, there were scenes of mass hysteria that prompted Han Yü, leader of a literary movement in favor of the "ancient style," to write a scathing diatribe.[18] If monks could so incite the gullible, the social order was at risk. In the years 842-845, the emperor struck back. The foreign religions were banned; their institutions were broken. On Buddhism, being the most prominent, the blows fell heaviest. The sequel was a reaffirmation of Confucian orthodoxy, but with changes. Some elements of Taoism and Buddhism were eventually incorporated into a synthesis that has been named neo-Confucianism.[19] In this form, and with some later refinements and modifications, China endured through the regimes of Mongol, Ming, and Manchu.

There is much in this history that is instructive. The experience of China demonstrates that a durable civilization requires a continuing social nucleus around which its members may cohere. The values that they most prize should be such as to harmonize with this social nucleus, reflecting and reinforcing it. Their function is to supply a rationale to the intellectuals and a morality to the masses. But because no large and complex civilization moves solely in one direction, across it flow the currents of a counterculture that seeks another channel. This, too, the Chinese cosmology is flexible enough to explain. Are not the twin phenomena of Confucian dominance and its Taoist or Buddhist alternatives an illustration of the complementarity of yang and yin?

The Indian Social Order

Moving the focus of the discussion from China's civilization to India's provides a revealing study of similarity and difference. The principal difference consists in the centrality of religious beliefs among Indian values and in the special nature of those beliefs. It is significant that Lin Yutang, a Chinese intellectual of the twentieth century, when editing a book of classic writings, *The Wisdom of China and India,* observed that "India is a land and a people intoxicated with God."[20] Comparing India with China means reversing the positions of yang and yin. The other-worldly attitudes supply the Sinic civilization with its secondary theme. In India, however, they predominate. Hinduism has no counterpart to Confucius. And in this century, when the movement for Indian independence from the British found a leader who could arouse the passive millions to nonviolent action, this was a spiritual and moral teacher, Mohandas K. Gandhi, called the Mahatma ("Great Soul"), an attorney turned ascetic. In no other country of the modern world has a saint evoked such a response. India is different.

But what is of special interest to a humanist studying civilization is that the difference accompanies a profound resemblance. The family unit, which we have seen to be the nuclear force in Chinese civilization, and which became the focus of Confucian ethics, is no less fundamental among the Hindus.[21] For three millennia at least, India, like China, has consisted basically of a mosaic of families. Yet the value system that evolved among the Hindus is in many respects a contrast to that which has expressed the ideals of Sinic civilization. What is this contrast, and can it be explained?

Although it is true that Hindu society is cemented together from family groupings, the resulting mosaic is arranged in a pattern that is absent from China. The big difference is India's caste system. This has consisted of the four main classes of *brahmins* (priests), *kshatriyas* (warriors), *vaishyas* (cultivators and traders), and *shudras* (laborers), and, beneath these four, the lowest of the low who performed the dirtiest tasks and were untouchable. Within this general framework was an elaborate subdivision into smaller groups, more narrowly defined, which were called *jati*. The effect of the *jati* was to assign each family its status within a predetermined hierarchy, thus prescribing for every individual the obligations and opportunities of that status. The consequences were far reaching. They included such social limitations as who could marry whom or who could eat together, economic restrictions concerning what occupation one could enter to earn a living, as well as ranking and precedence at religious or public ceremonies. All of this encumbered a person by virtue of heredity. You were born into a station in life, and in it you stayed.[22]

As far as current archaeological knowledge extends, this system of social classification did not exist in the original Harappan civilization of the Indus Valley. It was introduced by the Aryan-speaking peoples who migrated into India from the northwest after 1500 B.C. These intruders, or invaders, not only had to adapt themselves from a nomadic life-style to agricultural, and then to urban, conditions; they also needed to maintain their superiority over the indigenous peoples whom they had conquered. That could suggest the reasons—social, economic, and governmental—for wanting to organize their culture on the basis of the increasing rigidities of class and caste. The stratification of society followed the compulsions of political and military power.

The Myths of Hinduism

But what may originate in physical force and be maintained by coercion is more enduring—and much more endurable—if it is sanctioned by a body of beliefs that the credulous and the ignorant can be induced to accept. This is where myth and religion play their part, reinforced by metaphysics and psychology. Fortunately, in the case of India's civilization, we are not left to guesswork or surmise about the linkage between the values that evolved and the culture in which they were grounded. The evidence is written, the reasoning is there to be read. It is enshrined in the classics of Hindu mythology, philosophy, and religion—the Rig-Vedas, the Upanishads, and the Mahabharata, which contains the quintessential Bhagavad-Gita.

In his essay on Confucian thought, C. K. Yang generalizes that "the dominant influence of religion in many cultures stems from religious dominance over ethical values."[23] Invariably the link between religion and ethics arises because every religion contains a code of rules to regulate human conduct. Hence it follows that a moral philosophy is a part of religious teaching, and the character of that philosophy is, of course, based on whatever image of human nature is embraced by the religion in question. Start with the doctrine that all humans are sinners, and you will end up with codes of penance and punishment. Assume that our nature is mixed of good and evil, or that we are basically good, and other conclusions will follow.

In civilizations whose value systems are pointed toward another realm of Being, as is the case with India, there is a close connection between that doctrine and their ethics. It would be difficult, however, to prove that either is the source of the other. If one is searching for origins and causes, the probable truth is that this is one of those chicken-and-egg relationships, where both the theology and the morality are rooted in the same conceptual matrix. One thing, though, is clear, and on this point Yang is correct. Whichever of the two came first, in any culture with an other-worldly bias, the religious attitudes generally succeed in dominating the ethical ideals.

Central to the Hindu conception of life is the belief in *samsara* (reincarnation) with its corollary of a distinction between our mortal body and the immortal soul. These doctrines carry important implications in their train. One is metaphysical: namely, that this world that we perceive through the senses, and that our soul temporarily inhabits, is but *maya* (illusion). Reality exists on another plane. That is infinite and deathless, and, could we but attain it, would be the true object of our comprehension. A second implication is ethical: Because the soul that now occupies our body had other incarnations in the past and will have more in the future, it follows that the life we lead at present was conditioned by those previous existences—as will the soul's next incarnation be shaped by its experiences during this one.

That leads to two further doctrines. One is the concept of *karma,* which is the principle of causation or the relation between cause and effect. Simply stated, a person's action has consequences. Each is responsible therefore for the results of his or her deeds. As ye sow, so shall ye reap. Our actions, however, or rather our range of choice, are not entirely free, for we are subject also to the rule of *dharma. Dharma* is righteousness, or rightful conduct, which means doing whatever is appropriate to one's station. Applying that to the four classes, one can deduce that the dharma of a *brahmin* is not identical with that of a *shudra.*[24]

Now come the questions that matter. How do the ethics harmonize with the theology? Does their inner logic hang together? And what are the practical consequences for human conduct?

The answer to the first question is straightforward. The source of the four classes is described in the *Rig-Veda* itself, where each is depicted as growing from different parts of the original cosmic Man whom the gods had sacrificed.[25] Obviously, the purpose of this transparently disingenuous story is to impart divine sanction to the pattern of social discrimination on which the Hindu culture was based. That pattern, established by heredity, was intended to be rigid. When the four classes, the Hindu name for which is *varna* (color), were reinforced by the *jati* (meaning "birth"), families and their individual members were imprisoned in a man-made structure of discrimination designed to perpetuate the unequal advantages of a few. The chicken-and-egg style of logic is thus evident. The Aryan conquerors needed a system of superimposed classes to secure what they had seized. A mythology is concocted to explain and justify their way of keeping people in their place, and it acquires the character of "holy writ." Hence a theology, which emerges as the consequence of a preestablished social structure, becomes a cause of its continuation.

The second question to which the concepts of Hinduism give rise concerns their internal consistency. Do they fit harmoniously together? There is a problem both of logic and of psychology in the relations between the three crucial doctrines of samsara, karma, and dharma. The first of these involves the fundamental assumptions that the human being has a soul that is immortal, and that it is reincarnated in successive bodily existences. All that a rationalist can say of these beliefs is that they have never been proven to be either true or false. Their status, in the absence of proof, is that of dogma—that is, an assertion made on the basis of someone's authority that others are told to accept. For the faithful, this may be satisfactory; for the intellectually critical, it is not. To be fair to Hinduism, however, let us not forget that all religions rest on a substratum of myth; and whatever criticism one makes of this aspect of the Hindu faith applies with the same force to all the others.

The notions of karma and dharma present another difficulty. Are they mutually consistent and can they be reconciled with samsara? The issue at stake here is of deep concern for psychology and for moral philosophy. It is the age-old controversy over free will or determinism—the question being whether an individual, at the moment of deciding to act, is genuinely free to choose among alternatives or is so influenced by past events and the surrounding culture as literally to have no choice but to behave in a predetermined fashion. Hindu thinking on this subject reveals two contradictory tendencies. The concept of karma contains the notion that actions produce consequences, either good or bad, for which the doer must be held responsible. Logically, the idea of responsibility has to entail some sort of freedom of choice on the individual's part. For to state that contrariwise, if one's actions are in truth directed along the path that follows from past behavior or from the force of cultural influences, then in no sense is one a free agent to whom responsibility can be ascribed.

But, on the other hand, Hinduism also posits samsara and dharma, both of which appear to subscribe to determinism. If dharma is the performance of the duties of one's station—an inescapable view for a culture structured into hereditary classes and castes—and if one's current station is the result of the soul's actions in its past incarnations, then one's conduct can only be conceived as the inescapable outcome of the turns of the "wheel of existence." Indian metaphysicians have sought with much subtlety to reconcile their karma with dharma and samsara. But they cannot have it both ways. Determinism, to the extent that it is conceded, always negates the possibility of free will. The logic is self-contradictory, as is the psychology. What they end up with therefore is the triumph of fatalism over freedom.

A third question concerns the practical consequences that follow from believing in these ideas. If you accept them, what kind of behavior is likely to be approved? For an answer, we have only to turn to the most authoritative source—the holiest of holies among Hindu scriptures, the work that is often described as occupying in Hinduism the place that the Sermon on the Mount does in Christianity. I refer, of course, to the Bhagavad-Gita, or "Song of the

Blessed One." What does it tell us? To what conclusions does it point?

The Bhagavad-Gita forms part of the sixth book of the epic poem the Mahabharata, whose subject is the war between the five Pandava brothers and their cousins, the Kauravas. On the day of battle, one of the Pandavas, Arjuna, rides out on his war chariot, sees his kinsmen arrayed on the opposite side, and, knowing that he must kill them or be killed, has a change of heart. He tells his charioteer: "Therefore we ought not to kill these . . . who are our relations; for how can we . . . obtain happiness by destroying our own kinsmen?"[26] The main body of the Gita consists of the response of the charioteer, who first rebukes him for being unmanly and faint-hearted—conduct unbecoming an Aryan—then discloses the reasons that justify his fighting. The charioteer, we learn, is actually the god Krishna and, as such, a manifestation of Vishnu himself.

Krishna's arguments are these. Human nature is dual. The bodily part is mortal. It exists in the realm of the senses and it desires the sense objects to which it is attached. This is the part that will die, as some day it must, if the body is slain in battle. But the other part, the true self, cannot be slain, for it is immortal. It comes from the universal, all-encompassing, infinite Being—that is, from Krishna—which it can rejoin by acting without attachment to desire. Only thus does the soul find release (*moksha*) from the wheel of existence and become reunited with the All. Fight then and kill, if so it comes to pass. Each person during this transient phase must fulfill the dharma appropriate to his class. "Looking upon it even from the standpoint of thine own *dharma,* thou shouldst not waver, for nothing is higher for a *Kshatriya* than a righteous war. . . . If thou fallest in battle, thou shalt obtain heaven; if thou conquerest, thou shalt enjoy the earth."[27]

There is much more in the Bhagavad-Gita, but that is the essence of its message—a message that unites the metaphysically lofty with the ethically revolting. No metaphysical concepts are on a higher plane than these that postulate the union of everything that exists in a oneness that is deathless and infinite. But what purpose is this doctrine being made to serve? The answer, in the context of the Hindu civilization, was to do your duty within the position into which you were born. But be passionless while you do it, eliminating attachment to objects of desire. If thus you kill, there is no guilt, because that body had to die and what you killed was not the immortal part.

Could there be reasoning more specious or more spurious to justify the socially sanctioned slaughter of other human beings that

civilization has institutionalized as war? There will be more occasions where we shall discover that a civilization whose values are
other-worldly, and where ethics is consequently subordinated to
religion, will settle for a hell on earth pretending it to be ordained
by divine decree.[28]

Hinduism's Challengers:
The Jains and Buddhists

That some Indians were not satisfied to stay at the ethical level
formulated in classical Hinduism may be deduced from what happened in the sixth century B.C. By that time, the case for new
directions was strengthened by developments that had occurred
within Hinduism in its guise as an organized religion. The Brahmin
priesthood had devised elaborate rituals, complete with sacrifices,
over which they wielded a monopoly. Release from the wheel of
existence was available—but at a price. The priests would perform
the rituals that they pronounced to be efficacious, if you paid them.
Thus they were operating a lucrative business whose financial gain
to themselves was more certain than the spiritual benefit for their
customers.

Two radical thinkers, contemporaries, emerged at the same time
to challenge the orthodox tradition and the abuses practiced in its
name. These were Vardhamana, called Mahavira (c. 600-527), founder of the Jains, and the still more remarkable Siddhartha Gautama
(563-483), the Buddha. On two fundamental points that marked a
bold departure from Hinduism, their teaching was in agreement.
Neither had any place in his system for the gods, and both rejected
the separation of human beings into hereditary castes. In essentials, therefore, Jainism and Buddhism were ethical systems designed to show the way to moral perfection. Their founders did not
preach a religion in the sense of human dependence on supranatu-
ral powers requiring propitiation or prayer. That both movements—
more particularly Buddhism—later acquired the characteristics of
an organized religion was due to the followers, not to the founders.

The two movements have had very different histories. Jainism
has been confined to India, where it has perhaps a million and a
half adherents. Buddhism, however, has overleaped the frontiers of
nationality, race, and civilization. It has been more successful than
any other system of belief in providing a universal creed for eastern
Asia, and it is strongly entrenched in many countries—except for

India itself. Why the contrast between the two? And why did Buddhism not permeate the land of Gautama's birth?

The message of Mahavira, the "Great Hero," was not such as to appeal to the millions. A moral perfectionist, he was also an absolutist. When he applied the logic of his doctrine to daily life, the practice was extreme. His central principle, like Schweitzer's, was a reverence for life. This extended to all animate creatures, and even inanimate objects were considered to have their *jivas*, or souls. The injunction to hurt no one became a total prohibition on the killing of anything alive. *Ahimsa* (nonviolence) was the golden rule in one's relationships with others. To such lengths was the rule carried that strict Jains would mask their mouths so as not to inhale any insect and thereby destroy it. Many Jains, following Mahavira's example, were ascetics. Some sought death through starvation. Some remained "sky-clad"—that is, they dispensed with all clothing. These, let it be said, were not the majority. But logical absolutism can lend itself to strange aberrations.

Gautama never went to such extremes. Like Vardhamana, he had been raised in a luxury that he abandoned; like him, he turned for a while to asceticism. But when mortification of the flesh brought him no nearer to purifying the soul than had indulgence in sensual pleasures, he sought a middle path, the one of moderation. That was what he proclaimed in his first sermon after attaining enlightenment, when he enunciated the Four Noble Truths to liberate humanity from the pains of mortal existence and show the way to *nirvana.* Nirvana was the bliss awaiting the person who had at last extinguished all desires for the finite and found union with the infinite. The extent of Gautama's influence owed as much to the man himself as to his teaching. His personality was compounded of two seeming opposites: an intellect that in discourse could be as analytical as that of Socrates and a compassionate tenderness resembling Francis of Assisi. He must have radiated that spirit of sublime serenity that is the characteristic expression of so many of his statues. No moral leader in any civilization has surpassed the Buddha.

Buddhism, however, was not for India. Why not? For a few centuries, it made some significant advances, reaching the zenith of its political influence during the reign of Ashoka, who may have been a convert. Thereafter it slowly declined, while Hinduism regained both its intellectual vigor (e.g., the philosophies of Shankara and Ramanuja) and the loyalty of its following. The process was completed by the Islamic invaders whose militancy destroyed what

36 THE ETHICAL CRISES OF CIVILIZATION

was left of Buddhist influence in the northwest. The main reasons for this decline are not difficult to discern. Gautama had rejected the central institution of Indian society—the caste—and he dismissed the whole Hindu pantheon.[29] The former, however, was too deeply embedded in the culture to be uprooted by a moral innovator, however inspired. As for the latter, Gautama suffered a fate similar to the innovative Pharaoh Ikhnaton, whose monotheistic ideas spelled heresy to the priests of Karnak. The Brahmins were tenacious. They hung on and they survived. Possibly they were aided and abetted by later developments within Buddhism itself. Gautama had inaugurated the *sangha,* or monastic order, which became the kernel for institutionalizing his movement. Eventually, the worst happened—and contrary to the Buddha's own instructions. He himself became an object of worship, with images and incense and all that those entail. Thus was an ethical movement subverted into an organized religion. When that happened, there seemed less to choose between Hindu tradition and the Buddhist erstwhile "Reformation." Moreover, Hinduism itself, to cope with the challenges of Gautama and Vardhamana, had introduced some internal changes (correcting certain abuses of Brahminical power) that made it more acceptable. As Percival Spear has so aptly stated: "It was a counter-reformation which succeeded."[30]

Unfortunately, that was true. I say "unfortunately" because, comparing the two sets of ethics, one who is neither Hindu nor Buddhist, and is therefore detached from both, must surely judge the Buddha's teaching to be morally the superior because of its toleration, nonviolence, and universality. That teaching, however, must be distinguished from the Buddhism that latter-day monks have preached and practiced, much of which Gautama himself would surely have repudiated. Some important conclusions can, of course, be drawn from the fact that it was Confucianism in China and Hinduism in India that became the mainstream in the flow of these two civilizations. Both established and retained their dominance because they codified the basic realities of the social structure—that is, the family network in China and family cemented by caste in India. Confucianism and Hinduism were the specific cults of two particular cultures. Born into a Chinese family, you were taught a Confucian outlook. Born a Hindu, you were from birth a member of a family with an assigned caste status, which Hinduism reinforced. Neither of these systems aimed at universality. Being in the nature of the case culture-bound, they could not embrace others than Chinese or Indians.

The character of Buddhism was something else. Gautama offered an end to suffering and ultimate perfection, not through faith but through knowledge. Any individual could qualify, because salvation began with understanding. His was a message to all humanity, transcending the boundaries of culture and capable therefore of universal extension. This explains why the Brahmins, from their position at the top of a caste system restricted to Indians, opposed it so strenuously. It also explains why Gautama could spread to eastern Asia and be revered in Nepal, Tibet, China, Korea, Japan, Sri Lanka, Burma, Thailand, Laos, Cambodia, and Vietnam.

The links that connected Hinduism and Confucianism with the family are a point of similarity. The major difference, as we have seen, is that between India's other-worldliness and China's focus on this world. Without doubt, this contrast has had its influence on the attitudes and values of the two civilizations. Muller argues that "life-negation" has been the dominant theme in Indian religious thought and that "no civilization has been born by a renunciation of life."[31] Although that is true, the word *dominant* implies some degree of opposition. Life negation is not exactly the message conveyed by the erotic sculptures on the temples at Khajuraho and elsewhere. Nor is it the impression one receives from the legends about the gods—of Krishna, for example—or from the Kama Sutra. The top trinity of the Hindu pantheon is composed of a creator (Brahma), a preserver (Vishnu), and the destroyer (Shiva); while on the feminine side, the benevolent Parvati is balanced by the bloodthirsty Kali. Have we yang and yin all over again?

A friend who spent his whole life in India commented to me once: "Anything you say about India is true." This means, of course, that it is true of some part or aspect, and that its opposite is also true of another aspect or part. "Shiva," as Wolpert points out, "epitomizes Hinduism's reconciliation of extremes: erotic passion and ascetic renunciation, frenzied motion and unmoving calm, violence and passivity."[32] Seen in that light, Gautama's emphasis on moderation and toleration sounds decidedly un-Indian. Or possibly, his acute insight led him to advocate these ideals precisely because they were contrary to the propensities of his countrymen. A parallel that suggests itself is that of another brilliant and volatile people, the ancient Greeks, whose behavior oscillated similarly between extremes. That explains why the Delphic oracle pronounced the maxim "nothing in excess" and why Aristotle located virtue in the "Golden Mean." It is not uncommon for the sages to recommend those values that the surrounding culture conspicuously fails to practice.

That said, however, I return to the point that religiosity and other-worldliness have characterized the Indian mainstream, just as humanism and this-worldliness have been more typical of China. The stereotypes that one normally visualizes portray that difference. The Indian ascetic, his body emaciated, squats cross-legged, meditating with eyes closed and hair unkempt. The Chinese sage, in a loose-fitting silk robe, applies his brush in calligraphy, with a teapot conveniently close to his writing desk. The rationalist will argue that only by focusing our intelligence on the problems of this world can we expect to ameliorate the human condition. Moreover, we do know that we exist here and now, but we do not know for certain of any other plane of existence. The mystic insists, however, that this world is illusion and its problems are insoluble. You must therefore hold out to suffering humanity the hope of happiness at other levels of consciousness and in some future state of being.

Such opposites, one would naturally think, are hard to combine and impossible to reconcile. Suppose, then, that we examine a third civilization that has sought to do just that. If half of a civilization is like China and half is like India, will it work successfully? The civilization to which I refer is our own—this that we call Western. Our contradictions demand analysis.

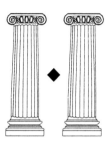

Two souls within me strive
for the mastery.

Goethe

3

The Split Personality
of Western Civilization

*A*mong the major civilizations, the Western is unique. We are a
bonding of incompatibles, a junction of opposites. Like the images of
the Roman god Janus, we look at the world with two faces pointed
in different directions. No wonder that we have an identity crisis. Can
anyone understand us when we ourselves are unclear as to what we are?

Western civilization is a hybrid growth, formed primarily by the
merging of four traditions: Greek, Roman, Jewish, and Christian.
Some might be inclined to add a fifth, the contribution of the
Germanic peoples. But their imprint was placed more deeply on
the socioeconomic system and on military techniques than on the
values that are central to this discussion. Among the four, there has
been a pairing. Rome stands in a special relation to Greece, Christianity to Judaism. From the standpoint of values, the crux of
Western civilization has been the never-ceasing tension, mounting
at times to direct conflict, between the Greco-Roman conception
of life and the Judeo-Christian—one centered on humanity, the
other on a deity. That is my theme. I shall explore it by discussing
the four traditions and the relations between the pairs.

Origins of Western Civilization

The tortuous history of Western civilization begins on an island
in the eastern Mediterranean. It was among the Minoans in Crete

that a culture emerged during the Age of Bronze which, though influenced by Mesopotamia and Egypt, was different in certain vital respects—so much so that its novel traits impressed the archaeologists who excavated its remains and are apparent to anyone who observes them nowadays at Knossos and Iraklion. There before your eyes is the visible evidence of an original and independent growth. What are the qualities that justify that statement?

Three should be mentioned. The first is the influence of the sea. Living on an island, the Minoans were perforce a maritime people. Their legendary ruler, Minos, is credited by Thucydides with being the first to build a navy, which commanded the seas.[1] The empire thus established over the isles of the Aegean (the Cyclades) had the means to develop a wide-spreading commerce. The effects of this can be seen in the palace at Knossos. That huge, multistoried structure (the original labyrinth) was a center of political power as well as of economic governance. Its most striking feature is the absence of fortifications—proof that its ruler must have dominated the island and controlled the surrounding sea. At Knossos, humanity had ventured beyond the river valleys. Here was launched a civilization that depended not on an army but on its sailors, who at distant ports along with their cargoes could load up with new thoughts.

In addition to not having walls, there was a second noteworthy absence at Knossos and at the other centers of Minoan settlement. No massive temples have been found, nor are there signs of a specialized and powerful class of priests. It appears that the rulers did double duty by functioning as priest-kings and conducting whatever religious rites were required in small shrines. Understandably, for a people who lived off their agriculture as well as from the sea, the Earth was venerated in the form of a fertility goddess—a very common belief in the eastern part of the Mediterranean. Fertility cults have the merit of celebrating life. How different from the bloodthirsty warrior-gods of Mesopotamia and the morbid underworld of the Egyptians!

The third trait that marks the Minoans as different is something attractively positive. It belongs in the realm of the spirit. Their art strikes a chord of feeling without parallel at that time, for its mood is joyous, blithe, fresh, and free. The men and women of the frescoes exude a natural charm that evokes a response after four millennia; and the flowers, fish, animals, and birds have grace and liveliness—sometimes, as with the dolphins, playfully so.[2] This does not look like the art of a society crushed by despotism and misery or withdrawing from a world perceived as illusion. It is the mood of humanists reveling in life.

In the origins of Western civilization, therefore, one already discerns that focus on this-worldly existence that has constituted one of its two antithetical themes. That same focus continued and was intensified in the next stage when this civilization embarked on the first of those westward migrations that have characterized its history from earliest times to the present. The second stage was enacted on the mainland of Greece. There, a power base was built up, first at Mycenae and afterward at numerous other centers, until reaching a climax in Athens. Here is not the place to recount the familiar outlines of a history that has been told so often and does not need restating. My concern is rather to extract its meaning. For that, I shall concentrate on the values that evolved among the Hellenes during their millennium (1300-300 B.C.) of spectacular flowering. What was it they bequeathed to us, their beneficiaries?

The Values of Hellas

The supreme achievement of the Greeks lay in their choice of the values that they most prized and to which, as ideals, their practice aspired. Among these, their performance, as distinct from their philosophical speculations, was not notably successful in the domain of ethics. They were preeminent, however, indeed conspicuously so, in their pursuit of truth and beauty. It is as thinkers, writers, and artists that the ancient Greeks made an imperishable contribution to humanity—one that has continued to yield fresh inspiration to generations long removed from antiquity, as happened in the Italian Renaissance. The greatest gifts of the Hellenes were those of intellect and imagination. Their use of those faculties laid the foundations for much that has since transpired in the civilization of the West.

Where does one begin an appraisal of the Greeks? I take my start from their key concept—the Good—whose inherent ambiguity conveys a split in their value preferences. The Greek adjective for "good" is *agathos;* and the abstract noun, signifying "goodness" or "virtue," is *arete.*[3] *Agathos* (like *bonus, gut, good,* and the similar words in other languages) can have two different meanings. One of these is functional, in the sense of a successful manifestation of skill or competence. We employ this meaning when we speak of a good knife, a good racehorse, a good quarterback, or a good play or painting. The other sense is ethical, as when we describe a good deed or a good human being. What happens in the thinking of the Greeks is that they begin with the functional and later formulate the ethical, which launches them into a wide range of speculative inquiry. The split in their attitudes occurs because at times they are admiring technical proficiency, whereas at other times they approve what is morally right.

The dilemma is clearly presented in the earliest literary portrayal of their society, the *Iliad*. Homer's subject is an incident in the Trojan War when Achilles quarrels with Agamemnon and ceases to take further part in the fighting. The circumstances of the rift between the king leading the whole army, and the chief of the Myrmidon contingent, who is the army's most formidable warrior, are primitive and trivial in the extreme. When raiding a town, the Greeks had carried off among the booty the daughter of the priest of Apollo, and Agamemnon took her for his prize. Angry at the insult to his priest, the god punishes the king by shooting at the army, killing men and animals. Agamemnon then decides that he must placate Apollo by restoring the girl to her father. But he demands an alternative prize, which one of the chiefs must surrender to him. When Achilles opposes this, the king insists on having Achilles' own girl for himself. Honor and rank are now at stake, and this is the "heroic" age! So Achilles stays in his tent sulking, while the Trojans, led by Hector, son of King Priam, get the better of the Greeks. After a while, Achilles' devoted friend, Patroklos, rejoins the fray, until Hector slays him. That galvanizes Achilles, who proceeds to avenge Patroklos by killing Hector. He then treats the corpse with the utmost indignity and drags it back to his camp.

Up to this point, neither the story nor any of the characters is especially edifying. Agamemnon, as a general, is ready to risk his entire army over the seizure of a girl. Achilles is nothing but an efficient fighting machine. He is *agathos,* in the sense of being good at killing. Because he surpasses others in this respect, it constitutes his *aretē*, his excellence.

But now a great poet lifts a brutal and sordid episode to a height of humanity seldom equaled in literature. Under cover of night, Priam slips out of his besieged city, makes his way to Achilles' tent, and there, humbling himself as a suppliant, pleads on his knees for the return of Hector's body. As the aged, white-haired king kisses the hands that have slain so many of his sons, Achilles thinks of his own father, far away in the Peloponnese, and relents. The ruler of Troy and the chief of the Myrmidons are transmuted into a father grieving for his slaughtered son and a son mindful of his own distant father. The humanness uniting them ennobles both. Priam returns to Troy with Hector in dignity; Achilles is purged of his murderous wrath. *Aretē* has now become the excellence of humanity. The instrumental good gives way to the moral good.

The Freedom to Speculate

Autres temps, autres moeurs, says the French proverb. The values to which priority is accorded at any given place or time bear some relation to the structuring of social classes and the interests to which they are attached. As the age of Homer's warriors receded into history, other groups emerged into prominence, and new forms of wealth gave rise to new antagonisms. Seafaring linked up a network of coastal cities and scattered islands. Commerce established relationships between producers and traders, who needed a medium of exchange that metallurgy was ready to provide. Economic development was proceeding so far and so fast by the seventh century B.C. as to result in social strains and political conflicts.

The great benefit in all this was that it offered a powerful stimulus to thought. This was the springtime when philosophy reached upward, putting out new buds. It all began in the Greek communities along the coast of modern Turkey and on the nearby islands of the eastern Aegean. Here on the westernmost fringe of the far-flung Persian Empire, at the seaward end of the caravan routes that reached to India and even China, speculative thinkers aware of the surrounding diversity propelled their minds into uncharted orbits. Two related questions obsessed them. Is there some unity, real although perhaps invisible, that underlies the innumerable varieties of phenomena presented to the senses? Amid the world of change and flux, are there any constants, fixed and permanent? To physicists and metaphysicians, such inquiries amounted to asking, "What is reality?" To logicians, they spelled out, "What is the truth?" To social theorists, they translated into the question, "What is the good?"

It mattered not that some of the initial answers were naive or that many were untenable. What counted was the profundity of the questions and the uninhibited daring of the questioners. As never before on this planet and seldom afterward, intellect and imagination were soaring self-powered in free flight. Civilization in the

West began taking shape in the minds of Greek philosophers. The circumstances were propitious because of the absence of those negative factors that operated elsewhere, as in Egypt and Mesopotamia. There was no hierarchy of priests powerful enough to proscribe speculation that deviated from its mythology. Nor were there sacred texts or revealed dogmas, sanctioned by institutional authority, that it was risky to challenge. Nor did the gods of the Olympian pantheon provide any kind of moral or spiritual influence. As the myths depicted them, they exhibited all the traits of human beings, writ large. Xenophanes, a poet and thinker of the sixth to fifth century B.C., acidly observed that "Homer and Hesiod attributed to the gods all that is a shame and reproach among men—theft, adultery, deceit and other lawless acts."[4] Add to these negatives the positive elements. The Greeks were people imbued with a lively curiosity and inquisitive minds. The faculty in which they excelled—their aretē—was reason, logos. The main focus of their thought was on themselves and their place in the scheme of things.[5] Rationalism and humanism together were their legacy to the civilization they launched.

The outcome was a wide range of vigorous speculation spreading over three centuries (from the sixth to the third B.C.), to which historians, poets, dramatists, and philosophers all contributed from their respective vantage points. Herodotus, the "Father of History"—a unique mix of raconteur, data collector, anthropologist-in-the-field, and tireless tourist—relates the contrasted customs of the Hellenes, the Egyptians, and the motley peoples of the Persian Empire. Comparative inquiry into human societies commences with his work. Thucydides, the Michelangelo of historians, depicts a Greek world tearing itself apart by the struggle between the two rival systems of Athens and Sparta and plunging into frantic excesses of atrocity and folly. The three tragedians—Aeschylus, Sophocles, and Euripides—use the traditional myths as their vehicle to explore the springs of individual behavior and trace the consequences for the doer. Euripides, in particular, skeptical and agnostic, exposes the shallowness of the "heroes" and the absurdities of the gods; while Aristophanes, writer of comedies and the right-wing satirist of a militant populist democracy, lambastes the new ideas and lampoons their exponents. This is heady stuff, exhilarating and even intoxicating. The mind, nous, was roaming free, and everything was called for question before the bar of reason.

In this milieu, it was Socrates, a man of powerful intellect and personality, who brought the restless probing to a climax. Socrates is the archetype of that character so well known in academia, the great teacher who never publishes. Fortunately, however, his disciples did, as well as his critics,[6] so that we know much about his highly individual style and habits. Socrates' principal contribution to civilization can be easily pinpointed. He it was who taught us how to use our minds. This doughty stonemason asked two basic questions of every statement made to him: What does this mean? Is it true?[7] Meaning and its truth or falsehood were analyzed by him with a relentless logic that no contemporary could parry. His fellow Athenians did not thank him for those inquiries that always left them knowing only that they did not really know anything. In a McCarthyite reaction to their defeat by Sparta and the tyrannies of the Thirty Oligarchs, the restored democracy, seeking scapegoats, executed this man of uncompromising integrity on charges of corrupting the youth and of impiety to the gods.

The fact that a majority of a jury, which was large by our standards, convicted this 70-year-old man tells us something important. It says that a gulf existed then, as it does today, between the mass culture and the intellectuals. The *man-in-the-agora* was as full of his prejudices as our contemporary in the football stadium or suburban shopping center. The glories of the civilization that have been so much admired and copied through the centuries were but a thinly laid veneer. They did not penetrate deep. Gilbert Murray has made the point in these words:

We must keep hold of two facts: first, that the Greeks of the fifth century produced some of the noblest poetry and art, the finest political thinking, the most vital philosophy, known to the world; second, that the people who heard and saw, nay perhaps, even the people who produced these wonders, were separated by a thin and precarious interval from the savage. Scratch a civilized Russian, they say, and you find a wild Tartar. Scratch an ancient Greek, and you hit, no doubt on a very primitive and formidable being, somewhere between a Viking and a Polynesian.[8]

Variations on the Greek Theme

That is a salutary caution for us to evaluate the Greeks as they were in their own day and age and not only as a small fraction of their number have endured *sub specie aeternitatis*. For Greece at its zenith—that is, the half century from the end of the Persian invasion to the outbreak of the Peloponnesian War (479-431 B.C.)—

THE ETHICAL CRISES OF CIVILIZATION

the reasons both for its greatness and for its downfall. At that time,
two major centers existed, each embodying its unique value preference and therefore exemplifying a different *arete*. These were
Sparta and Athens.

Sparta was a tightly knit community of late-immigrating Dorians,
sitting on the backs of a much larger Messenian population whom
they subjected and exploited (the Helots). To perpetuate their
power and privileges, they raised their male children in the most
rigorous discipline—hence the term *spartan*—of physical training,
character shaping, and martial arts. Sparta was an armed camp; its
culture, that of the landowning Helot-ruling soldiery; governance
was conducted in the spirit of a barracks.[9] Courage in combat was
the virtue most lauded. A land so deeply conservative, so xenophobic and fear ridden, was not fertile soil for the arts. To Spartans,
only one principle mattered: follow orders.[10]

How different from that city was Athens! The values that Athenians held highest were given tongue by their leading statesman
whose words Thucydides reported. On the solemn occasion of
burying those who died in the first year of the war with Sparta,
Pericles honored their sacrifice by expressing the ideals that Athens represented. He praised its democratic character (unique in
the world at that time), stressing the point that power was spread
among many and not restricted to a few. Democracy afforded
freedom in private pursuits and both the opportunity and the
obligation to take part in public affairs. The kind of citizen who
flourished in Athens was the well-rounded amateur rather than the
highly specialized professional. Versatility implied every activity
that could develop their potentialities, thus enriching themselves
and the community. Not only did the Athenians exercise their
bodies, but they gave full play to their imagination. "We love
beauty," said Pericles, "while practicing economy, as we love
wisdom without it making us soft." What is more, Athens was
inventive. It had created its own unique system without borrowing
from others. Its example therefore was an education to the rest of
Greece.[11] In fact, as later history shows, much more than Greece
has been educated by Athens. Democracy itself is a case in point.
This unique political system is the exception to all the other forms
of government in that it locates ultimate power in the mass of the
citizens, and not in their rulers. Thanks to its modern rebirth, it
can be appropriately described as Western civilization in its political aspect. And the original model was provided by Athens.

From Polis to Cosmopolis

To affirm ideals is one thing; to actualize them, another. The Greeks, I repeat, were more distinguished in thought than in action. Although they went to great pains to argue how superior they were to the "barbarians" (Persia included) in the sphere of morality, these claims cannot be substantiated. If one looks to the *Republic* as the climax of Greek social thought prior to the extinction of the independent *polis,* what is it that Plato is saying? Only in one respect does he advocate a major ethical advance—that was in his bold argument for equality between the sexes. For the rest, he is no less hidebound in his values than those whom he condemned for condemning Socrates. He takes slavery for granted, recommends that unwanted babies be exposed to die, and gives his full sanction to war.

But although their ethical accomplishments did not match their artistic or intellectual creativity, their rationalism was able eventually to exert an influence on their moral beliefs. This happened, however, only after the system of government through the polis collapsed, and the ethical advance was possible only because of that collapse. As long as the polis continued as the single, all-encompassing institution of society, it claimed a monopoly of everybody's loyalties. Its morality prescribed their morality; and when its government behaved unethically (as so often happened), the individual citizen was compelled either to resist—which meant revolution—or to swallow conscience and acquiesce, with the unavoidable result of cynicism. The pages of Thucydides are full of this. Read his account of the psychological effects of civil war, that *stasis* or internal war of factions which accompanied the conflict between Athens and Sparta, or of the moral degeneracy of the Athenians when they subjected the pro-Spartan islanders of Melos to the power of their naval empire.[12] Sophocles made this same issue the subject of his most moving tragedy, *Antigone,* where the heroine defies the despot of Thebes and performs a ceremony of burial for her brother's corpse, an act that she justifies by appealing to a higher law.[13] The moral crisis that overcame the polis is of the utmost relevance to us today, given that we confront a similar crisis in the behavior of the now obsolete system of nation-states—a problem about which there will be more to say anon.[14]

After the polis lost its independence, the Greeks could make a fresh start. Their response was the philosophizing of the third century B.C., most notable of which were the ideas of the Stoics. Their system was a novel response to a novel situation. After

Alexander's conquests, the political order was in flux. Across the eastern Mediterranean and through the Middle East, new kingdoms were taking shape and old empires were refashioned. When the polis was reduced to an agency of local government, its true parochialism was manifest. Where then was the focus of loyalty for its inhabitants? To what did they belong? Within the polis during its heyday, the human being was conceived not as an individual but as *polites,* a citizen. Now that individuals had become the reality, what, if anything, could unite them?

Addressing their intellects to these questions, the Stoic thinkers conceived an imaginative solution. For the polis, they substituted the concept of *cosmopolis.* All humanity is one; we are parts of a single, universal whole. Nay more, the principle pervading the cosmos is reason, *logos,* a spark of which animates each and every person. The law of reason is therefore the law of human existence, and it is the same for one and all. From the logic of these premises, revolutionary conclusions followed. Political subdivisions that separate human beings are of secondary importance. Slavery is against the law of reason. Neither Plato nor Aristotle, nor Socrates himself, ever rose to these levels. Western civilization was now embarked on a course whose terminus would be the City of Humanity.

The Roman Achievement: Latin, Law, and Legions

The Stoics occupy an important place in history, but not only as the philosophers of universalism. Their doctrines soon had some practical consequences, because for three centuries it was they who educated the Roman leadership. Educating was exactly what the Romans needed most, and this the bright Greeks were ready to supply. As Horace aptly expressed it: "Captive Greece captured its wild conqueror and introduced its arts to the bucolic Latins."[15] That did not happen, however, until the second half of the second century B.C. Prior to that date, the Romans were a staunch and dogged agricultural people, with a citadel and administrative center located on seven hills beside the Tiber. Surrounded by hostile communities, they broke out of their encirclement through a selective policy of alliances and attacks. As their sphere of influence expanded, they had to cope not only with the internal strains of class conflict but with successive invasions by Gauls, Carthaginians, and Macedonians. From three centuries of almost unremitting warfare, they emerged strong and hard, like tempered steel.

The Romans were a people who command respect, but whom it is difficult to like. They tended to be stern, humorless, and self-important, for they took themselves very seriously and performed their imperial role with obvious relish. Their own favorite self-characterization was *graves* (meaning "weighty," "serious," and "dignified") by contrast with the Greeks whom they dismissed as *leves,* literally "light-weights." When Virgil, writing in the tradition of the *Iliad,* composed his patriotic epic the *Aeneid,* he gave his hero the stock epithet *pius,* meaning someone who conscientiously fulfilled his duties, public and private[16]—a veritable Confucian *chün-tzu!* Early Roman history, as recounted by Livy and others, is replete with morally edifying stories of frugal farmers, brave soldiers, stern magistrates, and strict—often puritanical—heads of households.

If that were really their character in the early days, assuredly they deteriorated after they had acquired dominion. Transformed into the military overlords of all the lands surrounding the Mediterranean, their heads became giddy at the heights. Power brought wealth and limitless opportunities for plunder. Slave gangs labored under the bailiff's whip on the soil of Italy once plowed by citizen-farmers. Roman valor built an empire, and its empire corrupted Rome. But a system that endured for six centuries in the West and for yet another millennium in the East, and whose effects can still be traced in the Europe of our time, had to be sustained by positive qualities. What was the secret of the lasting achievement of the Romans? What did they contribute to our civilization?

The Roman forte was pragmatism. Intensely practical, they groped their way toward procedures that worked. When these succeeded, institutions developed that generated their own momentum. Thus were built their legal code (including the impressive *jus gentium,* or "law of the peoples"), the municipal colonies in the provinces that served as centers for Romanization, and the common citizenship that eventually conferred on every free male the status of a *civis Romanus.*[17] All of this arose piecemeal and evolved slowly as a result of devising expedients for problems that needed solutions. The Romans did not formulate theories and were averse to thinking deductively. One of the least speculative among the peoples who have made a lasting impact on history, their genius was inductive. Always they functioned empirically, extracting their principles from the crude ores of experience. Brilliant as engineers, architects, and builders, they could erect the Colosseum, or construct the water supply for a metropolis, or fling a network of highways across an empire. But not a single theoretical advance in science or mathematics is credited to a Roman name.

And that was why they needed the Greeks. One bond of similarity united this pair of otherwise contrasted peoples: the focus of values for both Greek and Roman was on this world. Their universe was not only geocentric but anthropocentric. This humanistic outlook made it possible for the theoretical reason (logos) of Greece to combine with the practical reason (ratio) of Rome. The result, from the first century B.C. to the second A.D., was a Roman body infused with a Greek spirit.

That was where Stoicism fitted in so well. In two respects, this philosophy proved attractive to the Roman conquerors. First, the Stoic ideal of the strong-minded person, combating difficulties with fortitude, harmonized perfectly with the Roman self-image of *gravitas*. Second, the Stoic arguments about universal reason and its law were thoroughly appropriate to the circumstances of jurists and administrators who needed to discover common principles uniting the diverse inhabitants of their scattered provinces.[18] Could not the *jus gentium*, reached by an inductive process, be considered an approximation to the law of reason, deductively conceived? This must be the explanation of why, from the Scipionic circle to Seneca to Marcus Aurelius, so many leading Romans, when they professed a philosophy, were followers of the Stoa. But let us not forget that Stoicism at Rome was a doctrine for the elite and for them alone. Its tenets were too intellectual, its ethics too austere, for the masses of the *populus Romanus*. The latter, to paraphrase an epigram of Hilaire Belloc, were less interested in the equality of human beings than in the unequal performance of the charioteers at the Circus Maximus.[19]

Such were the foundations that the Greeks and Romans laid down for the civilization of the Western world. Nowadays, in this century, those foundations still underpin its structure. We think with the Greeks; we organize with the Romans. But is that all? What about Western beliefs in those matters where reason has not yet discovered the answers to our questions? For the origins of these we must look further east. Let us consider the influences that have flowed from the area successively designated the land of Canaan, Palestine, and nowadays Israel.

An Other-Worldly Faith: The Judaic Model

The Judeo-Christian contribution to Western civilization revolves around one central, dominating concept: belief in the existence of a Supreme Being, creator of the universe and of everything in it—humanity included. To this Being, or God, all power is ascribed. Human life therefore is subject to divine will and ultimate judgment. We can expect to be rewarded if we live in obedience to God's commands, and punished if we do not. These basic assumptions differentiate the Judeo-Christian tradition from the Greco-Roman. The latter peoples, it is true, paid lip service to their rather ridiculous gods. They thought there was some kind of ghostly afterlife in a shadowy place they called Hades; they were superstitious enough to pay money to consult oracles and astrologers; and, like the Chinese, they engaged in divination. Such practices plainly indicated a belief in nonhuman forces operating in the universe that might be influenced by magical means or propitiated by sacrifice. Evidently that belief was strong, because it evoked from the Roman poet Lucretius his powerful denunciation of religion in the *De Rerum Natura.*

But when all due allowance is made for these facts, the contrast remains striking. The Greeks subjected everything—not omitting their deities—to critical inquiry, so that the natural outcome of their speculations was agnosticism or skepticism; while the pragmatic Romans, being primarily interested in results, cared mainly if their gods delivered what was expected of them. With the Jews and the Christians, however, the whole basis of the relationship between human and suprahuman was reversed. Instead of human beings creating a multiplicity of gods in their own image, a God in the singular was now assumed to have created humanity in its image. Or, to be more precise, in *his* image—because a male-dominated, pastoral[20] society, when personifying the supreme force in the universe, assigned it a masculine gender. God was imagined as the father. And how was all this known? The answer was pronounced in defiance of reason. Some personage—a Prophet, Messiah, or Son of God—claimed to be repeating what God had revealed to him. Their audience was then told to accept this on faith. Faith served the religious as reason served the humanist. Both Judaism and Christianity have professed to know on faith something that lies beyond evidence and proof.

Thus was Western civilization plunged into the great divide. The consequences, both positive and negative, for our values in general, and our ethical development in particular, have been far reaching. In our attachment to whatever values we cherish, the beliefs we hold about their source and sanction make a significant difference. It matters much whether we think their origin is human or divine. For one thing, if we believe that a deity gave them to us, who are we to question or change them? If, however, it was human beings who formulated them, then other human beings can recast them or adapt them to altered tastes. The essence of the Judeo-Christian tradition, in contrast to the Greco-Roman, has been to subject humanity to an imaginary external authority.

This explains the mentality of whoever thought up the story of creation in the Book of Genesis. Adam and Eve were forbidden to eat the fruit of the tree of knowledge of good and evil on the extraordinary ground that, if they acquired this knowledge, they would become equal to God—that is, free to make up their own minds, which of course is in conflict with the notion of obedience to revealed truth. In this fable, Adam's first human act occurred after he had tasted the fruit. He then observed that he and Eve were naked. In other words, he started thinking for himself. The strange theology of Western civilization has branded this mythical event a "Fall," when in reality it would have been a major leap upward in humanity's ascent. Pilate's question to Jesus—"What is truth?"—poses the central intellectual dilemma of Western civilization. A Greek philosopher or a Roman governor assumed that truth was discoverable by human beings using their reason; Jews and Christians have held that humanity receives it from God through revelation. Much of the history of Western civilization is the antagonism between these two opposing views, one that has been waged not merely in words but in blood.

What did Judaism contribute to this history? Three major innovations may be ascribed to the ancient Hebrews. First, in the midst of peoples who practiced animism or polytheism, they insisted that there was only one God. This monotheistic faith is proclaimed thus in the *Shema*: "Hear, O Israel, the Lord our God, the Lord is one."[21] Second, they believed that this one God—Yahweh by name—had made a covenant (*brit*) with them specifically, selecting the Hebrews to be the bearers of the divine revelation to all mankind. Third—and this is the contribution of direct relevance to the current discussion—the Jewish religion, as it evolved, became more and more concerned with ethical issues.[22] Not that morality started with the Jews: Breasted has demonstrated that many moral conceptions, in public relations as well as private, had been formulated by the Egyptians and that some of their thoughts and phrases were paralleled later in various passages of the Old Testament.[23] Be that as it may, the fact remains that in the Jewish writings the ethical concern is more intense and the moral code is developed to a higher standard than before.

Certain aspects of this code need to be stressed. To begin with, the ethics of Judaism derive from Yahweh and are contained in his law. The Pentateuch is full of injunctions and prohibitions—"thou shalt" do this and "thou shalt not" do that—with which the Lord instructs his chosen people. That instruction, or teaching, is expressed in the Torah, which is the Jewish holy writ and is generally translated as "law," though it means "instruction." Because this law is Yahweh's will, its ethics are those of Yahweh. And here one can observe an evolution in the conceptions of deity held by this ancient people. At one level, Yahweh is represented as a fierce tribal war god,[24] fighting the putative gods of other peoples and destroying them. The ethics at this level are quite primitive. They consist in obedience to Yahweh, solidarity with the group, and punishment of one's enemies. But there is another level, spreading like an overlay, which becomes increasingly prominent. This is a concept of Yahweh and his law as just and righteous. Justice, an ethical ideal with legalistic connotations, becomes increasingly merged with righteousness, a notion that is primarily ethical. The ideal Jew is one who walks righteously in the way of the Lord. At this level, Yahweh is a god of mercy, tenderness, and compassion. Help is assured for the orphan, the widow, and the poor. The stranger is to be loved[25] ("for ye were strangers in the land of Egypt") and peace shall reign among peoples, as in Isaiah's utopian vision.[26]

The great virtue of the Jewish teaching is its passion for righteousness, expressed in particular by the Prophets, those remarkable men whose sustained moral fervor has few equals in other cultures. Offsetting that, however, was a chronic fault, the proneness to legalism and correct ritual arising out of excessive attention to the meaning of the written text. When you are governed by a text, you become subject to an orthodoxy; and once orthodoxy is established, the mind is no longer free to create anew. Or if it does, it must be the mind of a rebel.

Jesus and the Values Revolution

The arch-rebel in this case was Jesus of Nazareth. Here was a Jew who challenged the rabbis,[27] was a nuisance to Rome, and, as events unfolded, started a new religious movement. The parallel is remarkably close between Gautama's reaction to the Hinduism of his time and that of Jesus to Judaism. The similarity also extends into later history when both of the religions launched in their names had hardened into restrictive institutions. Viewed as social and political organizations, Buddhism and Christianity can be seen to have shared much in common—including their later departures in practice from the tenets of their founders.

Jesus belongs in that tiny handful of individuals who, as exponents of ideas and teachers of values, have wielded the greatest influence on human civilization. In one respect, his achievement was even more remarkable than that of Socrates, Gautama, Confucius, or Mohammed, given that he was only in his early thirties when he was put to death. What are the reasons for the lasting effects of that very short life? His influence has been due primarily to two factors. The first is found in the character of his teaching while he lived; the second, in the beliefs that gained credence after he died.

What Jesus taught was revolutionary. A radical in his values, he confronted his contemporaries with a head-on challenge. In the Roman Empire of his time, and in the Judaic society that was a part thereof, respect was accorded to wealth, power, high status, and fighting ability. Jesus said simply, but very clearly, that the conventional wisdom was valuing the wrong things. The beatitudes of the Sermon on the Mount give their blessing to the poor, the meek, the righteous, the merciful, the pure in heart, and the makers of peace. The lowly not the lofty, the humble not the high up, are those preferred on Jesus' scale of values. Further, when it came to choosing one's behavior in relation to others, his counsel was not to join in conflict or resist an aggressor. "Love your enemies, bless them that curse you, do good to them that hate you."[28] Throughout the teaching of Jesus, love is the central theme—love of humanity and love of the deity. Indeed, the principal difference of emphasis between Judaism and Christianity is this, that the former is keyed to righteousness, and the latter to love.

All this spelled a complete reversal of the ways of the world. Jesus confronted the Romans, as he confronted the rabbis, by turning their systems upside down. Such thoughts as his were utterly subversive of the established order. That is why, like Socrates, he too was executed by the agents of the state. The lives of the two most original teachers in the history of Western civilization were forcibly terminated: one by the cup of hemlock, the other on the cross.

But what were the reasons for the subsequent spread of Jesus' ideas? The explanation lies in the readiness of so many persons to believe, irrationally, in the supernatural. In his lifetime, Jesus was credited with having performed "miracles"—meaning by that the production of effects outside the natural course of events, as, for example, the healing of a leper. Three days after his crucifixion and burial, Jesus' tomb was opened and found to be empty. Reports subsequently circulated that he had "reappeared" to those who had known him. Hence the Christian belief in the Resurrection. Rational explanations of such stories can, of course, be offered. But there are always credulous people to whom the abnormal and the irrational are more appealing. Such individuals abound today, and they would not have been less plentiful 19 centuries ago. One of the most influential of the early Christian writers, Tertullian, is famous for his comment, much quoted and as often misquoted: "It is certain because it is impossible."[29] When a person is in a frame of mind to say that, he is obviously prepared to believe anything. Let faith be in control, and reason takes a backseat.

What is more, this belief that Jesus had "risen from the dead" harmonized with his own references to God and his general conception of human nature. Here one enters the sphere of the supernatural and encounters assertions for which there can be no proof. The frequent allusions to God as his father gave rise to the doctrine that the Deity had sent his own son into the world (hence the legend of the "Virgin Birth") to redeem humanity. Allied with this was the notion that human nature is dual, being composed of the mortal body and an immortal soul. The latter, depending on the quality of one's life on earth, could face after the body's death the prospect of eternal bliss in heaven or eternal damnation in hell.

Here was where the Christian religion was responsible for radically changing the priorities of Western civilization. Judaism, it is true, believed in some form of existence after death, but its religious focus was firmly set on this world. For Christians, however, because the soul takes precedence over the body, a life of three score years and ten fades into insignificance when compared with a life everlasting. Augustine formulated the doctrine with unequivocating clarity when he drew a sharp distinction between the Earthly City and the Heavenly City.[30] Thus was the hierarchy of Christian values cast in a mold of other-worldliness.

The Power of the Catholic Church

Every major movement in civilization begins with a visionary. Thereafter, it is run by administrators. The latter are people skilled

in organization. Their concern is power, for whose orderly exercise
they establish institutions. These then recoil, often negatively, on
the values of the original vision. Such was the fate that befell the
teaching of Jesus. As the Apostles and their successors spread the
Gospel, Christian communities sprang up and, stone by stone, the
church was built. What followed had the elements of a Greek
tragedy. An other-worldly faith was corrupted by this-worldly success. After the emperor Constantine's conversion (312 A.D.), Christianity was installed as the empire's official religion. Thereupon
the church entered into a lasting partnership with the temporal
powers, each serving to underpin the other. From being the victim
of persecution, the church led the persecuting. Pacifist when weak,
an organization grown strong now flexed its muscles. Augustine
formulated the doctrine of the "just war" (*justum bellum*) as the
theologian's apologia for military action. Formerly poor, the church
amassed wealth. It thus had property to preserve and very earthly
interests to protect. Christianity had come a long way from the
Sermon on the Mount.

These changes, combining together, may be summarized as the
conversion of the church. They were accentuated after 410 when
Alaric's Visigoths destroyed the heart of the Western empire. The fall
of Rome made possible in the West the further rise of the church. The
Cross became the rallying symbol for a society that had to accommo-
date itself to the Goths, Ostrogoths, Visigoths, and Vandals, while it
attempted to repel Attila's Huns and, not long afterward, the aggressive Muslims. The fifth century and those immediately following (the
Dark Ages as they are conventionally called) formed the earlier of two
great turning points through which the Western civilization has
passed. Its significance requires analysis.

After the Roman Empire collapsed in the West, the separation of
the eastern and western halves of the Mediterranean became complete. What had commenced as a necessary administrative division
between Greek- and Latin-speaking areas widened into a political
gulf. Christianity reflected this same split, because the church of the
Greek rite was headquartered in Constantinople, while the other part
of the church, based in Rome, used Latin. The consequences for the
West were far reaching, and some were indeed disastrous.

For one thing, the Roman church proceeded by degrees to
acquire the characteristics of the empire whose place it had occupied. The Bishop of Rome evolved into a pope, wielding over other
prelates a power as autocratic as any emperor's. In a thousand ways—
ceremonial, ecclesiastical garb, language, and thoughts—Catholicism

acted in the Roman style.[31] The *imperium Romanum* lived on as the *ecclesia Romana,* propagating its dicta "from the city to the world" (*ab urbe ad orbem*). Not without reason, after the Catholic monopoly in the West was finally broken, did an English philosopher of the seventeenth century retrospectively declare:

> And if a man consider the originall of this great Ecclesiasticall Dominion, he will easily perceive, that the *Papacy,* is no other, than the *ghost* of the deceased *Romane Empire,* sitting crowned upon the grave thereof: For so did the Papacy start up on a Sudden out of the Ruines of that Heathen Power.[32]

The effects on western Europe of this merger of clerical power with the traditions of imperial Rome were most evident in the sphere of values. From the Dark Ages until the Renaissance, a period of almost a millennium, Christian ideology maintained a dominance over the minds, tastes, and morals of the Western civilization. What is more, that ideology became in practice whatever was sanctioned by papal authority in Rome. Because the church controlled such education as existed, and because Latin was its language, increasingly the West was cut off from its most stimulating heritage, the Greek portion. The break was admittedly not total because certain Greek ideas had been incorporated into Christianity, and a few Greek writers were deemed compatible with its tenets. The influence of Stoicism, for example, can be detected in the Gospel according to St. John and in the thinking of St. Paul. Platonism, too, especially in its later form as developed by Plotinus, could be harmonized with Christian teaching. After all, there are in Plato's philosophy strong elements of transcendentalism and mysticism, and he entertained such specific doctrines as the immortality of the soul and its reincarnation, with which Christians agreed. But the rest of Greek literature (including until the twelfth century the whole Aristotelian corpus, except for some of his *Logic*) was stigmatized as pagan, so that its study was prohibited. In any case, such study was ruled out by the fact that fewer and fewer of the clerics and scribes had any knowledge of Greek.

Papal Intolerance

Worst of all, during a millennium, western Europe was bereft of the greatest benefit that the Greek legacy conferred on its recipients: the spirit of independent critical inquiry. That was the very antithesis of the atmosphere prevailing under the dominion of the church, when everything had to be couched in a Catholic context. The pronouncements of the Papacy were stated as dogma. Orthodoxy was its dictate. Dissent was stamped out, for it was branded as heresy, which in those days was equated with sin. The establishment of the "Holy Office of the Inquisition" to discover and punish the heretic confirmed the character of the medieval church as a clerical police state. Throughout the period of its greatest power, its rule was stained by that most heinous of intellectual sins: intolerance.

Intolerance manifested itself in two ways—in requirements that non-Christians convert and conform as well as in overt hostilities against those who did not. Pagan temples, libraries, and works of art were wantonly destroyed. Individuals were sometimes attacked and killed, as when rampaging monks in 415 A.D. lynched Hypatia, a lady of a noble family in Alexandria. Jews were systematically persecuted, with the result, in Muller's words, that "the martyrdom that Christians suffered in their early history was negligible compared with the martyrdom they later inflicted on the Jews."[33] Islam, whose penetration of Europe from the south was halted by the Franks at Poitiers (732), was later counterattacked in that series of Crusades that pitted the "just war" of the Cross against the "holy war" of the Crescent. Internally within the ranks of western Christendom, those who dared to deviate from Rome (e.g., the Albigenses and the Waldenses) were exterminated.[34]

Apart from the ethics of such behavior, one cannot fail to note its paralyzing effects on the development of civilization in Europe. The leaders of the church exercised such comprehensive thought control that the growth of original inquiry was stunted at the source. When this was combined with unsettled, and often turbulent, political conditions, it is small wonder that in six centuries (the fifth to the tenth) western Europe had sunk into a backwater, which compared dismally with the level of learning and inventive skill then attained in Islam and China.[35] In the ninth and tenth centuries, the greatest center of cultural distinction on the European continent was Cordoba in Moorish Spain. There, such enlightened Muslim rulers as the first two Umayyad caliphs, Abd al-Rahman III and Hakim II, gave encouragement to literary, artistic, and scientific pursuits. Hakim was particularly famous for having collected an extraordinary library of some 400,000 volumes, which included Greek, Roman, and Hebrew writings in the original or translated into Arabic. Not only did they practice a liberal policy at this time toward their Jewish and Christian subjects, but they provided schools for the majority of the young throughout Andalusia. Women, as well as men, were employed in teaching and some became noted for their scholarship. Under such conditions, it was not surprising that this branch of Islamic civilization reached an early peak.[36]

In that same period, China, too, was blossoming. From the end of the sixth century, the empire, reunified by the Sui dynasty, expanded under the T'ang. The latter, as was discussed earlier, put an end to the threat of a stranglehold by the Buddhist clergy and facilitated the reassertion of Confucian humanism. China's accomplishments in scholarship, literature, and the arts, and also in social organization and technological know-how, were already at a stage that Europe was unable to reach until several centuries later.[37] The development of civilization in the West was arrested by the dominance of faith over reason, of other-worldliness over this-worldliness.

The Beginnings of Reform

Europe's eventual emancipation from its thralldom to the monopoly of a single organized religion was a long and arduous process that occurred in stages as a result of separate causes. One of these consisted in the efforts of certain churchmen to reform their institution from within and to bring it more into harmony with the teaching of Jesus. Some of the monastic orders attempted to live by a higher moral standard, which percolated through the surrounding society. A notable example was the influence that radiated outward from Cluny in the eleventh century. Contemporary with that was the enforcement of stricter rules on the clergy (e.g., celibacy), for which Hildebrand, as Pope Gregory VII, was responsible. The church also tried to limit private warfare within Christendom through the "Peace of God" (designed to protect its own institutions) and the "Truce of God," which forbade Christians to kill other Christians on certain days of the week.

The greatest ethical impetus, however, came from the extraordinary life of Francesco Bernardone, St. Francis of Assisi, the man who was perhaps closer to Jesus in spirit than any Christian has been. He it was who presented to the Papacy a challenge it could not possibly meet—to renounce its earthly power, to practice poverty and humility, and to embrace all living creatures with universal love. That was, of course, too much for the Princes of the Church, who were by no means saints and found it hard to cope with one. All attempts at the moral redemption of their institution became increasingly futile during what Barbara Tuchman has termed "the calamitous fourteenth century."[38] The wide-ranging corruption and internal dry rot, which permeated the Papacy, created the climate for the Reformation.

Europe's Renaissance

A second impetus for change in medieval Europe produced other lasting consequences. Its source was intellectual, and its focus was an institution not seen since Greco-Roman days: the university. Starting in Bologna and Padua, then spreading north of the Alps to France and England, new centers of learning sprang up, initially under clerical control and eventually with secular support. Paris was the earliest city to bubble with the yeasty ferment of independent inquiry.[39] This happened in the twelfth century when Abelard's ideas stirred controversy in the religious schools and again in the thirteenth when Albert the Great was teaching at the University of Paris. In philosophy and theology, Albert started a revolution no less profound than what St. Francis launched in ethics. For in contradistinction to the accepted dogmas of a Christianized Neoplatonism, it was he who represented the rediscovery of Aristotle.

Aristotle crept back into Europe by the side door. His return was due to the Arabs, who had become acquainted with Greek thinkers after their conquest of Syria and had the good sense to translate Greek works into Arabic. Both Avicenna and Averroës were influenced by him. When the University of Paris was organized, Aristotle was introduced there from Cordoba. "The Philosopher," as the scholastics came to call him, was studied in a medieval Latin translation of Arabic, which had been translated either directly from the Greek or from an intervening Hebrew translation. One needed a circuitous route to outflank Rome.

The impact of new ideas was soon felt in the universities. Rediscovering Aristotle was significant not only for what he taught but more for his method and spirit. Here was a metaphysician and logician who was also an empiricist with a scientific attitude. Aristotle searched for data; he weighed the evidence; he reasoned both deductively and inductively. Tertullian's nonsense—"it is certain because it is impossible"—could not survive the rigors of an Aristotelian analysis. Thought was therefore liberated, because reason was back on its throne. Other-worldliness, with its irrational beliefs in the supernatural, was placed on the defensive. Naturally, the church struck back. The Bishop of Paris detected heresies in the schools and persuaded the king to muzzle the faculty, with the inevitable result that Paris soon declined in intellectual vigor. But other centers of learning were ready to continue the inquiries, as happened at Oxford in the cases of Roger Bacon, William of Ockham, and John Wycliffe, all of whom became targets of ecclesiastical displeasure. From the thirteenth century onward, universities were being established in ever greater numbers in France, Italy, England, and Germany. Their function was to train for the lay professions (law and medicine) as well as for theology. Mathematics was also studied, thus laying the basis for novel theories in physics and astronomy. In the fifteenth and sixteenth centuries, the fruits of the new learning were ripe and ready for the plucking. Western civilization had arrived at its second great turning point.

Return to Humanism

No transformation in history was ever more dramatic than that which the West experienced before and after the twin movements called the Renaissance and the Reformation. The backwater, as it had been for a millennium, changed into a tidal wave whose cresting energies flooded out to irrigate the world. For the last 500 years, the other major civilizations—those of China, India, and Islam—have been in decline, whereas the West has been at its peak of influence. In later chapters, I shall be exploring various aspects of this phenomenon, but here is the place to analyze it in relation to that central characteristic that has been my explanatory theme: the tension between the values of the Greco-Roman and the Judeo-Christian traditions.

The chief reason why there was such a difference in the West before and after the Renaissance and the Reformation can be summarized in one sentence, which, though oversimplified, stresses the essential: The main source of Europe's inspiration shifted from Christianity back to Greece, from Jerusalem to Athens. Socrates, not Jesus, has been the mentor of the civilization that in modern times has influenced or dominated most of the planet. The West abandoned other-worldliness, becoming this-worldly for a second time. In the last five centuries, the West has been the dynamo, generating the power that has shaken and shaped our planet—and this dynamo is the product of that liberating spirit of independent critical inquiry that the ancient Greeks bequeathed and the Renaissance rediscovered.

Let me emphasize those aspects of the Renaissance that were responsible for this result. First, there was the inspiration of the classical world, an inspiration drawn from reading the literatures of Greece and Rome in the original and studying their art and history. The Romans provided models for social action (witness the use that Machiavelli made of them). But the Greeks were the teachers in all matters artistic and intellectual; and when one drinks from that source, the creative powers of the human mind are invariably unleashed. Second, the switch from Judeo-Christian influences to the Greco-Roman brought about a reaffirmation of humanism and rationalism. Human beings were seen to be the makers of their own destiny, in charge of their own fates. Third, the sciences made their great leap forward, because they were at last freed from the shackles of Christian theology. The effects were felt immediately in the fields of astronomy and physics. The combination of mathematical studies with the use of experiment and observation revolutionized our knowledge of the physical world. Copernicus, Kepler, and Galileo (all three of them products of the universities) threw out the Ptolemaic theory and put the Earth in its proper place within a solar system. The church blustered, as it did with Galileo—and still later with Darwin—but it always loses this kind of battle.[40] Fourth, the Reformation made its own unique contribution by destroying the Catholic monopoly in western Europe. Men like Luther and Calvin were as authoritarian as any pope. But their labors left society freer, because by splitting western Christendom they at least provided a choice. There were now so many different keys to the Kingdom that thoughtful people were bound to wonder whether there might also be several kingdoms, or even several gods—or possibly none.

The interest in human potentialities in this world can be stated another way. By contrast with the essentially corporate view of society that the medieval world had taken for granted, both the Renaissance and the Reformation gloried in the individual. It was the individual who could look through the telescope and observe the movements of Jupiter's moons.[41] It was the individual who could read the Bible (available now in print, and translated into German or English) and could form an opinion of what its words might mean. All this, to put it mildly, was liberating. Hence began what an economic historian has named "the European Miracle."[42]

With all this, it must be asked, what happened to ethics? The West achieved its intellectual liberation. Since then, it has led the world in scientific discoveries and their application through technology. It has amassed a formidable power, both economic and political. But have these achievements been accompanied by ethical improvement? Has the West displayed a moral leadership commensurate with the rest of its leadership? Is our civilization nowadays ethically superior to what it was at the time of its "takeoff"—during the age of Machiavelli and Michelangelo, of Leonardo and Luther, of Fugger and Erasmus? In other words, I am again restating the question that Rousseau tackled in his Essay: Has the progress in the arts and sciences contributed to purify morality or to corrupt it?

One could plausibly argue both sides of this question, and in later chapters I shall be presenting the contradictions. Here, however, let me suggest what is the crux of the issue. From the time when Rome's empire collapsed in the West up to the Renaissance and the Reformation, all ethical questions were submitted to the arbitrament of the Christian faith. In principle—though certainly not in practice—whatever Jesus reportedly said, as interpreted by the early fathers of the church and affirmed on papal authority, was binding. Morality meant conforming thereto. Outside Christianity, no ethics was admissible.

All that changed when Luther broke the papal monopoly. Various interpretations of Christian ethics were now possible. Indeed, every church, every sect, could offer its own. Some skepticism was therefore bound to ensue, because an intelligent person would have to ask which view was right. Voltaire was the understandable consequence of Luther's defiance of Rome. Into this maelstrom of polemics entered the scientists. It was they who had succeeded in breaking the stranglehold of the church over questions concerning the physical universe. They had reasserted in these matters the supremacy of reason over faith. Did the same hold for questions concerning human nature, especially the relations between human beings within society? Could ethics be emancipated from theology in the same way that science had been? Was it possible to formulate a humanistic ethic on rational principles, or must morality be grounded in religion? Could we match our increasing knowledge and control of physical nature with a corresponding knowledge and self-control of human nature?

Indeed, at an early stage in the development of modern science and technology, the issue was clearly faced by none other than

Leonardo. That many-sided genius, who engaged in military engineering, believed it practicable to invent a submarine, but decided
not to do so. This is the reason he gives:

> How and why I do not describe my method of remaining under water
> for as long a time as I can remain without food; and this I do not
> publish or divulge on account of the evil nature of men who would
> practice assassinations at the bottom of the seas, by breaking the ships
> in their lowest parts and sinking them together with the crews who
> are in them.[43]

These are weighty matters. They lie at the heart of any civilization that focuses on this world and whose values are human
centered. In the West, as we shall see, serious efforts were made
to formulate answers in the eighteenth century (the Age of Enlightenment) and again in the nineteenth (the Age of Progress).[44] The
twentieth century, as I shall argue, has been one of continuous and
unresolved contradictions between the pretensions and much of
the practice.

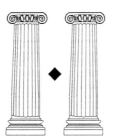

Man is explicable by
nothing less than all
his history.

Emerson

4

The Rise and Decline of Civilizations

*W*hat happens to a civilization with the passage of time? How does it develop? Does it pass through a series of stages, and, if so, do they follow a pattern? Do all civilizations change in the same, or a roughly similar, sequence? Taking a retrospective view of 5,000 years, can we detect any design, some rhythm perhaps, to connect and unify the data? Failing that, must we ascribe the sequences to chance, seeing therein the merely fortuitous play of individual personalities and random events?

The intellectual challenge in these questions has always fascinated the inquiring mind. They have been raised in one form or another ever since the historiographer began evolving from annalist into analyst. Thucydides, Polybius, Ibn Khaldun, and Vico—to cite but four of the eminent precursors—reflected on some of these issues. More recently, such speculations were revived after Gibbon had published *The Decline and Fall of the Roman Empire,* coinciding, as this did, with the revolutions in America and France.[1] Soon thereafter, new material for speculation was provided by the cumulative changes of the nineteenth century and the breakdowns in the first half of the twentieth. Queries of this kind are fundamental in any attempt to interpret history and decipher its meaning, if there be one. Should a common design be discernible in historical development, would it not indicate that the determinists may have a point—that human agents who believe they are acting freely are under an illusion, because in reality they are merely conforming to the laws of a historical process? But if no pattern can be found, if pure chance–Machiavelli's *fortuna*–apparently reigns supreme, would not the believers in free will be right?

Is There a Design in History?

The debate as to whether history exhibits a design has a still broader import than the issues in that age-old argument between free will and determinism, which, in a literal sense, is strictly academic. If a pattern is discovered, it would help us in a practical way to make predictions–always on the assumption, of course, that like causes yield like consequences, which is not universally true. The quest for predictability is not unreasonable. Indeed, if we hope to plan our future, we are crediting ourselves with at least some capacity to direct the flow of events. And if we seek a modicum of security in a world of turmoil verging at times on chaos, the knowledge that change is not utterly haphazard, if provable, would be of help.

The broad problems that this chapter explores are specially relevant to my central theme. Because I am inquiring into the ethical development of civilization in general and am asking whether we can achieve a major ethical advance within the next half century, for that to be possible, some prior questions have to be examined. How does a civilization evolve? What causes it to advance or decline? If there are general lessons to be learned from the course that civilizations have followed in the past, how are these pertinent to the circumstances of today? Before speculating on how ethical change can occur here and now, one must consider those general factors that contribute to change, whether for the better or for the worse. To learn from the past, somehow we must make it intelligible.

The search for a rationale in history has both its commendable and its dangerous aspects. On occasion, when reading the ingenious efforts to elucidate it, one wonders whether the pattern that the writer presents was in fact objectively "out there" awaiting its discoverer, or whether the latter's wish to find it was father to the thought. How much preconception, it is fair to ask, is injected into the data by the ways in which they are selected, linked, and labeled? Such processes involve a subjective element, because they depend upon the writer's judgment, which is influenced in large part by the focus of his or her interest.

Even the terminology employed in discussions of the subject has its own coloration that permeates the thinking. Here is an area of thought where metaphor is so commonly used that at times the metaphor itself becomes the message. Take the title of a book by Stuart Piggott, *The Dawn of Civilization*. Start thinking in terms of dawn, and you will be expecting noon and afternoon to arrive, followed inexorably by sunset and night. Toynbee exploits another much overworked metaphor. In his *Study of History*, he writes at length about "the geneses of civilizations," which leads into a treatment of "the growths of civilizations" as well as those that fail to grow and are termed "abortive" or "arrested."[2]

One can, in fact, distinguish three principal metaphors that have constituted the frames of reference for the bulk of the writing on this subject. Two of these have already been illustrated. They may be named the biological and the geophysical. The former interprets a civilization as an organism and, once that is decided, traces its supposed life cycle. The latter conceives of our subject in terms of the Earth's motion either during the day or throughout the year. Both these metaphors contain the same flaw. They imply that change in a certain predetermined direction is inevitable and that it proceeds through the same stages in the same sequence. Thus it is necessary for birth to be succeeded by growth, maturity, decay, and death. Similarly, dawn starts a process that must continue on to darkness, as must spring lead eventually to winter. A principal practitioner of this style of interpretation is Spengler, who uses the metaphor of the four seasons into which the history of all civilizations is made to fit. Spengler has often been criticized for wrenching and distorting the facts when they did not conform to his scheme.[3]

The metaphors of the biological or the geophysical sort are focused on the passage of civilization through time. In some discussions, however, geometry is recruited into service, so that changes over time are illustrated by figures in space. The favored ones have been the circle, the spiral, and the line. Cyclical theories were prevalent in classical Greece, where many believed that the course of history was like the motion of a wheel, rotating until it returned to its starting point. To this simple conception, a moral element was sometimes added, in the sense that the successive stages supposedly marked a decline from good to bad. Significantly, the Greeks who held this view were like Confucius in that they placed their Golden Age in the past, judging the present to be degenerate.[4] The spiral is more complex than the circle because its form is flexible. A spiral is open ended; it can narrow or widen. Hence its looser form may more accurately depict a civilization's development. Others, however, have preferred the simple line, which can zigzag or twist up and down. This image of a linear development was popular in the nineteenth century. The idea of progress was then in vogue and the line was drawn optimistically to point upward. Franklin D. Roosevelt alluded to this in one of his speeches. He recalled a teacher who had said that history recorded a succession of peaks and valleys, and that, if you drew a line connecting all the peaks and another through all the valleys, both lines would slant upward. Such, at any rate, was the view prevailing in the West until 1914.

In this book, I am attempting, as far as is linguistically possible, to avoid such metaphors. I do so not only because they have been overdone, but more important because they all involve the same defect. They are, and in the nature of the case must be, oversimplifications. As such, they can never do full justice to the truth. For truth is infinitely complex and contradictory. History is a long catalogue of special cases and exceptions, of reversals and breaks in continuity, of chance and the unexpected. It is impossible adequately to subsume its protean data under any of the formal categories proposed. Even the biological metaphor, the one that would seem to contain the greatest flexibility, is nevertheless misleading because it implies an inevitable end—that what is born must die. On this I part company with those who have colored their studies of civilization with such metaphorical treatments. Civilizations do not necessarily evolve through the same successive stages; nor do they terminate in a predestined end. They do not all conform to one and the same immanent logic or to some immutable laws of growth and decay. To imagine that these exist, and to claim to have espied their outlines in the fog of phenomena, is to chase after the "will-o'-the-wisp." The desire to uncover a systematic orderliness in the history of human societies is the "last infirmity of noble minds."[5]

The underlying error in these metaphorical interpretations stems from a misunderstanding of the nature of the subject matter. It is incorrect to interpret human societies by analogy with something else. To do so amounts to thinking about them as if they are what they are not. Let us recognize this basic truth: Human society is unique. It exists sui generis.[6] To treat it therefore as if it were an organism or a geophysical process or a geometrical figure is a mistaken starting point that cannot lead to other than distorted conclusions. In this respect, Spengler, Toynbee, and their like fall into the same trap—one that they gratuitously set for themselves.

If we wish to understand what is happening when major changes occur within a civilization, and if we are to avoid the pitfalls of the misleading metaphor, certain precautions are needed. First, the categories we employ must flow from the subject matter itself. They should not be imported into it, a priori, from another kind of material that is qualitatively and intrinsically different. Second, the language used to describe or explain the data must be accurate and precise in its meaning. That is usually not the case with metaphors, which, being symbolic, tend to be fuzzy. Let us then examine the problem of the rise and decline of civilization, keeping these considerations in mind. Under what circumstances does it rise? What circumstances attend a decline? Are the factors at work in different civilizations similar or different?

Continuity or Breakdown

(1) The Case of China

For a start, I shall return to a part of the argument in Chapters 2 and 3, where the values of China and of the West were examined. In discussing that subject, I begged a very large question. China was interpreted there as the seat of a single, continuous, Sinic civilization that emerged in a central geographic area during the second millennium B.C., which later expanded to include more people and territory and that has persisted through many vicissitudes to the twentieth century. Similarly with Western civilization: This, too, I have depicted as one and the same civilization that originated in Crete, first acquired a distinctive form among the ancient Greeks, and has lasted with accretions and contradictions to the present day.

Such an interpretation of these two major civilizations is not universally held. Toynbee, for example, states another view in his table of "the civilizations of the world, 3500 B.C. to 2000 A.D."[7] Here, Western civilization is shown to begin around 300 A.D. Its predecessor, which he calls "Hellenic," is listed as starting around 1500 B.C. and ending in 500 A.D. Within that time span, he notes a change in the first century B.C. from "political plurality" to a "universal state phase." The Sinic civilization he treats as lasting continuously from 1500 B.C. to the present, passing in 211 B.C.

from a long phase of political plurality into a universal state. Carroll Quigley goes further than Toynbee. He agrees with him that the Western world has experienced two civilizations in succession, stating that the earlier "Classical" civilization was "destroyed" in the fifth century A.D. but he then proceeds to say the same of China. There, he identifies a Sinic civilization that "rose in the valley of the Yellow River after 2000 B.C." and was terminated when it was "largely disrupted by Ural-Altaic invaders after A.D. 400." This is immediately followed by a Chinese civilization "which began about A.D. 400" and which he seems to think was "destroyed by European intruders in the period 1790-1930"—the latter date being exactly one year prior to the Japanese invasion of Manchuria.[8]

These tabulations are very revealing. The choices of dates for the beginning or ending of a civilization tell a great deal about what was going on, not only in the civilization under discussion but also in the writers' minds. They indicate which criteria are the decisive ones for them in determining whether a civilization continues in existence or has ceased to be. Both Toynbee and Quigley concur in the judgment that the civilization established around the Mediterranean after 1500 B.C. was shattered in the century between Constantine's conversion to Christianity in 312 and Alaric's capture of Rome in 410. The reasons for their opinion are plain. Two momentous events occurred during that century, which had long-range consequences. First, the Christian church vaulted into the seats of power as the Roman Empire's official religion. Second, the central structure of that empire's secular branch in the west was destroyed in 410, and despite several attempts was never effectively reestablished.

In the case of China, the circumstances are sufficiently similar and sufficiently different for Toynbee and Quigley to hold opposite views. The Sinic civilization acquired a centralized state in 221 B.C. and maintained it for four centuries until the Han dynasty came to an end. There followed a long period of political separatism, accompanied in the north by incursions of "barbarians," which lasted for three and a half centuries. In 581, however, China succeeded politically where Europe failed, for it was reunified under a centralized regime. Confucianism, which the Han Emperor Wu Ti had recognized as official doctrine, as was noted in Chapter 2,[9] was reestablished under the T'ang, who broke the power of the Buddhist clergy.

For the equivalent to have occurred in Europe, Charlemagne would have needed to act differently than he did when he inaugurated the so-called Holy Roman Empire in 800. On that celebrated occasion, he had himself crowned by the pope on Christmas Day, which invested the secular arm with ecclesiastical sanction. To parallel China, it would have been necessary for him to crush the church and then replace Christianity with the kind of Romanized Stoicism that Marcus Aurelius had enunciated. As it turned out, however, Catholicism was more deeply rooted in Europe by that time than was Buddhism in China, and Charlemagne, despite his remarkable talents, was no T'ang emperor.

The judgment that China has had one civilization evolving continuously since the second millennium B.C. hinges on the survival of three major components: its cultural identity, its basic values, and its central government. The connecting threads, in other words, have been the family system, Confucianism, and the empire. Of these, the first two are not only interrelated, but historically they preceded the act of political unification. So strong were family solidarity and its ethic that they could withstand the protracted shocks of a reversion to the earlier political fragmentation and the novelty of the Buddhist challenge. Once a centralized government was restored through a combination of political and military power, the value system that harmonized appropriately with the traditional family ties regained its primacy. I would agree therefore with Toynbee that in the case of China we are observing a single civilization which has survived thus far for three millennia and a half.

(2) The Western Experience

But what about Europe? Has the West experienced two civilizations or one? Did our present-day civilization originate in the fourth or fifth century A.D., as Toynbee and Quigley both argue, or are we the latter-day descendants of a line that stretches back continuously through Cicero and Caesar to Pericles and thence to Homer and to the wall paintings at Knossos?

Nobody would deny the importance of the changes that occurred in the West in the fourth century A.D. To describe them in Toynbee's own categories, a "universal state" disappeared, but its place was filled in part by a "universal church" whose monopoly of power endured for a thousand years. Moreover, a new population, bringing some novel cultural features, was added to western Europe during the centuries that we call the "Dark Ages," as had happened in northern China at about the same time—from the third century A.D. onward. The question at issue is whether such changes, taken together, are sufficient to designate the period after the fifth century as a new civilization.

One's answer to this question depends on which criteria are taken as central to the definition of civilization. If the presence or absence of a "universal state" or a "universal church" is the determinant in forming a judgment, then Toynbee and Quigley are right. If other factors are considered the determinants, they are wrong. Fortunately, the choice between these opposite interpretations does not have to be decided by semantics, that is, by argument about a definition. We shall be on more solid ground if our judgment is based on the irrefutable events of history. The facts that weigh heavily with me are these: Not only did China reestablish a central government under the Sui and T'ang dynasties, but even more important, it reinstated Confucianism on the pedestal it had occupied during the Han period. Given that this did happen, it is self-evident that enough of Confucian ideas and ideals lived on during the interregnum of political disunity, something that is easily explicable in the light of the continuity of the family system. Social institutions often survive political breakdowns. So do the values that they incorporate.

Now apply the same reasoning to western Europe. Toynbee and Quigley regard the collapse of the Roman Empire in the West and the advent to power of the Catholic church as marking an end and a fresh start. Add the further ingredient of the infusion of Germanic stock and the result, as they see it, was a new civilization. But this explanation, plausible though it may sound, overlooks and cannot explain a fact of supreme importance—that this Western civilization which they regard as evolving continuously since the fifth century A.D. underwent a reversal of its values a thousand years later. I am referring, of course, to the Renaissance. What inspired this dynamic breakaway was the rediscovery of the Greeks—especially of their intellectual and artistic values. When the Reformation followed quickly on the heels of the Renaissance, the church lost its monopoly as the sole arbiter of thought, of art, and of morality. The changes unleashed thereby were, in my judgment, no less momentous than those that occurred in the Dark Ages. The Renaissance and the Reformation marked a sharp break with the Middle Ages by reasserting the authority of the individual.[10] What followed was a new image of human nature, eloquently voiced by Pico della Mirandola, and with it a new ethic.

New? Yes, new to the Christian Europe over which the Catholic church had exercised its thought control for a millennium—but not new to the Europe of the Hellenic tradition. Italians of the *Rinas-*

cimento, especially the Florentines, were thinking and behaving much as the Athenians had done in their Golden Age.[11] What inference is to be drawn from that fact? If the return to Greek sources energized a cultural revolution, does this not tell us something important? Is it not apparent that enough of the Greek model of independent creativity had survived—latent and repressed, but never wholly extinguished—under the stifling rule of the "Mother Church"? For the Renaissance was not an original beginning but a rediscovery. Hence there had to have been some continuity. The century that elapsed between 312 and 410 did not finish off one civilization and inaugurate another. It marked a change of course by the same civilization in a different direction with a new element becoming salient and some of the older ones being submerged. A thousand years later, this was followed by a reverse movement toward the earlier direction and the salience once again of the original values.

I am stressing this point about the essential continuity of the Sinic and Western civilizations for two reasons that are fundamental to my argument. The first is the emphasis in this discussion on values as expressing the core meaning of a civilization. When one grasps that point, the perspective from which one views the duration of any civilization, as well as judgment on its successes and failures, will be different than those obtained at another angle of vision.

Not sharing Toynbee's belief in religion as the key to civilization,[12] I do not regard the advent to power of the Christian church as signifying the start of a new civilization in the West, and I am convinced by the capacity of the Chinese to maintain an enduring civilization wherein a humanistic morality effectively filled the place of religion.

Second, it is transparently clear that, when one assigns to these two major civilizations a time span of three or four millennia, and recognizes that they are still in existence today, some of those metaphors that have been employed to interpret them are seen as either misleading or meaningless. Those who couch their thoughts in such language draw the conclusion that the logic of the metaphor requires, not that which is called for by the historical evidence.

What the Historical Record Discloses

A different picture presents itself, however, if the interpretation leaps out from the facts and, as it were, hits the observer in the eye—instead of the latter molding the data with a priori preconceptions. What pattern, then, does the historical record disclose? Surely the answer must be that, if a pattern implies regularity, symmetry, and a recognizable design, none such can be found. The course of civilization is one of ups and downs, of periods of stagnation that can sometimes be very lengthy, of peaks of creative brilliance and of depths of horror, of revival and recovery. Actuality, viewed in retrospect, is devoid of a definite form; viewed prospectively, it presents an array of options, any one of which might conceivably be chosen. Only one reason can explain this: Nothing is determined, because everything results from acts of human free will. That is the beauty of civilization. That is the miracle. And how much more interesting to study than if the data we discover were conforming to a fixed design!

Having said that, however, I do not want to convey the erroneous impression that, because I think the unfolding of civilizations follows no overall design, everything that happens is haphazard and the observed panorama is chaotic. Not at all. Actions produce consequences—in the case of human groupings, no less than in the life of an individual. Assuredly, there are relationships between events, to some of which we can reasonably impute a causal connection. Hence it is possible to arrive inductively at certain generalizations concerning trends that manifest themselves during a civilization's history. When formulated, such generalizations are valid to the extent that they tell us "if A occurs, B is likely to follow." When we seek to apply this knowledge to our current circumstances, however, we must always keep in mind that, where we detect A in the contemporary world, past experience may demonstrate that it is possible for B to ensue, or even, in some instances, probable that this will happen. But this is never certain. To all her "laws," Clio provides exceptions, and they arise because of our free will.

The West and Islam—
Declines and Revivals

A point that strikes me forcibly when I scan the history of civilizations is their capacity to renew themselves periodically with fresh bursts of vitality. Not only does this happen at intervals of several centuries, but, just as interesting, it will occur in regions within the same civilization geographically removed from the place of origin. Let me illustrate this phenomenon from two civilizations: the West and Islam.

The Western civilization crossed the sea from the island of Crete to the mainland, where the Greeks manifested their creative impulse for some four centuries (the seventh to the fourth). Next, the locus of activity shifted to the midwest of Italy, where the dogged Romans were building their system. After their energies had petered out, new centers emerged north of the Alps in the early Middle Ages among the Germans and in France. In the late Middle Ages, however, as the church declined, Italy revived. Its signal achievement was the Renaissance, which the Germans supplemented by launching the Reformation. Then came the decisive geopolitical shift, set in motion by circumstances originating on Europe's far eastern fringe. When the Ottoman Turks captured Constantinople in 1453 and terminated the Byzantine Empire, they sealed off the access of Europeans to the caravan routes across the Middle East. That started a search for alternatives: hence the circumnavigation of Africa; hence the rediscovery by Europeans of America.[13]

Now begins the Oceanic Age. For three centuries, the peoples who lead Europe are the pacemakers in world history. They are those perforce who possess an Atlantic seaboard. Spain and Portugal, followed by the French, Dutch, and British, prosper at home while abroad they colonize and conquer. The political unit that they created, their nation-state, however, contradicts its own principles of sovereignty by establishing maritime empires. Eventually a colony rebels—or 13 of them, to be more exact—and the United States of America is founded, setting a model for Spain's transatlantic dominions a half century later. The Europeans then commit their final act of folly. As the Greeks forfeited their hegemony by wanton self-destruction in the Peloponnesian War, so Europe was the author of its own decline in two murderous "civil" wars, those of 1914-1918 and 1939-1945. Thereafter, the leadership of the Western civilization moved to North America, and the Atlantic Ocean has since shrunk into what the Mediterranean was for the Romans, a *mare nostrum*, or inland sea.

"Westward the course of empire takes its way,"[14] wrote George Berkeley, the Irish philosopher-bishop. Substitute one word and read: "Westward the course of civilization takes its way." Such, during three millennia, has been the steady direction of its movement.

Similar movements can be traced in the history of Islam. Among the major civilizations, the Islamic has features that are uniquely interesting. One is that it was founded by a single historical individual, the main events of whose life are not in doubt. Second, his teaching gained enough followers while he lived to have become a political and social force in its region by the time he died. Third, within the next two centuries, it spread across a huge area, east and west, with unparalleled speed, generating political and military strength as it went. For an Arab army to defeat the Chinese of the powerful T'ang dynasty at the battle of the River Talas in 751 would have been utterly unpredictable a hundred years earlier. Yet it happened—effectively halting the advance of the Sinic civilization into central Asia.

Islam arose in the Hejaz, on the western side of the Arabian peninsula, in an area not distinguished earlier for its ethical or cultural creativity. Mohammed was a merchant of Mecca, who in his fortieth year claimed to have heard the voice of an archangel, Gabriel, revealing to him the words of the one true God. Having become convinced that he was chosen to spread this message, Mohammed began his preaching. As he sought an audience beyond his immediate circle of family and friends, opposition developed from the ruling interests of Mecca. Their commerce seemed threatened by the stricter morality that Mohammed enjoined, and they saw no reason to give up their flexible polytheism for his uncompromising monotheism. When therefore the leaders of the more northerly city of Yathrib invited Mohammed and his few followers into their midst, he grasped the opportunity. This was in 622 A.D., Year One of the Islamic calendar, the year of the *hegira*. In the more hospitable environment of a community devoted to agriculture rather than commerce, the Prophet acquired political power and, with it, military force. From Medina, as Yathrib now was called, the Muslims extended the range of their influence, until Mecca, too, succumbed. When Mohammed died in 632, the western half of the Arabian peninsula was unified under his control.

Then commenced the expansion of the Arabs from their original homeland. In three decades after the Prophet's death, the principal center of Islamic vitality had moved north to Syria, where the Umayyads established their dynasty in Damascus. From that base, within only a century Muslim armies and converts had brought the religion of Allah as far east as China and westward across North Africa and into the Iberian peninsula. Damascus did not long maintain its primacy. In 750 the House of Abbas destroyed the Umayyads and transferred the leadership of Islam to Baghdad. One of the defeated clan, however, Abd-al-Rahman I, escaped to Spain and there, in Andalusia, established the kingdom that by the middle of the tenth century had made its capital, Cordoba, the most brilliant European city of that time. Meanwhile in the Middle East, the Abbasids presided over a civilization whose vigor slowly ebbed until in 1258 they were crushed in the onslaught of the Mongols.

But the enduring quality of Islam and its capacity to continue exploding were demonstrated anew in the next three centuries, as yet more empires sprang up under the emblem of the Crescent. These were the achievements of the Ottoman Turks, the Persian Safavids, and the Indian Moghuls. What they had in common was their adherence to the same faith, which in each region encountered strong resistance from a rival. The Turkic people, as they advanced westward across Anatolia into eastern Europe, were pitted against the Byzantine Empire expressing its Christianity through the Orthodox church. In Persia, the former center of an important civilization, it was necessary for Allah to oust Ahuramazda and for Mohammed to convert the followers of Zoroaster. In India, where Hinduism was deeply entrenched, Mohammed's teachings competed with those of the Buddha in attracting many of the Indians whom the Hindu caste system relegated to a lowly status. From Istanbul to Isfahan, from Ghazni to Agra, the variations on the Islamic theme were both as similar and yet as subtly different as those of the Western civilization in the hands of Italians, Germans, British, or French.

The parallels in the successive developments of these two civilizations have something to tell us. In each, one detects the same kind of movement. A creative vitality manifests itself for a while and its influence radiates from a particular center. Eventually this ebbs until stagnation sets in. But the original dynamic reappears in another location, where the output draws on the earlier stimulus while it expresses a new individuality. One can visualize this, perhaps, as the bubbles popping up in different places when the yeast ferments in the dough.

If a civilization is its values, as I am arguing, these are evidently transferable from people to people, from culture to culture. When and wherever they are introduced, something ignites and creative activity occurs. Its character, and the circumstances in which it develops, will be my subject in the next chapter. Here, for the moment, let us recognize the fact that it happens and explore its effects.

In civilization's house are many mansions. Not only can they be newly constructed on separate sites, but on the old foundations of a dilapidated structure something fresh and wonderful can arise. Think of China of the Warring States, then repeatedly demonstrating its peculiar genius under the Han, T'ang, and Sung dynasties, and again with the Ch'ing in the eighteenth century. Or compare the West as its civilization spread its wings with the Greeks and Romans, reemerged in the eleventh century after a decline, gained a new lease on life with the Renaissance, and made its influence felt around the world in the eighteenth and nineteenth centuries. The history of these changes exhibits no common pattern, no regularities. Nor are the outcomes predictable with any degree of certainty.

What Causes the Rise or the Decline?

Let me then restate the central question and consider how it can be answered. That question is this: What causes a civilization to emerge, to flourish, to decline? Many answers have been offered, so many indeed that by now the history of the phenomenon is accompanied by the voluminous annals of its countless explanations. I shall attempt a review of some of these.

The Views of Ibn Khaldun and Vico

One of the early attempts was that of Ibn Khaldun, the erudite historian from Tunis. Living from 1332 to 1406, he witnessed in his teens the devastating onset of the plague, the "Black Death," which killed both his parents. So many states were weakened through loss of population that his times gave the appearance of the ending of one world and the start of another.[15] This judgment was reinforced by his experiencing the effects of the Mongol assault on the Arabs, during which Ibn Khaldun was actually involved in negotiations with the dreaded Timur Lenk (Tamerlane). It seemed an appropriate moment to review the course of history and to take stock.

The area of the world with which Ibn Khaldun was familiar was North Africa and the Middle East. His *History* is therefore focused on only one civilization, the Islamic. Therein, he traces the vicissitudes of the Arabs and the non-Arabic converts to Islam during the seven centuries since the death of Mohammed. His scholarship, well in advance of anybody else at his time, reads nowadays as a strange mixture of critical analysis with uncritical faith, as a pair of quotations will illustrate. Of the historian's craft, he writes: "He must compare similarities or differences between the present and the past (or distantly located) conditions. He must know the causes of the similarities in certain cases and of the differences in others."[16] For anyone using a comparative method, this is an admirable approach because it raises significant questions for empirical inquiry. But, along with that, after criticizing the work of a predecessor, he informs us: "We, on the other hand, were inspired by God. He led us to a science whose truth we ruthlessly set forth. If I have succeeded in presenting the problems of [this science] exhaustively and in showing how it differs in its various aspects and characteristics from all other crafts, this is due to divine guidance."[17] What is his evidence for that statement?

Toynbee characterized Ibn Khaldun as "the most illuminating interpreter of the morphology of history that has appeared anywhere in the world so far."[18] That is high praise indeed, especially coming from one who, had he been less modest, might justifiably have applied such terms to himself. With that in mind, when one examines what Ibn Khaldun has to say, the content of his argument sounds essentially simple or even commonplace—an impression that may merely reflect the tendency for yesterday's insights to become today's truisms.

His reading of history, fortified by observation of the contemporary world, led Ibn Khaldun to the conclusion that peoples and the dynasties that rule them pass through periods of increasing influence and prosperity, followed normally by a decline. In fact, he analyzes the sequence with meticulous precision, assigning three generations (or 120 years) for a dynasty to complete the process and tracing five stages that make up the cycle from rise to fall. Why does this happen? The cause, he thinks, is located in a phenomenon that is fundamental to effective social organization—group feeling or solidarity (in Arabic, *asabiyah*).[19] According to whether this is strong or weak, a people rises or declines. When one inquires further what it is that fosters this solidarity, for a Muslim writing about Islam, there could be only one answer. It was religion that had supplied the unifying bond and was responsible for the intense fervor both of the Arabs and of their non-Arabic converts.[20]

Four centuries later, another thinker with a powerful, and in certain respects original, intellect addressed some of these same questions. Giambattista Vico—Neapolitan, Catholic, and a professor of rhetoric—published his ambitious *The New Science* (*Scienza Nuova*) in three successive versions between 1725 and 1744. Like Ibn Khaldun, his knowledge too was confined to the history of a single region—namely, western Europe—although, in contrast with a specialist on Islam, he had the advantage of analyzing a longer time span. Also like his predecessor, he exhibits the same incompatible mixture of the rational and the irrational. Thus, on the one hand, he asserts "the eternal and never failing light of a truth beyond all question: that the world of civil society has certainly been made by men, and that its principles are therefore to be found within the modifications of our own human mind."[21] That is a statement with which a humanist will fully concur. On the other hand, we read a few pages later: "In one of its principal aspects, this Science must . . . be a rational civil theology of divine providence"; and "our Science finds certain divine proofs by which it [providence] is confirmed and demonstrated."[22] Add to this the affirmation that "there is . . . an essential difference between our Christian religion, which is true, and all the others, which are false."[23] This assertion, be it noted, is offered by the author of *The New Science* without any attempt at proof. In conformity with that belief, Vico explicitly mentions the direct clash between Greco-Roman values and those of Christianity, which I discussed in Chapter 3.

> When, working in superhuman ways, God had revealed and confirmed the truth of the Christian religion by opposing the virtue of the martyrs to the power of Rome, and the teaching of the Fathers, together with the miracles, to the vain wisdom of Greece, and when armed nations were about to arise on every hand destined to combat the true divinity of its Founder, he permitted a new order of humanity to be born among the nations in order that [the true religion] might be firmly established according to the natural course of human institutions themselves.[24]

A rationalist reading these statements is reminded of Ibn Khaldun's similarly dogmatic quotations from the Koran, which he accepts without questioning as the words of Allah, and is bound to be skeptical about interpretations of history that issue from such premises. But be that as it may, what are the principal lessons that Vico teaches? He believes he has discovered through his New Science a theme or pattern that pervades "the course the nations run," and that this has always been manifest and always will be. "Our Science therefore comes to describe at the same time an ideal eternal history traversed in time by the history of every nation in its rise, development, maturity, decline, and fall."[25] In sequence, he thinks, there are three stages, which he calls divine, heroic, and human. Applying this triad, he develops a threefold analysis of natures, customs, natural law, governments, languages, characters, jurisprudence, authority, and reason—his list is virtually endless! What he is saying, in other words, is that all aspects of society are imbued at any one time with a common design that itself changes through successive stages. This is, of course, the cyclical theory all over again, which Vico had gleaned from Polybius and others. But he varies it in this sense that, while the process is circular, the ending is not a return to the original starting point. He conceives it more as a spiral, curving back upon itself but at another level.[26] This is how he interprets the two phases, as he sees them, in the history of the West, marked by a return to barbarism in the Dark and Middle ages.[27] Vico's treatment is ingenious. He offers fresh insights, derived from his comparisons. But they are intermingled with much that is forced and fanciful. As for his schematism, like some contemporary sociological models, it exists more in logic than in life. History is never that schematic. Even if there were such a succession of phases as he outlines, we are still left wondering why the changes occur.

In this discussion of Ibn Khaldun and Vico, one aspect of the subject has not been mentioned: namely, the ethical. For this omission there is a valid reason. Neither of them makes it a topic of central concern in his analysis. By this I do not mean that either is totally silent about ethical values. On the contrary, they do refer to the virtues that are practiced in the successive phases of the historical cycle. But for both it is religion that enjoins morality and supplies its precondition. Faith in Islam's Allah or in the Judeo-Christian God makes ethical conduct possible. Such an interpretation, ascribing to ethics a religious source and sanction, comes naturally to historians of civilizations whose dominant values are other-worldly. But that presents a difficulty in evaluating their ethics. For, in the nature of the case, not only is the ethics based upon a supernatural foundation, which removes it from the range of rational analysis, but in addition it is "culture-bound" in the sense of being restricted to what was supposedly revealed to one individual. When God and Allah are reported as speaking differently, or where Moses, Jesus, and Mohammed disagree among themselves, do we not need another standard, external to them all, for judging their discrepancies?

Two Modern Synthesizers:
(1) Spengler's Schematism

It is instructive to turn from two distinguished minds of the fourteenth and eighteenth centuries to the two moderns—Spengler and Toynbee, a German and a Britisher—who are the best-known contributors to this discussion in our century. Both had the advantage over their predecessors of a longer historical perspective and of being able to draw on a vastly greater volume of knowledge. Their work differs, however, in two major respects. Spengler, while drawing on the history of other civilizations for purposes of comparison and analogy, concentrates his attention on the Western one to which he himself belongs. In fact, he goes so far as to say that, because you cannot have true knowledge without experience, you cannot really understand any culture other than your own.[28] Toynbee, however, has a range of knowledge as universal as it was possible for one individual to acquire and he employs a method that was genuinely comparative. Even though Mumford criticizes his *Study* as "the product of Old World Ideology," which "never confronts its own unexamined premises,"[29] it must be recognized as the most comprehensive analysis of the record of human civilization undertaken by anyone thus far.

Another significant difference between the two is their message and the effect this has on how each develops his theme. Spengler is convinced that the Western civilization has arrived at the stage of terminal decline, and his aim is to explain why this had to be. All of his work therefore is special pleading directed to the conclusion expressed in the title. Toynbee, like Spengler, has his biases and preferences, but he is less dogmatic in stating them. Thus in sharp contrast with his forerunner, he manages at least to convey the appearance of being somewhat detached. Now let us examine what each of them has to say about the changes that a civilization undergoes.

The ideas that Spengler presents are couched in a framework of categories that he asserts in the most positive terms, without considering it necessary to argue their validity. His fundamental distinction is that between becoming and being. The former is growing, developing, alive. That is good. The latter is fixed, static, dead. That is bad. The world can be comprehended from both of these vantage points. If from the former, we observe the world-as-history, moving through time toward the future to which destiny summons. If from the latter, we study the world-as-nature, shaped across space by the principle of causality and therefore determined by the past. The former perspective is that of the historian and the poet. Preeminently this was the vision of Goethe, the primary influence on his thinking, as he declares, with Nietzsche in second place.[30] The other perspective is that of the scientists. Their universe is the one created by Newton and Darwin.

Applying this line of reasoning, Spengler equates human societies with living organisms that pass through a series of stages, necessary and unvarying. These are not a matter of choice, for it is the morphology of the organism—that is, its form and structure—that prescribes them. How and why a particular culture originates and emerges is a problem to which he refers but that he is unable to explain.[31] While a society is expansive and creative, he calls it a culture. Civilization, by his definition, is what follows the great period. "The Civilization," he asserts, "is the inevitable *destiny* of the Culture. . . . Civilizations are the most external and artificial states of which a species of developed humanity is capable. They are a conclusion, the thing-become succeeding the thing-becoming, death following life, rigidity following expansion."[32] On the basis of these assumptions, Spengler compares the West in the first two decades of this century with what he insists are the homologous periods in the life span of other cultures. Thus is he able to conclude that this civilization is engulfed and drowning.[33]

The ideas that took shape to form his book were developed by Spengler in 1911, at a time when, as he states, he believed a major war to be imminent. When it broke out in 1914, he reworked and expanded the manuscript, which was published as the war was ending in 1918. In Germany, its immediate impact was profound, because the pessimism of the conclusions suited the mood of a defeated empire. But its shock waves rippled out to the British and French, who could no longer be confident about their own future when they took stock of the price they had paid for "victory." As for the United States, the buoyant optimism of the American people lasted a bare decade. It plunged with the crash of the stock market in 1929.

(2) Toynbee's Contradictions

It was in this same context that a British historian, trained in the Greek and Roman classics, embarked on the lengthy research that culminated in a 12-volume work under the unpretentious title, *A*

Study of History. Arnold Toynbee had conceived his theme and outlined his research shortly after the end of World War I. He says that he was "racing" to complete it "against the coming Second World War,"[34] but he had published only the first six volumes when hostilities began. The remaining six appeared in print in 1954, 1959, and 1961. Thus it was the experience of twentieth-century warfare that created for Toynbee, as for Spengler, the context for reflections on the human condition and that dominated the conclusions reached by both men about the prospects for civilization. One other link between this pair is worth noting. Both drew heavily on Goethe for their inspiration. Indeed, the legend of Faust, especially the thoughts and myths that Goethe weaves into that drama, become the vehicle for some of the central ideas that Spengler and Toynbee have expressed.

Although Toynbee thinks and writes in the tradition of Ibn Khaldun, Vico, and Spengler, he transcends them all. His work— one of the outstanding intellectual achievements of this century—is extraordinary in two ways. Nobody before him had known as much about human history as he did, and every civilization yields grist to his mill. The second remarkable aspect of his work lies in the plan of the mill that he designed. To compare civilizations, he conjures up a conceptual framework whose elaborate machinery grinds the historical data into particles and recombines them in novel shapes and groupings. It is in this conjuring—a term I use with full awareness of its connotations—that his signal contribution and serious flaws are equally evident.

Here my concern is to focus on that part of Toynbee's treatment which seeks to explain the growth of civilization and its decay, a phenomenon that he illustrates with relevant examples and that he describes, as noted before,[35] in the language of the biological metaphor. How then does he interpret it? What factor, what principle, causes the growth or the decay to occur? He faces this question, as he must, and offers his answer. His explanation is compressed into the short formula of "challenge-and-response."[36] Human society, in the course of existing on this planet, encounters a sequence of challenges to which it must respond. When the effectiveness of the response is adequate, or on some occasions more than adequate, to the strength of the challenge, that society grows. When the response is barely sufficient, it becomes stagnant—or its growth is arrested. When the response is inadequate to the challenge, decay sets in and death may ensue.

This formula has echoes, of course, that are familiar to our ears. One hears the principles of Darwinian biology, of struggle for existence and the survival of the fittest, the stimulus and response of psychological doctrine, and the supply and demand of economic theory. In that sense, Toynbee's central theme—the grand explanation of why civilization runs its course—lacks the element of novelty, and one cannot help being surprised that the complex apparatus of his unparalleled scholarship did not generate a more original insight. But leaving aside the matter of novelty, a deeper criticism must be leveled. The real reason for feeling dissatisfied with "challenge-and-response" is that this formulation, to put it plainly, explains nothing. It is a redundant statement devoid of meaning. What Toynbee is saying amounts to this: If a civilization is growing, that itself is the proof that it has responded to its challenge, and, if it is decaying, that it has not. The so-called explanation merely restates in other language the facts that we already know. It affirms the results of a process, when we are trying to understand the cause. What it is incapable of telling us is what we need to know—namely, the reason civilization sometimes responds successfully to its challenge and the reason why at other times it fails. When his exhaustive comparison of 34 civilizations brings Toynbee to such a lame conclusion, my own feeling is that the massive columns of Karnak are here being used to support a yurt.

Aside from this inadequate response to his own challenge, Toynbee's work contains another fundamental flaw. In this complicated individual was a split personality. As a consequence, there are two streams in his thinking that run parallel and never mix. One side of him is the analytical historian trained in the classics and taking Thucydides as a model. The other side is a Christian mystic in search of an ultimate reality whose essence he insists is spiritual.[37] This is the Toynbee who has switched from the rational to the irrational, who writes passionately about the need for a universal church and who genuinely believes that human salvation is possible only through religion. Thus it is that the final sentence of his massive *Study* consists of the words from Goethe that he quotes several times: *Das Unbeschreibliche, Hier ist's getan* (Here is accomplished the indescribable). To this a rationalist can only inquire: Just what is the indescribable telling us? Toynbee is impaled on the horns of his own dilemma—Greek this-worldliness and Christian other-worldliness. By the schisms within his own soul,[38] he has personified the incompatibility between the two sides of Western civilization.

A Different Answer to the Question:
How Values Evolve

He who critically examines the works of others incurs both an obligation and a risk. The obligation is to offer something of one's own that is free from their faults. The risk is that this, too, will assuredly invite criticism. Fully conscious therefore of the hazard, let me try now to answer the question that has been raised throughout this chapter. I, too, have something to suggest, and I offer it as being derived a posteriori from the facts of history, and not as issuing a priori from the notion of a preconceived pattern.

Earlier in this chapter, I reviewed the sequence of changes in some major civilizations. The conclusion drawn from the facts is that they exhibit different patterns—or possibly, in the case of India, no pattern at all. As their course of development varies so markedly through time and through space, is it not plausible to suggest that those who have searched for a uniform pattern in the data, or who have sought to introduce it a priori, have proposed the wrong answers because their thinking was founded on the wrong assumption? If the conception one adopts flows from the data, instead of the latter being grouped to fit a preconception, one can drop the misleading idea of a common design and explore some other hypothesis.

What the events of civilization disclose is a series of alternations, following one another at irregular intervals in an irregular sequence. Advances are made in various sectors of society, generated by an outpouring of creative energy that eventually diminishes. What follows is either a period of stagnation, which can in some cases last for a millennium, or a breakdown that is marked by disintegration and upheaval. In the latter case, an invasion may occur because those beyond the frontier detect their moment of opportunity. That this is how civilizations change, how they rise or decline, is attested by the historical record. What has yet to be explained is why their changes occur in this fashion.

I base my own explanation on the argument that the clue to every civilization lies in its values, for these are what supply it with motive power and rationale. That is Point 1. Point 2 consists in a tendency of human nature with which we are all familiar. We find something that is appropriate in coping with a particular situation, some principle or modus operandi that works adequately when put to the test. Because success attends its application, we go on applying it—and we do so more and more until eventually its benefits are converted into vices. That this is a common occurrence is indicated by the fact that we have the phrases ready to describe it. We say we are suffering from the defects of our virtues.[39] Or we may cite the Latin tag *corruptio optimi pessima,* "the best, when corrupted, is the worst." This is an ancient insight, which Plato formulated in *The Republic* as a general psychological characteristic.[40] We go too far in one direction; a reaction follows; so we go in the opposite direction—also to excess. This is indeed a common tendency that history can amply illustrate. It is equally valid as an explanation of the changes that have overtaken civilizations. Consider some examples.

As I have cited Plato, let us think first about what happened to the ancient Greeks. Central to their social system, and therefore vital to their view of civilization, was the *polis.* What principle upheld it? Obviously its autonomy, meaning its complete independence from any external control. That principle enabled each polis to develop according to its resources and opportunities. It also opened up the possibility for some freedom of movement for selected categories of individuals—political exiles, for example, or traders, or the Sophists. That was freedom seen from its good side. This was offset, however, by the harmful consequences of a useful principle carried to excess. Internal faction fighting, and the pressure of population on food supply, led to indefinite splitting and the planting of colonies. Hence more and more *poleis* were planted around the Mediterranean. The result was the extreme of disorder—anarchy. No superorganization was ever established to regulate them all and inject a tolerable order into their relations. The more powerful states tried to do it by the methods of imperialism. But that only stimulated the creation of counterempires, whose struggles for hegemony led to the wars by which they were collectively weakened. It was then left to Macedon to gobble them all up. There was a clear and obvious dénouement, as foreseeable as the course of a Greek tragedy: The love of independence led to an excess of separate units of all sizes, which, in the absence of common controls, resulted in conflict and war, ending in an ultimate order imposed from outside.

The Romans exemplify the operation of the same principle, but in reverse. These were a people with a passion for system. Creating order out of disorder was their genius. Thus they unified Latium; then Italy; then, province by province, the entire Mediterranean. But, it will be asked, why did they succeed in building so vast an empire whereas the Spartans and Athenians failed in the same effort, although they were no less imperialistic and started from no smaller a base? The answer is that the Romans, being "doers" and therefore pragmatists, hit upon a device that would have been conceptually repugnant to the more speculative and rationalistic Greeks. At first the Romans treated the peoples they conquered as subjects, assigning them an inferior status. Naturally that bred sullen resistance or open revolt. So the imperial masters thought it prudent to begin sharing their privileges bit by bit, stage by stage, with trusted individuals, then with groups, then with whole communities. That process—the extension of Roman citizenship—culminated in the year 212 A.D. in the edict of Caracalla unifying under one politico-legal category all the inhabitants of the empire who were not slaves.

This solution to the problem of governing an empire was possible for the Romans because their lawyers were able to define citizenship as a collection of transactions—including, for example, the right to intermarry, the right to engage in trade, the right to sue in the civil courts (i.e., the courts reserved for the citizens), the obligation to pay certain taxes, and so on—which could be separated and granted piecemeal. An Athenian, however, thought of citizenship in a different way (witness the Funeral Oration of Pericles). Citizenship for him was the expression of a total functioning membership in the community where he lived and whose common life he shared. Active participation was therefore its essence, and those at a distance manifestly could not participate. Therefore citizenship must be restricted—good logic, but bad politics!

But the Romans too suffered the defects of their virtues. When order is your objective, certain consequences will follow. Order requires orderliness, and the latter is most efficiently maintained when a single authority is giving the orders. Thus the system tends to become centralized and, as we say, authoritarian. On matters that are not fundamental to the exercise of power at the center, diversity may be tolerated. But it is not permitted in whatever is deemed basic. Thus Christians cannot be exempted from taking part in religious ceremonies held in honor of those dead emperors who had been deified. Order, moreover, does not easily coexist with neighboring peoples beyond the *imperium* whose independence is disorderly in the eyes of systematizing Romans. Hence the neverending attempts at expansion, until the empire becomes unwieldy and unmanageable.

The empire was created while Rome was governed as a republic, but republican institutions were unable to administer it. Neither

the several assemblies, nor the annually elected consuls, nor even
the Senate could control the commander of an army in a distant
province whose troops were loyal to him and who had a political
following in the capital. Thus out of the need to hold an empire
evolved the emperorship whose tenure depended realistically on
the support of the army. But the resulting authoritarianism eventually had a stultifying effect internally. Establishing a single order
where none had existed before was the Roman achievement; carrying that order too far was a major cause of their downfall.

In further support of this generalization, two more instances of
this tendency may be cited: medieval France and modern Britain.
In the Middle Ages, there was a sharp contrast between French
preeminence in the twelfth and thirteenth centuries and decline
in the fourteenth. Why this dramatic change? Of the various contributing factors, one stands out as central—namely, the values that
motivated the governing elite. Because medieval France was a
feudal society, the landowning families were dominant. The maintenance of internal order and the conduct of war depended ultimately on the heavily armored knight mounted on horseback. This
figure, *le chevalier,* was not only an efficient killing machine but
also, like Japan's *samurai,* a person imbued with a special code of
ethics. As a fighting man, he attached great importance to physical
prowess and to courage in one-to-one combat. With this went also
a sense of honor, which supplied a code of fairness in regulating
some of the brutalities of martial strife and also the obligation on
the domestic front to succor the distressed.

At its best, this set of principles expressed itself in what today
we still call "chivalry." "Gaily bedight, a gallant knight," as Poe
pictured him, *le chevalier sans peur et sans reproche* (the knight,
fearless and stainless) was the stuff of which "romance" was
spun—a French term for a French fantasy. But reality was never
thus. The knight errant throve on adventure; hence the costly
tournaments where his skills were conspicuously displayed. Above
all, being trained to fight, he lived for war—and in it died with
honor, provided his wounds were in front.

Therein precisely lay the defect of his virtue. In peacetime, these
knights had limited usefulness, there being normally only a short
supply of distressed damsels for them to rescue. So they had to
create mayhem to give themselves a raison d'être. France was
plagued in the fourteenth century not only by the Black Death but
by an endemic sickness of human origin. This was the virulence
of the "free Companies," consisting of soldiers whose armies had

been disbanded and who entered the pay of any captain to lead a life of banditry and pillage. Many of the captains in these companies were themselves of the nobility, uprooted and footloose. Holding entire communities to ransom, they became the scourge of France.

But that was not all. When it came to fighting the wars on which the safety of the kingdom depended, the honor that spurred on these chevaliers was the fatal chink in their armor. Honor was an aristocratic value, beyond the reach of the vulgar mass. Only a few could attain it, because, if too many shared in its acquisition, it was not worth having. Such attitudes prevented the chivalry of France from changing the techniques of warfare when that would have meant according more tactical importance to common soldiers. As a consequence, at Crécy (1346), as later at Agincourt (1415), English archers, who were not noblemen, slaughtered French aristocrats. For similar reasons, when the French marched east in 1396 on a crusade to stem the advance of the Turks, they were destroyed at Nicopolis. "What basically defeated the crusaders," writes Barbara Tuchman, "was the chivalric insistence on personal prowess. . . . As long as combat was desirable as the source of honor and glory, the knight had no wish to share with the commoner."[41] It was left to a Spaniard to write, appropriately in the form of a romance, the epitaph to an institution that had degenerated from utility to futility. The values of Sir Galahad became the delusions of Don Quixote. Bred to ride in the whirlwind, the knight fizzled out on a windmill.

Modern Britain has retraced, in essentials, the story of medieval France, in the sense that the aristocratic virtues that once helped the country to greatness were corrupted into the vices responsible for its decline. The principal feature of English society, persisting for a thousand years, has been its class system. English men and women acquired at birth the social status of their family, which could be upper class, or middle, or lower. Movement between classes did occur, but very rarely before the nineteenth century. Under these circumstances, the influence of the upper class—few in number, but qualitatively different because of social position and education—was all-pervasive.

That aristocracy was very tenacious. Periodically, after a change of dynasty, or civil war, or revolution, its membership would be replenished. But those newly added were soon assimilated into the traditions of their predecessors. This English nobility retained its privileges because in return it performed the obligations of service. The fresh scions of ancient houses filled the great positions of the realm; they fought and bled in its wars. What they gave was leadership.

With its emoluments, they accepted the responsibilities and the sacrifices.

But an inherent vice accompanied such virtues, the vice of inequality. The status of someone's family was no necessary index to his or her native abilities. Talented individuals outside the upper class could seldom develop themselves to the fullest because of the barriers that the class system erected. By contrast with the peoples of the European continent, the English were guaranteed certain liberties, appropriately graded, of course, to their rank. But, although juridical rights were the English heritage, equality was not. It was in rebellion against such a system that Jefferson proclaimed that "all men are created equal."

Britain's society in the second half of the twentieth century is obviously different from that of 1776. What intervened was the Industrial Revolution, as it is called, the rise and dismemberment of the second British Empire, and the losses in the catastrophic world wars of this century. Throughout all this, the class system—though modified by economics and education—has remained a reality. The social classes yet survive; the hereditary aristocracy still is accorded an esteem that nowadays is unearned; and the monarchy still occupies the apex of the hierarchy. Here, without doubt, is one of the major factors contributing to the British decline. The downgrading of industry, trade, and commerce—in contrast with the professions—prevented enough of the country's talented men and women from filling positions of leadership in the economy. In the workplace—whether factory, department store, or suite of offices—the "two nations" of which Disraeli warned are palpably present to this day. A deferential society is one of inherent inequalities, and with inequality comes wastage of talent. A democratic polity cannot cohere with an undemocratic society.

After considering these four cases—the Greeks and Romans of antiquity, medieval France, and modern Britain—let us now translate the terms of the argument to a wider sphere, substituting a whole civilization for a single people. Does the same tendency operate across a broader span of time and space? What does the record of four major civilizations reveal?

Virtues Transformed Into Vices

Looking first at China, what strikes one so forcibly about that civilization's history is its undulating pattern. Advances occur and recur with a wavelike rhythm, interspersed with stagnation or breakdown. What causes this to happen? The explanation, I think, has to be found in those persistent features that endow this civilization with its unique character. Here is an area as large as Europe, with a population always greater than Europe's, cohering through time and space by cultivating this-worldly Confucian values. The latter, as was seen in Chapter 2, supplied the connecting link between the enduring family system and the centralizing authority of successive dynasties. These values, however, are alternately a blessing and a bane. They are a blessing, when they provide stable and dependable relationships to millions; a bane, when they become so rigid and ritualized that creative departures from tradition are inhibited. But because the values are basically humanistic and are focused on human needs in this earthly existence, the possibilities of renewal always exist whenever a new opportunity presents itself—whether a change of dynasty, or a technological innovation, or the shock of penetration by outsiders.

Next, consider India. Here the salient facts are markedly different from the Chinese record. As Hinduism is the authentic expression of India's civilization, it is worth noting that since the twelfth century A.D. Hindus have not been in control of their own destinies except in the deep south. Across the north and in much of the central region, they fell under the rule of Muslim invaders (the Sultanate of Delhi followed by the Moghuls) and subsequently of Europeans (the Portuguese, French, and British). For some eight centuries, therefore, Hinduism sank into a prolonged stagnation from which it is only now emerging.

If, therefore, we are seeking the true manifestation of the character of Indian society before foreigners overran it, we should look earlier at the two millennia prior to the twelfth century. During that time, India registered some major achievements, most of which were clustered within two shorter periods—from the sixth to the third century B.C. and from the fourth century A.D. to the eighth. Not only was the interval between these a long one, but the fact that only one such renewal occurred makes it impossible to treat India's history as parallel to China's. One revival does not a pattern make, and it would be stretching the facts to describe the Hindu experience as a series of undulations.

But as that is the case, there must be a reason for the difference. Why was it that Hinduism developed along separate lines? What caused the two earlier successes and, subsequently, the prolonged failure? Surely the explanation must derive from those features of this civilization that are peculiar to it. The first major respect in which India has differed is its other-worldliness; the second is its caste system. The effect of other-worldliness is to transfer human priorities from this existence to some hypothetical existence hereafter. That set of values induces passivity in regard to social arrangements here on earth. Hinduism did not provide a springboard for social reform or innovation. Protest movements had to originate therefore outside of Hinduism and in opposition to it—the prime examples being the Buddhists and the Jains. The great Ashoka, let us not forget, was a Buddhist. Then, too, there were the consequences of caste. How could there be regular renewals of vitality when the social order was so highly segmented and stratified—and petrified in addition? India has been the victim of its values: good for the Brahmins, bad for most of the others.

This brings me, third, to Islam. What picture does this civilization present and how is it to be explained? In terms of the problem under examination, it is the rise and decline of the Islamic culture that need elucidating. Here, as was discussed earlier in this chapter, the course of events exhibits a definite pattern, one that is obvious to the eye. We see a wavelike movement that can be traced from century to century and from country to country. Islam crests successively among the Arab peoples in Medina and Mecca, in Damascus and Baghdad; then it demonstrates a renewed vitality in Persia, in Moghul India, and among the Ottoman Turks. In each of these areas, however, after an initial advance comes the stagnation or the breakdown. Why does this happen?

The clue can be discovered in those traits that make Islam distinctive or even unique. Here is a civilization constructed around a religion and characterized therefore by other-worldliness. And what is the central doctrine of this religion? It is that which Islam signifies, complete submission to the will of Allah purportedly revealed to his chosen prophet, Mohammed, and written down by him in the Koran. As what is stated in the Koran consists of the words not of Mohammed but of Allah, its authority is supreme. What is more, no human being may change it.

In these beliefs lay Islam's strength and its weakness. Among people after people—throughout the Middle East, across North Africa, and in Spain, India, and southeast Asia—the message of the Koran, strict, stern, and charged with certitude, initially had a galvanizing effect. Hence the succession of centers of vitality. But after a while, rigidity overtakes the society that has submitted. The combination of other-worldliness with inflexibility is eventually deadening for the life here and now. If Allah rules the world, whatever happens must be Allah's will. The individual dare not question fate or challenge it when everyone knows "it is written." How could a civilization imbued with such values not stagnate?[42]

Fourth, let us apply this same analysis to Western civilization. Is a pattern observable here, too? If so, what form does it take? And how are we to explain whatever it is we find?

In the preceding chapter, I described Western civilization as having a split personality because it has attempted to incorporate two incompatible sets of values—Greco-Roman this-worldliness and Judeo-Christian other-worldliness. Historically, these have alternated in their dominance. Greco-Roman values were ascendant until the third century A.D.; Christianity, for the next thousand years. Since the Renaissance and Reformation, Western development has again drawn inspiration from the rational humanism of its Greco-Roman tradition, with Christianity in retreat but fighting a rearguard action. Within each of these three stages, forward thrusts have been followed by stagnation or breakdowns of varying duration. That raises the question of whether these changes are connected with the opposing sets of values. I think it can be shown that they are.

How the virtue of the polis was corrupted into its vice has already been discussed. That same tendency that led the Greeks politically from autonomy for each community to anarchy for all was also operating in another sphere where its social effects were quite mixed, namely, the relation between the critical intellect and social ethics. The work of the Sophists in the fifth century B.C. was successful in questioning traditional beliefs and in challenging the conventional wisdom to justify itself on rational grounds. But the overall effect of their inquiries was negative. They differed among themselves too deeply to supply any positive affirmation in face of the values that they undermined.[43] Then, to compound this intellectual restlessness that they engendered came the self-destructive catastrophe of the Peloponnesian War, lasting for a whole generation. Not until the time of the Stoics did a positive ethic emerge. But by then, the polis was past saving. By their excesses the Greeks had forfeited their independence.

As for the Romans, I have already described how they lost their innocence, embraced the "bitch-goddess"[44] of empire, and fenced in the Mediterranean lands with their legions and their law. But the structure they built became a shell that lacked an indwelling spirit. Their *virtus* gave the boon of order, and an excess of order corrupted them. The same sequence was repeated by the Christian church. Tragedy befell Christianity when the popes draped themselves in the *toga* of the Caesars. Once they were wedded to worldly wealth, political power, and military force, their spiritual mission was hopelessly compromised. In the localities where the priest was close to the people, or in scattered monasteries and convents, some good could be accomplished. But in Rome itself, *realpolitik* ruled. In medieval Europe as in Hindu India, the other-worldly focus was a convenient stratagem for deflecting attention from this world and inducing submission among those who suffered its injustices.

With the reaffirmation of humanistic values in the Renaissance, the Western civilization made a new start. Once again the critical intellect was unleashed. The individual was free to query the conventional wisdom, and the church, its monopoly gone, could no longer impose its orthodoxy. Spectacular were the breakthroughs that ensued—in political and economic innovation, in the arts and literature, and above all in science. But as the churches now encountered growing skepticism, morality had to be given another sanction than the religious. Here is where we can place our finger on the crucial weakness of Western civilization since the seventeenth century. Our gains in scientific knowledge and technology have been phenomenal. By comparison, our ethical progress has not kept pace. That is why in this twentieth century human civilization has peered into the abyss of horrors—of Hitlerism and now the nuclear bomb.

The Wavelike Rhythm

Such, as I read the history of our species, has been the general course along which the major civilizations have evolved. Wavelike alternations are the best summary description of what happens, but these do not always recur with enough regularity to constitute a recognizable pattern. In every civilization the values we choose have made us what we are, and it is our tendency—common, but by no means inevitable—to carry their benefits to an excess that in time becomes injurious. Thus we rise; thus we decline; thus we renew ourselves. Looking backward, one can discern the causal connections that link the sequence of events. Looking forward, as nothing is predetermined, one observes a bundle of possibilities, some of which are more probable than others. Always, there lies in human hands, directed by human will, our fortune or our misfortune.

This summary of the general causes of a civilization's rise or decline has particular relevance for ethical change. It is the essence of moral choice that it must be free. A civilization advances or regresses ethically by decisions about the values to which it assigns priority; and in choosing what to accept or reject, its freedom is made manifest. For anyone today who envisages the need for ethical improvement among humanity at large, that is a hopeful conclusion. It is better to know that we can determine our destiny. Should we fail to change, "the fault . . . lies not in our stars, but in ourselves." We are the ones responsible.

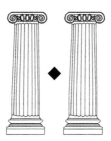

Many things are awesome,
and none is more awesome
than humanity.

Sophocles

5

Creative Eras and Areas

$\mathcal{A}$ll of us are aware of times in our lives when our performance rises to a level far above our normal capacity. Somehow, all of a sudden, we seem to be lifted up; we transcend our limitations. What previously was difficult, or even unattainable, is accomplished with an ease that is almost effortless. These are the "peak experiences" of which Maslow has written.[1] They are those special moments when a person functions gloriously at the heights. What happens thus to a single individual also occurs to individuals in groups. A community, whether small or large, an entire people, a nation, finds itself for a certain length of time collectively surpassing its previous record of achievement. Compressed into a short, spectacular epoch are works and deeds of rare quality that exercise a lasting effect on later generations and permanently enrich humanity. It is this kind of creativity that forms the subject of this chapter.

In this respect, civilization exhibits the same characteristics as a person or a people. On occasion, after a steady development that remains slow and gradual for several centuries, a civilization seems to lift off like a rocket. Inventiveness and energy, fired by sparks of audacity, combine in an outpouring of creative talent. Feats of mind and imagination break through the frontiers of the known, voyaging into the unknown. Out of the welter of experiment, some of it inevitably mistaken and misdirected, the genuine triumphs emerge that put their stamp upon their time and mold the future. We call such epochs the Golden Ages. They are variously described—by the name of a ruling family (e.g., the Guptas) or a leading personage (Pericles, for instance) or some broad movement in ideas and values (such as the Renaissance). What all these have in common is that they are out of the ordinary. When we are living in an age such as the present that, except in the fields of science and technology, cannot be included among the great ones, we may wonder with some touch of envy what it must have felt like to be contemporaries participating in, or even witnessing, the accomplishments that mark a Golden Age.

The occurrence of this phenomenon of the creative era is not in doubt. What is a matter for speculation is to discover its conditions and explain its causes. In a general sense, a discussion of this problem continues the analysis conducted in the preceding chapter, where I inquired into the rise and decline of civilization, into how it develops and why. Here, my theme is to explore a special aspect of that problem. Under what circumstances does civilization attain its highest levels? Not only is this question intellectually significant, but to study humanity during our past successes may give us hope amid the anxieties of the present. Could not the level of achievement, which was reached before, be reached again? This query applies with special force in the sphere of ethics. If, as is argued in this book, our several contemporary civilizations need at this point in social evolution to take a giant ethical leap, then it behooves us to inquire, first in general terms, how such movements have happened in the past and, second, specifically, how they have come about in the ethical sphere. This chapter concerns itself with the former question. The latter will then be the subject of Chapters 6 and 7.

The question propounded here has many facets and must therefore be approached from many angles. First, we must specify what the creative periods are. They need to be identified so as to clarify what we are talking about. Identifying them will help in answering two related questions. When do these ages occur, and where are they centered? In other words, which eras and which areas have been the creative ones? Those topics, although they invite differences of interpretation on certain points, are not too difficult to elucidate. Next, however, come the problems that are more complex. In what kinds of activity do the creative surges manifest themselves, and is there any relationship, positive or negative, between success or failure in a particular sphere and what happens in the others? Finally, there is the crucial question of causation. Why is it that civilizations become creative or fail to create?

Every major civilization has experienced its exceptional periods; but, as is to be expected, these are not very numerous. Nor, generally, has their duration been very long. The time span of the greatest achievements normally extends for one or two centuries, within which a couple of generations (that is to say, six or seven decades) constitute the peak. That generalization must be qualified, however, by the reminder that the highest level of performance is never reached in all spheres contemporaneously. What are conventionally described as Golden Ages tend to be so named because they excel in political dynamism and the economic growth that so often accompanies it. As a consequence of their amassing power and wealth, the rulers and the rich bestow their patronage on the arts—or at least on whichever of these affords them pleasure. In the Golden Age, therefore, more sectors of the society are simultaneously stimulated to creative effort of higher quality. But there are some human activities that are generated by other circumstances and follow other rhythms. Philosophy is one of these and, as will be noted in Chapters 6 and 7, some ethical breakthroughs are accomplished in understandable reaction against wealth and power.

Civilization's Creative Eras

Which eras then should be designated as the most creative? In the case of China, there were two occasions when this civilization is usually judged to have been conspicuously eminent. These were during the Han and T'ang dynasties. Clearly this judgment places heavy stress on the accomplishments in the political, economic, and military spheres wherein certain of the Han and T'ang emperors (e.g., Wu Ti, 141-187, and Hsüan-tsung, 713-756) distinguished themselves. Certain other activities, however, experienced their Golden Age at other times. Philosophy reached its peak long before a centralized state was established, given that Confucius lived toward the end of the "Spring and Autumn" period, and the "Hundred Schools" flourished soon afterward at the time of the Warring States. Artistic creativity attained a very high level in the T'ang dynasty, but so it did later under the Sung emperors[2] whose political strength did not match that of their T'ang predecessors.

Indian civilization offers some parallels with the Chinese in this respect. Here also, two periods, the Mauryan and Gupta empires, are customarily designated as marking the higher levels. Within them, the peaks can be pinpointed as the reigns, respectively, of Ashoka (269-232 B.C.) and Chandra Gupta II (375-415). But Hindu civilization had its other peaks that stand out in more solitary style.

Both Mahavira and the Buddha precede the Mauryas, and the philosophical speculations of Shankara (c. 780-82) and Ramanuja (c. 1025-1137) postdate the Guptas. In the realm of the spirit, humanity's timetables are not necessarily congruous with political preeminence.

Islam has had the shortest duration of the four major civilizations that are still active today. This particular civilization, being centered on a religious faith that spread from its Arabic origins to non-Arab cultures, has lacked a leading capital or a central institution since the Abbasid caliphate was destroyed by the Mongols in 1258. Consequently, it is characteristic of Islam to have risen to separate peaks at successive eras in scattered areas. During the half millennium of Abbasid rule from Baghdad (750 to 1258), the most distinguished period[3] was in the ninth century. To this, the Caliph al-Ma'mun (813-833) contributed by his vigorous encouragement of science and philosophy. The other major triumphs of Islam were accomplished away from its Arab core—in Moorish Spain, Safavid Iran, Ottoman Turkey, and Moghul India. These were the societies that nurtured Averroës and the Alhambra, Firdawsi and Avicenna, Suleiman the Magnificent, Akbar, and the Taj Mahal.

The Golden Ages of Western civilization display two dissimilar patterns. The earlier one suggests a parallel with China, where the achievements of the Warring States and the Sui dynasties preceded those of an empire unified, respectively, by the Han and T'ang. In like fashion the warring city-states of Greece abounded with genius during the century and a half from Marathon and Salamis to Plato and Demosthenes. Rome's Augustan Age, however, did not occur until the *imperium* of the Caesars replaced the *respublica* of the senatorial oligarchy after a century of savage civil war.

The later pattern resembles not China but Islam. Western Europe became fragmented after Rome fell to the Visigoths, as did Islam when Baghdad fell to the Mongols. Thenceforth, beginning in the eleventh century in France, one people after another in different eras takes the lead in creativity. What is more, within each culture the periods of most noteworthy advances in the various activities are not synchronized. In Britain, for example, philosophy flourishes in the seventeenth and eighteenth centuries—that is to say, in between the Elizabethan and Victorian eras. Similarly, in Germany music and literature are at their greatest before Bismarck forged the Second Reich *mit Blut und Eisen* (with blood and iron).

This brief review of creative epochs in four leading civilizations has already implied, or made explicit, certain points that deserve a closer examination. If we focus our attention on the twin categories of time and space, what can be learned from past history about the eras when, and the areas where, the highest creativity was generated? Do the data warrant any generalizations of significance? Have there been events recurring with sufficient similarity to suggest a pattern?

As a caution, I begin with the conclusion at which Alfred Kroeber arrived after his exhaustive factual analysis in *Configurations of Culture Growth*: "In reviewing the ground covered," he states, "I wish to say at the outset that I see no evidence of any true law in the phenomena dealt with; nothing cyclical, regularly repetitive, or necessary. There is nothing to show either that every culture must develop patterns within which a florescence of quality is possible, or that, having once so flowered, it must wither without chance of revival."[4] With that general summation I concur—in fact, it corroborates the arguments presented in Chapter 4. The denial "of any true law in the phenomena" and of anything "cyclical, regularly repetitive, or necessary" does not, however, preclude the recurrence of certain similarities that may supply some clues to possible causation. Let us proceed on the basis of this hypothesis: If one seeks to explain why the Golden Ages occur, no conditions can be said to necessitate them, but some may be shown to facilitate them.

Because creativity is both an intellectual and an imaginative phenomenon, one would expect to find that certain situations act as triggers that stimulate a community to rise to unusual heights. The experiences that can yield this effect are of various kinds—for example, successful resistance to invasion by a powerful foe, victory in a war of liberation from external rule, a revolution that brings into power a new social class with a dynamic leadership, or the advent of a new dynasty that initially displays both energy and vision. Some cases will illustrate these points.

The Triggers of Creativity

(1) The Athenian Case

Why was it that Athens demonstrated such brilliance in the fifth century B.C.? Surely because it had been one of the two city-states that made the greatest contribution to the Greek victory over the Persian invaders. Xerxes' army and navy were in fact defeated by the combination of Spartan land power and Athenian sea power. The pride and exhilaration that stirred the Greeks after their deliverance are reflected in the pages of Herodotus, who penned the history of these events and placed in the mouth of a Spartan the explanation of why their soldiers were motivated to fight and die for their independence.[5] Likewise, the first of Athens' three great tragedians, Aeschylus, who had fought at Marathon, wrote his play *The Persians* extolling the values of the Hellenic culture in contrast with those of the "barbarian" foe.

That raises the question of why it was Athens, not Sparta, that became, in Pericles' phrase, "the educator of Greece."[6] The answer lies in the differences, sketched in Chapter 3, between the social and political systems of the two states and the type of military force on which each was based. Athens had already begun evolving in the direction of democracy before the Persian invasion and completed that development within a few decades after the war ended. The foundation of its military power was the fleet, whose political stance was imperialist abroad but populist at home. This democracy was an open society that tolerated experiment and was hospitable to aliens. It became therefore the natural forcing ground for talent, not only of its own citizens but of other Greeks whom its liberalism attracted.

Sparta, by contrast, was the archetype of a closed society. Living in constant fear of domestic rebellion, this conservative landowning oligarchy perpetuated itself only by a military regimen. To pursue a vigorous foreign policy in distant areas was risky, because, if too large a portion of the army was sent far afield, might not the Helots be tempted to revolt? The constitution introduced by Lycurgus was rigidly resistant to major change. New ideas were unwelcome, and aliens were periodically expelled. Under such conditions, neither artistic nor intellectual greatness could be expected, nor did they occur.

(2) Florence in the Quattrocento

The Athenian case, though quite exceptional, happens not to be unique. The history of Western civilization includes the record of at least one other community that attained, in an equivalent time span, an eminence parallel to that of Athens. This was Florence during the spectacular *quattrocento,* the fifteenth century of our counting. Florence was an ancient settlement that initially derived its importance from its geographic location. It was situated so as to intersect two main routes for travelers and commerce—that which ran north-south between Rome and the Lombardy Plain, and the other that followed the east-west course of the River Arno. In the late Middle Ages, the arts of painting and literature were carried to great heights by men who either were Florentines or had some connection with the city—witness the names of Cimabue and Giotto, of Dante, Petrarch, and Boccaccio.

During this period, Florence was deeply embroiled in the rivalry between the Papacy and the empire. Each of those institutions had its partisans, the Guelphs and the Ghibellines, who sought ascendancy in the numerous city-states of a divided Italy. Florence was controlled in general by the *parte Guelfa,* favoring the papal cause. That brought the great Tuscan city into opposition to Milan, the principal center of Lombardy, which was pro-imperial and Ghibelline. Milan was ruled in the fourteenth century by the Visconti family, who had been appointed vicars of the emperor. In 1378 Gian Galeazzo Visconti came to power, and he then set in motion a carefully conceived plan to extend his dominions and unify the north and center of Italy under a centralized rule. The chief obstacles were the two republics, Venice to the east and Florence to the south. One after another, various cities fell under his sway, until he was master of the four that lay along the routes linking Florence with the outside: Bologna to the north, Perugia to the east, Siena to the south, and Pisa to the west. In 1402 after taking Bologna, his army was mustered and poised to strike at the heart. Florence appealed for help to the Venetians, but they, feeling secure in their lagoon, were indifferent to the fate of another republic. Isolated, Florence awaited invasion, when, by a fluke of fortune, its salvation came. Suddenly, Gian Galeazzo was stricken by the plague and died.[7]

The emotions of the Florentines at their deliverance were as strong as those of the Athenians after Salamis and Plataea. They had stood alone and had defied a dangerous enemy. Imbued with pride and self-confidence, the city on the Arno thenceforth outdid itself. Between the birth of Brunelleschi in 1377 and of Guicciardini in 1483, Florence was the center of creativity in all of the arts, as well as in historiography and political analysis. At the head of the long list of those who achieved greatly by any standard, two geniuses stand out: Leonardo and Michelangelo.[8]

To explain their Renaissance, Florentine intellectuals turned to history, finding therein the comparisons to suit their purpose. Situated in Tuscany, was not their city the heir to mighty Etruria, which had preceded Rome? In addition, was not Florence also the new Rome—but of its republican, not its imperial, tradition?[9] This principle of republicanism was emphasized by such a Florentine spokesman as Leonardo Bruni, chancellor for 18 years. In the eulogy he delivered in 1428 at the funeral of the wealthy patrician Nanni Strozzi, he spoke with echoes of Pericles in praise of the republic whose civic values inspired excellence.[10] The greatness of Florence was due to the measure of freedom that its institutions assured, to the patronage of enlightened men of wealth, and to the humanistic studies that stimulated ideas and strengthened ideals.

This last point is especially significant. The same invigorating intellectual climate that had existed in Athens in the fifth century B.C. was re-created in Florence of the quattrocento by a succession of artists and humanists. Humanistic studies, their seeds planted by Petrarch, flowered in Florence. Their influence on the life of the city was demonstrated by the fact that four distinguished humanists served as chancellor in the Florentine government for almost a century (Salutati, 1375-1406; Bruni, 1410-1411 and 1427-1444; Marsuppini, 1444-1531; and Poggio, 1453-1459). In what other major Italian city—or, indeed, where else in Europe—would this have been possible at that time? Thus Bruni could make this claim: "Florence harbours the greatest minds: whatever they undertake, they easily surpass all other men, whether they apply themselves to military or political affairs, to study or philosophy, or to merchandise." Likewise, of classical studies, the core of humanism, he asserted: "These are the best and most excellent of studies, and most appropriate to mankind . . . they took root in Italy after originating in our city."[11] Continuing with this theme, Marsilio Ficino, who founded a Platonist academy in Florence, said exultantly: "It is undoubtedly a golden age which has restored to the light the liberal arts that had almost been destroyed: grammar, poetry, eloquence, painting, sculpture, architecture, music. And all that in Florence."[12] The art historian, Vasari, evaluating these achievements a century later, speculated why it was this particular city that had been the home of such perfection in the arts. He found the cause in "the spirit of criticism: the air of Florence making minds naturally free, and not content with mediocrity."[13]

(3) The English and the Americans

To Athens and Florence we could add another well-known case of a people whose creative capacities rose to a peak soon after they had freed themselves from a grave external threat. This was England in the reign of Elizabeth I. The defeat of the galleons of the Spanish Armada in 1588 by the smaller ships of the English navy, an exploit so similar to that of Athens at Salamis, ended a long period of anxiety. The heightened sense of self-esteem which followed that event expressed itself in a new boldness and assurance. What Shakespeare wrote in *Henry V* and in the speech of John of Gaunt in *Richard II* captures the mood, the élan, of a risen nationalism. After centuries of fruitless efforts to hold northwestern France, the English set sail across the wide oceans and liked the brine-laden breezes. What is more, their imagination was voyaging toward uncharted shores. Within a century of the Armada, England had given birth to Bacon, Hobbes, and Locke; to Harvey, Boyle, and Newton; to Milton, Purcell, Pepys, and Wren. The offshore island was on its way to becoming a planetary force.

Another kind of collective experience that can trigger an outpouring of creative activity is success in achieving independence from external rule. Witness the familiar instance of the United States. At the time of independence, the 13 colonies were unusually rich in political talent. Think of Franklin, Adams, Jefferson, and Hamilton, as well as Madison and Marshall. A generation later came the philosophers, writers, and educators, centering in Boston and Concord or, in Walt Whitman's case, New York. *The Flowering of New England* is the name with which Van Wyck Brooks described this phenomenon in his now-classic work of that title. In Emerson and Thoreau, and certainly in Whitman, new thoughts and new accents are heard, no longer colonial but authentically American. It is the poets and the intellectuals who are now creatively writing their own Declaration of Independence.[14]

New People in the Seats of Power

Thus far the circumstances favorable to creativity that have been discussed originate in a successful opposition to outsiders. But there are other factors, purely internal in character, which can so galvanize a community that its achievements become qualitatively superior. Such is the advent to power of a new ruling dynasty or a revolution that opens up new opportunities for an erstwhile inferior class.

The history of China offers a preeminent example of the former. Consider the case of the T'ang dynasty during its first 14 decades (from 618 to 756). Three unusually capable men reigned in that period. They were the second emperor of this dynasty, T'ai-tsung (626-649), his immediate successor, Kao-tsung (649-683), and Hsüan-tsung a generation later (713-756). The first two of these initiated the military expansion into central Asia, which extended Chinese influence into northern India and even to Sassanid Iran. From the capital in Ch'ang-an, the "Silk Road" stretched through valleys, oases, deserts, and mountain passes, linking the Middle Kingdom with the Middle East. This made possible a confluence of cultures, and a resulting ferment of ideas, which is vividly described by Michael Sullivan:

> Ch'ang-an . . . now became a city of a size and splendour rivaling, if it did not surpass, Byzantium. . . . In its streets one might have encountered priests from India and Southeast Asia, merchants from Central Asia and Arabia, Turks, Mongols and Japanese, many of whom are humorously caricatured in the pottery figurines from T'ang graves. Moreover they brought their own faiths with them—which flourished in an atmosphere of rare religious tolerance and curiosity.[15]

Indeed, the confident spirit of that place and time is vividly conveyed to us today in the T'ang ceramics. They exude a dynamism, a strength, a lively vigor, appropriate to a people whose influence stretched for a century across the width of Asia.

The creative impulse of new rulers who seek to excel is not altogether uncommon, and that example, taken from China, can be paralleled elsewhere, such as the Guptas in India or the Umayyads and the Abbasids of early Islam. What is much rarer is an internal revolution that not only terminates a set of traditional values and exterminates those whose privileges rested on them but at the same time enunciates new values, so that the former underprivileged benefit from gaining access to education, wealth, and power. The three most deep-seated revolutions of modern times—those of France, Russia, and China—have erupted within different civilizations. The question they pose is this: Did any of these revolutions inaugurate an age of creativity?

The Modern Revolutions

The one that prompts a clear and positive answer is the French. The principles which that revolution proclaimed—*liberté, égalité, et fraternité*—deliberately repudiated those of the Old Regime. In course of time, after the Napoleonic Empire and the Bourbon restoration, the majority of the French settled for the values of the petit bourgeois that guided the lives of the peasants and the lawyers, shopkeepers, teachers, and local officialdom in the innumerable villages and small towns of the provinces. What the revolution had accomplished was the opening of careers to the talented and the provision of public education exempt from church control. The result was that in the nineteenth century France made distinguished advances in the aesthetic and intellectual realms—in philosophy and the sciences, in literature and the arts.

The same cannot be said of the twin revolutions in Russia and China, both drawing their inspiration from Marxism. How the communist system evolved in those two countries—one occupying the biggest area of the planet, the other containing the biggest population—will be discussed in Chapter 9.[16] Here let it suffice to say that neither has succeeded to date in inaugurating the brave new world whose dawning was proclaimed in Moscow in 1917 and in Beijing in 1949. Despite some genuine social gains—notably the provision of health services and education for the mass of the people—the economic and political failures have been notorious. The ideal of a classless society, with its goal of ending human exploitation, was never realized. Vanished, too, is the dream of creating a new Soviet man and woman, along with their Chinese counterparts, whose ethics would be demonstrably superior to those of the decadent "bourgeois" societies. If there is to be a modern revolution that will remake the human being, it awaits a future century. Neither Russia nor China has pointed the way.

Which Are the Creative Areas?

This leads to another aspect of the general topic of what fosters creativity in civilization. The cases I have cited were chosen as examples of creative, or would-be creative, eras. But the dimension of space must be added to that of time. What has been the location of the creative areas? Were certain sites more conducive to creativity than others? What kind of environment has been host to originality?

The first point that strikes one about the great centers of inspiration in the past is that by modern standards, with few exceptions, their size was so small. Some could even be described as minute. We need to remember that until 150 years ago the vast majority of human beings lived in rural areas or in very small towns. Cities have existed, of course, for at least 8,000 years, and there is a direct connection between their development and that of certain aspects of civilization.[17] But they did not abound, nor did their inhabitants constitute a large proportion of the total population. The prevalence of the modern megalopolis, so incisively dissected by Lewis Mumford,[18] is part of the cost that industrialization has imposed upon humanity. Athens at the peak of its glory in the fifth century may have contained a population of 250,000—a huge figure for that time made possible only by seaborne commerce. Rome is estimated to have housed a million people in the third century A.D., because its engineers had designed aqueducts that could carry water higher into the hills. Constantinople embraced half a million when Justinian ruled it in the sixth century. China's population, when the first census was conducted in 2 A.D., had reached a total of 57 million, which already included some large cities. Most of the exceptional cases in the past were due to the fact that they were capitals, where the governmental and economic network of a wider region received central direction.

On the other hand, one thinks of centers of creative achievement, whose performance was quite disproportionate to their size. Medieval Paris before the Black Death had 100,000 inhabitants, much the same as Florence in the heyday of the Renaissance. Geneva, in the period between Calvin and Rousseau, was even smaller. And how does one explain such a phenomenon as tiny Concord, which in the first half of the nineteenth century housed not only two geniuses, Emerson and Thoreau, but also Hawthorne and the Alcotts?

The crux of the problem is not size per se, for there is no necessary connection between quantity and quality. The factors that are most relevant to creative effort are the psychological stimuli and the values pervading the community, as well as access to certain necessary facilities. But these are related to size in opposite ways. Sometimes the larger concentration of people can have a more stimulating effect, as it provides a greater diversity and more ample resources (e.g., libraries). Could Leonardo have developed as he did if his father had not brought him from Vinci to Florence? Indeed, creativity may require the fellowship with others working in the same field, given that cross-fertilization can generate innovation. In this respect, however, excessive expansion may be counterproductive. Aristotle comments caustically in the *Politics* on Babylon having been so vast that, even three days after it had been captured, some of its inhabitants were unaware of what had happened.[19] Are there not many obstacles to creativity nowadays in such environments as Tokyo, Los Angeles, or Mexico City? The small communities—the Concords—that preserve relationships on a human scale may yet be the seedbeds of significant advances.

Because community flourishes with communication, many of the areas that distinguished themselves in the past were centers of movement and transportation. Think of some of the place-names that are associated with notable epochs and the connection becomes obvious. Athens, Venice, Amsterdam, London, Boston, and Istanbul were seaports. Ch'ang-an, Florence, Baghdad, Damascus, and Vienna were inland nodal points where routes converged and travelers moved in and out. Many of these were also capitals whose power attracts as a magnet, bringing the ambitious and the adventurous within their field of influence and giving them scope.

The Clusters of Creative Individuals

This concentration of creative activity in time and place relates to another aspect of the topic that is well documented, yet somewhat puzzling. We know for a fact that individuals of exceptional ability often cluster together in the same century and region. Consider these instances. Athens produced four dramatists of preeminent quality during the fifth century: Aeschylus, Sophocles, Euripides, and Aristophanes. Neither before nor afterward were there others of the same class.[20] China's greatest philosophical speculations occurred between the sixth century B.C. and the third, a period that extends from Lao-tzu and Confucius to Mo-ti, Mencius, and Hsün-tzu. Other examples are the Dutch School of painters, all in the seventeenth century,[21] and the musical efflorescence in Vienna, which within the space of seven decades was hearing the compositions of Haydn, Mozart, Beethoven, and Schubert.

This phenomenon has recurred throughout history in scattered centers at sporadic intervals. It was sufficiently evident in ancient times for the Roman historian Velleius Paterculus to take notice of it early in the first century A.D.[22] He attempts to explain it in terms of the human propensity to emulate others either from admiration or envy—which would imply that, whenever somebody stands out from the crowd or branches off in a new direction, others are impelled to match the effort and compete. But is that explanation adequate? Does it tell why the society happens to contain enough

individuals whose abilities are at the same high level and who exert
themselves contemporaneously in precisely the same field?

The puzzle consists in a relationship between two separate
factors—the presence of the requisite talent and the environmental
conditions that encourage its development. Unless these are present simultaneously and interact, the clustering will not take place.
If we assume that abilities within any community are distributed
at any time according to a normal curve—a big "if," but let us grant
it for the moment—then it follows that a certain number of individuals of exceptional talent are always present in our midst. From
this small group there comes, very rarely, the undoubted genius,
the person at the level of Plato, Gautama, Michelangelo, Shakespeare, or Einstein. The difficulty is that every society goes through
some periods of general mediocrity. Nothing very distinguished is
accomplished. Nobody out of the ordinary emerges. Why does this
happen if the assumption of a normal distribution curve is correct?
If the exceptionally talented are there, why do they not display
themselves?

The answer, on Kroeber's reasoning, has to be found in the
environment. He is, as he repeatedly emphasizes, a cultural anthropologist. Consequently, for him the cause of whatever happens in
a community is embedded in its culture. When the outstandingly
able fail to show themselves, it is because of cultural deficiencies.
The situation is then like that which Gray imagined in his *Elegy*,
fantasizing that under the gravestones might be buried "some mute
inglorious Milton" or "village Hampden" for whom the placid and
limited locale could not provide a springboard to greatness.[23]

But this explanation, if universally applied, runs into difficulties.
How can one account for those rare, yet genuine, cases of a lone
genius who stands like a single mountain peak rising out of a level
plain? Kroeber duly mentions such instances of what he calls
"exceptional isolated genius." Those whom he names, all from the
Western civilization, include Copernicus, Tycho Brahe, Leibniz,
Goya, Thorvaldsen, and Villon. Each of these was isolated in the
sense that alone in his culture at his time he occupied a pedestal
of special eminence in his field. To the cultural anthropologist, this
is troubling, as Kroeber frankly admits, because here is an effect
of which culture cannot be the cause. Yet to concede another,
independent cause of social phenomena must undermine the foundations of the culture concept.

One who is not wedded to this doctrine, however, has no such
problem. Why not adopt the explanation that accords with common

sense and happens to fit the facts? What we are considering is the operation of two independent factors and their recurring interdependence: the presence of a few exceptionally able people and a social context that either stimulates or inhibits them. The truth is that the highest ability does not develop according to any pattern or conform to a set of rules. This is especially so in the case of geniuses who are what biologists call "sports." They carry within themselves the resources that others receive from outside. Take Abraham Lincoln as an example. Here was a farmer's son, born and raised in the backwoods of Kentucky and southern Illinois. Yet his development was utterly different than that of other boys of his area, exposed to similar stimuli. Culture cannot explain the difference. That this one child grew into the historic Lincoln must have been due to his innate qualities, which had to find their expression and did so without any help whatsoever from the environment.

On the other hand, when a clustering does occur, it is reasonable to look to the surrounding society to discover why the capacities of the exceptionally talented were channeled in a certain direction. Here the influence of culture is strikingly manifest. Consider some examples, and the circumstances that made them possible.

Western civilization supplies some well-known instances of the concentration of ability in a particular field at a certain place and time. One thinks of Italian accomplishments in painting, architecture, and sculpture during the fifteenth and sixteenth centuries, of Dutch painting in the seventeenth, of German and Austrian music in the eighteenth and nineteenth. In these cases it is surely true that the influences of the culture directed the creative energies of the most talented into specific channels. Painters, sculptors, and architects were not only practicing their art in those periods so as to "express themselves," as current idiom has it; their art was also responsive to the demands of the market. Artists depended on their patrons and customers, whose wishes and tastes helped to determine the choice of the product and the character it assumed. The Renaissance popes wanted to embellish the Vatican or construct a larger Saint Peter's in rivalry with Hagia Sophia or build a monumental tomb for their mortal remains. Similarly, the Medici, the Strozzi, the Sforza, and other leading families made their wealth and power visual by commissioning the works of Michelangelo, Leonardo, and Raphael for the adornment of their palaces. The mercantile guilds and the richest burghers of Amsterdam glorified themselves by paying Rembrandt to execute their portraits; whereas the Viennese court and nobility would grant a stipend to Haydn, Mozart, or Beethoven for chamber or symphonic compositions that bore their name. The Roman satirist, Martial, had said long ago: "Let there be patrons, Horace, like Maecenas, and poets such as Virgil will not be wanting."[24] At the same time, it is clear that the style or fashion prevailing in the culture at those times shaped the purposes for which funds were forthcoming. The elite of Amsterdam wanted portraits, not string quartets; Viennese aristocrats wanted music, not canvases. These preferences are a large part of the explanation of why no great music was produced in seventeenth-century Holland, nor any great painting in Vienna of the late eighteenth.

The Patrons and Their Influence

The arts just mentioned—painting, architecture, and sculpture—have a public or quasi-public aspect and two of them are costly to execute, which is why wealthy institutions or persons were needed to authorize and commission the artist. Creativity in these fields was limited therefore by the tastes of the patron. But there are other spheres where the stimulus to creativity has not been so related to external demand, where individuals could rely more on their own resources, where the market was not a major magnet attracting the talent. I am thinking of literature and philosophy and of the early scientists whose pioneer work did not require the superelaborate and superexpensive apparatus of our contemporary laboratories. Pen and paper, plus rudimentary materials and equipment, were all that was needed before the twentieth century by those who combined a first-rate mind with a fertile imagination.

Nevertheless, in these spheres, too, although the original creative act might be a private and intensely personal experience, the subsequent publishing of the results took on a public character. A written manuscript, if it was to be read by others, had to be copied or printed. When publication took the latter form, the authorities might impose their censorship, prohibiting certain books because of their contents while licensing others. Directly or indirectly, many governments still exercise this power today, as does the Catholic church. Moreover, the scope of publication was enlarged or restricted by the size of the reading public, that is, by those who were not only literate but better educated and by the growth of libraries in the homes of those who could afford them. In these respects, therefore, cultural factors played their part by shaping if not the origination of ideas at least their subsequent dissemination.

Nor, while stressing the political and economic aspects, should we overlook the effects of religious doctrine. Religious institutions have exerted a considerable control over the creative, both positively and negatively. During the period of the Papacy's greatest power, religious subjects preoccupied the painters, who treated them with due respect for the conventions of theology. God was depicted as a venerable old man with a long white beard, angels looked beatific, saints had halos, the devil was loathsome. Architects and sculptors, when not employed by the court or the nobles, were designing or decorating churches, whose Gothic style was symbolic of humanity's upward aspiration. And for a thousand years, the speculations of the philosophers were governed by notions about the dualism of human nature and the need to stake out the independent jurisdictions of church and state. Prohibitions, too, when based on sacred writ, define for the artist the bounds of the permissible. Jews are forbidden by the Second Commandment to make a "graven image." Hence their aesthetic talent shied away from sculpture. But because the Old Testament abounded with occasions of song and dance, music was an art in which a Jew was free to excel.

These generalizations about civilization in the West can be fortified by parallels from the East. In China, for example, most of the principal dynasties brought to the throne some emperors who either were artistically inclined or had the wit to perceive the utility to society of scholarship and technology. They therefore attracted the talented and the learned to their court and encouraged them to be productive. It was under imperial patronage—such as Yung-lo (1403-1424) of the Ming dynasty and K'ang-hsi (1662-1722) of the Ch'ing—that encyclopedic compilations of knowledge were assembled, extending into thousands of volumes.[25] Naturally, the values approved by society's elite, whose consequences we noted in Amsterdam and Vienna, were shared by the emperor himself. Thus there were emperors who painted. This was possible for them because scholars set a high value on painting, seeing it as an extension of the calligraphy in which they were proud to be proficient. No emperor, however, would take hammer and chisel to sculpture a stone, for such activity had an affinity with manual labor.[26]

In China, as in Europe, there were times when metaphysical or religious belief gave the artist his themes. The Taoist emphasis on nature, and on the human need to be attuned thereto, exerted a powerful influence on landscape painting, as it did on lyric poetry.

Subsequently, when Buddhism was introduced, the resulting fervor found expression in the arts. All the rock carvings in caves and on cliffs are testimony to the faith inspired by Gautama's teaching, a phenomenon comparable to the Indian carvings at Ellora and Ajanta and to the cathedrals of medieval France.

Yet another parallel can be traced in the ways whereby the prevailing philosophy of an epoch, its Weltanschauung, communicates its qualities to those who are creative in various spheres—a valid example of Kroeber's point about culture influencing the individual. A striking case is the experience of the Sung dynasty (the tenth century to the twelfth). The China that flourished then was so different from its T'ang predecessor or the much earlier Han that Gernet titles it "The Chinese 'Renaissance.' "[27] The difference resulted from changes in the makeup of the elite and in a consequential transformation of tone and spirit that reflected their taste. Where T'ang was aristocratic, warlike, expansionist, and influenced by its contacts with the peoples of central Asia, Sung was more urbanized, commercial, pacific, and introspective. This was an era when China could once again settle down after the Buddhist tidal wave had abated, reasserting its older rational humanism. The work of the intellectuals—artists, scholars, and philosophers—was marked by an elegance, a sophistication, a maturity that had not been matched before and was not to be repeated. Look at a piece of Sung celadon, and you know what I mean. It is with justice that Michael Sullivan writes: "The art of the Sung Dynasty which we admire today was produced by, and for, a social and intellectual elite more cultivated than at any other period in Chinese history. The pottery and porcelain made for their use is a natural reflection of their taste."[28] Europe had to wait six centuries before it attained such a level during the Enlightenment, as in the tone of Voltaire's writings and the tones of Mozart's music.

The Social Context:
Stability or Conflict?

The effect of the social environment on individual creativity can be considered from yet one more angle. Do the creative eras and areas, one may ask, tend to be characterized by stability, security, prosperity, and peace—in other words, by a combination of orderliness with well-being? Or is the contrary the case? Does creativity flourish amid insecurity and turmoil?

On preliminary reflection it may seem plausible to argue that creativity is best fostered by a calm environment and peace of mind. Someone who feels harassed or hungry, who faces the privations of an economic depression or suffers the alarms of war, is not in the best mood, it may be thought, to write, invent, compose, or design at the heights. Historical evidence backs up these assumptions. Several of the Golden Ages were notable, in point of fact, for domestic stability and an ensuing prosperity. The Augustan Age at Rome was one such. So was the Gupta period in India or Safavid Persia in the time of Shah Abbas.

But this is one of those fascinating questions where evidence of the opposite can also be presented, indicating how contrary "causes" can yield a similar "effect." Indeed, on this issue the cases that support the other view are quite spectacular. Consider these three: Greece in the fifth and fourth centuries B.C., the contemporary China of the Warring States, and Italy during the Renaissance. Anyone who was challenged to identify half a dozen of the most creative epochs in the history of civilization could not fail to include these three. All are equally remarkable for the high quality and rich diversity of what they produced. At the same time, their political and social conditions bordered on the chaotic. Corruption, conspiracy, lawlessness and violence, factionalism and warfare, were the common misfortunes plaguing the peoples of Hellas, China, and Italy in those periods. The sadness of Confucius, the mordant exposés of Thucydides, the bitter analyses of Machiavelli indicate how three extraordinarily perceptive men reacted to the perils of their epoch. On one level, those were highly civilized societies; on another, their behavior was barbaric. How can this conjunction of seeming incompatibles be explained? Why the paradox?

The answer to these questions is most illuminating because it demonstrates how careful one must be when drawing inferences about causal relationships in the sphere of social and political phenomena. The point is that the same factor, which lay at the root of the prevailing insecurity, was itself the means for talent to emerge. The root cause of the disorder was the subdivision of a single culture into separate and independent units, each with its own ruling authority.[29] What followed from these circumstances was competition. Each ruler jockeyed for position, trying to obtain security by winning an advantage over rivals who were potential enemies. The advantage in this situation might consist in welcoming creative individuals, either because their presence at court enhanced the ruler's prestige or because their inventiveness could contribute something utilitarian to augment his material power.

The lives of several geniuses offer testimony to these generalizations. When Leonardo da Vinci decided in 1482 to leave Florence and transfer his service from Lorenzo di Medici to Ludovico Sforza, he wrote a letter to the ruler of Milan in which he detailed under nine headings the several military devices he could construct, while cursorily mentioning in 6 lines out of 34 his skills as painter and sculptor.[30] He knew, in other words, what his prospective patron valued most. Born illegitimately and living in a turbulent age, this enigmatic, multifaceted genius never married, left no children, had no home, but moved restlessly from one Italian court to another until he died in France.

The fact that he could move, that his creative talents were transferable, however, tells us something important. Michelangelo, too, shuttled between Rome and Florence, often quarreling with those who had paid him or who had failed to pay. Confucius became an itinerant sage because his own Kingdom of Lu did not welcome his advice. Herodotus of Halicarnassus and Protagoras of Abdera were examples of the fifth-century intellectuals who spent several years in Athens because of its stimulating atmosphere of free inquiry. The Persian poet Sa'di (c. 1184-c. 1291), who lived in what Toynbee has called "the stormiest century of the Islamic world's history,"[31] wandered incessantly across the region from North Africa to Asia, only returning to his native Shiraz when he was already advanced in years and then producing his two greatest works. Mozart finally escaped the tyranny of the Archbishop of Salzburg and sheltered under the more tolerant patronage of the Hapsburg Emperor, Joseph II.

There is a pattern in these events, and from them are lessons to be learned. The rootless expatriate is a not uncommon type in the intellectual history of civilization. Is this because the universal genius, who belongs to all humanity, is at home nowhere because such a person's home is everywhere? Some geniuses, it is true, have remained in the country or region of their birth, finding an environment hospitable to their efforts. A few were fortunate enough, as was Goethe, to locate their Weimar. But others—more particularly those concerned with the arts or with ideas—have been wanderers over the face of the Earth.

In that case the multiplicity of regimes, itself the basic source of discord, afforded a haven because continued creativity depended on alternatives being available. Driven from one prince's table, the artist or intellectual might sup at another's. Many of history's autocrats, including some of its most repulsive despots, offered their protection to the talented that they might bask in reflected glory. Sigismondo Malatesta, whose cruelties were legendary even in an age that had no shortage of evil, was enlightened in his appreciation of artists and the arts. Similarly, Timur Lenk besought the services of Ibn Khaldun. And if amid the multiplicity of regimes one area happened to stand out as freer, more liberal, than the rest, that served as the honey to draw the bees—hence fifth-century Athens, hence fifteenth-century Florence, hence seventeenth-century Amsterdam. By contrast, the worst fate for the creative was to live at a time when all power was concentrated in a single comprehensive despotism from which there was no escape. In China, the reaction to the Warring States was unification by Ch'in Shih Huang-ti, during whose merciless, but mercifully brief, reign the books were burned (except for treatises on medicine, agriculture, and divination) and scholars were executed by the hundreds. But his atrocities do not begin to compare with those committed in this century by Hitler and Stalin after they consolidated their grip. Freud and Einstein managed to escape while it was still possible, finding refuge, respectively, in Britain and the United States. But for the creative person who is trapped, and is not enough of a threat to be eliminated, a despotism is a living death. Here is what Yehudi Menuhin has to say about a gifted Russian composer:

> The artist in our day cannot altogether escape his role in history or in his society. I have often thought of Dmitri Shostakovich, a timid and anxious person, struggling all his life within the state system without ever quite breaking through. . . . It is sad that a man who had such genius and so much to say was not able to reach the very apogee of his capacity because of political disapproval. Great honors were accorded him and he had to live up to them, ending his life in such terror that he trembled constantly.[32]

Mutual Stimuli Among Varied Fields

The points raised in this discussion have touched on a large issue of general significance. I have been commenting on the varied influences, positive or negative, which flow between a society's political system and its creative output in thought or art. This is one aspect of a yet broader question. Does any discernible relationship exist, overall, between creative achievements in different spheres, the mode of governance being one of these? Can it be shown, for example, that a community's excellence in field A can facilitate its success in B or possibly prohibit success in C? If any such patterns disclose themselves, they should be explicable in terms of one of two factors. Either, objectively, there exist in the society strong interests or institutions that stimulate creativity along certain related lines while at the same time discouraging others, or, subjectively, there are certain psychological traits or intellectual preferences that produce these same effects. What light is thrown on these suppositions by the evidence of history?

The former possibility—namely, the effect of powerful social interests or institutions—harks back to the earlier discussion of cultural factors and their influence on the creative. To take an obvious example, whenever a potentate or an organized religion embarked on a massive building program, not only would the architects be stimulated but so would the sculptors and, sometimes, the painters, as well as the related arts and crafts. The history of civilization abounds with occasions of this kind. Think of the successive pharaohs who ordered the construction of the pyramids and of their tombs in the Valley of the Kings, or the priests of Amun-Re who carried to completion the gigantic complex at Karnak; of emperors who planned and built new capitals (Ch'ang-an in the T'ang dynasty, Fatehpur Sikri by Akbar, Isfahan by Shah Abbas, St. Petersburg by Czar Peter), of the Counter-Reformation popes redesigning Rome after its sack by the Spanish army, of Buddhism and Catholicism stimulating a widespread demand for pagodas, cathedrals, stupas, and shrines. For all the creative talent that a civilization could muster in the arts of construction and decoration, there indeed were bonanzas in the eras of elaborate edifices, both secular and sacred. And this is observable in the biographies of many of the great practitioners. Pericles placed Pheidias, the sculptor, in charge of planning the buildings that were to crown the Acropolis, and it was his collaboration with the architects, Ictinus and Callicrates, that bore fruit in the Parthenon. A few exceptional individuals have even managed to combine several talents in their own person. Michelangelo was sculptor, painter, designer, and architect. Leonardo's genius covered a still broader range. Not only was he a painter and a sculptor, but in addition a scientist and inventor.

This reference to Leonardo's many-sidedness is a reminder not only that progress in the arts is often related to or contingent on progress in the sciences but also that scientific discovery and technological inventiveness are themselves both cause and effect of the growth of civilization. Very early in their history, during the Shang period (roughly 1550-1030 B.C.), Chinese metallurgy developed a skill in the use of bronze that has seldom, if ever, been surpassed. The surviving objects belong mainly in two categories: those used in rituals or public ceremonies and weapons of war. The design and construction of a war chariot, for instance, was a complex undertaking that united several crafts and techniques.

That suggests a broader generalization. The warfare, which has been a continuous accompaniment of civilization, has directed human ingenuity to the discovery of ever more efficient ways to kill other human beings and destroy their habitations. In consequence, much inventiveness has occurred in periods when society's rulers were preoccupied with military needs. I noted above that Leonardo had introduced himself to Ludovico primarily in his role as a military engineer. Gernet points out that Chinese civilization, which he describes as "first and foremost a technical civilization," experienced great advances in technology between the fourth and second centuries B.C.[33] This was, of course, the time of the Warring States, and Gernet makes a direct connection between the persistent warfare and the technical innovations.[34] That this connection has been regularly maintained during two millennia is a commonplace of history. We need only remind ourselves of events as recent as those of this century's Second World War, whose exigencies speeded up the exploration of the physics of the atom and culminated in the explosion of the first atomic bombs. It is indeed a paradox of human motivation that the impulse to destroy is twin to the impetus to create.

That brings me to consider from the subjective standpoint the linkages between different kinds of creativity, or their absence. Are there any psychological or intellectual factors that make different fields of endeavor compatible or incompatible?

A clue to the answer to this question is contained in this insightful remark by Renan: "The religious inferiority of the Greeks and Romans was the consequence of their political and intellectual superiority. Contrariwise, the [religious] superiority of the Jewish people has been the cause of their political and philosophical inferiority."[35] Burckhardt, who quotes this in his discussion of the influence of the state on religion, comments as follows: "If the Greeks and Romans had had priests and a theology, they would never have created their perfect State on the basis of human needs and relationships."[36] The point is well taken. It implies the distinction that I drew in Chapter 2 between values that are focused on this world and place the human being at the center and those that give priority to another world with a deity at its center. The Greeks and Romans were guided by reason. (Or so they professed, practice not always conforming to their claim.) Being humanists, they of course constructed their gods in their own image. The Jews, however, were dominated by faith, believing in Yahweh, the omnipotent One. What Renan and Burckhardt are saying, essentially, is that you cannot have it both ways. Exalt reason and you will subordinate faith, and vice versa. Reliance on the critical intellect is incompatible with the uncritical acceptance of belief.

That was a negative correlation. Now consider a positive relationship. If I were to pick the two peoples who have excelled in their contributions to metaphysics, my choices would be the Indians and the Germans. In addition, those same peoples have been responsible for some outstanding discoveries in mathematics. Is not the connection evident? In both metaphysics and mathematics, what is needed is a capacity to reason logically at a level of the highest abstraction. There is thus a natural carryover of excellence from one to the other. Pythagoras, Plato, Descartes, Leibniz, and Russell are conspicuous examples of these abilities combining in the same individual.

Contacts Between Civilizations

In addition to the influence that creativity in a particular field may exert upon performance in another, the meeting of civilizations and communication between them can also be a source of stimulus. "An isolated people," says Christopher Dawson, "does not invent or advance."[37] To illustrate his point, he refers to Egypt, which was more isolated geographically than other civilizations and eventually sank into stagnation and decline. Dawson conjectures that Egypt's two major periods of cultural achievement— those of the pyramid builders and the Eighteenth Dynasty—"were set up by the intrusion and assimilation of new racial elements, first in the Delta, and in the second case (from 1700 B.C.) in upper Egypt."[38] The same factor—namely, the mixing of cultures—has been adduced by some historians as the underlying reason for the creative flowering of the people who always figure most prominently in the discussions of this subject. "The Greeks of history," writes J. L. Myres, "are now clearly revealed as the product of intense fusion." Invaders of northern nomadic origin came south and succeeded in conquering the older indigenous stock. What followed was a mixture of the two cultures. The result, in Myres's striking phrase, was "a Greek nation of magnificent mongrels."[39]

If geographic isolation meant a reduction of stimuli, to live in a crossroads would correspondingly be an advantage. This fact, according to McNeill, explains why in the religious sphere the most fruitful thinking of the first millennium B.C. did not occur in either Egypt or Mesopotamia, the ancient centers of Middle Eastern civilization, but in the marginal areas of Palestine and Iran. The former, situated between Egypt and Mesopotamia, felt the influences of both. The latter, in between Mesopotamia and India, drew similarly on its two neighbors.[40]

There are indeed examples by the bushel of the ways in which the caravan routes that spanned the length of Asia not only were trod by merchants, armies, pilgrims, and envoys but served as the medium for transmitting ideas, beliefs, and patterns of culture. Already I have mentioned the eastward spread of Buddhism, its introduction to China in the period of the Sui dynasty, and its impact on the empire during the early part of the T'ang dynasty. But India had other gifts for China in addition to the teachings of Gautama. From the fourth to the eighth centuries, the Indians were advanced in mathematics, as well as in medicine and astronomy, in grammar and phonetics. In all of these fields the Chinese debt to India was considerable.[41]

China, too, was itself an exporter of civilization on a grand scale. The influence of the Middle Kingdom radiated outward in all directions through the various agents of military expansion, economic exchange, and cultural dissemination. Japan, Korea, Manchuria, Mongolia, and Southeast Asia all felt the impact of China and incorporated aspects of its life-style into their own societies. More even than silk and ceramics, the two Chinese products that found the widest usage in other civilizations were their inventions of paper and gunpowder. A process for manufacturing paper was discovered in the first century A.D. and was later perfected. According to the traditional account, the Islamic civilization learned the process from Chinese taken prisoners in 751 at the battle of the River Talas. The Arabs adopted paper avidly, as it had clear advantages over parchment or papyrus. The art of papermaking moved steadily westward—across the Middle East and North Africa into Spain. There, the backward Europeans learned it from the

Moors, and Italians were manufacturing paper late in the thirteenth century—more than a thousand years after the Chinese had hit on the idea.[42]

Gunpowder, too, was another early "gift" of Chinese science.[43] The formula for making it was first mentioned in a text of 1044, although it was in use earlier. It is true that the Chinese applied gunpowder to fireworks, but the often-repeated belief that Europeans were the first to employ it in war is erroneous. In the tenth century, the T'ang were inserting it in projectiles that produced smoke and fire. Later, they discovered the principle of the rocket by setting off an explosion in a hollow bamboo guided by arrows. It was the Mongols who borrowed explosives from the Chinese after their encounters with the Sung armies. These they fired from mortars made of metal, which they introduced to Hungary at Sajo in 1241. The Europeans proved to be most adept and eager pupils. That was what the Chinese learned in the nineteenth century, when the expansive empires of the West brought their gunpowder with them—back to its place of origin.

In this respect Islam, too, conforms to the general pattern that civilizations give to one another and borrow in return. When the armies of the Prophet overran the Hellenistic kingdoms of the Middle East, the Arabs began absorbing from their subjects the arts, the scholarship, and the speculations in which Greeks had distinguished themselves. From the resulting mix of ideas in areas as far apart as Spain and Persia came the works of Averroës and Avicenna. Still farther east, when Islam penetrated northern India from its base in Afghanistan, the Moghuls left their imprint by combining Persian and Turkic elements with the Hindu styles. The Taj Mahal, incorporating these several strains, represents the sublime culmination of their union.[44]

The influences that flowed between the Islamic civilization and the Western operated in both directions. The Arabs had learned much from Hellenistic Greeks; they later became teachers to medieval Christians. E. L. Jones has noted that, when the Muslims were driven out of Sicily in 1090, the libraries they had accumulated fell into the victors' hands, and Latin translations of Arabic writings ensued. The same occurred in Spain after the fall of Toledo, Cordoba, and Seville. Because of the Crusades, Europeans could observe the Islamic civilization firsthand, and they brought home with them whatever they liked or could use with good advantage. Thus, as Jones points out, they acquired the veil, the four-poster bed designed for draping mosquito nets, and the cone-shaped hat, which also was draped in muslin. In addition, Europe acquired some items that Islam had found in China—the compass, crossbow, chain mail, and types of rigging, along with the paper and gunpowder already mentioned.[45]

When Europe's turn came, the peoples who inhabited its Atlantic seaboard deployed their sea power across the oceans, making conquests, converts, and commerce. No civilization known to history ever registered such global impact as has western Europe in the Americas, Asia, and Africa since the sixteenth century. The physical means that initially made this possible were ships and guns. Sailing out for trade, or in some places to settle, the Europeans needed a base with a garrison to provide security. They were helped further by the clergy, Catholic and Protestant alike, who saw their opportunity to spread the Gospel to the "heathens." The indigenous peoples reacted differently to the shock. In the Americas—north, central, and south—they were broken, or even in some areas exterminated. Africa, too, was devastated by the penetration of Europeans, who used the peoples of the west coast for their source of slaves, as had Arabs on the continent's eastern side. With some rare exceptions, such as the martial Zulus, the African tribes were too backward in their technology or too divided among themselves to be able to offer an effective resistance.

In Asia, Western domination proceeded on other lines, both because its population was so immense and because its historic civilizations were so deeply rooted. What was it that made possible that extraordinary phenomenon of the control exercised by the relatively small populations of western European states over huge sections of humanity halfway across the world? I would ascribe it principally to the purely fortuitous effects of timing, which combined in the eighteenth and nineteenth centuries to give Europe the advantage and to place India and China at a disadvantage. Europe had been in turmoil during the sixteenth and seventeenth centuries when the Oceanic Age began. It was beset with the problems of ending the medieval division between temporal and ecclesiastical jurisdictions, of breaking up the Vatican's monopoly of religious power, and of developing a mercantile economy. To cope with this situation, a new system of government by nation-states was emerging, the first of which were located on the Atlantic seaboard. At this same time, philosophical speculation, liberated at last from clerical control, joined hands with scientific experimenters to usher in a series of discoveries that gave rise to technological inventions. Denied access by the Turks to the land routes across Asia, boldly and brashly the western Europeans took to the water with the Cross in one hand and a musket in the other.

For their arrival in India the time was opportune. The Moghuls after Aurangzeb had run to seed. Their empire across India's northern plains was ripe for plucking. South of them, the Marathas expanded beyond the Deccan, but their power too was broken in 1761. It was thus left to the French and British, having supplanted the Portuguese and Dutch, to fight each other for supremacy. The Indians, weak because they were divided, were their pawns on the chessboard.

China's decline came later. Europeans had been arriving on its coast since the mid-sixteenth century and Jesuit missionaries sought to make Christians of Confucians. But of the two instruments of infiltration that the Europeans carried with them—their technology and their religion—whereas both had a deadly effect on the indigenous cultures of Africa and the Americas, only one was of any use in Asia. Hinduism, Buddhism, and Confucianism were generally resistant to Christianity. But there was no gainsaying the widening technological gap between Asia and Europe. For the Chinese, who until the fifteenth century had been ahead of Europeans in shipbuilding, metallurgy, and explosives, were starting to lag behind. Indeed, the Jesuits astounded the court at Beijing with their knowledge of mathematics, astronomy, and other sciences.

What delayed the European takeover was that, unlike India, China under the Ming dynasty, and in the first century and a half of the Ch'ing, was ruled by a centralized regime with sufficient power to grant or deny the entry that "foreign devils" were seeking. But its appearance of strength was illusory, because it was ill-informed of the changes then taking place in Europe, and most of all in Britain. Few documents in history exude a higher degree of unjustified complacency than the famous response of the Ch'ing Emperor Ch'ien-lung to Lord Macartney leading a delegation from George III to Beijing in 1793:

> As to your entreaty to send one of your nationals to be accredited to my Celestial Court and to be in control of your country's trade with China, this request is contrary to all usage of my dynasty and cannot possibly be entertained. . . . Our ceremonies and code of laws differ so completely from your own that, even if your envoy were able to acquire the rudiments of our civilization, you could not possibly transplant our manners and customs to your alien soil. . . . Swaying the wide world, I have but one aim in view, namely to maintain a

perfect governance and to fulfil the duties of the State. . . . I set no
value on objects strange or ingenious, and have no use for your
country's manufactures.[46]

From these sublime heights of overconfidence, the descent was
indeed rapid. Early in the nineteenth century, internal dry rot had
begun to weaken the pillars of the Celestial Empire. Once the
process started, the deterioration was unchecked. After the Opium
War of the 1840s, the British—George III's granddaughter being
then on the throne—were able to dictate their terms. Seriously
shaken in the next decade by the T'ai P'ing rebellion, Beijing could
no longer repulse the invasive foreigners—British, Russians, Japanese, French, and Germans—nibbling away at its frontiers. A century of humiliation overtook this once-brilliant civilization. In
1900 after the Boxer uprising, the joint forces of foreign governments sacked Beijing. In 1931 the Japanese seized Manchuria, and
from 1936 to 1945 they occupied China's principal cities. Not until
the second half of the current century did China regain its independence and begin to regain its self-respect.

Some lessons can be drawn from this account of contacts between
civilizations. It is clear that too much isolation, whether self-imposed
or due to geography, can be harmful, as it induces stagnation. Those
who are situated at the crossroads are fortunate in being exposed to
numerous stimuli, but they can also be unfortunate in that they risk
being walked over too often. The Poles are a tragic case in point.
When one civilization has contact with another, much will depend
on the stage of development at which each has arrived relative to the
other. In other words, in encounters between a dynamic society and
one that is decadent, it is evident which of the two will prevail. At
the same time, history demonstrates that a culture that is backward
in technology or in other respects can, when it has contact with one
more advanced, stay in charge of its destiny and experience a new
creative impetus if it has the social solidarity and political strength to
determine for itself what flow of innovation is acceptable. I am
thinking here of the striking contrast between China and Japan in
the later decades of the nineteenth century. The Japanese, after the
shock of Commodore Perry's uninvited intrusion, overthrew the
Shogunate, reinstated the authority of the emperor, and then experienced the Meiji Restoration. Thereby they could invite the British to
modernize their navy and the Germans to train their army—but on
their own terms. When civilizations meet, who stays in control of
the contact and directs its consequences makes all the difference.

The Daring of the Audacious

Creativity originates in individuals. It begins whenever somebody has a novel idea and plays with it—feeling the way, groping, exploring the unknown. That takes audacity, as well as imagination. Whether the new idea gains credence or not depends on its inherent validity and on social factors. It may challenge established interests and powerful institutions. It will, by definition, run counter to the conventional wisdom in one respect or another. If the timing is unfavorable, the new idea will be placed in cold storage. It may even be deliberately suppressed and forgotten, perhaps to be independently rediscovered at a later date. But when and where the circumstances require change, a new movement, a new process, a new doctrine, will be launched. It is then that a society finds itself transformed.

Creativity, as we have seen, is rare. It occurs but on few occasions and in few locales. Every civilization has had its share of these experiences—all of them in some spheres of activity, some of them in most. Seldom do they last for more than two generations, because, even if humans are capable of scaling Everest, no one can remain there very long. But it is from these amazing outbursts of exceptional achievement that civilizations acquire much of their character. Indeed, such peaks transcend the horizons of the particular civilization in which they arose. They become the treasures of the whole human race. One does not have to be European to be inspired by Plato or Beethoven, or Indian to be moved by Gautama or the Taj Mahal, or Chinese to love Sung porcelain. When the creative spirit functions at the highest, its outreach is universal. Only the lower levels nurture the parochial.

But if that be true of creativity in general, can the same be said of the most important of all human enterprises? By this I mean the task of improving the individual self and those relations between persons that constitute society—in a word, our ethics. Do similar conditions apply to ethical creativity? Or are different factors pertinent in this sphere? These questions will form the subject of the following chapters.

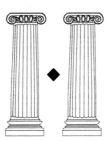

Of the tree of the
knowledge of good and
evil, thou shalt not eat of it;
for in the day that thou
eatest thereof thou shalt
surely die.

Genesis

This, then, which imparts
truth of the things that are
known and the power of
knowing to the knower,
you may affirm to be the
Form of the Good. It is the
cause of knowledge and
truth.

Plato

6

Humanity's First Great Moral Advance

*I*s there such a phenomenon as ethical creativity? Has our moral development had its Golden Ages comparable to those in the arts, in literature, in science and technology? Does ethics have its Michelangelos? Can we point to the moral equivalents of *Hamlet,* the Taj Mahal, the Ninth Symphony, the special theory of relativity? When and where, how and why, does the human spirit, so brilliantly manifested in feats of mind and imagination, take off and soar in the spheres of social enterprise, community life, and our relationships with one another?

In this chapter and the next, I shall inquire whether the same factors that were discovered in Chapter 5 to be pertinent to creativity in general hold equally true for human society. We need to know which ethical gains in the course of civilization have been both enduring and significant and under what circumstances they occurred. This topic is highly relevant to our turbulent world of today, so sorely in need of an ethical leap forward. If it appears that such advances have happened in the past, it is reasonable to expect that they could happen again.

Any inquiry into ethical progress must hinge on the prior assumption that this is possible. How can we be sure this is the case? There is a weight of opinion, supported by considerable authority, that holds the opposite view. The arguments on this side take one of two forms. Either they rest on a belief in the uniformity of human nature, or they assert that our nature is basically so bad that

we can never be made over. Let us look at these doctrines and see
what image of humanity they present.

How Skeptics and Pessimists
View Human Nature

The notion that human nature remains fundamentally unchanged
is an old one. It has been voiced repeatedly by historians and
theorists who compare widely separated periods, wherein they
detect similarities in the behavior of individuals and of groups.
Thucydides, describing the calamity of civil warfare as it compounded the evils of a war between states, engages in this broad
generalization: "Also in the course of factional strife, many hardships befell the cities, such as happen and always will occur while
human nature remains the same."[1] Machiavelli writes in like vein
in the *Discourses*: "Wise men say, and not without reason, that
whoever wishes to foresee the future must consult the past; for
human events ever resemble those of preceding times. This arises
from the fact that they are produced by men who have been, and
ever will be, animated by the same passions, and thus they must
necessarily have the same results."[2]

Later in the same century as Machiavelli, the French essayist
Montaigne endorses this judgment: "It is one and the same Nature,"
he asserts, "that rolls on her course, and whoever has sufficiently
considered the present state of things might certainly conclude as
to both the future and the past."[3] Closer to modern times, we find
Jacob Burckhardt basing his reflections on the self-same premise:
"We . . . shall start out from the one point accessible to us, the one
eternal centre of all things—man, suffering, striving, doing, as he
is and was and ever shall be. . . . We shall study the *recurrent,
constant* and *typical* as echoing in us and intelligible through us."[4]
To this we may add the views of a British historian, writing both
before and after World War II. In *Christianity and History*, Herbert
Butterfield offers comments that echo Plato's story of the ring of
Gyges. Civilization he depicts as a veneer thinly covering the
passions of our animal nature. "On the operation of certain safeguards which in normal times work so quietly that the superficial
observer may miss them altogether depends all the difference
between civilization and barbarism. In this connection we may say
indeed that the difference between civilization and barbarism is a
revelation of what is essentially the same human nature when it

works under different conditions." "The infirmities of human nature," he insists, "are always with us and the twentieth century can hardly complain to high heaven that the basic human material with which the world is endowed is any worse nowadays than it was in other periods."[5]

What is apparent in all these statements, stretching across 24 centuries, is the pessimism underlying their professed realism. They accept it as given that the fundamentals of our nature do not alter. To expect otherwise is self-delusion. Burckhardt pours scorn on Buckle's naiveté in looking for evidence of progress and being astonished that he could discover none.[6] All of them persons with powerful minds and great erudition, these writers resign themselves to what they present as a realistic conclusion: Learn from history, for the same traits that operated in the past continue today and will be manifest in the future. Patently, if that be true, any hope of significant ethical progress is so much wishful thinking.

Inevitably the same pessimistic outcome is reached by those who insist that human nature is basically bad—a belief predicated on uniformity of a special kind. This image that evil is ingrained in us and cannot be eradicated is sketched from several perspectives. Three of these can be illustrated: the biological, the theological, and the psychological.

The biological argument is grounded in the fact that the human being is one of the animals. Hence is deduced the proposition that, as all animals seek their survival, they must struggle to obtain whatever they need, for which purpose, if necessary, they kill. A stark expression of this belief is that which Hobbes presents in his *Leviathan,* where the analysis of human society is preceded by the imaginary construction of a state of nature, so characterized because all social institutions and their accompanying restraints are absent. Under these conditions, human beings are driven inexorably to ensure the security of their lives and possessions by enhancing their power in relation to others. "So that in the first place," he affirms, "I put for a generall inclination of all mankind, a perpetuall and restlesse desire of Power after power, that ceaseth only in Death." The result is a "warre of every man against every man," wherein, not surprisingly, he finds "the life of man, solitary, poore, nasty, brutish, and short."[7] In the twentieth century, when civil war and revolution persisted in Russia from 1917 to 1921, the novelist Boris Pasternak has described what ensued in terms that remind us of Hobbes: "That period," he writes, "confirmed the ancient proverb, 'Man is a wolf to man.' Traveller turned off the road at the sight of traveller, stranger meeting stranger killed for fear of being killed. There were isolated cases of cannibalism. The laws of human civilization were suspended. The jungle law was in force. Man dreamed the prehistoric dreams of the cave dweller."[8]

Thinkers, like Hobbes, who reason from the premise that human beings are naturally competitive and aggressive, are driven to the conclusion that very strong restraints are required to keep us in check. Hence they advocate a government with absolute powers—precisely that *Leviathan* whose total sovereignty commends itself to Hobbes. Such being the obvious logical deduction from this psychological doctrine, one is not surprised that a similar line of reasoning had been followed by a Chinese thinker almost 2,000 years earlier. Hsün-tzu, two centuries after Confucius, begins with the proposition that "human nature is evil." Anything good therefore has to be acquired through the social training we receive. But because the evil is so fundamental, a tolerable social existence is only possible under total power. Hsün-tzu's reasoning was not without practical effect. The two leaders of the Legalist School who followed him, Han Fei-tzu and Li Ssu, were his students. This was the school whose ideas helped to reorganize the western state of Ch'in and launched it on the successful career of conquest from which Prince Cheng emerged triumphant as Ch'in Shih Huang-ti, unifier of China.

A second source for the belief that we humans are naturally bad is theology. It is here particularly that the dogmas of Christianity have exercised so long and baneful an influence. Taking as literally true the account in Genesis of the origins of the universe and of humanity, Christian theologians have argued that the transgression of Adam and Eve—the Original Sin—was transmitted to all their descendants. Hence at core the human race is sinful and depraved. The extent to which this notion could be carried may be illustrated by a statement of the Protestant leader Calvin. "Infants themselves," he wrote, "as they bring their condemnation into the world with them, are rendered liable to punishment by their own sinfulness, not by the sinfulness of another. For though they have not yet produced the fruits of their iniquity, yet they have the seed of it within them; even their whole nature is as it were a seed of sin."[9] Such beliefs have for centuries supplied fodder for the Sunday sermons of priests and pastors fulminating from their pulpits. The harm thus done to Western civilization has been incalculable.

In yet a new guise the same old doctrine that we are fundamentally dangerous and destructive creatures was reformulated in modern times by the Viennese doctor who founded the practice of psychoanalysis. As sin has served the church, so has guilt served the Freudians. Sigmund Freud depicted humanity as impelled by antisocial drives that required strong repressions, both internal and external, to prevent the damage they could cause. In his *Group Psychology and the Analysis of the Ego*, he explains the social relationships of human beings by citing, with concurrence, the parable of the porcupines written by the nineteenth-century misanthrope Schopenhauer. "A company of porcupines," the story runs, "crowded themselves very close together one cold winter's day so as to profit by one another's warmth and so save themselves from being frozen to death. But soon they felt one another's quills, which induced them to separate again. And now, when the need for warmth brought them nearer together again, the second evil arose once more. So that they were driven backwards and forwards from one trouble to the other, until they had discovered a mean distance at which they could most tolerably exist."[10]

This image of our species as creatures projecting sharp spikes forms the central theme of a work that Freud wrote between the two world wars, translated into English under the title of *Civilization and Its Discontents.* Like a Wagnerian leit-motif, the refrain is repeated in phrase after phrase—"this aggressive cruelty," "this tendency to aggression," "this primary hostility of men towards one another," "the natural instinct of aggressiveness."[11] And here is the summation: "The bit of truth behind all this—one so eagerly denied—is that men are not gentle, friendly creatures wishing for love. . . . Aggression is at the bottom of all the relations of affection and love between human beings, possibly with the single exception of that of a mother to her male child."[12] On this supposition, the function of civilization is to prevent those aggressions from erupting. As they flow, however, from a natural instinct of whose existence we are aware, the tension between aggressiveness and civilization causes a feeling of guilt. From the burden of guilt, as from the burden of sin, release is at hand for those who will be guided by authority. Bring your sins to confession, says the priest, and, if you repent, you may find salvation. Bring your guilt to the couch, says the analyst, and understanding its causes may bring you release.

Whether the case is argued from the premises of psychology, theology, biology, or historical comparisons, the conclusions are essentially the same. The facts about humanity, as presented, are rooted in our nature. There is nothing one can do to alter them.

The wise course is to accept reality, adjust to its compulsions, and discover by trial and error, as the porcupines did, a tolerable means of surviving. Above all, be not sanguine about the prospect of a higher civilization emerging. *Plus ça change, plus c'est la même chose.*

The Possibility
of Ethical Improvement

How does one evaluate such a point of view? How much of it is true? How much exaggeration? The rest of this chapter and the next will attempt a response. If it can be demonstrated from history that there are significant facts that these theories cannot explain, their foundations will have been cut away, or at least weakened. Let us proceed on the hypotheses that human nature is not uniform and that some improvements have occurred that belie the pessimism cited above. First I shall state my conclusions and then marshal the evidence in their favor.

Because ethics constitute the moral quality in the relations between human beings, the lowest place on the scale is taken by egoism or pure selfishness. At the highest level is the altruism that acts on the maxim "love thy neighbor as thyself." The latter cannot be better illustrated than by the story told of Sir Philip Sidney, the Elizabethan nobleman regarded as the perfect embodiment of Renaissance ideals. Wounded on the battlefield, he was given a cup of water. As he was about to drink, he saw a soldier near him in extreme pain who looked at the water longingly. Sidney at once offered him the cup, saying: "Take it, friend. Thy need is greater than mine." Indeed, Westermarck has affirmed in his exhaustive study of the *Origin and Development of the Moral Ideas* that "progress in civilization is generally marked by an expansion of the altruistic sentiment."[13] Others who have undertaken the most comprehensive studies of ethics, comparing numerous societies at different levels of development, are in general agreement about their finds.[14] They point out that the central principles of the world's major ethical systems are substantially similar, that these were first enunciated long ago, and that in essentials they have not changed. Most of the progress, when it occurred, has lain in applying them more consistently and in extending them to widening circles of humanity. T. H. Buckle, one of the earliest of the moderns to write a history with civilization as his central theme, summarized "the great dogmas of which all moral systems are composed" in these phrases: "to do good to others; to sacrifice for their benefit your own wishes; to love your neighbor as yourself; to forgive your enemies; to restrain your passions; to honor your parents; to respect those who are set over you."[15] In short, that boils down to altruism and deference. Commenting on these precepts, Buckle goes on to say that "they have been known for thousands of years." One century later, Crane Brinton, writing his *History of Western Morals,* arrived at a somewhat similar conclusion: "The three or four thousand years of our Western recorded history show an unmistakable constant element. Honesty, loyalty, kindness, self-control, industry, co-operativeness are virtues; lying, treachery, cruelty, self-indulgence, laziness, conspicuous and uncontrolled aggressiveness, and selfishness are vices."[16]

If that were all, the task of discussing the relation of ethics to civilization would be fairly simple. But the whole truth—alas!—is more complicated. Ethical precepts may converge; morals, however, diverge. They not only differ from one another, but quite frequently they are at variance with the precepts. Reflecting on ethics in this sense, one observes that the record of civilization comprises both gains and losses in the moral quality of life but that overall the gains have outweighed the losses. The gains were achieved in one of two ways. During some finite period, either in one civilization or in several concurrently, major advances were registered within a few generations; alternatively, a long series of incremental improvements cumulatively produced a genuine transformation. Human progress, however, has never followed an even, steady course, and in certain eras and areas the losses have reversed the gains. Some of these losses—the persistence of warfare, of poverty, and of divisions between social and economic classes— have been intensified by civilization itself. Our findings therefore will be very mixed—as also, in later chapters, will be the diagnosis of contemporary society and the prognosis for our possible future.

No one who is concerned about human well-being and who speculates on the future of our species can fail to be perturbed by the continuing plight of so many of our fellow creatures and by the paradoxical mix of potentialities for good and evil that the advances in our knowledge have placed in our hands. In the final decade of the twentieth century, no need is more urgent than that of applying in practice the best of the ethical ideals that contemporary civilizations profess. The remainder of this book is devoted to an inquiry into whether this is possible.

The Great Eras of Ethical Progress

What eras in history were outstanding in ethical creativity? I would select two as being preeminent. The earlier one extended from the seventh century to the fifth B.C., the peak occurring in the sixth. Geographically, the entire Asian continent, which then already comprised several distinct civilizations, contributed to the gains; and the ripples from this ethical wave lapped across the eastern Mediterranean to the shores of Greece. The second occasion of a spectacular ethical advance was in the eighteenth and nineteenth centuries—what are called the Enlightenment and the Age of Progress. This originated in the Western civilization, where its effects were immediate and most apparent. In addition, one may cite numerous scattered instances in every civilization when ethical development took a surge forward. Generally these occupied a shorter time span and were confined to a particular country. They are often associated with the endeavors of a particular individual whose creative impulse found its vent in an ethical direction. Some examples are India during the reigns of Ashoka and Akbar, Palestine at the time of Jesus, Rome in the Age of the Antonines, Arabia under the impulse of Mohammed, western Europe in parts of the twelfth and thirteenth centuries, China under the Ch'ing emperors of the eighteenth century. The list is illustrative, not complete. Let us now explore the principal cases of ethical progress and inquire into the conditions that may have caused them or made them possible.

Of all the instances mentioned, the earliest is unique and is the most extraordinary. What happened in the ethical realm during two centuries across Asia, and in Europe among the Greeks, has no parallel, either before or since. A succession of inspired individuals suddenly emerged and enunciated ethical teachings at a very high level, with or without a religious or metaphysical content. Some of them were contemporaries, and their lives overlapped in sequence so as to form a continuous chain. Who were they? Those in question, with the dates of their births and deaths as known or estimated, were the following:

in Persia, Zoroaster (?630-553);
in China, Lao-tzu (?600-531) and Confucius (551-479);
in India, Gautama (?563-483);
in Palestine, the Hebrew Prophets, culminating in deutero-Isaiah (eighth to sixth centuries);
in Greece, Socrates (470-399).

How did this clustering occur? Why did it take place at this time in these widely separated regions? Did any of these individuals influence any of the rest, or were they wholly unaware of each other?

The Axial Age

Because the phenomenon that prompts these questions is so important and so exceptional, it has long attracted the attention of scholars searching out its significance and seeking to explain both the parallelisms and the contrasts. Early in this century, the California historian Frederick J. Teggart noted and discussed the synchronicity. Later, the existential philosopher Karl Jaspers suggested the description "The Axial Age" (*Die Achsenzeit*) to characterize a period that marked in his view a turning point in ethical and religious development. Lewis Mumford in *The Transformations of Man* makes use of Jasper's concept in a chapter called "Axial Man." More recently, at the initiative of the Sinologist Benjamin I. Schwartz, an issue of *Daedalus,* the journal of the American Academy of Arts and Sciences, was devoted to the discussion of this topic.[17] I am using the essays in that stimulating volume as the starting point for my own treatment, because theirs is the most carefully focused examination of the subject thus far.

The *Daedalus* discussion proceeds along these lines. Several of the contributors offer a specialized analysis of one civilization, in which they explain the social context of that period and its accompanying ideas. Those described are China, Greece, India, Mesopotamia, and Palestine, but not Egypt or Persia. Other essays tackle the task of drawing together the threads, of formulating generalizations based on the data, and of tracing whatever common pattern they reveal. Hence, if any significant conclusions emerge from the evidence, it is here that we can expect to find them.

Unfortunately—or disappointingly, if one is looking for clear-cut answers to a complicated question—the writers are unable to offer anything positive and definite to explain why such major ethical developments occurred at approximately the same time in the several civilizations. What they do present are some generalizations about the period as a whole, which, although suggestive, are rather vague. As for the essays on particular civilizations, these tend to such a degree to stress the factors peculiar to each that comparative inferences are hard to draw. Let me illustrate this by summarizing some of their arguments.

Benjamin Schwartz, in addition to writing his analysis of China, has introduced the volume with an essay, "The Age of Transcendence." This is the term he chooses to characterize the Axial Age, although, when employing it, he is careful to explain that he is not using "transcendence" in the technical connotations of philosophy or theology. "What I refer to here," he states, "is something close to the etymological meaning of the word—a kind of standing back and looking beyond—a kind of critical, reflective questioning of the actual and a new vision of what lies beyond."[18] This transcendence, as he sees it, consists in the phenomenon of the simultaneous "breakthroughs" occurring at that time in all the known civilizations except Egypt and Mesopotamia. The breakthroughs do not all have the same emphasis. In some, the theological element is very strong, as with the Hebrew Prophets; in others, the ethical dominates, as in Confucian China; in others again, the intellectual factor is uppermost, as among the Greeks. But all are alike in that they constitute a significant forward leap in values. Even so, Schwartz hastens to add the cautionary note that along with the leap there are the continuities. "Like all breakthroughs in history," he affirms, "the age of transcendence had its antecedents."[19]

Breakdowns and Breakthroughs

This reasoning is advanced a step further in an essay by Eric Weil, who inquires: "What Is a Breakthrough in History?" His discussion speculates on the problem of why a breakthrough occurs, and the explanation, tentatively submitted, is that it happens because of a breakdown. "Breakthroughs," we read, ". . . follow breakdowns. This would appear to be self-evident. Why should people change their ways unless they are no longer satisfied by them?"[20] Tempting though this sounds, Weil immediately dashes our hopes, if we are thinking that here at last we have the answer. "Unfortunately," he writes, "for those who crave overall explanations, breakdowns in history are common; breakthroughs are extremely rare." How true! Which means that we are then left with the further problem of explaining why only certain breakdowns result in breakthroughs and others do not. Causation, as I have commented before, is the trickiest topic on which to speculate. So often do we find that like "causes" do not always yield like "consequences" and that like "consequences" may sometimes issue from unlike "causes"—a fact of human behavior that is frustrating to schematic minds.

Were there then, in the judgment of this group of scholars, any general characteristics pertinent to all these civilizations that could explain why the same or a similar breakthrough occurs at approximately the same stage of their development? One common factor was an underlying technological revolution, the spread in the use of iron. As to its significance, Schwartz suggests: "The transition from bronze age to iron age, by accelerating the advance of agricultural and military technologies, may have hastened the emergence of those conditions that elicited transcendental responses. On the other hand," he continues, "if the breakthroughs can be spoken of as effects, they are 'effects' that often stand in the relationship of dialectic tension with their 'causes.' "[21]

The warning is justified. If one were to assert that the advent of the Iron Age in metallurgy was responsible for the Axial Age in morality, what is being said? The spread of iron in place of bronze cannot be cited as the direct and immediate cause of certain individuals voicing unusual ethical ideas. There are too many other factors, intermediate links in the chain of causation, that must be taken into account. One might cogently argue that the introduction of iron altered the weaponry of war, the implements of agriculture, and the utensils of domestic living; that, because iron was more abundant than copper, the social elitism of the Bronze Age was challenged and that new economic possibilities brought new social groups to the fore, and that finally the resulting tensions within society produced clashes that evoked the moral-intellectual-religious breakthroughs. But can such a complex series of developments as that be described as causation? Romila Thapar, in her essay "Ethics, Religion, and Social Protest in the First Millennium B.C. in Northern India," subsumes the whole sequence under the single, broad category of "change." "The primary concern of the new attitude is with the perception of change," she tells us, "the recognition that the context during this period was different from any that had existed before."[22]

But if change be suggested as the explanation, is this not even more tenuous, even broader, than iron technology? And what are we to say of all the periods of history when changes occurred and were perceived but no corresponding ethical breakthrough took place? This leads us back to the point that no such breakthroughs occurred in Egypt or Mesopotamia. Iron, however, was replacing bronze at that time in the valleys of the Nile and of the Tigris and Euphrates, just as it was across the Gangetic plain and along the course of the Hwang-ho. Neither change itself, nor the perception thereof, was absent from Assyria, Babylon, or Egypt. What was missing was the breakthrough. Why?

A reasonable answer, I think, would be the following. The substitution of iron for bronze at that time did set in motion a series of changes, pervading many aspects of the society, unsettling the preestablished order, and thus helping to produce a general ferment. In this situation, persons with speculative minds and strong convictions about right and wrong are likely to explore alternative models for human conduct. Whether their thinking has any effect, however, depends on the social structure and on how that opens up or closes the avenues of expression. Add to all this the final, necessary, but incalculable, condition of the presence of the requisite individual personality at the appropriate time—something that no amount of alleged sociological causation can predict or determine.

In this light, let us examine some of the cases that contributed to the Axial Age. Their circumstances, as we shall see, were far from uniform. Some might be described as "breakdowns." Others could not properly be so designated. As for the responses, or "breakthroughs," these, too, ranged all the way from the rational humanism that focuses on this world to the transcendental or mystical flights into another sphere of consciousness or existence.

Zoroaster and the Conflict of Good and Evil

Zoroaster, the Hellenized version of Zarathustra, heads the list chronologically, whatever the exact dating of his life may have been.[23] His position, both in space and in time, reveals something of significance. He lived toward the end of the period when the Persians were governed by the Medes and died shortly before Cyrus the Great defeated the Medes and laid the foundations of the Persian Empire. His habitat was not in the more developed, urbanized areas of the west, nearer to Mesopotamia, but far away in the northeastern region of Chorasmia where the River Oxus waters a valley in the midst of mountains and deserts. The people there were not agriculturalists but nomads whose social conditions were disorderly. Zoroaster himself possessed moderate wealth in the form of livestock, enough at any rate for him to have retainers in his service. The religious practices of the region were those of traditional polytheism, which required the placating of numerous nature deities (*asuras*)—each with its flock of ministering priests who received the mandatory offerings and sacrifices.

Into this unpromising situation, Zoroaster infused an unusual set of values and beliefs. Rejecting polytheism, and thereby provoking the ire and opposition of its priests, he interpreted the universe in terms of a fundamental dualism. Two antagonistic principles, as he thought, were arrayed in eternal conflict. One, symbolizing the light, was named *Ormuzd* or *Ahura Mazda*. This was the principle of goodness, manifested as truth, justice, and life. Its opponent—*Ahriman*, or darkness—epitomized evil and took the form of lying, injustice, and death. Between these must human beings choose.

This dualistic philosophy has two features—one ethical, the other intellectual—to commend it. The ethical merit is that it places on each individual the responsibility for choosing. You can take sides with Ormuzd or with Ahriman, and you will harvest the consequences of your actions. Morally, this doctrine is vastly superior to those notions of fatalism or predestination or original sin under which a person has lost the prerogative of choice.

The second great merit of Zoroastrian dualism is that it deals with the problem of evil in an intellectually satisfying manner. That problem arises from the fact that evil exists in the world. If so, how do we explain it? In their attempts to answer this question, all three monotheistic religions—Judaism, Christianity, and Islam—have failed. Their reasoning starts with the basic assumption of one Supreme Being (Yahweh, God the Father, Allah) to which, as the criterion of supremacy, they attribute omnipotence. In addition, however, this being is conceived as good, just, and merciful and, by Christians, as loving. How then can anything so beneficent allow the evil that causes pain and suffering? Is Satan reconcilable with the goodness of an omnipotent God? Theologians of the monotheistic faiths have tied themselves up in knots trying to resolve this problem, which is purely of their own making. They present themselves with an inescapable dilemma and then become enmeshed in a tangle of illogical contradictions. Because evil exists, a God that is all good cannot be omnipotent, for, if it were, its goodness would require the destruction of the evil. Conversely, a God that is omnipotent cannot be all good, because it is responsible for permitting the evil to continue. Zoroaster's solution to the problem—dualism—is logically consistent. Significantly, his reasoning on this point is paralleled later by no less a philosopher than Plato, who has this to say in the *Laws*: "We cannot suppose that the universe is ordered by one soul; there must be more than one, probably not less than two—one the author of good, and the other of evil."[24] Unprovable though this supposition may be, at least it makes rational sense—which the assumptions of monotheism, when applied to ethics, do not.

Certainly Zoroaster's teaching may fairly be called a breakthrough on the ethical and theological planes. But it is stretching the facts to suggest that it was the response to a breakdown. As far as is known, Zoroaster was offering a corrective to the chronic maladies of a traditional society, which was not deteriorating catastrophically but was merely continuing along the lines of its past—just as was to be the case later when Mohammed blazed forth in Mecca. As events soon showed, the Persians of the mid-sixth century B.C. were girding themselves for a creative surge that launched their empire and their contribution to civilization. To this achievement, Zoroaster supplied the spiritual force, and Cyrus, the political. In his lifetime, the prophet was able to convert the local ruler, Hystaspes, to his teaching. Later on, the successors to Cyrus in the Achaemenid dynasty proclaimed the primacy of Ahura Mazda. But the tenets of Zoroaster were eventually diluted by the reabsorption of some of the earlier polytheism. It is ever the fate of prophets that subsequent generations muddy the purity of the original doctrine.

The Buddha, in Time and Place

The purity of the flowering lotus rooted in the muddy ooze below was the simile employed by the Buddha to illustrate his point that the enlightened person could blossom even in a corrupt environment. Like Zoroaster, Gautama rejected much of what he saw in the society around him. He rejected the values of wealth, power, and high social standing—all of which had been his by accident of birth. He rejected the caste system, the deities, and the mercenary ritualism of the Hindu priests. What he offered in their place was an escape from suffering in the endless cycle of rebirths.

Gautama's prescription for curing the ills that flesh is heir to resembles Zoroaster's in that the possibility of choosing lies with the individual. To every person he holds out the hope of enlightenment, which can be attained by those with the understanding and the self-discipline to follow the right path. But in Buddhism, the end result—the extinguishing of desire—goes beyond the formulae of the Persian sage. Here Gautama is in the same camp with Jesus, urging a revolutionary reversal of those values that evolving civilization was prizing most.

What prompted such teaching at that time? Obviously, we have here the phenomenon of an extraordinary personality endowed with rare intellectual acumen and imaginative vision. But was there, in addition, anything in the social circumstances of his time that stands in some causal relation to his emergence? Why was it then and there that Gautama so thought, so felt, and so acted?

Romila Thapar tackles this question in the essay she wrote for the *Daedalus* study.[25] Her principal argument to explain why India was part of the Axial Age was, as noted before, the perception of changes in society. She details what these changes were. The civilization at Harappa and Mohenjodaro in the Indus Valley had petered out, and the peoples of the Gangetic plain were shifting from the bronze technology to iron. In the rural areas, land and money were replacing cattle as the index of wealth; while in urban centers, the cities were developing not, as earlier, to house the court, garrison, and temples but to organize a market for trade and finance. The result was a growth of banks and guilds—not unlike Florence in the fifteenth century. As the Hindu caste system did not accord a high status to the trader, he would be receptive to a new message. Hence the appeal of Gautama, as also of his contemporary, Mahavira.[26] The former, says Thapar, won many adherents precisely because he emphasized causation and personal responsibility. Each individual was the cause of his or her own fate. Each could shape the future.

A breakthrough assuredly this was, but, once again, not in response to a breakdown. The north Indian society of the sixth century B.C. was swirling with crosscurrents, but it was not in dissolution. We are still left with no satisfactory explanation of why the Buddha preached as he did. Indeed, when Thapar stresses the need of the urban commercial entrepreneurs for a new doctrine, one fails to see how they could be attracted to Gautama's insistence on extinguishing desire. If people ceased to desire possessions, what would happen to economic activity? Understandably, therefore, Schwartz expresses some skepticism about the chain of causation that Thapar infers. "Buddhism," he rightly remarks, "hardly strikes us as a 'bourgeois' philosophy."[27]

So far, then, a comparison of Zoroaster with Gautama suggests only this tentative conclusion: A society on the eve of profound change, or one already experiencing the stress of change, is prepared for a radical departure from conventional precepts and practices. Why, however, the departure should be in such directions as were proposed by Buddhism or Zoroastrianism has still not been explained.

Let us turn therefore to two other instances of breakthroughs that differ from both the Persian and the Indian in that these were clearly associated with breakdowns. Those that I have in mind are Palestine and Greece. The comparison of this pair is indeed instructive. The two societies were similar in that they fell from a peak of high attainment. They were dissimilar, however, in the kind of breakthrough that their most vigorous minds envisaged for them. The prescription in Palestine was other-worldly; in Greece, it was of this world. Both the resemblance and the contrast need explaining.

Other-Worldly Israel;
This-Worldly Hellas

There is no other succession of preachers in history that quite compares with the Hebrew Prophets. Fearless and independent, flailing around in every direction, they spared no one. In their denunciation of wrongdoing, king and people alike are lashed by their wrathful tongues—and the circumstances of the eighth to the sixth centuries provided much material to kindle that wrath. With all its variations, their message reiterates a single theme. You have strayed from the path of righteousness and have forsaken the Lord. The Lord is therefore punishing you for your transgressions. Return to the Lord, heed his commandments, and you will be requited. What was the context that evoked these contents?

The descendants of Abraham had taken on a formidable task, which, as events demonstrated, was beyond their strength and resources. They sought to make a homeland and build a state in a region that, geographically viewed, lay in a crossroads where a north-south route between the Black Sea and the Red Sea intersected with an east-west flow between Mesopotamia and the Mediterranean. Whoever sought to occupy the crossroads had to withstand the converging pressures. Translated into political terms, this meant that the Hebrews must be prepared to cope with Egyptians and Philistines, with Babylon and Assyria, with Medes and Persians. For a small people, this was a big undertaking. Under two kings, David and Solomon, they were sufficiently united to project their power outward. Later, after they fell apart into the two kingdoms of Israel and Judah, they could not maintain their independence. The north therefore fell victim to Assyria; the south, to Babylon. Both came later under the more tolerant suzerainty of Persia.

Why would Yahweh, who had made a covenant with the Hebrews, allow this to happen? Had Yahweh forsaken his people? No, said the Prophets. It was the Hebrews who had forsaken Yahweh. He was using Assyria and Babylon as instruments of his rightful wrath against a "stiff-necked people." So, what must be done? Repent, return to the Lord, walk righteously. Thereafter, in the vision of deutero-Isaiah, will Yahweh's Golden Age come to fruition. Granted the assumptions of Judaic theology, the reasoning hung together. Yahweh, the one and only God, was omnipotent. All attributes were therefore his. "Shall there be evil in a city," asked Amos, "and the Lord hath not done it?"[28] Project that argument into this century, and it would follow that the same Lord had to be responsible for Hitler. Once you grant the transcendental premise, which lies beyond reason and is believed through faith, you dispense with the logic of human rationality.

That logic was developed, however, by the leading thinkers of the most intellectual of ancient peoples, the Greeks. For the Greeks, the fifth was the critical century. Opening in triumph, it ended with tragedy. From the level of heroism that could confront and conquer the Persian invaders to the deep pessimism of the Peloponnesian War, the descent is as swift as it is shocking. Contrast the soaring mood of Herodotus with the biting reflections of Thucydides, the grandeur of Aeschylean drama with the sick neurotics of Euripides, the loftiness of the Funeral Oration with the piercing satires of Aristophanes, and you can trace the change in morality and morale.

The worst you can say against the Greeks is that their mortal wounds were self-inflicted. Only a people bent on self-destruction could have done—with due judicial process, to boot—what the Athenians did to Socrates, executing their most fearless thinker whose unforgivable crime was to raise basic questions that the conventional wisdom was unable to answer. Was Socrates a rationalist or a transcendentalist? Some might argue for the latter by stressing his belief in that in-dwelling spirit—his *daimon*—which cautioned him, always in the negative, not to do this or that. Also, he believed the soul, *psyché*, was immortal, and he devoted the last hours of his life, before drinking the hemlock, to proving this supposition. As for the gods, like Confucius, he never analyzed their meaning or attempted to disprove their existence. He duly observed the rituals and offered sacrifices as custom required. In all this there was nothing to lift him out of the ordinary. Had that been the "true" Socrates, he would not have left so deep an impression on his contemporaries, nor would he have been singled out for execution.

No, the "true" Socrates was the intellectual with the relentlessly probing mind whose inquiries caused the Delphic oracle to pronounce him the wisest of the Greeks. This was the Socrates who demanded of every proposition submitted to him a reasoned argument as to whether it was true. Testing the statements made in everyday conversation by the criteria of their internal coherence and their consistency with known data was the hallmark of the Socratic method. He may have "proved," to his own satisfaction, that we possess souls and that the soul is immortal. But what he demonstrated by the practice of his own teaching was the sovereignty of truth, discovered by the human reason critically weighing the pros and cons. Socrates' thrust was the humanism of this world, not the transcendentalism of another. And was it not significant to be teaching thus when the civilization around him, all that world of the Hellenic polis that he knew so intimately, was encompassing its own extinction? The Greeks were starting to destroy themselves through *hubris,* overweening arrogance. Might they not save themselves, thought Socrates, with *logos,* reason?

What China Demonstrates

That brings me to the Chinese. Their contribution to the Axial Age is the one that I purposely left to the last, because of the special light that it throws on the problem under discussion. There are two features of the Chinese case that stand out. The first concerns the period when they made their breakthrough and the circumstances then prevalent in their civilization. Lao-tzu lived during the sixth century B.C.; Confucius was born in the middle of that same century and died in 479. In Chinese history this is known as the "Spring and Autumn" period and is the immediate precursor to the era of the Warring States. It was a time of insecurity and, according to Confucius, of a decline in moral standards. Although the clashes between states were compatible, as we have seen,[29] with cultural creativity of a high order, public ethics were deteriorating. To call this a breakdown would be exaggerating. Knowing the outcome, we can now see with all the benefits of hindsight what Lao-tzu and Confucius could not—namely, that this was the travail of a time when China was undergoing that process of consolidation which led, two and a half centuries after Confucius died, to the unified empire. The then separate kingdoms were jockeying for advantage, which augments tension and tempts unscrupulous rulers to discard the accepted canons of conduct.

Under these conditions, how does a sensitive person, with high intellectual and moral standards, respond? Here we can detect the second feature of the Chinese breakthrough, which not only is arresting in itself but distinguishes this civilization from the others of that time. It is the simple fact that the effort to improve human life provided not just one highway to salvation but a forking into two paths leading in opposite directions. There was the way of Lao-tzu, the *Tao,* along with the alternative way, that of Confucius. For this discussion, it does not matter whether the Lao-tzu of tradition was a historic person or not. If he was, his life is said to have covered the first two-thirds of the sixth century, which means that he would have overlapped with Confucius for perhaps two decades. Indeed, a story is related of their having met. But even if there was no Lao-tzu, the text that makes up the *Tao-te-ching* existed. It was known and recited; it had an influence. Taoism, therefore, became a fact.

Now my point is that this self-same epoch in China—call it Axial or the Age of Transcendence, or what you will—produced two major, but contradictory, philosophies. You could embrace the world of established institutions and social relationships and elevate it to a higher moral plane, suffusing order and hierarchy with a humane benevolence; or you could withdraw and seek inward communion with the natural rhythms of the universe. We know, again with hindsight, which of the two philosophies subsequently prevailed, that Confucianism became the established doctrine while Taoism remained the protest of a counterculture. But the outcome was not certain in the fifth century, when the Chinese were being offered either an improved this-worldliness or an other-worldly escape.

What does that tell us? Reviewing the circumstances in the contemporary civilizations of the Axial Age suggests some conclusions about how breakthroughs may occur and whether they are caused by breakdowns. First, it would appear evident that ideas for a major ethical transformation are likely to be generated at a time when society is undergoing widespread changes, deep seated in their origin. Such a factor, in the case of the Axial Age, was the advent of the iron technology, which had the effect of opening up new possibilities. When alternatives exist, and different routes are explored, inquiring minds will speculate on the respective advantages and disadvantages. That is a time therefore for ethical searchings. Can the outlines of a Good Society be traced, bringing in their train the improved humanity of the Good Person? Or, if society is to continue as a mixture of contrasts and contradictions, can the Good Person survive on another level of consciousness through inward enlightenment?

The social circumstances of the Axial Age, as we have seen, were not breakdowns everywhere, though all were transitional phases of stress and crisis. As the conditions varied, so did the remedies proposed. The latter extended across the gamut from rational to mystical, from humanistic to transcendental, from this-worldly reformism to other-worldly utopianism. And when attempting the intellectual task of drawing inferences about causation from all of these varied histories, I come back to the Chinese case as the convincing one. Here the same set of facts was the genesis of opposite teachings. Does this not demonstrate once again that in the history of civilization outcomes are never predetermined? Each epoch encounters a number of possibilities. What differs in each civilization at any given time is the extent of those possibilities. The Axial Age remains uniquely interesting because at that time the opportunities available to the major civilizations covered an unusually wide range, which prompted original speculations by individuals of exceptional gifts.

That last point reminds us that in two civilizations of that period there was no comparable ferment. The two in question were Egypt and Mesopotamia. Why did no significant philosophy emerge at that time in the valleys of the Nile and of the two rivers?

The Social Acceptance
of Ethical Change

The answer, I suggest, is to be found in the social structure of those civilizations and in its dampening effects on intellectual creativity. Egypt, Babylon, and Assyria suffered from the same vice. These were societies in which the intellectual realm lay under the domination of priestly hierarchies. The temples of the god—of Amun-Re and Osiris, of Marduk and Ashur—were the institutions that formed the basis of the power of the organized priesthoods. Theirs was the monopoly of conducting official ceremonies for the kings as well as rites for private persons. What is more, the dogmas enshrined in their system of beliefs so pervaded the whole society that they constituted a formidable obstacle to independent thought.

Under these conditions, from what source could any new ideas—moral, metaphysical, or religious—be generated? These might have issued from within the hierarchy itself, had there been a priest bold enough to defy the temple bureaucracy. But neither in Egypt nor in Mesopotamia do we hear of a Martin Luther challenging his pope. A second possibility would have been for some individual outside the official hierarchy, like Zoroaster or the Hebrew Prophets, to speak with a different voice. But what happened in Palestine and Persia never transpired under the rule of the Pharaohs or in Babylon or Nineveh. That leaves the third possibility. Innovation—a breakthrough in ideas—would have had to come from the ruler, if one was prepared to challenge the priests. That there was one we know—but only one—the maverick pharaoh Ikhnaton, the man with an original mind and undoubted political courage, who defied the priests of Amun-Re and initiated a form of monotheism in the worship of Aton, the Sun-God. Here is proof that, in these two civilizations, such was the power of the priesthood that only a ruler could venture opposition. But let us not forget that this happened only once, and his endeavor ended in failure. The stultifying social effect of a priestly monopoly explains why no breakthrough arrested the steady decline of Egypt, Assyria, and Babylon. Not until the new faith of Islam replaced the older cult was a renaissance possible in those societies. Mesopotamia had a second spurt when the combination of Islamic culture with Abbasid power radiated outward from Baghdad. Subsequently Egypt, which had served so long as the battleground for Macedonians, Romans, and Christians, regained some vitality of its own under the Fatimids.

The experience of the Axial Age, both in the civilizations where its effects were manifest and in those where they were not, suggests some hypotheses that can be tested in later history. There is first the question of the connection between ethical improvement and religious belief. Frequently in the history of civilization, these have been linked—for the very obvious reason that every religion includes a set of ethical values which are presented as following from its theology. Zoroaster illustrates this, as do the Hebrew Prophets. So does the Brahminical Hinduism from which Gautama recoiled. Such a morality is set therefore in an other-worldly framework.

Gautama himself, however, like Confucius and Socrates, has no need to import a deus ex machina to be the source and sanction of the ethical system. The Buddha's teaching, as we have seen, consists essentially in a psychological transformation, a change of consciousness, which will extinguish suffering and pain; and the

Eightfold Path, which leads to *nirvana,* omitted the worship of god or gods. As for Confucius and Socrates, their fundamental humanism, although compatible with the performance of conventional religious rites, is in no way intellectually dependent on them. What is more, the ancestor worship of the Chinese made every head of household his own priest, thereby dispensing with the functions of a priestly class. The humanistic focus on this world has the effect of deriving ethical values from reason, not from revelation. The difference between basing morality on the one or the other is that between worshippers bowing their heads in prayer and individuals using their heads to think. In the Axial Age both types of breakthrough emerged, and they have been with us ever since. The notion that ethics and religion are necessarily interdependent is disproved by history, as it is by logic.

Another question of importance concerns the sequel to the Axial Age. What happens after an inspired teacher or preacher has delivered his message? How is it spread? How does it become accepted? How long does it take for an ethical system, with or without a religious component, to establish itself?

The answers display a considerable variation. Zoroaster initiated one pattern by converting the ruler of his region, whose subjects were then induced (if that is the correct word) to follow his example. Not long thereafter, Cyrus is said to have adopted the new faith for his Persian Empire. Here is a case, then, of a practice much repeated in later centuries, that is, the exercise of political power from the top to inculcate a change of ideas and values. The Hebrew Prophets were in a different situation. Theirs was not a new doctrine but a passionate cry for a return to the old religion. Invariably that was seasoned with dire predictions of the doom to come, if the sinners—whether king or subjects—failed to mend their ways. Of course, those who venture on prophecy are taking a chance, for what happens if the sky does not fall? Jeremiah was one whose dismal forecasts were ignored for much of his life but who was tragically vindicated when the Babylonians destroyed Jerusalem.

Seldom does a new teaching gain widespread acceptance rapidly, for the resistance to change is normally stronger than the appeals of innovation. Moreover, as has been noted, not every breakthrough follows a breakdown and not every breakdown is succeeded by a breakthrough. Witness what happened to the ideas of Confucius and Gautama. The former attracted some followers during his lifetime, and much of the philosophical outpourings of the "Hundred Schools" during the Warring States period consisted of variations on, or rejections of, Confucian themes. But his vindication had to wait for three and a half centuries after the sage had died. Gautama had less success, at least in the country of his birth. When the Buddha played Luther to the Brahmins' Vatican, the latter mounted a Counter Reformation,[30] which was effective enough to hold the ground for Hinduism. Later on, what remained of Buddhism in northern India was virtually wiped out by the Muslim invaders. As an export, however, into the regions east and southeast of India, the Buddhist triumph was phenomenal. Except for China, where the T'ang emperor clipped the soaring Buddha's wings,[31] the latter's doctrine developed into the universal religion of eastern Asia, along with all the cultism that this term implies.

As for Socrates, his was another kind of breakthrough on yet another plane. What he demonstrated was the probing, questioning intellect. For an Athenian, that too embraced an ethical content. The Socratic maxim that "nobody errs voluntarily"—often freely rendered as "virtue is knowledge"—was his way of saying that, to act aright, one has to know what is right. Knowledge therefore is the necessary precursor to virtuous conduct. The doctrine of Socrates was a subtle one—too subtle for his fellow citizens whose majority, unable to answer his questions, voted to execute the questioner. Its transmission to posterity would not have been possible without Plato, who, unlike his master, was also a writer and duly fulfilled the obligation of the disciple to propagate what he had learned. Because in this instance the latter was as eminent a thinker as his teacher, we cannot always be certain, when reading the dialogues where Socrates participates, whether these are Plato's arguments, or those of Socrates, or some combination of the two. Yet there is enough that has a distinctive and uniquely individual flavor for some of the teaching to be identified as Socratic. Anyway, content apart, about the method there can be no doubt. The uncompromising logic of Socrates, never deviating in its search for the truth, has been his lasting legacy to civilization. He therefore, par excellence, is the intellectuals' intellectual. But this rationalism is an influence that ebbs and flows through history in the never-ending combat against ignorance, bigotry, and prejudice. Today, that struggle is still being waged with undiminished intensity.[32] In many contemporary countries, were a Socrates to emerge, he or she would be banished, jailed, or shot.

Morality and the Mores

There is another question arising from the Axial Age that is of supreme importance but on which it is difficult, if not impossible, to speak with certitude. I have been referring to breakthroughs, to ethical advances, to a group of inspired individuals whose teaching (whether moral, intellectual, or religious) had a profound and lasting effect. But how far did their influence extend? How much of the traditional mores gave way to the new morality? Did the philosophers, preachers, and prophets find their audience generally at the upper heights of the social structure, from which elevation some droplets of the new wisdom trickled down to the grass roots? Or, to change the metaphor, was their message a fire that swept across the plains and then flared up to scorch the treetops? How noticeably did the ethics of civilization improve after the Axial Age?

For definitive answers to such questions, one would need to produce authentic empirical data describing how the various relations between human beings were translated into the numerous activities of everyday life—how parents related to their children, husbands to wives, masters or mistresses to servants or slaves, rulers to subjects, officials to private persons, and so forth. That is outside our capacity, given that the information available is sparse and scanty and sometimes contradictory.[33] For most of the history of civilization before two centuries ago, the records we now have consist of isolated glimpses, of a few close views of detailed scenes, of events or situations that in some instances were recorded because they were atypical. If the purpose of the historian's craft be, in Ranke's phrase, to describe the past "as it actually was,"[34] the chapters on ethics will contain many blank pages.

But although the variations that have existed in practice, and the gap between practice and precept, are undeniable, the formulation of ideals is itself an integral part of reality. The prevailing social conceptions of what people ought to value and how they ought to behave have their effect on what they actually think and do. The majority of human beings are socially conditioned to obey authority. That manifests itself in different ways. We know that states have the means to coerce, that religious bodies capitalize on the awe of the supernatural and fear of punishment, that individuals can win respect both by the nature of their teaching and by their example of personal integrity. For reasons such as these, the values that a society happens to consider important have their influence on conduct. It makes a great difference, therefore, which values receive priority. For these are the signposts pointing in a direction that some will travel for at least part of the distance.

Confucius, for example, gained a following of disciples in his own lifetime. But his influence was vastly extended when Wu Ti gave his teaching the imperial sanction, so that Confucianism permeated officialdom. If entry to the ranks of the mandarins was open only to those who could pass an examination in the sage's writings, something was bound to rub off—in the same way as the values conveyed in Britain's classical education molded the graduates of Oxford and Cambridge who entered the Administrative Class of that country's Civil Service. Likewise, in the literally millions of families that formed the cellular units of China's social organism, the Confucian ethic set the norm. From its canons only the very bad, the very bold, or the very bemused would overtly or flagrantly deviate.

It is needless to repeat this point for each of the other civilizations that participated in the Axial Age. Instead, a summary of the results will suffice. What was accomplished at that time was a significant advance in the ethical standard of the major civilizations, truly a great forward leap. The teachings of Gautama, Zoroaster, Confucius, Isaiah, and Socrates invited agreement or dissent. But they could not be ignored. They had brought the basic problems of right conduct to the forefront of human attention, and much of the discussion since then has been couched within the frameworks they presented. The subsequent history of civilization would record advances in several other spheres—in scientific knowledge and technical know-how, in the capacity for political and administrative organization, in literature and the arts. But the handful of eminent thinkers who emerged in the seventh, sixth, and fifth centuries had held out the greatest possibility of all, that humanity could improve in its essential humanness. From their time to the present, that vision has always lain before us.

The Political Context
and the Impact of Religion

In the millennium that followed the Axial Age, each of the major civilizations went through a process of political consolidation. Cyrus created the Persian Empire for which Darius provided a structure and a system. China was unified and its influence ranged far afield during the Han dynasty. India experienced the two great periods of the Mauryan and Gupta empires. In the West, the polis was absorbed into kingdoms, all of which in turn were absorbed by Rome. The organization of these much larger units had the effect of both enlarging the area and increasing the population under a common framework. For the spread of new ethical values, this could be either a help or a hindrance, depending on the aims and attitude of whoever ruled at the center.

We have seen that Zoroastrianism and Confucianism became established when the king or emperor gave their doctrines official approval, which happened fairly rapidly with the former, but belatedly to the latter. In India, Buddhism maintained itself in opposition to Hinduism largely through the institution of the *sanghas,* the bands of monks clustering around a monastery. Official encouragement fluctuated. It was at its strongest in the reign of Ashoka, many of whose famous pillars, erected throughout his realm, were inscribed with precepts of a Buddhist flavor. Later on, the tolerant attitude of Chandra Gupta II created a climate in which the Buddhists could thrive along with Hindus and Jains. Because Buddhist ethics, however, insisted on nonviolence, rulers who hoped to survive amid the insecurities of northern India were unlikely to follow Gautama consistently. Even Ashoka's change of heart, be it remembered, occurred only after he had attained his political objectives through the slaughter at Kalinga.

The experience of Rome throws yet another light on the problem of humanizing power. After the empire was consolidated and its political framework had been organized, two attempts were made to infuse the structure with a higher ethic. Both, interestingly enough, were imports. These were the Stoic philosophy and the Christian religion—one a construct of reason, the other of faith.

Stoicism produced its greatest effect in the second century A.D., during the reigns of that unusual succession of "good" emperors: Nerva, Trajan, Hadrian, Antoninus Pius, and Marcus Aurelius.[35] For Edward Gibbon, whose account of the empire's decline begins with the death of Marcus in 180 A.D., the preceding period spanned by the rule of those five (96-180) marked not only the culmination of classical antiquity but the highest point in civilization up to his time. "If a man were called to fix the period in the history of the world during which the condition of the human race was most happy and prosperous, he would, without hesitation, name that which elapsed from the death of Domitian to the accession of Commodus."[36] Thus runs the much-quoted judgment, rendered in the Age of Enlightenment by one of its notable representatives. Peter Brown has remarked that "reading the literature of the classical upper classes, we can agree with Gibbon . . . for in this, he was accepting the judgment of a group of contemporaries on themselves."[37]

Those who were perched near the apex of the social pyramid had reason, it appears, to be satisfied with their lot. Yet uneasy doubts remain. Prosperous they certainly were. But were they happy in addition, as Gibbon opined? Consider the view from the highest point of the apex. It was expressed by the philosopher-emperor himself, by Marcus Aurelius in his own *Meditations.* This thoughtful and sensitive man, a Stoic of the best, reflects on the human condition as he knew it or had been told, and his general picture is not heartwarming. "Death hangs over thee" is his constant refrain. "One man after burying another has been laid out dead, and another buries him; and all this in a short time. To conclude, always observe how ephemeral and worthless human beings are, and what was yesterday a little mucus, tomorrow will be a mummy or ashes." Before that day comes, however, in what does life consist? "The idle business of show," is his answer, "plays on the stage, flocks of sheep, herds, exercises with spears, a bone to cast to little dogs, a bit of bread with fish-ponds, laborings of ants and burden-carrying, runnings about of frightened little mice, puppets pulled by strings."[38] To this one can only append the comment of Lewis Mumford: "If life was as repulsive as this at the top, what must it have been at the bottom?"[39] Despite the "goodness" of the Antonines, and in plain defiance of Stoic doctrine, slavery persisted under their regime. So did the gladiatorial contests that had disgusted Seneca a century earlier. Even Marcus Aurelius did not shrink from persecuting Christians when "reasons of state" persuaded him of its necessity. For how many in that civilization would Gibbon's verdict hold true?

The head that wears a hollow crown is supported on feet of clay. One is not surprised that the empire faced a crisis of disintegration less than two generations after the death of Marcus. Armies were routed, the frontiers were breached, 25 "emperors" appeared and disappeared within half a century. The breakdown, in this case, was severe, and it provided the occasion for the breakthrough. Hence Constantine's conversion to Christianity and his decision to adopt as the Roman creed the faith that his predecessors had treated so cruelly. The Christian conquest of the Romans is one of history's most dramatic stories, particularly when one contemplates the direct contradiction between the values of the *imperium* and those of Jesus. No less dramatic was the later dénouement, when the imperium reestablished itself through the power of the Papacy and the institution of the church, appropriately named in Latin *Ecclesia Romana*.[40] The Roman pontiffs have been more notable for turning the screw than the other cheek.

When ethical teaching combines with a religion that believes in divine justice and places its hope in another world, it has abandoned hope for this one. The Stoics could not save Rome from decline because their metaphysics were too intellectual. Moreover, their profound distrust of the emotions prevented their engaging the feelings of ordinary people on behalf of principles that contained some admirable features. Other-worldly religions, however, go to the opposite extreme. Such is their faith in the irrational that they can arouse the most powerful passions in the name of assertions that defy all reason. They can even persuade people to seek their death in the confident expectation of rewards in another life on some other plane of existence. It has been thus with Christianity; it has been equally so with the next major religious faith that emerged six centuries later.

Islam, like Christianity, marked a breakthrough, although it was not the consequence of a breakdown. This, too, is an other-worldly faith, whose single, central tenet is complete submission to the one god, Allah. Belief in Allah's omnipotence underpins the social structure and the ethical precepts that the prophet enjoins. What is the reason for this religion's unique feature—its extraordinarily rapid spread? A hint is supplied in the judgment of Machiavelli "that all armed prophets have conquered and unarmed ones failed."[41] The kernel of truth in that somber generalization is obviously exaggerated. But if one were to select the single instance that best illustrates the first part of the statement, the career of Mohammed comes at once to mind. Leaving aside its ethical and theological teaching, Islam from its inception was a martial and a political movement. Submission to Allah was promoted by the joint persuasions of the word and the sword. Mohammed himself initiated this technique by leading a military force from Medina to Mecca and subsequently compelling those who had previously rejected him to come to terms.

But though arms were instrumental in spreading the words of Allah, they were nothing more than an instrument, and it would be simplistic to ascribe the success of Islam to their potency alone. The character of Mohammed's message was of equal importance.

His was a creed well suited to the conditions of the desert, which, as a camel driver, he knew so well. The irrational element was confined to the two basic propositions that there is only the one God, Allah, and that Allah had revealed himself to Mohammed. Those being granted, the rest that followed was rationally arguable or could be defended as good social policy. Islam did not require of the credulity of its believers that they accept the myths surrounding the life and death of Jesus with which Christian theology has encumbered itself—the doctrine of the virgin birth, of God being the father of a son in human form, the story of the resurrection, the concept of the Trinity, and so on. Islamic doctrine was simple, clear, and direct. It did not impose too great a demand on either the intellect or the imagination of its adherents.

Islam represented itself as the climax in the evolution of religion through the two earlier stages of Judaism and Christianity. In truth, its ethical values were not nearly as radical as those of Jesus. But in its time and place, the message of Mohammed was revolutionary enough. He preached to the Arabs a kind of moral puritanism that deviated so sharply from prevailing practices that society would be genuinely transformed if a majority of Muslims were actually to base their lives on the Koran. What is more, as the military power of the Arabs expanded and Islam extended its sway beyond the Arabian peninsula, Mohammed's teaching proved itself to be adaptable to conditions and cultures as diverse as those of the Iberian peninsula, the Gangetic plain, and the Indonesian archipelago.

The fact that this happened contains some important implications. Earlier in this book, I drew the distinction between civilizations whose focus was on this world and those setting their sights on another. Here let me suggest a further dichotomy. There are those ethical systems and religions that are culture-bound and those that have the potential for universality.

By the former, I mean those that are specifically restricted to a particular people. These inherit its body of values or ideas and cannot transfer them to others. Examples are Confucianism, Hinduism, and Judaism. The first, being so intimately connected with the family relationships, is a product of Chinese history, and is not for export. Hinduism, too, remains rooted in Indian soil because of its serving as a rationale for perpetuating the castes. Judaism, likewise, was never a proselytizing faith because of its doctrine that the Jews were the "chosen people" with whom Yahweh had made his covenant. In consequence, Confucian ethics are for the Chinese; Hindu ethics, for Hindus; Judaic ethics, for Jews.

There are other ethical and religious systems, however, to which these restrictions do not apply. Consider the cases of Buddhism, Islam, and Christianity; also of Stoicism and, as we shall see later, of the Enlightenment. The doctrines of each of these have been addressed to human beings in virtue of our common humanity. Potentially, their scope is universal. Each has succeeded in stressing some aspects, some needs, of our nature that pertain to human beings everywhere. That explains why these movements could do what the culture-bound systems could not. They leaped across the boundaries of culture, race, and language. Buddhism could penetrate China, where Hinduism could not reach. Islam, unlike Confucianism, could extend across central Asia. Christianity could embrace the peoples excluded from Judaism. The universal systems invited conversion. Hence, they were able to spread.

Mohammed marks an end, as well as a beginning. Both he and Jesus lived many centuries after the Axial Age, and Mohammed is the last individual in the history of civilization to have succeeded in founding a major religion. That, in itself, tells us something significant. The Age of the Prophets—if one may so designate the whole period from the seventh century B.C. to the sixth A.D.— ended 13 centuries ago. Religious development since then has consisted in organization, in splits and secessions, in doctrinal elaboration, but not in basic innovation. Consequently, ethical values that have been founded on religious belief have not advanced significantly during this period. They have been interpreted, restated, clarified, codified, but not radically altered. In the history of Christianity, for example, the most revolutionary figure of the last millennium was not Luther but Francis of Assisi. What the latter did was to challenge the church—an institution enmeshed in this world, if ever there was one—to return to the values enunciated by Jesus. This, the power structure of the Papacy was wholly unwilling to undertake. Luther's Reformation consisted primarily in setting up an alternative power structure, breaking Rome's monopoly. His innovations lay in his nationalism (the German versus the Italian) and his use of the vernacular instead of Latin. In ethical values, however, he was no innovator—far from it. He voiced anti-Semitism and he supported those German rulers who crushed the Peasants' Revolt.

What this means is that the principal ethical developments of the last thousand years in the major civilizations have not flowed from a religious source, nor is their point of origin to be found in suprarational faith—quite the contrary. They have been constructs of reason and are ascribable to this-worldly humanism. In most civilizations—especially those of Asia—both the institutions and the intellectual traditions became so rigid that no significant breakthrough was generated from within. India, China, and the areas of Islam and Buddhism were not stimulated to think and behave untraditionally until they felt the impact of revolutionary change in another civilization, that of the West, from the seventeenth century onward. This revolution will form the subject of discussion in the following chapter.

Nature has set no bounds to
the perfectioning of human
faculties. . . . The
perfectibility of Man is
really limitless.

Condorcet

7

The Enlightenment and the Age of Progress

Like the Axial Age 2,000 years earlier, the second great leap in ethical consciousness contained features that mark it as unique. Although starting in one civilization, the Western, its effects were felt in all. For this, there were two compelling reasons. First, the character of the new technology, made possible by advances in scientific knowledge, enabled the West after the seventeenth century either to dominate the other civilizations or to exercise a profound influence on their development. In addition, that influence was facilitated by the kind of values that the West espoused. For these were not restricted to westerners, but held true universally for all human beings. Hence, in principle, there were no limits to their extension.

The ferment in the Western civilization has been a long process, lasting from the fifteenth century to the present. Significantly, it did not begin with ethics but arrived there eventually in the eighteenth and nineteenth centuries. There were successive stages in this process, each with its own focus. Five can be distinguished. In rough chronological order (allowing for some overlaps), these were the Renaissance, the Reformation, the discoveries in science and mathematics, the Enlightenment, and finally the social reforms launched in the nineteenth century, which called itself the Age of Progress. Ethics therefore was not the early catalyst but a later resultant.

The sequence is indeed interesting. At every stage an advance was made that contributed to what followed, although at the beginning no one could have intended or foreseen the outcome. The Renaissance, by reviving classical studies, stimulated the artists and the intellectuals with the inspiration of the Greeks. The Reformation stimulated freedom of thought by presenting alternatives; for, after the Protestant churches had established themselves, any pope who tried to repeat what Urban VIII did to Galileo was unlikely to be successful. Together, these two movements ended the domination over the intellectual realm of theological dogma as certified by one single organization. Scientists were then free to observe the physical world and report their observations, to speculate and hypothesize without having to conform to Holy Writ or to Ptolemy or Aquinas or the Inquisition. Thus when Descartes gave logic and metaphysics its new start, and augmented this with his mathematical innovations, he provided the concepts and categories, plus a method of applying them, for a different image of the universe and of humanity's place therein.

The seventeenth century was the turning point (the start of this second Axial Age, if you will) in the modern evolution of the Western civilization. There is a striking contrast between its first half and the second. The first half experienced the prolonged misery and devastation of the Thirty Years War directly caused by the mutual intolerance of Catholics and Protestants. Barbarism was rampant in Europe during this period, no less than in "the calamitous fourteenth century," which Barbara Tuchman has so vividly described. The torture chamber, the gibbet, and the stake represented the agonized convulsions in this world of a continent bedeviled by the antagonisms between other-worldly churches. Thousands of women were killed as "witches" by bigoted men who convinced themselves that they were doing God's work, while the armies of the Reformation and the Counter-Reformation marched and countermarched across the center of Europe like devouring locusts.

As a contemporary to these horrors, Pascal had abundant evidence for writing that "men never do evil so completely and cheerfully as when they do it from religious conviction."[1] It all ended in a stalemate, simply because neither side was able to exterminate the other. Thus, not because they wanted it, but because there was nothing else they could do, the survivors learned to live and let live. What slowly emerged was a new atmosphere, that of toleration, which helped the spirit of scientific inquiry.

Some scientists had managed to do their research even in the days when religious bigotry was at its worst. Copernicus worked in the sixteenth century; and Descartes, Harvey, and Galileo belong in the first half of the seventeenth. But Galileo's case shows what risks they ran. After 1648, when the Peace of Westphalia confirmed the division of Europe into nation-states (some Protestant, others Catholic), the scientist who might need protection had broader options and opportunities. In the second half of the century, Newton and Leibniz did their work. After them, there was no turning back. Significantly, Newton's contemporary and compatriot was John Locke, whose philosophy—a product of reason penned in a spirit of reasonableness—embraced the concept of tolerance in matters of religious faith.[2] Europe was beginning to relearn the truth that it had forgotten throughout the Christian era, that it is possible for individuals to hold different religious beliefs and be equally good citizens. The advent of a more tolerant attitude had its moral and social consequences. If you discover on closer acquaintance that the Devil is a gentleman, will you not treat him with appropriate consideration?

The benefits of this reasonable outlook matured in the eighteenth century. By this time, a civilization that had grown infinitely weary of religious polemics and was bent on exploring the unmapped vistas of the scientists' universe was ready for a philosophical departure. This included a major ethical component, because the time had now come to redefine the image of humanity. Here is a valid example of a breakthrough consequent upon a breakdown. One century after the Thirty Years War, revivified Europe blossomed in the Enlightenment. What kind of a movement was this? What difference did it make?

The Enlightenment
and the Age of Reason

Unlike the Renaissance, which generated no major advance in philosophy, philosophical speculation was central to the process that the Enlightenment set in motion. As this was a period of creative ferment, numerous ideas were explored in different directions and the systems of thought thus generated were as divergent as those of Descartes, Locke, Leibniz, Hume, and Kant. But certain assumptions—metaphysical, scientific, and moral—were held more or less in common and characterized the movement as a whole. If unanimity was absent from their conclusions, at least the thinkers stood on common ground.

The basic idea of the Enlightenment was that the individual could acquire knowledge of the truth by the exercise of reason.[3] Look inside yourself, and you will discover how human beings think, how we are impelled to act, how we formulate concepts, how we perceive and interpret the data of experience. Next, look outside yourself at the natural world, and you may learn through direct observation and experiment how the Earth and its creatures, how the universe, are constituted and function. Certain truths then become self-evident. In the physical universe, regularities occur that derive from the properties of its constituent elements and the relations between them. These are explicable through the logic of mathematics, and, because that allows for predictability, some measure of certainty is possible in human affairs.

These regularities, made manifest in nature, consist in sequences of cause and effect and may be expressed as laws. Among them are laws of nature that govern humanity—for are we not ourselves a part of the natural world? Hence, to live aright, both as individuals and as social creatures, we must learn not only what natural law is binding on us but also what rights this law confers on us. Inherent in this logic is the premise that these rights belong equally to us all in virtue of our common humanity. One is justified in assuming that, if the laws applying to the physical world are universal in their scope, their counterpart—the natural laws that apply to humanity—must also be universally valid.[4]

In contrast to the theological assumptions that had prevailed during the ten preceding centuries, the doctrines of the Enlightenment represented a veritable Copernican revolution. Once you insisted that the source of knowledge was the individual's unfettered exercise of reason, your image of the universe again became, what it had been for the Greeks and Romans, anthropocentric. Divine dispensation was ruled out of court, simply because no one could prove it. Humanity was seen to be in charge of its own fate. The concerns of this world had regained the priority.

Although the philosophy of the Enlightenment exploded with the force of novelty, certain of its concepts can be paralleled in the earlier history of Western civilization. In fact, it contains some similarities to Stoicism, a philosophy that also emerged to calm a troubled region after a breakdown. A like parallel may be drawn between the two philosophies in their practical effects. Stoicism, translated to Rome, appealed to many of the nobility and was espoused in the second century A.D. by the "good emperors" culminating in Marcus Aurelius. Similarly, in the eighteenth century there were autocratic rulers who paid their dues to the Enlightenment. Frederick the Great invited Voltaire to Potsdam; Catherine the Great corresponded with Diderot. The "enlightened despot" exemplifies a maxim of Machiavelli's statecraft: An outwardly civilized demeanor may be wise policy.

But there is one other aspect of the Enlightenment that distinguishes it from the Stoa. Its outlook, to express it in contemporary idiom, was decidedly upbeat. After two murderous centuries of fanaticism, intolerance, and pessimism, there was a disposition to be optimistic. This mood expressed itself in two ways, both significant. One was the belief that human nature is fundamentally good. If that is so, why does evil exist? The answer was that a small number of persons, bent on their own self-aggrandizement, gain positions of power in our social institutions and use it to thwart and pervert the natural goodness within each of us. The remedy for this is to rebel against the powerful and sweep away their corrupt institutions so that the good in human nature can freely express itself. Thus argued Voltaire in his terse denunciation of the church: *écrasez l'infâme* (stamp out the infamous thing). Thus fantasized Rousseau, who portrayed his radical ideals on education in *Émile,* on love between a man and woman in *La Nouvelle Éloise,* and on the state in the *Contrat Social.*

Optimists and Reformers

The optimism of the thinkers of the Enlightenment was nowhere more evident than in their confidence in progress. They interpreted the history of humanity in terms of a rising trend to higher levels of civilization. This would be brought about increasingly by the spread of knowledge as reason discovered it in all the sciences. Robert Shackleton has written that "implicit in the conception of the *Encyclopédie* is the theory of intellectual progress, the belief that knowledge itself is a liberating force."[5] For the intellectuals of the eighteenth century, that belief was not a utopian myth. Freedom of thought had been severely limited in the West throughout the Christian era when secular authoritarianism, combining with theological dogma, imposed restraints on intellectual development and, *pari passu,* on moral growth. If knowledge, as such, could not grow freely, how could the knowledge of good and evil? But after papal power had been successfully challenged, and political absolutism was curbed in Britain, the Netherlands, and Switzerland, the same occurred in Paris and posed a threat to Vienna, Berlin, St. Petersburg, and Madrid.

Moreover, the possibility of a civilization being infused with the union of knowledge and morality gained further credence in the eighteenth century from an unexpected source. China was now becoming better known to the West. Thanks to the Jesuit missions and the contacts established by merchants and traders, the trickle of information about all things Chinese was increasing to a flood.

Leibniz[6] had expressed an interest in learning as much as possible about the Sinic culture, and by Voltaire's time the *salons* of Paris were accepting (often uncritically) the conclusion that China was the living demonstration of a people ruled by gentlemen-scholars animated by high ethics.[7] What was believed to be a fait accompli in Asia must also be possible in Europe. Nay, more than that, the progress which now lay within human grasp could, and would, be extended to all humanity.

Of those Enlightenment figures who arouse our admiration, there is one whose life and thought and death personify the climax of what was best in its ideals. This is Condorcet. In his final work, he sums up his optimistic hopes for humanity in these uncompromising words: "Nature has set no bounds to the perfectioning of human faculties. . . . The perfectibility of Man is really limitless."[8] That was written by a man in hiding from the Terror, daily expecting his capture and execution. Of him, Muller has said: "Among the truly glorious scenes in man's history—the scenes that make one feel honored to belong to the human race, and not simply unhappy at the thought of dying for it—is that of Condorcet in his wretched garret: a fugitive from the French Revolution he had helped to bring about, living in the shadow of the guillotine, and on borrowed time working on his outline of human progress, to hearten mankind by his vision of its indefinite perfectibility."[9]

The values formulated by the thinkers of the Enlightenment expressed their aspirations. But they were far from being the complete reality of an age about which Voltaire had said: "We live in curious times and amid astonishing contrasts: reason on the one hand, the most absurd fanaticism on the other."[10] The Enlightenment was much more, however, than a philosophical movement and its influence cascaded beyond the salons of Paris. In the political arena, the American and French revolutions, although not caused by the Enlightenment, employed its concepts when seeking to justify what they had done and to build a new system for the future. Both Paine and Jefferson repeated the ideas—and even the phrases—of Locke, while the authors of the Constitution of the United States drew heavily on Montesquieu when they established the three branches of the federal government. In France, Rousseau's ambiguous[11] concept of the *volonté générale* (the general will) was much invoked by revolutionary orators who represented themselves as its spokesmen. The philosophies that Aristophanes depicted as floating in the clouds have a habit of descending to earth.

More than that, a wave of enlightened thinking began flooding not only the body politic but also the body social. The emphasis on the oneness of humankind, and on universal rights that transcend governments, opened up the possibility that people of conscience and compassion would turn from the contemplation of humanity to the practice of humanitarianism. Thus were inaugurated in the nineteenth century some new and impressive achievements in the field of ethical progress—that is to say, a qualitative improvement in human relations. To illustrate the link between the Age of Reason and the Age of Progress, one instance will suffice.

The oppressive injustice of the old order was nowhere more patently evident than in its penal code. By defining which acts were crimes and designating the punishments for each, those in positions of privilege were setting the tone of public morality. That tone was harsh indeed. So lengthy was the list of crimes; so severe were the penalties. Against this monstrous inhumanity, an Italian wrote a book that became famous for its content and its impact. This was Cesare Beccaria's *Dei Delitti e delle Pene (On Crimes and Punishments)* published in 1764 when the author, a nobleman of Milan, was 26 years old. Brinton calls this "one of the clearest examples that books do work in this world."[12]

What Beccaria did was to inject a new humanitarianism into the philosophy of criminology. In his preface he incorporated the famous principle of "the greatest happiness of the greatest number," which the British philosopher Francis Hutcheson had propounded in his *Inquiry Concerning Moral Good and Evil*. Beccaria argued that public policy should be more concerned to prevent crime than to punish it. Penalties, he thought, should be proportionate to the offense, and it was more important that they be certain than severe. He was critical of the death penalty, of the use of torture, and of secret judicial proceedings. All of this was a rational and humane approach to a social evil. Beccaria was a child of the Enlightenment in the sense that he had been stirred intellectually by reading Montesquieu. Through Jeremy Bentham and Samuel

Romilly, his ideas were translated into British jurisprudence. Eventually, they contributed to reforms of that country's brutal penal system. This is as clear an example as may be found of the unfettered use of reason to enhance the understanding of good and evil and thereby to bring about an improvement in ethical values. It was but one of the several revolutions that the Enlightenment helped to inspire and that altered the ethical practice of the following century.

To move from the Age of Reason to the Age of Progress is to shift from principle to practice. When the emphasis switches, however, from the concepts to their application, the refractory nature of the empirical evidence is a challenge to its would-be interpreter. Contradictions abound, and institutions now play a dominant role. A preliminary comment on these two factors is needed therefore before the Age of Progress, as some of its contemporaries chose to call it, can be properly understood.

The most accurate short summary of the history of civilization would describe it as an unending succession of paradoxes. In point of fact, that same coexistence of contrasts to which Voltaire referred in his day can be paralleled from any century for which sufficient records survive. Every age incorporates, in one form or another, the good and its alternatives. Every epoch manifests its prevailing climate (sometimes called "the spirit of the age") and, alongside it, various countercultures wedded to other values. These latter include the survivals from earlier times together with the forerunners of tomorrow's fashion—for at any given moment some elements of both past and future will always be found coexisting with the traits that dominate the present. Summary characterizations of an epoch should always be read with this caution in mind: The truths they tell are never the whole truth.

That reminder is particularly relevant when attempting to estimate the improvements in our practices, for the course of their development has been markedly erratic. Even if overall the movement has been in the direction of raising both our ethical standards and our actual behavior, the gains are marked by so much asymmetry, by so many reversals, that clear-cut generalizations are precluded. The story of civilization remains a welter of contradictions, among which it is sometimes impossible to state definitively just where the weight of the evidence lies. Moreover, ethics, in the simple, basic sense of doing good to others, can manifest itself on occasion in ways that do not fit the conventional stereotypes. In this connection, a remark of Muller's is worth quoting. "A philosophy of history," he wrote, "might well begin and end with a report I have heard on the French underground that took care of Allied airmen and escaped prisoners in the last war [i.e., World War II]. The report was that the most effective workers in this underground were priests and prostitutes."[13] Does this not indicate that, when civilization breaks down (as happens when war is being waged), a group that is not publicly accepted as part of the social order may for a while be perceived in some other guise?

How Institutions Alter Values

In addition to being strewn with paradox and contradiction, the path of history exhibits another constant characteristic that bears directly on the possibility of ethical progress. Although I am chary of propounding historical laws, there is one tendency in human affairs that recurs so frequently that it could qualify under this heading. What I have in mind is a process that unfolds in the following sequence. Somebody enunciates a concept or an ideal that, when first presented, exists only in the realm of the intellect. If others are similarly persuaded, both their thinking and their behavior are shaped accordingly, and, as they become more numerous, their collective influence spreads. After a lapse of time, their movement builds an institution. This means that, to spread the doctrine and accomplish its objectives, an organization is established, complete with its functions and functionaries, its structure and system, its revenues and regulations. Once that happens, the institutional apparatus generates its own logic, which then reacts upon the concept or value whose inspiration was its original raison d'être. Invariably the demands of the institution set limits to the doctrine it purports to serve. In the interest of being "pragmatic" or "realistic," appropriate compromises are made. The ideal descends from heaven to earth. Or, as Henry of Navarre observed so cynically when he converted to Catholicism: "Paris is worth a Mass." The needs of the institution—particularly the retention of its power and its will to survive—take priority over its ideal objectives. If successful, the structure may continue for centuries. The institution flourishes, but its spirit withers.

This general tendency whereby values atrophy in the course of being institutionalized permeates the history of all civilizations. It epitomizes the two horns of the dilemma on which humanity is forever impaled. Without some institutional form, an ideal cannot

have effect in practice; yet, with it, atrophy sets in. Earlier, I alluded
to some instances of this tendency in mentioning the deviations of
the church from Jesus and of Buddhist monks from Gautama. An
example in the same genre is the fate that befell Francesco of Assisi—
truly a saintly man, if ever there was one. He had seen enough of
worldly wealth and power to know the corruption that possessions
and status bring to those who have them. Once, when a novice asked
for a psalter, he replied: "When you have a psalter you will wish to
have a breviary, and when you have a breviary you will sit in a chair
like a great prelate and say to your brother, 'Brother, bring me my
breviary.' "[14] Despite the insight that remark reveals, Francis himself
took the fateful step of journeying to Rome and seeking papal authority to establish an Order. Truly a dramatic confrontation! Picture the
young, frail monk, clad in the simplest garb, pleading with burning
eyes and passionate conviction for official sanction to institutionalize
his ideals. And there sat Pope Gregory IX, the former Cardinal
Ugolino, enthroned in a church at the pinnacle of its power and
pomp, rich in land and buildings and tithes, potent enough to bring
kings and emperors to their knees, and hearing the message that
Christians must embrace poverty and humility as did Jesus.[15]
Gregory, in effect, had no choice but to grant Francis his Order. Yet
a man of his statecraft must have known that the request was
self-defeating, because the Order, once established, would not forever
remain poor and humble and so could not, by the effect of its example,
challenge the Mother Church to abjure its worldly goods. In fact, it
did not take long before Brother Elias's enterprising efforts at fund-
raising had struck a mortal blow at Franciscan ideals.

But it is not only in organized religion that one discovers the
cases to support the generalization. The theater might be considered a sphere of creative endeavor somewhat removed from the
spiritual and the other-worldly. There, too, however, as in the other
arts, instances abound of the creative person struggling for emancipation from the fossilizing effects of the institution that their art
has generated. Listen to these words of the great actress, Eleanora
Duse, as passionate in her role as was Francis in his: "To save the
theater, the theater must be destroyed, the actors and actresses
must all die of the plague. They poison the air, they make art
impossible. It is not a drama they play, but pieces for the theater.
We should return to the Greeks; play in the open air. The drama
dies of stalls and boxes and evening dress, and people who come
to digest their dinner."[16] If you doubt this, take a glance at Broad-
way or Hollywood, at Covent Garden or La Scala.

These general features of the historical process are observable in the special sphere of ethical progress. Here, indeed, the contradictions are mind-boggling. How does one sum up an age in which Genghis Khan (1167-1227) was the contemporary of Francis of Assisi (1182-1226)? Whose work should we say had the more widespread or longer-lasting effects? Or consider the lives of two contemporaries born within the same culture—Albert Einstein (1879-1955) and Adolf Hitler (1889-1945). Whom would we regard as more representative of German values in the first half of the current century? As we attempt to trace the pattern of ethical development, we should bear in mind the cautionary thought that every generalization has its exceptions. Likewise, when contemplating how institutions corrode the values from which they sprang, one is simply recognizing the gap between our visions and our deeds. Theory, being abstract, can embody perfection; practice must abide the imperfect.

The Ethical Revolution of the Nineteenth Century

The conversion of good principle into effective practice was the task that enlightened individuals set before themselves in the nineteenth century. The French *philosophes* and their kindred spirits in Scotland and elsewhere had provided the intellectual rationale for the moral reforms that blossomed forth when the Napoleonic Wars ended. Not that the intellectuals of the 1780s confined their endeavors to the metaphysical plane or failed to instigate remedial action in the workaday world around them. Suffice it to remember that Voltaire—the Enlightenment's presiding genius, if there was one—actively immersed himself in vindicating some of the victims of the law's injustice; while Rousseau, that self-tortured neurotic, struck out in Quixotic outrage against the windmills of his restless mind, whether real or imagined. I noted earlier that Beccaria was influenced by his reading of Montesquieu and that he took from Hutcheson the formula of "the greatest happiness of the greatest number" that Bentham was soon to make famous. These were some of the precursors of the lengthening list of reformers who in the nineteenth century applied their energies and talents—and in some cases also their private fortunes—to infuse a higher ethic into society's institutions and to mitigate the hardships of the masses of humanity. The names, and the fields in which they made their impact, are indeed impressive. John Howard, the contemporary of Beccaria and Bentham, initiated reform of the prisons, and his pioneering was continued by Elizabeth Fry. Shaftesbury, an aristocrat, was responsible for the legislation that began the long process of correcting the inhumane treatment of those working in the mines and factories, especially the women and children. Robert Owen humanized the mills that he owned and managed, and launched experiments in utopian communities. Edwin Chadwick inaugurated measures to improve the public health in the industrialized cities, while Florence Nightingale dedicated herself to heal the soldiers wounded in war and to make nursing an honorable profession. William Wilberforce led the movement that resulted in the abolition of slavery in the British Empire. Meanwhile, in literature the novelists—notably Charles Dickens— created a wider audience for the public discussion of social issues, at the same time as a group of gifted women—the Brontë sisters, Mary Anne Evans (George Eliot), and Harriet Martineau—demonstrated their talents in the teeth of a sexist society.

These whom I have cited were all British. As that was the country where the Industrial Revolution started, it was there that the appalling social effects of its early, unregulated phase were first apparent and were first brought under some control. In Britain, moreover, the authority of Parliament and the practice of periodic elections to the House of Commons made it possible for public opinion to influence the governing class. Somewhat similar conditions pertained in the United States from the 1830s onward. There too, especially in New England, educated men and women with a social conscience turned their minds and energies to the reform of their institutions. Thus William Lloyd Garrison campaigned against slavery; Channing, the Unitarian minister, and Emerson and Thoreau, both transcendentalists, conceived and taught a higher ethic; Bronson Alcott, Elizabeth Peabody, and Horace Mann initiated radical educational experiments; Emily Dickinson and Margaret Fuller excelled in poetry and prose; and Elizabeth Cady Stanton led the crusade for women's suffrage.

It would be hard to find at any other time or place so many contemporaries who were both individually gifted and socially constructive. On each side of the North Atlantic, the period that opened in the 1770s was a second Axial Age, comparable in the sphere of ethical action to the teachings of its earlier counterpart in the seventh and sixth centuries B.C. One resemblance lies in the fact that both movements were spearheaded by private persons acting on their own without positions of leadership in the established order.[17] It was neither kings nor emperors, neither popes nor archbishops, who injected the new moral stimulus. The leadership came from well-educated, conscience-stricken, men and women reacting to the harsh injustices of the prevailing system. The Age of Progress had its origins almost entirely outside of society's established institutions because the governments of state and church belonged to the core of the power structure in need of reform. Later these bowed to the inevitable; but at the outset their leaders resisted change. Moral initiatives normally flow from the altered consciousness of private individuals, rarely from officeholders whose respect for higher principles is so often compromised, or corrupted, by their own privileges and by the demands of the institution they serve.

Essentially what distinguished the ethical progress in Western civilization during the nineteenth century was its range, its depth, and its durability. In earlier times the ethical gains had been limited in scope or in duration. However wealthy the individuals who endowed orphanages or hospitals, or founded schools or libraries, their resources were never adequate to supply all those in need. When Buddhist monasteries and Christian churches distributed alms and aided the weak, they too were perforce selective in the help they administered. Even when a compassionate king or chief minister—an Ashoka or Wang An-shih—dedicated his regime to moral ends, the effects were only temporary. The principles they espoused, the programs they launched, were invariably attenuated under their successors, who had other priorities. To raise the ethical standard of a whole society requires considerable resources of money and personnel, together with a zeal and staying power that must endure beyond a single generation. These in turn depend on the doctrinal stimulus that generates the inspiration and on a psychological jolt, like an electric shock, to alter people's values. Both jolt and stimulus were felt at the end of the eighteenth century and the start of the nineteenth. The Enlightenment had expanded the intellectual horizons of thinking individuals. The French Revolution, followed by Napoleon's wars, had demonstrated the hollowness of the Old Regime in society and politics. Industrialism was starting to revolutionize the manufacturing process. With the advent of the modern world, ancient inequalities seemed out of place.

For civilization the possibilities envisioned in the Age of Progress were indeed revolutionary. In their different styles, Immanuel Kant and Jeremy Bentham enunciated principles that, if practiced, would drastically reshape the social relations between human beings. "So act as to treat humanity," said Kant, "whether in thine own person or in that of any other, in every case as an end withal, never as means only."[18] In other words, do not use or exploit another person to serve your ends. In the same spirit, Bentham affirmed the equal worth of all human beings with the formula that each should count for one, and nobody for more than one. Such assertions chimed with the universality of the "Rights of Man" as the Enlightenment had conceived them.

The Stimuli of
Democracy and Industrialism

To translate principle into practice began to come within the range of the possible during the first half of the nineteenth century. As the democratic ideal gained more acceptance, its concepts were applied to ever larger areas and populations through the representative process. Because freedom would be limited in scope if it was not linked to equality, the extension of the suffrage, accomplished by gradual stages in both Britain and the United States, led to the eventual transfer of ultimate power from the privileged few, who had always held it, to the many underprivileged, who had never previously shared it. To bring universal adult suffrage to completion in Britain required a century (1832-1928). When that was finally accomplished, a genuine revolution had occurred in the all-important process of choosing and ultimately controlling those who would wield the power to govern. Under a system where all adults were entitled to vote, and two or more parties sought their votes with competing candidates and programs, the government would be responsive to the wishes of the majority. Thus for the first time in human history the masses of humanity held in their own hands a constitutional means of making government serve their needs. That made it possible for them to use the state as the agency for encompassing the ethical improvement of society at large.

Simultaneously with these political developments, equally revolutionary changes were transforming the economic system.[19] By applying energy to machines, then by assembling the power-driven machines under the roof of a factory and by accumulating the capital to pay for them, "the captains of industry," as Carlyle called them, could produce all manner of goods in larger quantities at lower cost. Thereby, many of the articles of consumption that had hitherto been the luxuries of the few were increasingly available to broader groups of consumers.

A novel kind of political economy evolved as a consequence. In the sphere of government, opposing parties outbid each other in the offers they dangled before an enlarged electorate. On parallel lines in the industrial economy, producers competed for customers in a market whose purchasing power was expanding beyond any that had ever existed. The stage was then set for fundamental changes in the social order. A new materialism coexisted in tension with a new idealism. The resulting conflict of values has been a central theme in the history of Western civilization since 1850. What should be the aim of society as a whole and of its members individually? As both a superior standard of living and a higher quality of life were within reach, was it possible to combine them in some semblance of harmony? If not, which should take precedence? In either case, would the benefits be spread equally throughout society? The record of the Age of Progress demonstrates that in such matters the questions can be formulated more clearly than the answers. The gains for humanity were positive and unmistakable. But ancient evils did not disappear; in fact, they persisted, sometimes assuming new forms.

The advent of the industrial society as a direct consequence of the new technology changed the economic base of civilization and set in motion tendencies that contained the potential for either cooperation or conflict. The inner dynamics of industrialization fostered a greater concentration of power, both human and financial. All the structures that had to be created—the factories, mines, railroads, ports, canals, and highways—were more extensive than heretofore and much more expensive. Such development only became possible through the accumulation of capital. Hence the big private fortunes of the newly rich, plus the joint stock corporations with a host of shareholders large and small, characterized the growth of capitalism in this particular stage.

Along with it, a parallel concentration proceeded apace—this one, of human beings. When the new manufacturing methods replaced the domestic handicraft with the factory product, an immediate result was that those who worked the power-driven machines had to assemble where the machines were located. Thus the sons and daughters of village folk were sucked into the congested alleys of what quickly became city slums. For the first time in history, more than half of the population of the most industrialized countries dwelled in urban areas rather than rural. This very process of congregation and congestion, however, not only created conditions that required a remedy, but by its very nature provided the opportunity for the underprivileged to organize in concerted action.

Thus it was as actors—in the literal sense—that the mass of the population now occupied the stage. From their activities a novel drama proceeded to unfold. In all its earlier phases, civilization had relied perforce on the labor of the masses of ordinary men and women. Society was in fact so structured that they would produce whatever their superiors required within the limits of the available technology. But their roles had invariably been passive. They were cast as subordinates—as slaves, serfs, subjects, or servants. To their overlords, these were the common sort, the working class, the mob, the rabble, the meaner kind, *la canaille, das Lumpenprole-tariat*—all derogatory terms. Whenever they rebelled—one thinks of Rome's *bellum servile,* China's Yellow Turbans, the Peasants' Revolt, the Florentine *Ciompi*—such uprisings were always suppressed in blood. To the ancient evils of civilization—its inequalities, class divisions, and mass poverty—the enlightened humanitarians of the Age of Progress addressed their energies.

The results were two-pronged. There was an outcropping of voluntary organizations—created, staffed, and financed by private individuals—and with these a mounting stack of laws enacted for the benefit of the poor and the weak and designed to improve their conditions. Some examples will illustrate the trend.

Private Initiatives
and Public Enterprise

No branch of human society was left untouched by the ethical zeal of the nineteenth-century reformers. Slavery was abolished in the British Empire by the new Parliament in 1833. This occurred just one year after the adoption of the first of the reforms that in half a century (1832-85) would extend to all adult males the right to vote in elections for the House of Commons and apportion its voting districts more nearly in accord with the distribution of population. The legal position of married women, whose subordination to their husbands was branded "subjection"[20] by John Stuart Mill, benefited from legislation in 1870 and 1882. As a result, in Hobhouse's opinion, English law, which had been "the most backward in Europe" on this point, became in 12 years the most forward.[21] To help the young—especially to offer them some protection from a drunken or brutal father—a Society for the Prevention of Cruelty to Children was founded in 1884. That was six decades after a similar body was organized to prevent cruelty to animals, which tells us something about priorities in Victoria's Britain. Private philanthropy also endowed many orphanages during that century, and the conditions did improve somewhat—partly as a result of the effect of books like *Oliver Twist.*

In the workplace, both women and children were helped by statutes limiting their hours of labor and setting a minimum for their wages. This mode of regulating the capitalist economy was then applied to men. "The dark Satanic mills," as William Blake had glimpsed them, were starting to be less hellish. The formation of unions was illegal in Britain when the century began, but was permitted after 1824. This development was fraught with momentous consequences for both political and economic history.

The more humane outlook also exerted its influence on the penal code, which had been notoriously harsh. Hobhouse alludes to "the ferocious penalties of the old law,"[22] as well he might. In George III's reign, around 200 offenses were punishable by death. These included such unspeakable crimes as slitting someone's nose or stealing from a boat on a navigable river (though not on a canal).[23] Between 1832 and 1861, the list was reduced to only four—namely, murder, treason, piracy with violence, and arson against arsenals and docks.[24] So pervasive indeed was the official brutality of Britain's Old Regime that Kenneth Clark has this to say: "We forget the horrors that were taken for granted in early Victorian England: the hundreds of lashes inflicted daily on perfectly harmless men in the army and navy; the women chained together in threes, rumbling through the streets in open carts on their way to transportation [i.e., to the colonies]."[25] In the second half of the century, convicts, whether women or men, were no longer deported and military discipline was becoming a shade less cruel.

Even the government of the empire began to feel the new influences. In 1813 Parliament considered, but defeated, a resolution declaring that Britain's first duty to India was to promote the interests of the Indians. Only 20 years later, however, the reformed Parliament embodied this principle in the Government of India Act. In the years 1841-42 Queen Victoria's gallant men fought to compel the Chinese to keep their ports open to the opium that Britain was shipping from India—one of the most disgraceful episodes in the empire's history. Two generations later, however, the House of Commons pronounced the opium trade to be "morally indefensible," and it was ended in 1917.[26] The arch-imperialist, Disraeli himself, referred to "that justice without which the possession of power would have no charms."[27]

Meanwhile, on the domestic front the effects of industrialism on population and on the patterns of its distribution created new social conditions that public policies were required to rectify. Britain's population not only quadrupled during the nineteenth century, but the proportion of urban to rural was radically altered. When the century began, one-third were living in cities; at midcentury, one-half; by the century's end, more than three-quarters. The size of London increased fivefold. Manchester, which had numbered only 75,000 inhabitants in 1800, by 1910 housed 720,000.[28] Many of these in the early decades of an unregulated, laissez-faire capitalism lived in grim and grimy conditions where malnutrition and disease brought early death. Periodically, too, the mortality statistics were augmented by epidemics, such as cholera in the early 1830, which endangered the rich as well as the poor. Remedial measures, the products of altruism and of self-interest, were therefore introduced. The necessity of public health programs was recognized after Chadwick published his report, *The Sanitary Condition of the Laboring Population of Great Britain* (1842). A Public Health Act was adopted within six years, and others followed. Such intelligent action by the state brought positive results. The average life expectancy in the cities at midcentury was only 40 years. After two generations it had lengthened to 56.[29]

Action by the state was also the necessary means for battling the age-old vice of ignorance. Scotland, although a poorer country, had provided public education for all its children long before England deemed this desirable. But in 1870,[30] three years after the second extension of the suffrage, the saying "we must educate our masters" became the accepted wisdom of the English upper class. Primary education for all children, paid for by taxes, was adopted as national policy, and inevitably the same principle was later broadened to the secondary level. Ignorance and illiteracy were no longer to be the stigma of "the lower orders."

All of those innovations had this in common. They were based on the concept that one of the Levellers, a Colonel Rainboro, had affirmed in the seventeenth century with these words: "Really I think the poorest he that is in England hath a life to live as the richest he." To feel concern for the well-being and dignity of everyone in the community was to write a new chapter in the history of civilization. No less remarkable were the means employed to achieve the ends. The rebirth of democratic values after a long dormancy was accompanied by two momentous changes that appear contradictory on their face but were in fact complementary. The individual, of whom so much had been heard since the Renaissance, now came into his own—and subsequently into her own. The barriers that had traditionally prevented the majority of individuals from developing their potentialities—barriers of class, wealth, race, religion, and sex—were being lowered. A society that valued freedom was beginning to comprehend that this could only be achieved when specific freedoms were equalized. Equality, however, could not be left to chance or to Adam Smith's "hidden hand" or to market forces. It called for purposeful policy, ethically animated and intelligently planned. The public sphere—or, rather, that of the re-public or common-wealth—had to supplement and complement the private. Collective effort was therefore required through the one social institution that in principle derived from all and existed for all: namely, the state. The modern state was called into being to redress the inequities of the Old Regime. A revolution in the opportunities for the individual combined with a revolution in the ethos and techniques of governance. For this reason the Age of Progress was the culmination of a second Axial Age.

Nor were those engaged in the work unaware of its significance. William E. Gladstone, the prime minister and Liberal party leader, who was responsible for much innovative legislation, wrote that the five decades from 1840 to 1890 would be known as "the half-century of emancipation."[31] A. R. Wallace, a biologist, published in 1898 a book titled *The Wonderful Century*. In it he declared: "Not only is our century superior to any that have gone before it, but . . . it may be best compared with the whole preceding historical period. It must therefore be held to constitute the beginning of a new era of human progress."[32]

The Limits to Progress

Reading those words at this point in time, one cannot but reflect on what preceded the "wonderful century" and what happened soon after it had ended. In the eighteenth century the Age of Enlightenment was immediately followed by the French Revolution out of whose inner conflicts emerged the Terror and then the autocracy and wars of Napoleon Bonaparte, a paradoxical dénouement to the rationalism of Voltaire and the romantic visions of Rousseau. Likewise, within two decades after *The Wonderful Century* appeared in print, World War I had broken out. For four years, young Britons—together with young Frenchmen and Belgians and Germans and Austrians and Serbs and Turks and Armenians and Russians and Americans and Italians and Canadians and Australians and Indians and New Zealanders—were slaughtered across the length and breadth of Europe, a sacrifice to the failures of their elders. Something had gone terribly wrong. What was it? Why did civilization revert to such savagery?

There are various answers to these questions at different levels of analysis. One obvious explanation is that the progress was not all-inclusive. It was felt in some sectors of society, but not everywhere. After all, one would not reasonably expect that the evils of gross inequality, class division, and war could be eradicated within the space of a single century, no matter how progressive some of its leading figures may have been. In formulating generalizations about a period of history, even in using such terms as the *Age of Enlightenment* or the *Age of Progress,* one is emphasizing certain facts and minimizing others. This resembles the situation when two persons observe the same bottle and one describes it as half full, the other as half empty. The Age of Progress did accomplish a number of ethical advances in the treatment of its less fortunate members. But it had its horror stories also. The British stopped fighting the Americans and the French. But that did not prevent their going to war with Russians, Chinese, Indians, Zulus, Maoris, Afghans, Burmese, and Boers. During the century when Great Britain was the wealthiest and most powerful country in the world, hundreds of thousands of its people emigrated to North America, South Africa, or the South Pacific because they could not live decently in the British Isles.

As for progress on the domestic front, one should not forget how low was the starting point from which improvement was measured. In addition to the judgments of Engels, Dickens, or Mill—none of them sympathetic to the Establishment—consider what Disraeli, the future Conservative prime minister, wrote in his novel *Sybil: Or the Two Nations,* published in 1845: "There is more serfdom in England now than at any time since the Conquest [i.e., the Norman Conquest of 1066]. I speak of what passes under my daily eyes when I say, that those who labor can as little choose or change their masters now, as when they were born thralls. There are great bodies of the working classes of this country nearer the condition of brutes than they have been since the Conquest. Indeed I see nothing to distinguish them from brutes, except that their morals are inferior. Incest and infanticide are as common among them as among the lower animals."[33]

That indictment dates from the decade known as "the hungry Forties." But at the turn of the twentieth century, reforms notwithstanding, the gulf between the two nations still persisted. London was then "the greatest city in the world, both in size and sphere of influence," as Roger Fulford describes it. "Within the . . . City beat the golden heart of the empire. The great god was gold. . . . Deplorable poverty and deep disillusion existed side by side with great prosperity. . . . The squalor and degradation of life in some quarters of the East End were scarcely to be credited."[34] It was at this time that Charles Booth published *The Life and Labor of the People of London,* the results of his investigations into their social conditions. Thirty percent of Londoners by his estimate existed in dire poverty—only a few miles distant from the wealth that was concentrated in the City and the West End.

But there is another explanation, also valid, for the contrasts I have been describing, and this one runs deeper. The contradictions existed because they accurately reflected the conflict of values in Western civilization itself. Not only did different groups hold different values in higher esteem, but individuals who were possessed of clear minds and sensitive consciences were literally torn apart by the struggle within themselves. What Toynbee in another connection has termed "the schism in the soul" was a deep cleft dividing the British during the century when they emerged temporarily as the Western civilization's leading edge.

What form did this conflict take? The conflict centered on the use of the potentialities unleashed by the Industrial Revolution. The hereditary inequalities of the old class system, rooted in a largely static and mainly agricultural society, had to adapt themselves to the radical dynamics of factories, cities, and wealth derived from industry and commerce. "The morals of no age or people," says Myers, "have been proof against suddenly acquired riches."[35] The amassing of new fortunes within a single generation in manufacturing or trade constituted a new pyramid of power, and its presence was threatening both to the old wealth whose main resource had been the land and to the urban poor whose labor contributed to its profits.

The result was a conflict not only between divergent material interests and the social classes based upon them but also between alternative values that could be held in esteem or opprobrium. The central issues were questions of ethics, and they were the old ones that civilization has been confronting for more 3,000 years. Were all human beings to be considered equal in their basic humanity? How much inequality was tolerable? Should positive steps be taken to eradicate poverty? Should wealth be redistributed, and, if so, through what agency? Was it always right for people to do whatever a new technology enabled them to do?

The Economists' Declaration of Independence

In the nineteenth century these old familiar questions were debated from a novel angle. The new protagonists in the fray were the economists. They presented an argument that offered a challenge to the previously unquestioned assumptions of Western thought. Before the middle of the eighteenth century, it had been held as an axiom that economic activity was to be controlled by government wherever the public interest and a public need were paramount. As a corollary, it was argued that the economy should conform to the ethical principles generally accepted within the community. In no sense was economics considered a sphere of activity whose laws were independently derived from the inner compulsions of its own processes. Displaying a consistent consensus, the Greeks and Romans, the medieval governments and the Papacy, and the first nation-states imbued with mercantilist economic notions had all taken it for granted that economic matters were a subordinate aspect of social activity. Governments could appropriately conduct economic functions without having to answer the objection that they were interfering in a realm where they did not belong. The church, too, had no hesitation in attempting to regulate economic practices—as, for example, when it enunciated the doctrine of a "fair price" (*justum pretium*) or when it condemned rates of interest above a certain level as usurious.

The kind of capitalism, however, that was emerging between the sixteenth and eighteenth centuries challenged these restraints on its freedom of action in a revolutionary break with tradition. In this it was aided by the Protestant stress upon the individual who, when animated by the appropriate "work ethic," was fully entitled to the fruits of his enterprise. Thus was launched the attack on the enveloping system of regulations and controls that mercantilist doctrines had imposed on manufacturing, transportation, and trade. *Laissez nous faire, laissez nous passer* (let us make whatever we wish, let us and our goods pass freely from place to place); this was the protest of the entrepreneur against the paternalist, absolute monarchies and their self-styled "sovereign" states.

The year 1776 witnessed the publication of two Declarations of Independence. Jefferson's text announced that the 13 American colonies would no longer be subject to imperial commands from a distant capital. Adam Smith's work *The Wealth of Nations* affirmed that capital in private hands could energize the economy most efficiently if it was allowed to maximize its profits without let or hindrance from political fiat. "Leave us alone," said the businessman to the statesman. The demand might have been ignored, as often in the past, had it not been for one irresistible fact. The new wealth acquired in industry spelled power—power enough to stand up to governments, power to blunt the censure of the churches by sufficient donations to charity, power to control the masses of people whose livelihood depended on the work that industry created. It was for these reasons that the new doctrines—call them classical economics or *laissez faire*—gained their ascendancy in the decades that followed the ending of the Napoleonic Wars, and it was in Britain, being then the industrial leader, that their formulation was the most explicit.

What effect did all this have on determining which values were the most prized? What ethical consequences ensued when businessmen were left unhindered in their competition for profit?

In a society where for centuries a hereditary, landowning aristocracy had defined what was good and what was bad, the immediate outcome of the new thinking was a drastic shift in priorities. Edmund Burke railed against this when he declaimed: "The age of chivalry is gone. That of sophisters, economists, and calculators, has succeeded; and the glory of Europe is extinguished for ever."[36] In similar vein the poet Wordsworth laments:

> The world is too much with us; late and soon,
> Getting and spending, we lay waste our powers.

And again:

> To think that now our life is only drest
> For show; mean handy-work of craftsman, cook
> Or groom! We must run glittering like a brook

In the open sunshine, or we are unblest:
The wealthiest man among us is the best.[37]

A generation later, when the American moral philosopher Ralph Waldo Emerson reflected on what he had observed in his two visits to Britain, his conclusion supported Wordsworth's. "There is no country," he wrote, "in which so absolute a homage is paid to wealth. In America there is a touch of shame when a man exhibits the evidence of large property, as if after all it needed apology. But the Englishman has pure pride in his wealth, and esteems it a final certificate."[38]

This emphasis on getting and spending, this pride in wealth, was obviously appealing to greedy individuals who seized the opportunities to make their pile and stash it away. But it touched a raw nerve in a body politic that professed itself Christian. The Christian faith had traditionally viewed Mammon with the same wary suspicion as Caesar. Had not Jesus chased the money changers from the Temple? Did he not favor the poor as more likely to reach Heaven than the rich? St. Augustine had branded business as "in itself an evil." St. Jerome stated categorically that "a merchantman can seldom, if ever, please God."[39] Although such attitudes did not deter the Venetian plutocrats or Amsterdam's guildsmen or Fugger of Augsburg or Geneva's bankers, they had at least the effect of placing the successful entrepreneur morally on the defensive; and some of the uneasy consciences thus induced might be salved—if not finally saved—by disgorging a portion of their gains to succor the wretched. But the attractions of Mammon generally outdid the abnegations of Jesus. Toynbee has stated this categorically in language whose studious moderation barely conceals its bitterness: "Since the thirteenth century Western man has professedly honored Francesco Bernardone, the saint who renounced the inheritance of a lucrative family business and who was rewarded with Christ's stigmata for his espousal of the Lady Poverty. But the example that Western man has actually followed has not been St. Francis's; Western man has emulated the saint's father, Pietro Bernardone, the successful wholesale cloth-merchant."[40]

What is more, the church itself—or, after the Reformation, the churches in the plural—succumbed to the same earthly temptations. Organized religion needed revenues to finance its activities. So, like Faust, it made its compacts with the devil. Henry Willets, writing about Poland during the sixteenth and seventeenth centuries, has made a comment that admits of wider application: "Though the Catholic Church in Poland never lacked learned and pious prelates, the hierarchy at large showed greater zeal in protecting its worldly goods than in combatting heresy. A common clerical attitude was summarized in the words ascribed to a Bishop of Cracow, 'Believe in Old Horny, but pay me my tithes.' "[41] Much the same was true of the Protestants in Britain. In the eighteenth century, churchmen of the higher ranks held similar opinions, and lived in a style that assimilated them, to the landed nobility. To the lower orders and the poor, their message was contained in the unctuous advice that they should remain content in that station of life to which it had pleased God to call them. Burke said it explicitly: "Patience, labor, sobriety, frugality and religion should be recommended to them; all the rest is downright fraud."[42] Echoing the chorus, as written by the establishment, is this prayer in the *Poor Girls' Primer* distributed to the inmates of the Girls' Charity School of Sheffield: "Make me dutiful and obedient to my benefactors. . . . Make me temperate and chaste, meek and patient, true in all my dealings and industrious in my station."[43] Whether in Cracow or in Sheffield, these utterances were not the preachings of Jesus. They were the pronouncements of the spokesmen for inequalities entrenched in the society of which organized religion had become a central pillar. Churches that were themselves a part of the problem could not be the source of its solution. The latter had to emanate from individuals inspired by the rationalist humanitarianism of the Enlightenment or simply stirred by the promptings of their consciences. It was thus that the captains of industry, the Arkwrights and the Gradgrinds, were to be confronted and controlled.

The New Wealth and Its Fruits

There were two sides, then, to the Age of Progress, and one's judgment on what it accomplished must depend on where the emphasis is placed. One can agree with Hobhouse that "humanitarian ethics has had a large share in the distinctive changes that have made the modern state and the civilization of the modern world."[44] These ethical changes were genuine and prominent during the nineteenth century. At the same time they were accompanied by such a revolution in the processes of manufacturing that the whole economy was flooded with vast quantities of commodities for sale, and the standard of living in its material sense was transformed. Mill was quite right therefore to mention this as a

continuing trend in the history of his time. "In the leading countries in the world . . . ," he wrote, "there is at least one progressive
movement which continues with little interruption from year to
year and from generation to generation: a progress in wealth, an
advancement of what is called material prosperity. All the nations
we are accustomed to call civilized increase gradually in production and in population."[45]

True enough! Yet while this was going on, we have seen that the
endemic ills of civilization were not eradicated. To a certain extent, they were even intensified because greedy men had new
opportunities for amassing money and power. Surely it is significant that in the middle decades of the nineteenth century two men
of towering intellects, but opposite social philosophies, Benjamin
Disraeli and Karl Marx, the Conservative and the Communist,
should be looking at Victorian Britain and arriving at the same
diagnosis. Disraeli's "two nations" and the Marxian bifurcation of
society into two opposed classes express the same point in different language. To each the inequalities arising from internal divisions were the besetting sin of the contemporary social order.

Meanwhile, from his precinct in Basel, the Swiss historian
Burckhardt was contemplating the characteristics of the time in
which he was living and, judging them in terms of a long perspective, arrived at a conclusion that will appear balanced to some and
pessimistic to others. "Morality as a power . . . ," he comments,
"stands no higher, nor is there more of it, than in so-called barbarous times. Good and evil, perhaps even fortune and misfortune,
may have kept a roughly even balance throughout all the various
epochs and cultures." He thought "our assumption that we live in
the age of moral progress is supremely ridiculous." In his most
biting tones he castigates the optimists of his day: "It is a general
mistake to suppose that a dominion built on egoism, lies, and
violence cannot be solid, as if the powers of this earth were, as a
rule, built on anything else." "Satan is prince of this world," he
affirmed, "and evil is certainly a part of the great economy of
history."[46]

Burckhardt, be it remembered, was a European who witnessed
the conflicts between states—France and Germany, Austria and
Italy, Russia and Turkey—which in the twentieth century were to
tear the continent apart. With deep insight he detected the rise of
militarism and its accompanying tendencies to despotism. The
outbreak of World War I, only 17 years after his death, was assuredly in line with his misgivings, and that tragedy compels us to

speculate on the quality of the advances made during the Age of Progress. That there were genuine improvements in economic productivity and in the domestic policies of governments is undeniable. That ethical changes were fostered in personal relations is also clear. But, that these were insufficient to restrain the ambitions of the powerful or the greed of the wealthy is equally evident. Otherwise, would two catastrophic wars have engulfed the world between 1914 and 1945?

It is therefore to the contradictory tendencies of the twentieth century—this age compounded of hope and despair—that the next two chapters will be devoted.

If . . . there is ethical
progress, . . . it is to be
found, not in the
development of new
instincts or impulses of
mankind or in the
disappearance of instincts
that are old and bad, but
rather in the rationalization
of the moral code which, as
society advances, becomes
more clearly thought out
and more consistently and
comprehensively applied.

Hobhouse

8

The Two Profiles of the Contemporary World

Our Rights and Duties, and Our Education

Staggering is the record of human progress in the twentieth century; but no less staggering is the catalogue of our disasters. Humanitarian advances have been matched by the cruelest inhumanity. Scientific discoveries have been employed both to save life and to destroy it. Our knowledge has steadily expanded, but truth has been systematically suppressed or distorted. These contrasts have been raised to a higher pitch than ever, and thus appear all the more glaring, because the instruments we now command are so vastly more potent. The result has been an increase without precedent in our capacity to reach our ends—whether good or evil.

How does one interpret, how evaluate, the contradictions of our time? Can a valid judgment be offered on the whole when the opposites are so extreme? Can any middle ground support a balanced summation? Let us review our own age with such queries in mind.

Wherein Contemporary Civilization Is Different

But first, some preliminary cautions are in order. Any attempt to characterize the major developments of our own times and to render an ethical judgment encounters two problems diametrically opposite to those involved in the subjects discussed earlier. For one thing, our information about earlier centuries is always incomplete and is often quite sparse. On many topics it is nonexistent. When we pass judgment therefore on the prior stages of civilization, it can only be on a portion of the total record. No student of the current century, however, would complain about the lack of data—far from it. When it comes to understanding today's world, we swim in oceans of facts and figures, we drown in documentation. To navigate the flood, we are aided nowadays by computers that store information, calculate rapidly, and make complex correlations. But computers are unavoidably limited. Being restricted to processing the data they receive, they do not engage in original thought. Unendowed with imagination, they cannot leap beyond what is known. Creativity, vision, insight, are beyond them. For these, we must rely on the best existing faculty—our own minds.

Moreover, the computer, being no more than a machine, is in a genuine sense value-free. It will thus tabulate the data on Idi Amin or Pol Pot, on drugs or AIDS or terrorism, with the same mechanical disinterest as it stores the thoughts of Albert Einstein or the ideals of John XXIII. The capacity to value—whether the values are intellectual, aesthetic, or ethical—is quintessentially and uniquely human. Consequently, however Herculean the labor, we must somehow keep our heads above the flood, applying a selective judgment and sorting out from the mass of materials those items that human insight rates significant.

The second difficulty is inherent in the effort to comprehend events to which one is contemporary. Many of these have directly affected our own lives and the lives of those we love, in addition to the well-being of our country. In such matters no one can be wholly detached. Our emotions enter therefore into our judgment. Even though I seek at the intellectual level to approach all history as if I were actually a contemporary participant, manifestly I can be more dispassionate about Attila and Genghis than I could ever be about Hitler and Stalin. Students, which is what we are when we study the past, are less personally involved than actors, which is what we are in the present. In this, be it said, there is nothing inappropriate unless it should induce us, when evaluating our own era, to omit or minimize any aspects of the truth that may be relevant to a fair conclusion.

The development of civilization during the current century exhibits certain features that mark its character. One noteworthy fact is the sharp contrast between the first half of this century and the second. During the three decades 1914-1945, the international system collapsed three times. Two of those occasions were military—that is, World War I (1914-1918) and World War II (1939-1945)—the third, occurring between the wars, was the economic depression lasting from 1929 to 1935. The recovery that followed those disasters was accompanied by new institutions and new programs expressing new values. Here, inviting comparison with the seventeenth century, is one of history's clearest examples of a breakthrough consequent upon a breakdown.

There is another aspect of the current century that endows its problems with a distinctive character. Manifestly, some profound changes of substance are taking place within civilization itself. Nowadays, the contacts between civilizations are numerous; their reciprocal influences far reaching. The result is the emergence of new syntheses constituting a new reality. In past eras—until the eighteenth century, at any rate—most of the activity of a civilization was self-contained in the sense that it was little affected by external influences. True enough, various civilizations had contacts with one another, which in some cases were regular and continuous. But the essential core of each civilization remained basically unaffected. Indeed, in those instances where foreign intrusion directly challenged the central values or institutions of any civilization, the latter would resist and would either succeed in rejecting the intruder or be subdued by it. One thinks in this connection of China's rebuff to Buddhism or the resistance of France and Italy to Islam and, for contrast, the conquest of the Aztecs and the Incas by Catholic Spain and the ensuing destruction of their civilizations.

But something new has happened in the last few centuries as a result of the transoceanic expansion by the Atlantic peoples of the Western civilization. Acquiring empires over large portions of other continents, they brought with them their belief systems, their social institutions, and their technology. Never before in history had the representatives of one civilization been able to penetrate and dominate so much of humanity. In this century, although the political controls of Western states have ended, their cultural, technological, and economic influences remain. Indeed, the westernization of the way of life in the traditional civilizations and cultures of Asia, Africa, and Latin America is one of the salient facts of contemporary global development. And this has been compounded in recent decades by the modern revolution in communication. The rapid transportation of persons and goods by air, along with the instant transmission of information, speech, and visual images, have prepared the way for what Marshall McLuhan has strikingly called "the global village." We now stand on the threshold of an evolving world society, in which the boundaries of historic separations are increasingly blurred. Consequently, when one reviews the course of civilization in this century, it cannot be adequately conducted from less than a worldwide perspective. To do anything else is to stay culture-bound within the parochialisms of the past. Such a requirement, while stimulating to the imagination, enormously complicates the intellectual problem of reaching generalizations that are sufficiently inclusive and at the same time fair to the diverse aspects of a complex subject. In this day and age, no one civilization can be sufficient unto itself.

Ethical Pluses and Minuses of the Twentieth Century

If we are to appraise the record of civilization in the twentieth century, it would help to compile a list of the principal pluses and minuses. In the accompanying table I have grouped the various goods and evils, as I perceive them, under four headings—human rights and duties, education, social patterns, and politics— with the proviso that certain aspects of the subjects mentioned could belong under more than one heading. This tabulation will form the structure for the discussion in this chapter and the next. I shall review the several topics, balancing the positive side and the negative. And where better can one begin than in the sphere of human rights and duties? Respect for the dignity of individual human beings, and their treatment by the society to which they belong, is the be-all and end-all of civilization. No civilization that conspicuously fails in this regard is really worthy of the name.

Toward Equality Between the Sexes

In the field of human rights, the first topic to discuss is the liberation of women, and this for reasons both evident and compelling. Because women are one-half of the human race, any general raising of their status in relation to that of men constitutes a major ethical gain for civilization as a whole. John Stuart Mill had good reason to say in his essay *The Subjection of Women*: "Historians and

TABLE 8.1
Ethical Pluses and Minuses in the Twentieth Century

	Pluses	*Minuses*
Human Rights and Duties	Women's liberation	Continued sexism
	Movements for racial equality	Continued racism
	Altruism, humanitarianism	Selfishness, greed
Education	Public education, literacy	Ignorance, the semieducated
	Advances in knowledge, scientific gains	Fanaticism, bigotry, religious fundamentalism
	Wide dissemination of books, art, music	Disharmony and ugliness in contemporary arts
	Global transmission of information	Controlled propaganda
Social Patterns	Health care, medical treatment	Poisoning the environment
	Conservation	Power of the polluters
	Alleviation of poverty, social security	Survival of the have-nots
Politics	Democracies	Authoritarian regimes
	The Welfare State	The Warfare State
	Universalism, interdependence, United Nations	Nationalism, aggression
	Peace movements	Militarism, wars, nuclear weapons

philosophers have been led to adopt their elevation or debasement as on the whole the surest test and most correct measure of the civilization of a people or an age."[1] In the preceding chapter, I stressed that one of civilization's besetting vices has been the subjection of its women, but that in the period of the Enlightenment the Western civilization embraced new values, which began to take hold during the nineteenth century. Those advances continued in the twentieth century, with the Western civilization in the van. From this center, progressive changes have spread to the civilizations of Asia, Africa, and Latin America, where the inequalities to be surmounted are more extreme. Overall, as this century draws to a close, and we inaugurate a new century and a new millennium, for most of the human race the work yet to be accomplished in the emancipation of women still greatly exceeds what has thus far been achieved. That is by way of summary. Now let us take a closer look at the gains and the gap, or in many places the gulf, between actuality and aspiration.

The original dynamics and the leadership propelling the movement for the liberation of women have emanated from various Western countries. Here therefore is where the results are most pronounced. But even in this region there have been setbacks; and after more than a century of increasingly vigorous organizing, women are a long way from being equal to men. The most notable gains, and those most easily documented, have been a series of legal changes designed to remove the disabilities from which women have traditionally suffered. As a general consequence, a woman in the Western civilization can nowadays own property and inherit in her own right, retain whatever she earns outside the home, sue for divorce, hold a passport, and travel abroad without the consent of her husband. Certain of these rights, however—for example, obtaining a divorce—are more restricted in Catholic countries than in Protestant ones. The same holds true, even more strongly, in the sphere of sexual relations and on the specific issue of the mother's right to terminate a pregnancy by abortion. On family matters in general, the official policies of the Roman Catholic church remain uncompromisingly sexist and reactionary. It is paradoxical that a hierarchy of priests, composed exclusively of male celibates and headed by its elderly members, issues instructions to both sexes concerning physiological functions and emotional bonds, of which their own rules forbid them to have had personal experience.

Outside the circle of their home and family, Western women have also scored gains that appear spectacular in comparison with their previous opportunities. The changes are evident all across the economy, including nowadays many of those occupations—whether blue collar, white collar, or professional—from which women were always excluded. Significantly, in this century it was the actions of males that gave women their best chances of employment outside the home. I refer to the long duration and intensity of the two world wars—war being a barbarism habitually perpetrated by civilized men with the object of killing others equally civilized.

The countries that are the most progressive on economic issues have enacted legislation since World War II to prohibit sexual discrimination in hiring, promoting, or firing and to prescribe the same remuneration for the same work. But whatever the intentions of enlightened lawmakers, experience discovers here another example of the familiar lag between forward-looking public policy and backward-minded social practice. That lag is all the greater when the social practice not only translates into vested interests but has also generated the institutions (e.g., corporate management and labor unions) to defend them. Thus the successes recorded in formulating new and more equitable principles are marred by the obstructions to their enforcement.

On this subject the facts speak for themselves. Study the data for country after country, and a coherent picture emerges. The number of women gainfully employed has increased steadily both as an absolute figure and as a percentage of the total work force; but inequalities continue. Many women work outside the home only part-time because the roles prescribed for them by society require that they take care of the children, clean the house, and cook the meals. It is still infrequent for men to share equally in these latter tasks. Moreover, in the workplace itself such equality as women have gained exists primarily at the lower levels. The higher the rank in the managerial hierarchy, the fewer the women. The tenure of those employed is also more precarious than that of men. When the economy is prosperous and expanding, more women are recruited. But when recessions occur, they are the first to be fired for the obvious reason that generally they lack seniority.[2] As for equal pay for equal work, although in many sectors there has been a marked improvement, nowhere yet do the realities of the market conform to the requirements of the law. In the United States during the 1970s and 1980s, the average earnings of women were estimated to be around 60 percent of those of men. In Britain that figure was 74 percent; while in the most advanced countries—Sweden, France, Denmark, and the Netherlands—it ranged between 80 and 90 percent. Even in Sweden, which leads the world in this respect, women were still at a disadvantage in the higher echelons of corporate management, academia, and the professions.[3]

A similar pattern can be observed in the sphere of public activity. In countries that are democratically governed, women have participated in politics during the twentieth century to a degree for which civilization supplies no earlier precedent. The big breakthrough was the achievement of the rights to vote and to be a candidate for elective public office. Here it was the English-speaking democracies that led the way, followed by those on the continent of Europe—the last of all being Switzerland. As a result, women have been elected to the U.S. Congress, the British Parliament, and the European legislatures; and by the early 1990s in four European countries—Britain, France, Norway, and Poland—a woman had served as prime minister.

That being said, the fact remains that, although the doors of opportunity have been opened to women, only a few have yet been able to enter the citadels of power. In the United States, as I write this, one woman serves as a justice on the Supreme Court—one out of nine; six now sit in the Senate, beside ninety-four men. A few women have been elected as governors or mayors, and the number serving in state legislatures, who in 1983 were 13 percent of the total, rose to 20 percent in 1993.[4] For the first time in history a major political party, the Democrats, placed a woman on its ticket in 1984, Representative Geraldine Ferraro being then nominated for the vice presidency. But the conservative tide ran strongly in the United States at that time and the Democrats were defeated. That followed the still sharper conservative setback to women that had occurred in 1982. In that year, after a decade of campaigning for and against, the proposal to add an Equal Rights Amendment to the Constitution was finally defeated. An opposition—consisting of women who did not want legal equality, of conservative men, and of corporate employers objecting to the requirement of equal pay—was able to prevent ratification by the necessary three-fourths of the state legislatures.

With variations, this theme repeats itself in other Western countries. In all the national legislatures, as on local councils, women nowadays hold seats both on the left wing and on the right. But they are generally a small handful. Governments now make it a practice to include one or two women, but seldom are they assigned the politically significant portfolios. Even when Margaret Thatcher was Britain's prime minister, she did not bring other women into her cabinet, nor did the Conservative party markedly expand the numbers of women in the House of Commons during her leadership. The great exception to these limited gains is Norway. There the Labor party adopted a rule that at least 40 percent of the candidates chosen for an election to the Storting had to be drawn from each sex. Consequently, in the mid-1980s as many as 43 percent of the Labor members were women, seven of whom served in the cabinet under the female prime minister, Gro Harlem Brundtland.[5] Could this be the shape of things to come? Indeed, that is a possibility for the future in many more countries than Norway. For the time being, however, the government and misgovernment of Western civilization remain essentially in the same male hands, where they have always been.

Conditions in the Third World

The difficulty of summarizing the changes in Western civilization in this century is compounded when one turns to consider the others. Throughout Asia, Africa, and Latin America, the social position of women when this century started was generally further back than in the West. In addition, if their opportunities and disabilities were diagrammed on a scale, its range would be longer compared with that of the West and the extremes would lie much further apart. The liberation of the female half of the population from their traditional servitude has indeed begun. But before their condition even approximates to equality, mountains of discrimination—all codified in law, politics, religion, economics, and traditional social attitudes—must be leveled.

Two external factors have helped the women of the Third World in their recent and current efforts at emancipation. One has been the influential example of changes in the West, which stimulated the bolder women in other civilizations to demand the same for themselves. A second source of help is the activity of the United Nations, which has focused international attention on the problems of women's inferior status. The world organization proclaimed the ten years from 1975 to 1985 the Decade for Women, and initiated three conferences—at Mexico City (1975), Copenhagen (1980), and Nairobi (1985)—for which documents and data were prepared and to which most governments sent official delegations. At the same time, unofficial groups held parallel meetings of their own, independently of their governments, to compare their situations and explore ideas for improvement. There resulted not only a great increase in the information available but a heightened awareness of common problems existing in different regions and cultures.

A United Nations report in 1980 summarized the economic condition of women globally in these terms: They perform nearly two-thirds of the world's working hours; they receive only 10 percent of world income; and they own less than 1 percent of world property.[6] The very lowest standards are those in many African countries and some in Asia. There, in the traditional society of the villages where the majority live, women serve their menfolk by unremitting toil in agriculture, by fetching water and firewood and preparing the family meals, and by delivering yet another baby at least every second year. Overworked, undernourished, and uneducated, their lives are—to borrow from Hobbes—poor, nasty, brutish, and short. From these worst possible cases, across Asia and in Latin America, the position of women ranges all the way along the scale of emancipation to the opposite end, where a handful of educated, urbanized, professional women earn independent incomes and live in a Western style.[7]

The influence of the Western civilization has been many-sided in its effects on the status of women, not all of those effects being beneficial. The initiatives for improvement have come from innumerable sources, both from the grass roots and at the level of officialdom. Many governments, themselves male dominated, have enacted legislation or issued decrees or signed international conventions whose text purports to guarantee equal rights for women and assure them equal access to education and jobs. Enforcing these provisions, however, and carrying them out consistently in practice are tasks deferred to the future. The old inequalities die slowly for they are buttressed by the entire social structure, one of whose foundation stones has been the inferiority of the female.

Several age-old beliefs and practices have to be abandoned, several male-run institutions must be challenged and changed, before the civilizations of Asia, Africa, and Latin America begin to do justice to their womenfolk. Let me cite some of the obstacles. One of the major ones almost everywhere in the world is the strength of the organized religions, staffed always by their male hierarchies. Invariably, their theology is sexist; and their myths, based on no other authority than that of some self-designated prophet, are employed to sanction a social structure that makes women permanently subject to men. The three principal monotheistic religions—Judaism, Christianity, and Islam—in their orthodox forms are permeated with male chauvinism. In terms of the number of adherents whom they influence, the world's most reactionary institutions, as seen from the standpoint of contemporary efforts to emancipate women, are the Vatican and the fundamentalist mullahs who interpret Islam's *shariya*. The Vatican contributes directly to the prolongation of human misery in Latin America by its uncompromising opposition to abortion and to the use of contraceptive devices. The mullahs not only endorse polygamy, but they continue to affirm that a Muslim woman counts one-half as much as a man in terms of basic legal rights. Only when it is imbued by a secular and rationalist outlook will civilization accord to women their due.

But there are other man-made obstacles aside from those traceable to the other-worldly assumptions of sexist theologies. Societies that are still encased in their traditional forms incorporate many objectionable practices whose origin is either psychological or economic. An example of deeply rooted psychological prejudice is the *machismo* endemic in the Latin culture and among those peoples who extol the male warrior. In the social beliefs of such cultures the woman exists as the object of male virility. Sons are more valued than daughters, and thus are inequalities perpetuated. A by-product of such attitudes is the mutilating practice of female circumcision, still in vogue in more than 25 African and Muslim countries and estimated to have between 30 and 80 million victims.[8]

No less repellent are some of the economic consequences that flow from the domination of the male. One example of this, over and above the unequal rewards for work, has been the close link that civilization has forged between its cherished institutions of marriage and property. This is seen at its most blatant in the requirement of the dowry or "bride-price" that a woman brings to her husband as part of the marriage contract. One test of whether a culture is advancing in the direction of emancipating its women is the progressive abolition of the dowry. Here again is a situation where social conservatism obstructs a government that tries to act in an enlightened way. Take the case of India. Legislation against dowries went into effect there in 1961. But the practice continues. The Indian press is constantly printing stories about the demands for dowries and the intolerable burdens that these at times impose on the bride's family. This custom also has consequences that are tragic. The Hindu civilization used to require the self-immolation of a widow on her husband's funeral pyre.[9] In keeping with that cast of mind, which had the "sanctity" of religious approval, it is still not uncommon among Hindus in contemporary India for the husband or members of his family, if dissatisfied with the dowry they have received, to kill the bride by setting her on fire in a manner that can be represented as an accident in the kitchen. Nor is this practice confined to the villages. In Delhi itself, as many as 610 cases of wife burnings were reported as recently as 1982—and, if that was the number reported, the actual total must have been even higher.[10] Yet, at the other extreme of Indian society, one observes educated women pursuing professional careers, actresses earning huge salaries in a country obsessed with movies, and the daughter of Pandit Nehru becoming prime minister and ruling with a mailed fist until she was assassinated. What generalizations about India are valid?

From this survey of the changing status of women in the twentieth century, two conclusions clearly emerge. First, there have been significant gains that in one form or another have been recorded in all of the major civilizations. These gains, as they result in removing injustices, are decidedly ethical. Taken all together, what has been accomplished by women and on their behalf during the last century and a half is revolutionary when compared with previous history—so far, so good. But the second conclusion qualifies the first. Nothing in human society is harder to change than an age-old practice, sanctioned by widely held beliefs and constantly reinforced by institutions that perpetuate the power and privileges of their leading group. To initiate improvements under these conditions, it is necessary first to challenge the underlying beliefs. That is why the thinking of the eighteenth-century *philosophes* was the vital precursor to the stirrings of the nineteenth century and the broader movements of the twentieth. Once the beliefs begin to alter, it becomes possible to enlist the help of the state, that powerful motor for social reform. Then can public agencies and private individuals, armed with the force of new law, do battle with social conservatism and reaction. Resistance, though, can be strong because it is backed by civilization's most sacrosanct systems—marriage, property, and religion. These are formidable, but the facts demonstrate that they are not invincible.

Meanwhile, as the struggle for equality of the sexes continues, our world will exhibit the greatest differences simultaneously. Scandinavia will be in contrast to Saudi Arabia, the National Organization for Women to the Vatican, the topless beaches of the Riviera to the *chadors* on the streets of Teheran. The broad spectrum of human diversity defies easy generalization.

Changes in Race Relations

The gradual movement toward greater quality that has characterized relations between the sexes is paralleled by changes in the relations between races. Here, too, gains have been registered in both the public domain and the private that are spectacular when compared with the situation existing only a hundred years ago. It is when one looks at the tasks yet to be accomplished, and the resistance to equality that still manifests itself so powerfully, that negative judgments are in order.

Civilization hitherto has been no less racist than sexist. There is not one of the major civilizations that has not contained an underclass within its midst, and that underclass has often been differentiated from the dominant group by its race. Although in modern times, because of the expansion of European empires to other continents, the world has been most aware of light-skinned peoples ruling over those of darker skin, a wider historical perspective reveals that discrimination and exploitation of one race by another are universal sins of which no group of any pigmentation can plead innocence. During the centuries when Christian Europeans were raiding the west coast of Africa to obtain supplies of slaves, Muslim Arabs were behaving similarly on the east coast. Indeed, in recent decades the United Nations has documented the continuance of slavery on the Arabian peninsula and elsewhere.[11] Slavery is, of course, one of the two extreme forms of inhumanity—the other being war—practiced by our species upon our own members. But the abolition of its legal forms—between the 1830s and 1930s—has not meant the immediate elimination of the modes of inferiority associated with that institution. In none of those societies where peoples of different race commingle today in substantial numbers are their relations equal in terms of political power, economic opportunity, or social status.

Nevertheless, although the goal is far from attainment, some of the changes in the world since 1945 have been truly remarkable. What triggered them was the defeat of Nazi Germany and the worldwide revulsion at the horrors perpetrated by Hitler's barbarically racist regime. German occupation and military destruction so weakened the countries of western Europe that they could no longer maintain, without much difficulty, their control over distant colonies that the Japanese had seized in eastern Asia. Independence from imperial rule—whether British, Dutch, French, or Portuguese—resulted in a proliferation of new, and so-called sovereign, states whose governments (whether democratic or dictatorial) were now headed by their own nationals. Their admission to the United Nations accorded them a position of equality in international law that entitled their official representatives to the customary privileges of diplomatic status. Thus was inaugurated a period of global politics in which the principal actors made up three recognizable groups: a "first world" consisting of the developed economies of the West, a "second world" composed of the Soviet Union and its Communist partners, and a "third world" formed by the underdeveloped societies in Asia, Africa, and Latin America. In terms of power, the last of these was the weakest; but it comprised more than half of humanity and its members had votes and voices at the United Nations and in other world forums.

This novel international phenomenon was not without its domestic effects. In the United States, was the black head of an African government to be received in the White House as an honored guest while a black American citizen was denied access to exclusive clubs, hotels, and restaurants in New York and Washington? Were African delegates to be seen voting at the United Nations while blacks were barred from the polling place throughout much of the South? Many African Americans raised such questions. One, namely, Martin Luther King, put them effectively to the test, using pacific means to break the pattern of discrimination in the public facilities of the southern states. When his nonviolent protests met with violence from the local police, public opinion nationally was so swayed that the federal authorities brought their power to bear on the local agents of white supremacy.

During the decade and a half that began in the mid-1950s, the United States embarked on a veritable social and political revolution in the field of race relations. This event is of deep international significance both because of the power that this particular country wields in the contemporary world and also because it is the only one in the Western civilization whose population includes a sizable minority racially different from the majority. More than that, the relations between its component races are peculiarly significant for a people who won their nationhood proclaiming the principles of universal humanism. The Declaration of Independence asserts as a self-evident truth "that all men are created equal"; must this not apply to all human beings irrespective of skin color? The three amendments to the federal Constitution adopted after the Civil War (the Thirteenth, Fourteenth, and Fifteenth) had altered the legal status of black Americans, but initially that alteration was only formal. Until World War II, blacks were denied a share in political power; everywhere they were social inferiors; and in the economy they functioned either as entertainers or as hewers of wood and drawers of water.

Since the 1960s there has been a perceptible change. Politically, more blacks have become involved and they now participate actively. Witness the numbers who register to vote, and actually vote, in all sections of the country, plus the election of black mayors in many large cities including New York, Atlanta, Chicago, Los Angeles, and Philadelphia. In 1988 the first black was elected governor, and that was in Virginia. A black congressman has chaired the powerful Appropriations Committee of the House of Representatives; a chairman of the Joint Chiefs of Staff has been black; and a black candidate ran so effective a campaign for the presidency in 1988 that in various Democratic primaries he attracted a sizable proportion of white voters. All this would have been unthinkable half a century earlier.

Socially, as well as in the economy, the gains are also visible. Due to a combination of legislative measures and judicial decisions, the older policy, which permitted public facilities in transportation and education to be separate provided they were equal, has been abandoned—for the compelling reason that, when separate, in fact they never could be equal.[12] Increasingly, this doctrine has been extended to commerce, to recreation, and to private clubs. As for the economy, the most positive evidence of general improvement can be found in the emergence of a new black middle class, especially evident in the California city of Oakland. This consists of entrepreneurs, executives, and professionals, whose life-style and tastes are assimilated to those of whites in the same occupations and at the same level of income. All of that is on the plus side, and it constitutes a major ethical gain in social justice.

But there are also the negatives to be taken into account. Unfortunately, they are considerable. True, the doors of opportunity have been opened. But relatively few have thus far succeeded in entering. Until 1992 only one black had served in the Senate; only one had been elected governor of a state; only two have served—in succession—on the U.S. Supreme Court. In presidential cabinets and on corporate boards there has been token integration, as with women, but that is as far as it goes. In higher education the number of black students, both undergraduate and graduate, has grown, but it is not yet nearly enough to make up for the deficiencies of the past. Few blacks have received positions of tenure on the faculties, principally because the supply of those with the requisite qualifications still remains limited.

In the economy, too, although a minority of blacks have broken through the barriers of discrimination, the great majority continue at the bottom end of the scale. In any society it is hard to emerge from poverty, and in the United States a larger percentage of blacks are poor than of any other racial or ethnic group. In the labor statistics, the highest rate of unemployment is always among black teenagers. This helps to explain why so many young blacks turn to crime and why they constitute a disproportionate segment of the prison population. In the older American cities the inner core nowadays contains large sections of dilapidated buildings, mainly inhabited by blacks. These are ghettoes. Their occupants fester in hopelessness, punctuated by periodic outbursts of violence. Civilization has never been color-blind and is far from distributing its goods with an even hand.

The values pervading American society have been primarily those of its English-speaking Protestants. For a comparison, consider the case of the largest country in Latin America, Brazil, whose basic values were introduced by Portuguese-speaking Catholics. Brazil's population is composed of three races: the indigenous Indians, the European settlers, and the Africans whom the latter imported as slaves.[13] In human terms, how these coexist is Brazil's central problem and the test of its ethical success or failure.

As a legal institution, slavery did not end in Brazil until 1888, later than in most other countries; but the act of abolition was peaceful. The Portuguese had enslaved Africans to provide labor on the large sugar plantations of the northeast. There, a symbiosis developed between the two races, aided by the somewhat relaxed attitude of the Portuguese toward differences of color. The mulatto offspring of sexual unions were in some cases raised by their fathers in the plantation's "Big House," or *Casa Grande,* and were educated so that they could advance socially.[14] The fairly tolerant practices of the empire (1822-1889) were continued under the ensuing republics, to the extent that modern Brazil has taken pride in regarding itself as a model of equal opportunity for persons of different races. This national policy has found expression in legislation explicitly prohibiting discrimination against any individual on racial grounds. In this respect, both the official position and the legal texts are unimpeachable.

But what the people of the country themselves refer to as "the Brazilian reality" (a realidade Brasileira) is something else. Here one encounters a familiar problem that has many parallels elsewhere. Racial differences are not the only major lines of division within Brazil. Equally important are distinctions based on social class and on inequalities of wealth. Among Brazilian values, status and money have always been the preponderant weights in the balance, and it is here that the scales are overwhelmingly tipped in favor of persons with white skins. In all sectors of Brazilian life, the higher one's position in the hierarchy of influence, the lighter the skin color. And the same applies to wealth. In general, the darker are poorer; the lighter are richer. I say "in general," for there are some individual exceptions. A dark-skinned person who succeeds in acquiring wealth can move up the social ladder. Conversely, a poor white is relegated to the social level of a black.[15] When the hundredth anniversary of the abolition of slavery was reached in May 1988, official celebrations were held. But many blacks refused to take part, saying that they had no reason to celebrate.[16] The Brazilian reality remains one of profound inequalities, of which race is still a major part to this day.

I have discussed the United States and Brazil as cases to illustrate the issue of race relations in contemporary civilization, both because of the size and importance of these two countries and also because at the governmental level serious attempts have been made to counter age-old patterns of social discrimination. But no review of this century that concerns itself with ethics in civilization would be balanced if it did not refer to the two most repulsive examples of the opposite: namely, Germany under the Nazis from 1933 to 1945 and South Africa under the Afrikaner Nationalists after 1948.

Germany and South Africa in Our Time

The German case is especially horrifying, not only by reason of what happened but also because of where it happened. Here was a regime that seized power in the depths of a major economic depression and for 13 years established a total mastery over all aspects of the life of a people who were systematically barbarized. Hitler's program was to rearm, to place the entire country on a war footing, then to launch a series of wars of aggression with the ultimate design of making Germany supreme throughout Europe. Domestically this was accompanied by the imprisonment or execution of political opponents, and by singling out a Jewish minority of 600,000 persons as the ones responsible for the military defeat in 1918 and the economic debacle of 1929-33. As their rationale for these actions, Hitler and his followers announced a doctrine of the racial supremacy of the Aryans, with whom they identified the Germans, and of the inferiority of all other races and particularly of Semites. In pursuit of those beliefs the Nazis conducted a mass slaughter, in camps constructed for that specific purpose, of all the Jews they could seize in Germany itself and in the other parts of Europe that their army had occupied. Within the space of a few years, some 10 million are estimated to have been deliberately murdered. This deed was perpetrated by Germans imbued with Nazi beliefs in a country professing Christianity.

One reads in earlier history of instances of the mass killing of helpless victims in cold blood by some conqueror or despot, and one shudders at the extent of inhumanity of which our species is sometimes capable. But this Holocaust to which I am referring took place not in the remote past but in this century and in living memory. Moreover, the country where it occurred could on no objective basis have been described as savage. On the contrary, the Germans of the eighteenth and nineteenth centuries had made glorious contributions to civilization; and their country, ranked by any indices of social development, would have been placed among the world's leaders. That 2,000 years of civilized progress could have been sloughed off by such a people within a bare decade gives us cause to wonder how fragile indeed is our progress.

With the example of the Nazis so recent and vivid, one would not expect another people to emulate them almost immediately after Germany's defeat by enforcing a regime of white supremacy in a racially divided society. But that is exactly what happened in South Africa from the late 1940s through the 1980s. It is one more tragic instance of the truth that the human species too often disregards the lessons of its past blunders. In the South African case the tragedy is compounded by the certainty that the government's policy of *apartheid* was doomed to fail. Irrespective of the moral objections that can be leveled against it, apartheid could not possibly succeed for economic and political reasons. The Afrikaner Nationalists, who constitute the dominant political party, remind one of the characters in a Greek tragedy who of their own volition take the actions, step by step, that bring about their own disaster.

The political reason why their policy was doomed is that they are hopelessly outnumbered. The whites who seek to perpetuate their supremacy form only one-fifth of South Africa's population. The human rights which have been denied in that country are those of the huge majority, who in addition are supported by the sentiment and sympathies of others of their race elsewhere on the African continent. No doubt, the white elite can maintain its dominance for an extended period because it is well armed and ruthless. But it cannot do so forever. In the long run the weight of numbers will tell against it. A second reason fortifies the first. The Achilles' heel of the white South Africans consists in what appears to be their strength, the economy. The standard of living among the whites is very high. But to achieve and sustain it, they have been exploiting the black underclass on whose labor they depend. This, too, cannot go on indefinitely. The blacks are now organized into unions whose activities necessarily acquire a political dimension because they have been denied a share in the central government. Inexorably, black grievances erupted every so often into mass violence, which no less inexorably the white authorities suppressed with utmost brutality.

At the end of the 1980s, after four decades of such cruel injustice, there were signs that a growing number of Afrikaners realized that their policies must change. The most repressive aspects of apartheid were moderated or discarded. But the big test remains: Can South Africa continue as a single multiracial country unless all groups accept the basic principle of a truly democratic regime in which every person has one vote and every vote has the same political value?

The cases that I have been discussing happen to be instances where the whites are privileged and the blacks are disadvantaged. But notions of racial superiority and the practice of racial exclusiveness are no monopoly of white-skinned westerners. The Islamic civilization, as I noted earlier, has a long and sorry record of enslaving Africans, which only international pressure compelled the Arabs and other Muslims to discontinue in this century. Nor does one forget India in this connection. The four basic classes of Hindu society rest on a racist foundation, each *varna* being identified with its specific color: white if you were *brahmin,* red for the *kshatriya,* brown for a *vaishya,* black for the *shudra.* As a historian of India has said: "Acute color consciousness thus developed early during India's Aryan age and has remained a significant factor in reinforcing the hierarchical social attitudes that are so deeply embedded in Indian civilization."[17] Today, like the United States and Brazil, India is legally and officially free of racism; in social practice, however, it is certainly not. But the changes at the governmental level constitute a positive gain. In this respect, the second half of the twentieth century has marked a definite improvement over the first half. Moreover, there is a steady, worldwide shift in public consciousness on this issue. Before this century, there were many places where racism was customary and respectable. Since Hitler, it has lost respectability and is on the defensive. Many people today consider the contemporary racists either immoral or kooky. Backlashes notwithstanding, the Enlightenment has had results. The social glacier may move slowly; but move it does.

Our Duties to Others

There are no rights without duties related to them. A right is an assertion of how I wish to act and to be treated. But it is conditional on my respecting the same rights in others, that being my duty. Rights and duties are correlative and inseparable. They are the obverse and reverse sides of the same coin.

In the history of civilization, the emphasis has been placed on one side or the other at different times. A good example is afforded by the Western civilization, where in the last three centuries the pendulum swung to each side in turn. The Enlightenment focused on rights, with the result that the great declarations were formulated in the United States and France in the later part of the eighteenth century and were authorized by official bodies. In the challenge to the ancien régime, the Individual was accorded recognition, and what individuals wanted most in that day and age was emancipation from the shackles imposed on their freedom to act by society and its government.

After the middle of the nineteenth century, the emphasis shifted, as it had to, when industrialism was creating the large cities where much of the population was employed in manufacturing. These new social units generated within them new social relations. If the millions who labored in factories and lived in slums were to have their rights respected, those of great or moderate wealth had to discharge their obligations. Not surprisingly, the individualistic doctrines of the eighteenth century were complemented and corrected by the socialist concepts of the nineteenth. The task of the twentieth century has been their synthesis and reconciliation. With the one notable exception of the Universal Declaration of Human Rights,[18] our age has not resounded with ringing formulations of principles because these were not the primary need. It has, however, generated innumerable good works.

What I am referring to is the collection of practices, far more widespread than is generally realized, consisting in the work of people who cooperate voluntarily in specific projects to improve their local communities and who devote their time, skill, and resources to help others less fortunate than themselves. There are many names for this. You could label it altruism or neighborliness or humanitarianism, or call it love and compassion for one's fellow creatures. Whatever term applies, the fact exists and it is the cement of civilization as a social phenomenon.

This is a subject of immense importance but it is exceedingly difficult to describe and evaluate. If one is observing a public program—authorized, directed, and financed from some central point—that is fairly specific and definable. The continual activities, however, of private citizens, doing good and useful things individually or in small groups, are too diffuse, too amorphous, too multifarious, to fit into neat categories. Still less can they be quantified and charted. But they are fundamental to what civilization is all about. Societies can function without competition; they could not even begin to exist without cooperation.

For evidence of this, look around you. Assuredly you will find instances in the community where you happen to reside. For several years I have been keeping a file of articles and newspaper clippings that report such activities, and their scope is truly impressive. One learns, for example, of the South Bronx, a blighted section of New York City with countless derelict, abandoned buildings and vacant lots, where the population that remains consists of impoverished blacks and other minorities. Few of the teenagers graduate from high school; instead, they take to the streets, where, untrained in useful skills, many engage in crime, join a gang, become addicted to drugs or sell them. Yet, in such an unpromising area as this, successful programs have been developed at minimal cost to rehabilitate the physical surroundings and re-create a community of self-respect.[19] The key to their success lies in arousing the energies of the residents themselves. Helped initially by outside advice, they take charge, organize self-government for their neighborhood, and together construct something needed and useful from which all can benefit—whether a children's playground, a vegetable garden, a bakery, or a day-care center. Their sense of achievement overcomes the feelings of helplessness and hopelessness and generates a justifiable pride.

All around the world, projects of this kind are under way. In the urban ghetto and the rural slum, to which civilization relegates those whom it ignores, examples can be found of local self-help and cooperative renewal. These extend from New York and Chicago and San Francisco to Villa el Salvador, which started as the bleakest of shanty towns in the environs of Lima and has grown into something of an international model;[20] to Danilo Dolci's encouragement of rural cooperatives in regions of Sicily that the Mafia have tyrannized; or to Indian villages where Gandhi's spirit awakened so many to the rich resources that lay within themselves.

In the nature of the case, it is impossible to gauge how much of this happens worldwide or to estimate its total impact. For what it is worth, a survey in the United States early in the 1980s calculated that 84 million Americans were working as volunteers in some kind of community service, each giving about two hours a week.[21] If close to the mark, that figure comprises a large slice of the population, and the cumulative effort week after week must have significant results. But nobody knows by how much, in proportion to population, such numbers exceed or fall short of what people were contributing, say, a hundred years ago. The publicity and the data collecting, which are so characteristic of our contemporary culture, often leave one wondering whether it is the realities that have changed or our awareness of them.

Awareness is also crucial in judging a topic that is closely related—the purely altruistic behavior where one human being helps another without thought of personal benefit. In this category are the labors of Mother Teresa and the members of her Order on behalf of the destitute and the dying in the streets of Calcutta and similar cities. Here also belongs the pioneering work of Albert Schweitzer, who established his hospital at Lambarene in Gabon and won the confidence of the tribespeople by practicing Western medicine with sensitivity to their culture. More recently, in the 1980s, the world was shocked by photographic scenes of the effects of famine in Ethiopia, Somalia, and the Sudan—a famine caused by civil war, prolonged drought, and corrupt governments. Internationally there was an outpouring of sympathy and of money to help the sufferers.

As further instances of pure altruism, one recalls the acts of thousands of individuals who rescued victims of the Nazis during World War II. The name of the Swedish diplomat, Raoul Wallenberg, is conspicuous because of the audacity of his exploits and the mystery surrounding his final disappearance. Similarly bold was the Papal Nuncio in Turkey at that time who saved Jewish children by issuing them false certificates of baptism. This was the priest who was later to be John XXIII, the most widely revered of modern popes. In addition, there were those in Germany itself and in the surrounding countries who hid and fed Jewish families in their homes—such as Anne Frank and her parents—always at the risk of death to themselves. These were Christians helping Jews, or Dutch aiding Germans, motivated solely by a feeling of common humanity. To no higher level can ethics ascend.

Tragically though, the human being can similarly descend, and by no less a degree. If it was the good in humanity that evoked the selfless actions to which I refer, the evil in humanity caused the Nazis to do what they did. The potential for both good and evil is rooted in human nature and hence in civilization. I doubt whether any who wrote so optimistically about the Age of Progress a hundred years ago could have foreseen in their wildest speculations the mass cruelties committed in our time by Hitler and Stalin and their smaller-scale imitators. Nor is it only in the political sphere that such bestiality manifests itself. Not a week goes by without one's learning in the mass media about some horror story of sadistic brutality whose victim was helpless before the aggressor. In New York, a city inured to crime and violence, there was an incident in 1964 that so shocked the public conscience as to evoke a prolonged discussion about the causes and their possible prevention. That was the attack on a young woman named Kitty Genovese, ending in her murder. The assault took place out of doors on a built-up street where more than 30 persons inside their apartments heard the victim's screams, not one of whom came to her assistance. If the origins of civilization are associated with the building of cities, as some have averred, what is one to say of the quality of civilization in a city that has bred such fear and alienation as to result in this depravity? Nor is New York unique in this respect. Comparable tragedies could be cited from many a major metropolis. Not without reason are large sections of the modern city described as jungles.

As the ethics of civilization extend along a scale between the extremes of sheltering Anne Frank and killing Kitty Genovese, so are there negative counterparts to the influences of neighborliness and humanitarianism that I mentioned. Many human beings are primarily selfish in the sense that they habitually place their own needs first and proceed to manipulate others for their own benefit. Selfishness manifests itself in various ways, all of them bad and all profusely inscribed across the records of civilization. The selfish are avid for power, which they use to bend other persons to their will. They are animated by greed in acquiring whatever their hearts desire—whether wealth or social status or political authority. This prompts them to compete, generating behavior that begins aggressively and ends destructively.

The civilizations of the world continue to display these tendencies as they have always done. The grossest evidence can be found in the inequalities of wealth and status that have characterized practically all cultures. The few exceptions exist either at the primitive level or in some of the smaller democracies of northern Europe and the South Pacific. The phenomenon of the privileged few who live in luxury can be observed not only in societies possessing rich resources but also where it is less to be expected—in poorly endowed countries where a large segment of the population lives out its brief existence in destitution. There is scarcely an underdeveloped society that lacks its quota of overdeveloped individuals, flaunting their affluence and strutting with arrogance amid the surrounding misery. If the ethics of civilization can be weighed in the scales by its measure of social justice, what are we to say of a culture, like the United States, where some heads of business corporations receive annual salaries whose dollar amounts run into seven figures while other Americans are sleeping in the streets; or of such countries as India or Brazil, where powerful industrialists in Bombay or São Paulo wallow in luxury while millions endure the most abject poverty? These contrasts are inseparable from the history of civilization. Of the current century, the best one can say is that, while the inequalities continue in some sectors of every civilization, in certain places they have been considerably abated. What is more, there is nowadays a rising public conscience in this regard, which is able to give voice at various international forums, notably at the United Nations. The greedy and the powerful do not surrender their privileges without a struggle. But the events of the twentieth century have demonstrated that more persons are daring to take the risks that that struggle involves. Sometimes, they actually win.

The Universal Declaration of Human Rights

To cap this review of some of the accomplishments of our century in the sphere of human rights and duties, there is one event that forms a fitting climax. That was the adoption by the United Nations in 1948 of the Universal Declaration of Human Rights. This document, whose title and contents belong so much in the tradition of the American and French revolutions two centuries earlier, is noteworthy because of the character of the institution that gave it moral sanction. The American Declaration of Independence and the French Declaration of the Rights of Humanity and of the Citizen, although their reference was potentially universal, were statements by national agencies to accompany one people's revolution. The United Nations declaration, however, was adopted officially by the new organization in which most of the world's governments were represented. No government voted against its adoption, although a few—such as Saudi Arabia and South Africa—abstained. It was the first time in history that a world body had drawn up a list of rights applicable universally to all humanity. Moreover, the contents reflect the fact that it was drafted only three years after the conclusion of a world war in which an exceptionally revolting brand of barbarism had been defeated at tremendous cost and sacrifice. The phrasing of the declaration acknowledges the emergence of a global community; it emphasizes rights of a social and economic nature along with the basic political, intellectual, and juridical freedoms; and it balances a respect for rights with insistence upon duties.

Yet another aspect of the Universal Declaration should be noted. Securing its adoption by the General Assembly of the United Nations at that time was a political achievement of the highest order. Joseph Stalin was then dominant in the Soviet Union, and many articles in the declaration affirm the opposite of what he was practicing at the Russian people's expense. Why then did he acquiesce in it? A cynic would assert that it made no difference to the realities of his regime, because in any case he would disregard what the declaration prescribed. But there is another factor that weighed with him. The commission that drafted the declaration was chaired by no less a person than Eleanor Roosevelt, widow of the late president of the United States, who was the wartime ally of the Soviet dictator. A great human being in her own right, Mrs. Roosevelt was able to utilize her diplomatic skills, fortified by her reputation for absolute, selfless integrity, so that even Stalin thought it impolitic to obstruct her.

Eleanor Roosevelt's prominence in the world scene at that time prompts a further reflection. Her contemporaries included Mahatma Gandhi, Albert Einstein, and Albert Schweitzer; and in the following decade the world would become acquainted with Pope John XXIII and the Reverend Martin Luther King, Jr. Those six had much in common. All believed in the oneness of humanity; their thinking and their actions were universal in scope. In their persons, so soon after the horrors of Hitlerism, humanity produced new models for our progress in ethics.

The strange thing is that this cluster of extraordinary individuals, all active together in the period from the 1940s to the early 1960s, has not been followed by equally outstanding successors. With the solitary exception of Mother Theresa, there are no comparable figures alive today who are widely known and are capable of reaching out to the conscience of humanity at large. Why is this, I wonder? It is a point of some importance to which I shall return later, because it may tell us something about the condition of civilization as this millennium draws to a close.

Educating Humanity

Next after human rights and duties comes the topic of education. I am using that term in a very broad sense to cover the full

enrichment of the individual—intellectually, culturally, and artistically. In itself, this is not a part of ethics, but it has consequences
that are profoundly ethical. Civilization's mission is to provide for
the development of its human members in accordance with the
values it espouses. This is clearly its moral responsibility, for,
depending on what a civilization fosters or prohibits, people's lives
will become the richer or the more stunted. Hence the need for the
educational facilities through which all individuals can develop
their potentialities. My question is this: How has civilization fared
in this respect during the twentieth century?

The immediate answer has to be very positive. Ours is a century
in which greater gains have been recorded in education than in
any known period of the past. This has been a worldwide movement. Its results can be traced in every civilization, although their
actual performance has varied considerably. What has been achieved
is a great increase, both in absolute figures and in proportion to
those of school age, of the number of students now receiving
instruction at all levels and in the number of institutions offering
it. Furthermore, the facilities have been substantially extended to
large sections of the population that previously were mainly or
wholly ignored—namely, women, the poor, and the inhabitants of
rural areas. The ideal, of course, would be to ensure for all persons
an education up to the highest level of their intellectual capacity.
That is more easily said than done and is still a long way distant
from today's realities. Nevertheless, the results of the large-scale
and systematic programs throughout the world, especially since
World War II, form a landmark in the history of this topic. Whatever index or criterion you care to take, the available statistics—and
on this topic there are statistics galore—are impressive. There have
been significant increases in the numbers of schools and universities, of the students entering and graduating, of teachers with
improved qualifications, and of adults—especially seniors—raising
the level of their knowledge. One particular program, which has
been a central policy of UNESCO, was to raise the rate of literacy.[22]
The results have varied greatly from country to country, the signal
successes occurring wherever the government accorded this a high
priority on its political agenda.

The net effect can be summarized thus: In every civilization
nowadays a larger number of persons have received some education and possess some store of knowledge. All this is to the
good—in the ethical sense of the term—because it indicates a
growing number of individuals who are better equipped intellec-

tually to develop their potentialities and take charge of their lives. For civilization, that is a moral gain.

But there is also the negative side to take into account. If it be true that "all that glitters is not gold,"[23] so must one recognize that not everything labeled education is necessarily praiseworthy—nor are all of its offshoots or by-products unqualifiedly beneficial. Higher education is not synonymous with higher morality. It may merely strengthen the competence to do evil. Again, let us remind ourselves that it was in Germany in the 1930s and 1940s, among a people with one of the world's highest levels of formal education, that the most heinous mass evil of this century was perpetrated. Joseph Goebbels, Hitler's minister for propaganda, had received a doctorate from Heidelberg University.

The Quality of Progress

Apart from any traceable relation between education and ethics, the gains referred to above are not always as genuine as the statistics would indicate. Figures express quantities; they say nothing about quality. One should be cautious about taking them at their face value. Many of the governments that collect and publish data on this subject are more concerned with their public relations than with truth. Standards vary enormously in different parts of the world, and what is called a school or university in country X might not receive accreditation in country Y. Of the students who graduate from college, one may ask whether the principal goal of the majority is to acquire knowledge or a degree. And how often is learning associated with wisdom? This skepticism, these reservations, come naturally to one who has spent his professional life in the academic community and is accustomed to search for the substance behind the outward form. Nor can one omit the political dimension from a calculus of the benefits of education. What boon is literacy if the regime is so constituted that those who can read have access only to what a Hitler, a Stalin, or a Khomeini permits?

That last question has even broader implications. In the 1980s one adult out of three in the world was estimated to be illiterate—the worst cases being in central Africa and in parts of the Middle East. That in itself is one measure of the problem, viewed at the bottom end of the scale. But what about the top end? Consider the situation in the United States, ours being the largest in population of the world's wealthiest societies. I emphasize our wealth because this means that Americans possess the resources to do whatever, as a people, we consider important. If we fail in something, it is for one of two reasons. Either we give it a low priority; or, while we may attach a high priority, our judgment is in error as to how we should proceed. Education is one of three values that the great majority of Americans generally esteem—the other two being individualism and commercialism—and, while fortified by the former, it is often weakened by the latter.

The consensus of innumerable studies, books, and reports is abundantly clear. Two trends have been pronounced in recent decades. Our educational facilities have been continuously extended to more persons; simultaneously the standards overall have declined. So serious has been the decline that in 1983 the report of a national commission described the United States as "a nation at risk," warning that we were committing "unilateral educational disarmament." Although 99 percent of Americans are counted as literate in the Census Bureau's statistics, many experts have rated one adult out of five as "functionally illiterate"—meaning that their skills in reading and writing are too low for them to comprehend the printed material, or fill out the various forms, or conduct the necessary calculations that the contemporary culture requires of its participants.[24]

Is there some causal relation between the declining standards and the laudable effort to extend education to ever more people? It is reasonable to suppose that there may be, because the inclusion into the mainstream of students whose problems require special attention results initially in the diversion of teaching time and financial resources. Another, quite different, reason for the drop is the so-called permissive philosophy adopted in many school districts in the 1950s and 1960s. That movement sought valiantly and rightly to eliminate the overrigid discipline and excessively formal content of the traditional curriculum. But at the same time, as classroom atmospheres became more relaxed and course contents were broadened, the basic subjects that are fundamental to everybody's education—knowledge of history, mathematics, science, and the language we speak and write—were no longer required as essential, and the results have been disastrous.

There are, however, other, broader reasons that have contributed to the drop in quality. Some are the direct result of social and technological changes that have affected the home and the general culture in which children are raised. For one thing, the structure of the family, as well as its economy, is being altered. There are many more families in which both parents work, so that neither is home when the child returns from school. Also, numerous households now contain only one parent, either because of a divorce or desertion, or because there never was a marriage. With inadequate parental guidance, the child seeks other distractions and the instrument is ready to its hand. The ubiquitous television has become the dominant cultural influence of most American households, which in the 1980s had their sets turned on for an average of seven hours a day![25] This figure is appalling, in view of the inferior intellectual and cultural quality of most of the programs shown in daylight hours on the commercial channels. The contents of television programs are shaped by advertisers whose primary concern is to sell some corporation's product. This they do by entertaining the public, and it is the level of that entertainment which conditions the public taste.

Nobody needs convincing that television makes a more powerful impact than any medium of communication that human beings have yet devised. Being visual, its impact is immediate and vivid. A television program normally consists of a succession of fleeting images passing before the eye too rapidly for critical judgment. Potentially, if it were wisely employed and carefully controlled, television could be a valuable adjunct to education. But it has unfortunately become the substitute for reading. Too many children and teenagers in today's culture are viewers, not readers—and that is an enormous difference. Viewers are passive; they are virtually hypnotized by the screen, which deadens the critical faculty. Readers, however, are active. The reader stays in control, determines the pace, and can reflect critically on what is written on the printed page.

What has resulted is the kind of public that exists nowadays—a public that has passed through a system of mass education, leaving a large number, perhaps the majority, only semieducated. Hence the millions who consult astrologers (including a president's wife, who passed on to her husband the advice she received from that source), who slavishly follow religious charlatans, who gullibly act on the urging of advertisements both commercial and political, whose tastes have been vulgarized by the "hype" of Madison Avenue and the "glitz" of Hollywood. With such influences at work around the clock, how wisely will a democracy make its decisions? What happens then to the quality of our civilization?

This point is worth pursuing further given that the relation between the acquisition of knowledge and its social application constitutes a profound paradox. The extension of human learning in all branches is one of the spectacular achievements of the last century and a half. Nothing in the past compares with it either in range or in depth. The advances have been notable in each of the major subdivisions—humanities, social sciences, and physical sciences. But it is the last of these whose social impact has been the greatest. Not only have the discoveries in physics, chemistry, and biology changed our thinking, but their subsequent application through technological invention has transformed our behavior, individual and social. Traditional institutions, linked to the older doctrines, were reformed or superseded. New ones have emerged in their place. The work of Darwin, Marx, Freud, and Einstein, taken together, revolutionized our understanding of ourselves, of our social systems, of life on our planet, and of the universe. Today we continue to explore the uncharted paths opened up by their speculations. Those in former centuries whose curiosity for knowledge was boundless—a Leonardo or a Jefferson—those who were the great unifiers and systematizers—such as Aristotle or Ibn Khaldun—those who manifested a free intellect in defiance of established power, whether political or ecclesiastical—Roger Bacon, Galileo, Voltaire—such individuals, were they living now, would have a field day for the exercise of their genius.

The paradox arises when one relates the undoubted gains in knowledge to their social use or misuse. Early in this century Ernest Rutherford demonstrated through experiments in his laboratory that the atom—so named in the belief that it was the ultimate indivisible constituent of matter—could in fact be split. Within four decades, humanity had put this knowledge to its first practical use, inventing an atomic bomb, which was used to destroy the centers of two Japanese cities. Or take the case of television: Daring and imaginative intellects made the discoveries in physics and devised the technology through which television became possible. Since then a crass commercialism has used this medium to offer programs marked so often by triviality, vulgarity, and sensationalism. These examples, this litany, could be extended endlessly. Suffice it to say that they illustrate the contradictory tendencies that contemporary civilization displays. Humanity is equally capable of rising to creative inspiration at the highest level and of descending to the depths of the banal or the bestial. Hence questions of ethics arise. Both the learning process and the discovery of new knowledge are purely intellectual pursuits; but the social use of what has been learned frequently carries ethical implications.

The Power of Religious Belief

That brings me to a related matter—the strength of religious belief and the continuing power of the institutions of the organized religions. Touching on both education and ethics, this subject reveals in sharp focus some of the deeper contradictions in civilization today. It is a further aspect of the theme discussed previously, namely, the difference between civilizations that locate their highest values in this existence and those that place them in another.

First consider this fact. During the 1970s and 1980s we have witnessed a wave of movements in many of the major organized religions exhibiting a similar character. Not only do they reject the values that became influential as a result of the Enlightenment and scientific research, but they express their reaction by strongly reasserting the foundations of the ancient faith in its most uncompromising form. What is so significant about the contemporary phenomenon of fundamentalism is its worldwide range. You find it within Christianity both in the Catholic church, which elected a highly conservative pope from Poland in the person of John Paul II, and among various of the Protestant denominations, the Baptists being a conspicuous example. In Islam the traditionalism of the *shariya* has been vigorously revived both by Sunnis and Shiites, though more virulently by the latter under the impetus of the theocratic revolution in Iran. In Judaism the orthodox groups, fired by the emotional charge of returning to the land of their biblical forefathers, have engaged in militant crusades against reformers and liberals. Such developments within the three monotheistic religions have also had their counterparts among Hindus and Buddhists. Why, one asks, has all this been happening at this time?

Some of the reasons vary in the various cases. It is clear, for example, that Islamic fundamentalism is a way of expressing that civilization's hostility to the West. The mullahs wage Holy War on the hated infidels by anathematizing our values, our ideas, and our morals—although in the process they take the fullest advantage of such products of "the Great Satan" as the airplane, tape recorder, television, tank, and time bomb. But when a phenomenon is as widespread as this upsurge of fundamentalism and cuts across as many civilizations, there must also be generic reasons. Is it possible to identify them?

Two can be suggested that share these common features: They originate in technological change and they generate a great anxiety.

The first of these is the simple, inescapable fact that all through this century one major new invention after another has come into general use, enlarging the range of individual behavior and creating networks of social relationships that never existed before. In my own lifetime there have been the automobile, airplane, and rocket; radio and television; computers, copying machines, and tape recorders; gene-splicing, contraceptive pills, artificial insemination, and conception outside the womb—the list goes on and on. The net effect upon the ordinary person, unversed in the advanced knowledge of the pioneering scientists and inventors, is bewildering and mind-boggling. These are marvels, and they work. Exciting though they are, their total effect also creates anxiety. They have rendered obsolete many of our traditional modes of conduct and they call into question the concepts and the values that underpinned them. The family, the community, the school, the city, the nation—entities that once seemed so firm and solid have become blurred shapes with fluid outlines. The old securities, the ancient certainties, have disappeared. The new frontiers are very challenging, but they offer both promise and peril. In these circumstances many people feel unsettled and insecure. The values they were taught, the institutions that shaped them, are being questioned or even superseded. The ground is shifting under their feet. Consequently, they want some reassurance and they grasp at the firm, authoritative pronouncements of those who claim to know and evince no doubt. This is a climate of feeling and opinion in which the alleged certainties of fundamentalist dogma find ready listeners.

Add to all this the second, and closely related, cause: the fission and fusion of the atom and the energy thus unleashed. Again I revert to the traumatic consequences of nuclear weapons for contemporary civilization. For four decades humanity lived with the knowledge that a few individuals in the governments of the United States and the Soviet Union held in their hands the means to destroy civilization and exterminate most forms of life across broad regions of this planet. The fear of this happening, whether conscious or unconscious, drew many persons not only to the flocks of the priests and pastors, the rabbis and mullahs, who expound the old religions, but also to the sects and cults of self-constituted prophets, shamans, gurus, and "holy men," offering salvation to those who would heed their voice and hand over their money. Here is an unregulated free market of irrational enterprise to lure the credulous. From the social standpoint the trouble with all this is that it fosters dogmatism, bigotry, prejudice, and intolerance. The semieducated, lacking critical judgment and being emotionally troubled, are easily converted into true believers. When that happens, they surrender their reason to another's authority. How often does the quest for Heaven make a hell on earth![26]

Mass Culture
and Mass Communication

The same two-sidedness that is manifest in the successes and failures of the educational system reappears in another aspect of the contemporary culture where education both molds and reflects the quality of our civilization. Consider the mass production of books, music, and copies of works of art, plus their widespread sale and dissemination among the general public. The classics are nowadays available for everybody to acquire. The world's masterpieces of writing, composing, painting, and sculpture can be enjoyed in one's own living room. And not only that: The modern world is notable for the number and quality of its libraries, museums, art galleries, theaters, and concert halls. Many of these were, of course, founded in the past, some of them by "enlightened despots." But in no earlier time was there ever such a proliferation of these institutions, enabling so many to benefit. Also, in addition to the large professional organizations—the major symphonies, opera companies, and so forth—there are nowadays thousands of small private groups assembling to play music, to read poetry, to act in a drama, to dance—not as spectators in an audience but as participants. Not only are older works thus performed, but the new can also be experienced. Today's civilization offers more cultural enrichment to more persons than ever before. In this respect, it is truly carrying out its mission—that of fostering human development to higher levels.

That being said, however, there are also the negative factors that balance the positive. The households that have the works of Shakespeare on their shelves or listen to tapes of Mozart or Beethoven are not the majority. In many houses there are no books at all; or, if there are, they are generally of the inferior kind. The records of a fashionable "rock star" sell in the millions. Such is not the case with Beethoven's Ninth. There is a vigorous popular culture in contemporary civilization, which millions of enthusiasts support with millions in hard cash. But the standard of taste exhibited there is seldom high.

Nor are the serious arts in much better shape than their popular counterparts if they are to be judged by what they tell us about the values of civilization. To put it bluntly, our century is not distinguished for its artistic achievement.[27] Hundreds of thousands of individuals have been writing, composing, painting, designing, sculpting, and performing. We have seen and heard much talent, much virtuosity in technique. But has this century produced a Michelangelo or a Shakespeare, a Tolstoy, a Rembrandt, or a Beethoven? Does any contemporary composer or painter or literary figure rank with them? The genius of the twentieth century has been prolific in science and technology, where the mind has burst through the frontiers of knowledge so that marvels have been invented for human use. What one sees and hears in the arts of today, however, is something that expresses a truth but is also very depressing. Much of the writing, whether in novels, poetry, or drama, much of the painting, sculpture, music, and architecture, faithfully mirrors the discords, the anxieties, the disharmony of our epoch. All too often, the mood is jangling, jerky, jarring; seldom does it inspire. This is a true reflection of the disorders in our culture to which artists are acutely sensitive. If Ruskin was right in perceiving our art forms as the most important of the records that a people leaves behind, a future generation will read in the book of twentieth-century art what Barbara Tuchman has appropriately described as an "age of disruption."[28]

Before leaving this general topic of education, one further feature should be mentioned that has enhanced the quality of contemporary civilization but also augments its dangers. I have referred to the tremendous proliferation of knowledge in all its forms and its availability to the public at large. That is linked nowadays to media of communication, which permit the global transmission of information in the swiftest manner conceivable. A televised news program instantly brings pictures and voices, summit conferences or wars, from any corner of the planet. Not only are we made aware of the problems of other human beings beyond the horizons of our personal experience, but the awareness creates a shared concern that could ultimately lead to a wider sense of community. The vision of the unity of humanity has a meaning today in practical terms that it never had before. Once more, in the long run this can be a gain for civilization, if we use the opportunity wisely.

But as always in human affairs, the gain is accompanied with attendant risks. The same media of communication, which liberate the mind when they open up new sources of information, can be perverted into agencies for propaganda and control. Past history is replete with the records of authoritarian regimes, political and ecclesiastical, seeking to keep their subjects quiescent by limiting the ideas and data to which they had access. How much more skilled, how pervasive, have been the arts of censorship and propaganda in the twentieth century. Examples of the very worst of these abound in each of the three forms they assume: in the deliberate suppression of the truth, the alteration of factual information, and the inculcating of beliefs that suit the interests of those in control. All this does violence to the mind, in the same manner as torture does violence to the body. Its purpose is the wholly unethical one of converting the human being from a free individual, capable of employing a critical intellect, into an automaton responding with a programmed reaction to the stimuli that the propagandist imparts. When an authoritarian regime has modern technology at its command, the means of enslavement are greatly enhanced. For when the mind is made a prisoner, it is unnecessary to place shackles on the body.

Such in summary form are some of the ethical pluses and minuses that the record of human rights and education in this century reveals. We observe so many crosscurrents and contradictions that the total picture is neither of one kind nor of the other. It is a blur of interpenetrating lights and shadows. This is not the whole story, however. Still to be discussed are a number of social factors, including the economic, plus the political flavor of the regimes by which humanity is rule or misruled. Their relevance to the ethics of civilization is direct and immediate. These topics therefore will form the subject of the chapter that follows.

We live in curious times
and amid astonishing
contrasts: reason on the one
hand, the most absurd
fanaticism on the other.

Voltaire

9

The Two Profiles of
the Contemporary World
(Continued)

Social and Political Patterns

Some years ago I served in a project conducted in Rio de Janeiro by the United Nations. At that time major economic changes were taking place whose effects permeated Brazil's social system. Observing them led me to two major conclusions. The first was that many sectors of a society are so interrelated that significant innovations in one area not only affect the others but depend for their success on consonant changes elsewhere. Second, I noticed that changes in the different sectors occur at different speeds. What was obvious in Brazil in those days was the dynamism and rapidity of its economic growth. The economy acted as a powerful locomotive pulling behind it a train of cars, some of which exerted a drag on the engine. At the rear of the train, in particular, were social institutions—such as the family, the church, and education—that either resisted innovations or were slow to adapt to those required of them. In the middle, reflecting all the manifold contrasts of Brazilian life, was the government, pulled forward headlong by the speed of economic development but slowed down by the brakes of social conservatism.

What was special about that particular instance was the position that each sector happened to occupy on the train at that time—the economy taking the lead, the social institutions lagging in the rear, with the political system coupled up in between. That pattern, however, is by no means universal. In Turkey after World War I, Mustafa Kemal initiated the westernization of its Islamic culture and modernized its economy, using his political leadership to shake up the whole society by the force of governmental power. Contrariwise, in Iran during the 1980s, it was a religious leader, the Ayatollah Khomeini, who launched his fundamentalist counterrevolution, turning the government and the economy inside out to compel them to conform to his traditionalist interpretation of the *shariya*. This indicates that basic transformations, whether in a forward or a backward direction, can originate in any branch of a culture; but when they do emerge, the speed of the changes they set in motion varies in different spheres.

Such reflections are relevant to this chapter whose subject is the ethical pluses and minuses in social and political behavior. Here, too, as with the topics discussed in the previous chapter, the contrasts are glaring. Our century has recorded some monumental gains, but some of our follies and failures have been tragic. First I shall review the social factors, then the political.

A Healthier Planet

To begin on a positive note, consider the advances in the field of health, which have been truly spectacular during this century. The results of progress in medical science have been applied to both the prevention and the cure of disease. Many of the beneficial effects are widely known and are incontestable. In numerous countries the mortality rates of infants and mothers have been steadily reduced, notably in the Western civilization and in the others that introduced its techniques. Many diseases that were scourges as recently as the first half of the twentieth century—tuberculosis, for instance—no longer take the same terrible toll. Nor are large populations decimated nowadays by the notorious epidemics of earlier centuries—those of plague, cholera, typhus, and smallpox. A consequence of the general improvement in health is that the average expectancy of life in many parts of the modern world is far higher than it has ever been. The contrast is indeed dramatic. One is astonished to read nowadays a letter written by Michelangelo in 1517 in which he refers to "the fact that I am old."[1] In that year he was actually 42. In the 1980s the average Italian lived to be 73.

What has happened to bring about such a change? The basic cause, which made everything else possible, was the advance in medical knowledge that has had cumulative effects since the seventeenth century. The science of medicine, as it is today, exemplifies the triumph of rationalism when it is focused on something as humanistic as our own bodies during their life cycle from birth to death. By employing the methods of research and experiment, medical scientists were able to test hypotheses by their congruence with the facts. In addition, they had to disregard religious taboos, such as those that had once prohibited the dissection of cadavers.

After the knowledge was acquired, to have any practical benefit, it had to be put to social use. For this to happen, there were two requirements. The public at large needed educating in the essentials of the new doctrines, and the powers of government had to be mobilized against outdated social practices. Such needs called for revolutionary ways of thinking about how to promote better health, and the new concepts had to be spread by leaders whose views commanded respect. Moreover, if governments were to act effectively, the political parties in the democratic systems and the more enlightened of autocratic rulers elsewhere must encourage a public opinion favorable to programs of public health. It took the combination of many skills therefore to install a pure water supply or an effective method of sewage disposal; to persuade the public at large to participate in programs for vaccination and inoculation as well as regularly to consume a healthy diet. To the extent that contemporary civilization has adopted measures of this kind, the gains have been more than physical. As a general rule, healthier individuals living in healthier communities have greater opportunities to lead happier and more creative lives—although what use they will make of those opportunities is something else.

In another respect, also, has medical progress been translated into public policy with corresponding ethical improvements. I have in mind the various programs of socialized medicine, initiated by progressive governments, which in many countries since World War II have provided comprehensive coverage for the entire population. The ethical aspect of these programs is plain. They are founded on the principle that medical care from birth to death is a fundamental human right rather than a privilege to be distributed differentially according to the capacity of individuals to pay for the services received. The greatest advances in this direction have been made in various of the democracies of western Europe and of the South Pacific. The United States, however, is the notable exception. This country has not established a comprehensive national system of medical care because of the antipathy on the part of conservative-minded citizens, of many doctors, and of private insurance companies to having social services operated by the government and to paying for them by tax increases. As a consequence, millions of Americans suffer poor health or live shorter lives, simply because of their lack of funds to pay the hospital or the doctor.[2]

Since World War II intelligent international action has also made its essential contribution to improvements in health care—essential because diseases are no respecters of political frontiers. The World Health Organization, the medical branch of the United Nations, has launched some indispensable programs to eradicate endemic diseases and to reduce the force of epidemics in both tropical and nontropical regions. Just now, as I write, the world body is working in conjunction with the medical authorities of many countries to cope with the onslaught of a new malady currently rising to epidemic proportions. This is AIDS—the acquired immunodeficiency syndrome—which in the 1990s is claiming its victims on every continent. When one hears about the scientific research now being conducted in laboratories to discover the cause of AIDS and therefrom develop a cure, one is struck by the contrast with what happened in the fourteenth century when the Black Death decimated western Europe. In 1348 the King of France, as Barbara Tuchman relates, "asked the medical faculty of the University of Paris for a report on the affliction. . . . With careful thesis, antithesis, and proofs, the doctors ascribed it to a triple conjunction of Saturn, Jupiter, and Mars in the 40th degree of Aquarius said to have occurred on March 20, 1345. They acknowledged, however, effects 'whose cause is hidden from even the most highly trained intellects.' The verdict of the masters of Paris became the official version."[3] In today's world many persons still seek advice from astrologers and presumably would give credence to this sort of nonsense; while others consider AIDS to be a punishment sent by God and curable therefore only by prayer. But apart from such surviving examples of the medieval mentality, in the temper of our times the great majority prefer to look to the white-coated medical researchers for rational analysis of a physical problem. Civilization certainly has some gains to its credit.

The Sickness of the Third World

Alas, though, there is more to be told, and its tenor is far from positive. Although it is true that the best medical treatment available today is superior to anything practiced before, and that in many modern countries the standard of care for the population at large has improved substantially, the fact nevertheless remains that provision for the health of much of humanity is still utterly inadequate. One-fifth of the population of the globe suffers severe health problems, according to the annual report of the World Health Organization (WHO) in 1989. Glaring disparities exist both between countries and within them—the worst conditions being those in south and east Asia and in sub-Saharan Africa, where as many as 40 percent of the people are undernourished and diseased.[4] The average life expectancy in 1983 was as high as 77 years in Iceland and 76 in Norway, Sweden, the Netherlands, and Japan. But it was almost half that figure—40, to be exact—in Chad and Ethiopia. Infant mortality in many countries of the Third World is as much as 200 babies of every 1,000 that are born—a number 15 times greater than in the West. The mortality of children between the ages of 1 and 5 in the Third World is 30 per 1,000, a rate 250 times higher than the western; and maternal mortality is 300 times as high.[5] Humanity may live in the One World that Wendell Willkie designated, but assuredly we operate on a double standard.

Why is the life span of an Ethiopian only half that of an Icelander? Why do babies and young children, as well as mothers giving birth, die in such large numbers in much of Asia, Africa, and Latin America? Of the many reasons that combine in those results, a few will suffice to mention. One has always been the sheer lack of the necessary scientific knowledge, although that is no longer the case today. The medical knowledge and the appropriate techniques for promoting better health are there for those who wish to learn and apply them. Some of the potential beneficiaries do not take advantage of the knowledge available because of fear. They harken to their religious leaders or to witch doctors or they distrust the methods of the foreigner. Then, too, there are the entrenched attitudes of those who rule the roost and wield authority. The social systems of the traditional civilizations were persistently hierarchical in structure; their governments, invariably authoritarian. Those at the top always took good care of themselves; but the masses below them were dirt in their eyes. Life was cheap, anyway; and if the majority died early, there were always others to take their place. So why trouble to lengthen the lives of the expendable? In the Western world, too, this attitude used to prevail. But our democratic revolutions put an end to that immorality. Ordinary people began to count when their votes had to be counted. Much of the Third World, however, continues to be misruled at this time by a motley crew of despots, dictators, autocrats, and thugs who are not accountable.

This political factor is part of the explanation of why health programs lag so badly in the regions that need them most. Look at the budgets of governments in what are euphemistically named the "developing countries." What do you find there? Annual expenditures on health in the poorest countries, as the WHO reports, averaged less than $5 per person in 1989, as compared with an average of $400 in the developed areas. The same budgets reveal all too clearly the values and priorities of those who govern the poor. What is it that their rulers seem most eager to develop? The answer in many instances is the military. In numerous poor countries the government spends more on the military than on either education or health.[6] In certain cases the military budget exceeds the expenditures on both health and education combined. These are political decisions, which carry obvious ethical implications—particularly where a dictatorship equips and trains its armed forces not because it is in any danger of invasion but because it is at war with a large segment of its own people and can only survive by repression. This general subject of the cancerous spread of militarism, and its appalling social costs, is one to which I shall return later in this chapter.

Threats to the Environment

But before leaving the field of health, another negative aspect of the topic must be mentioned for which the inventive technology of Western civilization is directly responsible. In the very same century when medical science has been reducing the incidence of diseases that used to kill our great-grandparents, new threats to health and even to life itself have emerged as by-products of the latest techniques that contemporary science makes possible and the economy finds marketable. Two industries in particular are culpable—that which generates nuclear power and that which manufactures chemicals. Both of these make and sell the substances that, if misused, can be lethal to the human organism. Radioactivity and pesticides—to mention two of the most dangerous—enter into the soil, the water, and the atmosphere and thence into our bodies, where cancer may result. Sometimes this happens by accident. There can be a breakdown in the manufacturing plant due to mechanical failure or human error, or both; witness what occurred at Three Mile Island in the United States, at Bhopal in India, and at Chernobyl in the Ukraine. Or the cause can be the careless, or even reckless, disposal of hazardous wastes, as happened at Love Canal; or the fallout from nuclear explosions conducted by the military, as in Utah and Nevada. Sometimes it is the consumer who is at fault through excessive use of a product that could be relatively harmless in smaller amounts. Sometimes again, a new substance, such as a "wonder drug," is advertised and promoted for sale without research over a sufficient length of time and therefore without full knowledge of all the side effects. The latter are only discovered years afterward when much damage has already been done. The examples I am citing—all based on actual experiences in recent decades—are the adverse accompaniments of what, viewed from another angle, are the striking benefits of scientific discovery, technological innovation, and vigorous marketing. What they demonstrate is that social responsibility should always govern the application of inventions, overriding considerations of either prestige or profit, which brings the discussion back to ethics.

Similar pros and cons arise when one considers the deterioration of the physical environment in general, a subject that has been the focus of intensive study and sharp controversy in recent decades. As is often the case in such matters, the basic facts are not in dispute. But because of uncertainties about the relative strengths of different causal factors, to allocate responsibility and to prescribe remedies can be difficult.[7]

The central problem can be simply stated. Since the 1950s many features of our physical environment have been deteriorating, in urban and rural areas alike, at the same time as population and economic growth have increased. There can be no doubt that the two trends are connected. Greater numbers of people create more demand for material commodities and consume ever larger amounts of the planet's resources. The consequence of these developments has been pernicious. Not only are we using up our resources—including those that cannot be replaced—at faster rates, but in the process we have done, and continue to do, untold harm to what remains. Most seriously of all, we are constantly contaminating—and in fact poisoning—much of our land, air, and water, the three essentials for sustaining life.

The evidence for this lies all around us. In addition to being regularly reported in the mass media and argued back and forth in public debate, the facts of pollution are there for everyone to see, smell, taste, and breathe. They are immediate and palpable, in the smog of our cities; the oil spills in the oceans; the fouling of rivers, lakes, and inland seas; the steady destruction of forests; the extinction of whole species of living organisms; the ominous spread of deserts; the storage and disposal of toxic chemical wastes and radioactive materials; the emission into the atmosphere of man-made gases that destroy the ozone and thus can drastically alter the Earth's climate—the list of perils goes on and on.

The Responsibility for Pollution

Granted all this, you may be thinking, but where does ethics come in? Are not these matters of concern for science and technology, for politics and the economy? Where is the ethical dimension? The question is both appropriate and important, and the answer is clear. The ethical aspect of this issue is one of responsibility. Who is responsible for causing the pollution? Who should clean it up? Who should take measures to prevent its recurring? Who should compensate the victims?

There is no difficulty in locating the responsibility. First, in an ultimate sense, each of us is responsible to some degree. When I drive my automobile, I contribute to the smog. When I purchase something packed in a nondegradable plastic, I add to the mountains of garbage that will not disappear. When I use a spray can operated by fluorocarbons, I help to deplete the ozone layer that protects our atmosphere from deadly cosmic rays. Such is our contemporary technology, and such the pervasiveness of its products throughout our economy, that it is extremely difficult nowadays for anyone, however well intentioned and well informed, to avoid causing some of the pollution from which we all suffer. It has been said with truth that every human being on this planet is downstream or downwind from somebody else. The responsibility therefore is truly collective because the machines, the gadgets, the objects that we use and discard not only recoil on ourselves but also do harm to others.

That being said, however, the fact remains that the responsibility varies in degree and in directness or indirectness. Although each of us, knowingly or not, does some damage on a very small scale, there are others who pollute on a very grand scale, hurting thousands of individuals and entire communities. Moreover, the causal relation between their actions and the resulting damage is immediate and direct. When a specific locality has a higher incidence of physically impaired babies or of cancer among its adults, when the water supply is contaminated by the efflux from an industrial plant, when the sky is darkened by the clouds of gas and particles issuing from smokestacks, when the spring is silent because the birds were killed by chemical pesticides, when beaches are made filthy and wildlife is destroyed by leaking oil, when poisons seep into the soil from discarded waste, the responsibility rests squarely with the corporations that made, marketed, or disposed of the products. In an economy dominated by private entrepreneurs, the great polluters are the business firms. Examples abound in the most highly industrialized countries such as Great Britain, Germany, the United States, and Japan. But lest it be thought that these antisocial practices are solely generated by greed and stimulated by the profit motive in a competitive culture, the fact that similar harm was done to the environment in the Soviet Union and in other societies that professed the principles of Marxism should lead us to seek a broader explanation. Pollution is a worldwide phenomenon that everywhere accompanies industrialism, and its adverse social effects are the same no matter whether the industrializers are votaries of Adam Smith or of Karl Marx. The underlying reason for the similarity seems to be that the principal organizations responsible for the mess are very large ones. As structures increase in size, the quality of their humanness is correspondingly diminished. Their leadership becomes impersonal; they are engrossed in the perpetuation of their power and privileges. The ways in which the spokesmen for the chemical companies attempted to discredit Rachel Carson after she published her epoch-making *Silent Spring,* like the self-interested reactions of the tobacco corporations in response to medical studies on the link between cigarette smoking and lung cancer, resemble in spirit the behavior of Communist bureaucracies, which, before Gorbachev introduced his *glasnost,* repressed their critics and punished dissent.

In the 1970s two major reports were published about the long-term implications of these trends for human survival on this planet. These were *The Limits to Growth,* which was sponsored by the Club of Rome's "Project on the Predicament of Mankind," and *The Year 2000,* a study conducted by a commission of the U.S. government established by President Carter. The central findings in this pair of reports were essentially similar. Examine the figures for three trends of recent decades—population growth, consumption of resources, and pollution of the Earth's biosystem—then project these into the future, and the conclusion emerges that the world is heading for disaster. Therefore the three trends must be reversed; and to bring this about, determined action by governments is necessary. For who else has the power to control the polluters?

Leaving aside for a moment the validity or otherwise of these judgments—and I am one who agrees with them—what was so interesting to observe was the division of opinion that they evoked. Those whose values might be called liberal, progressive, or social democrat accepted the findings as grist for their philosophical mills. Many conservatives, on the other hand, strenuously rejected them. The conservative and influential newsmagazine *The Economist* attacked the assumptions on which both reports were based. Editorially, it used to deride their authors as "econuts." In the United States the Hudson Institute, which expressed through Herman Kahn the thinking of the leaders of the military-industrial complex, launched its optimistic rationales for still further growth; while the Reagan administration, succeeding Carter's, quickly swept aside the notion of preserving the environment because that required regulation of business corporations and limits on their freedom to make a profit. It is worth adding that the disasters at Three Mile Island, Bhopal, and Chernobyl occurred after, not before, the publication of *The Limits to Growth* and *The Year 2000* and lend credence to their warnings. So did the explosion that destroyed the shuttle Challenger, a tragedy caused by technological defects of design compounded by managerial irresponsibility both in the U.S. Space Agency and in the principal corporate manufacturer, Morton Thiokol. So did the extensive oil spill from the Exxon Corporation's tanker Valdez, which devastated so much of Alaska's coastline. When individuals in positions of authority, whether public or private, allow harm to be done to others from carelessness, recklessness, ignorance, or bureaucratic defensiveness, they are morally responsible for the consequences. If a higher ethical standard were in force in our contemporary civilization, these disasters would not occur.

Nor is it impossible to prevent them. Nor, for that matter, is pollution in any of its manifestations an accompaniment of industrialism that must be accepted as inevitable. Far from it! During the 1970s and 1980s there were many instances of successful resistance to the poisoning and uglifying of the environment. The air over London is now much cleaner than it used to be, as is the once filthy River Thames. The condition of the Mediterranean and the

Baltic, of the Great Lakes and Chesapeake Bay, is improving. In the cities of California, where the sunshine contributes to the chemistry that aggravates the smog, state legislation has been responsible for slowing, and in some areas reversing, the deterioration of air quality. All of these successes, as the last sentence indicates, were caused in the same way. The governments had to take charge by regulating the polluters—both individual and corporate—and enforcing penalties against offenders. This in turn was made possible only when and where a sufficiently strong public opinion was aroused to impel the government to act. It takes a sense of outrage felt by masses of individuals to imbue officials, whether elected or appointed, with the strength to stand up to the corporations whose processes and products are the source of much of the harm. In countries that are democratically governed, the means exist for expressing this outrage and mobilizing it to political effect. Hence it is in the democracies that many of the remedial measures are beginning to show results. Even under authoritarian regimes, however, the leadership can sometimes be induced to act—at least in those instances when the menace is too widely known to be covered up. In Japan, where deference and hierarchy still permeate the social structure, the president of a business corporation was forced a few years ago to lose face and make public apology to the inhabitants of an area whose health had been injured by the filth spewing from his factories.

The ethical rights and wrongs of all this are perfectly clear. They can be expressed by quoting a judgment of Machiavelli, whose values on some matters were more moral than is generally recognized. "For the aim of the people," he declared, "is more honest than that of the nobility, the latter desiring to oppress, and the former merely to avoid oppression."[8] Something similar may be said of the polluters and their victims. It was the technology of contemporary civilization that made pollution possible on its present-day scale. It was the owners and managers of the economic system who exploited the possibilities. Only through enlightened politics can remedies be enforced. Only the public ethic, as expressed through public opinion, compels the politicians to respond. Good or bad, it is always our ethical priorities that shape the character of our civilization.

Poverty in Civilization

I turn to another aspect of the twentieth century where our concern for ethics—or the lack of it—is decisive. Along with ignorance, disease, and war, a persistent curse from which all civilizations have suffered is poverty. "The poor always ye have with you."[9] At the time when Jesus spoke those words, civilization in his part of the world had already evolved through two millennia. Another two millennia have since been added, and still the poor are with us. But this much may be said in favor of the twentieth century: More than in any age of the past, our generation has attempted systematic efforts on a large scale to raise the minimal standards of living and, if not to eradicate, at least to lessen the wide financial gulf that has traditionally separated the social classes. This was attempted in markedly different ways by the two contrasted political systems—the liberal-democratic form of the West and the Marxist type of the East. The differences between their social philosophies and fundamental assumptions have been the subject of voluminous comment, which needs no repeating here. Less noted, however, is the fact that both systems employed the same agency to bring about the desired reform. That agency was the state. No matter whether the prevailing concepts were those of Mill and Jefferson or of Marx and Lenin, it is the state that is everywhere called into service to rectify social injustice through positive political action.

The circumstances under which this has happened tell us much about the values of contemporary civilization. A society that acquiesces in poverty, and takes no systematic steps to alleviate or abolish it, is one that can accept the presence of inequality without an affront to its conscience. Inequality is then explained, and even justified, by references to the fact that individuals differ qualitatively, or it is interpreted by some religions as part of a divine dispensation that offers the rich an occasion to ensure their niche in "heaven" through charitable donations.[10] Indeed, there have been those who have argued on economic grounds that poverty is the necessary precondition for the creation of wealth through labor and is thus essential to civilization. Witness this statement of Dr. Patrick Colquhoun, organizer of the modern preventive police force: "Without a large proportion of poverty there could be no riches, since riches are the offspring of labour, and labour can exist only in a state of poverty. . . . Poverty is therefore a most necessary and indispensable ingredient of society, without which nations and communities could not exist in a state of civilization."[11]

The contrary notion that inequality in the form of poverty is unacceptable, and the ensuing conviction that society must take positive measures against it, has been an ethical revolution of a character that distinguishes the modern world from its predecessors. In the Western democracies this new ethic is linked with the affirmation, so strong since the Renaissance, of the basic worth and dignity of every human being. In the Communist regimes, it was the product of that impassioned preaching against social injustice in which Marx engaged with all the fervor of an ancient Hebrew prophet.

The Welfare State

The results are certainly impressive. Many states in this century have developed comprehensive programs in the fields of education, social security, housing, and health designed to assist those members of society who suffer the deprivations of the bottom quarter on the economic scale. Such programs have varied in their details from country to country; and the extent of the coverage, plus the degree of generosity, have reflected both the resources available and the political intentions that determined their allocation. Because graduated taxation provided the principal source of financing, the effect was a partial redistribution of income, whereby the state took from the richer and gave to the poorer. The social services have thus become a characteristic of the contemporary political system; and by contrast with past regimes, which have been variously described as the trading state, the garrison state, or the law and order state, our century has accorded priority to the welfare state—an ethical concept reminiscent of the Aristotelian "good life."

Granted its intent, how effective has the welfare state been in practice? No clear-cut general answer is possible because the variations are so enormous. How can one generalize about a world whose realities range from Haiti to Holland, from Calcutta to Copenhagen; from the hovels of the indigent to the palaces of the affluent? All that one can do is draw certain necessary distinctions and then make the comparisons that, to be valid, are relative to time and place. The first appropriate distinction concerns the distribution of wealth within a country; the second, its distribution among countries.

As to the first, it is clear that there are certain countries where poverty has been eradicated in the sense that every inhabitant is fed, clothed, and housed and also receives medical treatment, at least above the necessary minimum standard. Which countries are these? I would include the Scandinavian region—Denmark, Finland,

Iceland, Norway, and Sweden—plus the Netherlands and Switzerland, together with Australia, Canada, and New Zealand. All of these, it will be observed, have certain features in common. They are small in population, though not necessarily in area; they govern themselves democratically; they are all peaceful, though some were very warlike in the past. Also, it is worth noting that several of these countries—such as Denmark, Iceland, the Netherlands, and Switzerland—are not endowed by nature with an abundance of resources that could make them "lands of plenty." On the contrary, where nature has been niggardly or even threatening—as is the impact of the North Sea on the Dutch or of the Alps on the Swiss—they have turned their best possible resource, their own human qualities, to the best possible advantage. I emphasize this because, when one reads statistics indicating that the inhabitants of some emirates in the Persian Gulf possess some of the highest gross incomes per capita in the world, they deserve no credit for that. Indeed, it would be disgraceful if this were not the case in a world economy dependent on their oil. By contrast, the Danes, the Dutch, and the Swiss achieved what they have by their ingenuity, their hard work, and their ethical resolve to deal fairly with one another.

It will also be obvious that all the countries listed above belong in the Western civilization. That is, I believe, an objectively valid judgment and is not ascribable to ethnocentricity on my part. The fact is that the attack on poverty was launched in this civilization as a result of the humane philosophy of the Enlightenment reinforced later by a sense of moral outrage at the social evils for which unregulated capitalism was responsible after the Industrial Revolution. The spread of democracy, culminating in universal adult suffrage, gave voters the means to convert their power into legislative policies for the benefit of the underprivileged. Later on, several governments in other civilizations followed suit, but the stimulus to do so came to them from the example provided in the West.

The West, however, is far from perfect. One should not forget the subtle rebuke in Mahatma Gandhi's reply, when asked his opinion of Western civilization: "I think it would be a good idea." I singled out ten countries as recording the greatest success in combating poverty. All these, however, are small countries, whose combined populations form a minority even of this civilization. In Western countries with the larger populations—France, Germany, Great Britain, and Italy—and in the United States, with the largest and most diversified population of all, poverty continues to afflict an underclass whose social and economic adversity contrasts glaringly with the affluence of the well-to-do.

During the first two decades after the end of World War II, many constructive measurers were adopted whose general purpose was to establish a minimum level of treatment—or living standard—below which nobody should fall for reasons of economic or social disadvantage. Consequently, a country's success or failure in bringing its civilization to a higher ethical plateau could be tested by the number who remained at or close to the minimum and by later efforts to raise that minimum. Judged by those tests, some major countries of the Western civilization began to slip backward in the 1970s and 1980s when adverse economic conditions, signaled by the rise in oil prices and mounting inflation and unemployment, led to the election of reactionary political leaders in Great Britain and the United States. The policies of the Reagan administration in Washington and of the Thatcher ministry in Westminster were directly designed for the benefit of those already rich. Their natural result was to make the rich still richer and to widen the relative gap between them and the poor. The British press in the 1980s repeatedly revived Disraeli's phrase of "the two nations" to describe the gulf between haves and have-nots, accentuated by Thatcher. In the United States, many figures are cited as evidence of how the American people regressed socially during the eight years when Reagan and his right-wing advisers occupied the White House. But there is one that stands out: Two out of five of the children in New York City were living in poverty[12]—and that in the capital of the capitalist system, only a short distance from the gleaming glass towers along Park and Madison avenues and the financial fortresses of Wall Street! The means exist to eradicate poverty; the will has been lacking.

"The Wretched of the Earth"

Beyond the domestic divisions, there is the other aspect of this problem—the gulf within humanity at large between have and have-not peoples. Ethiopia, Mali, Bangladesh, and Haiti stand in the sharpest contrast to the United States, Germany, Sweden, or Japan. The full dimensions of poverty, worldwide, are hard to grasp. Reading the sober prose of official reports by agencies of the United Nations or the grimly vivid accounts in responsible newspapers, one is overwhelmed both intellectually and emotionally by the weight of the facts and figures and the extent of human suffering that they contain. No statement can claim to be precise and accurate, because statistics in many areas are unreliable. Moreover, there are disagreements over definitions. In the United States, for example, a family of four was classified as poor in 1986 if its cash income was less than $11,203. By that measure, there were 32.5 million poor persons, numbering more than 15 percent of the American population.[13] But many of those were living in conditions that would be envied by the poor of Haiti or Bangladesh. The first annual report of the United Nations Fund for Population Activities offered this estimate of the world's poor in the mid-1970s: 500 million were malnourished, 100 million lacked clean water, 800 million were illiterate, 350 million were unemployed or earned less than $50 a year, 250 million lived in slums, and 1.6 billion were without basic health care.[14] Ten years later, another United Nations report stated this: "For the developing regions (outside the centrally planned economies of Asia), a global estimate that finds broad support puts the total number living in poverty at the beginning of the decade at about 1.3 billion. To this must be added an unspecified but large number in the Asian centrally planned economies."[15]

The glaring disparities between haves and have-nots were further documented in two official reports made public by international agencies one week before Christmas 1988. The World Bank revealed that, as a result of the debts they had incurred, poorer countries that needed aid from outside were actually "transferring their wealth to richer nations" in amounts 50% higher than they had been in 1987.[16] The social consequences of this relative increase in the poverty of those already poor were stated by the United Nations Children's Fund (UNICEF). In 1987 they estimated that 14 million children died under the age of 5. Half a million of those deaths were attributed to the slowing of economic development in the debt-burdened countries.[17] This same point—that poverty is a major underlying cause of disease and of high mortality rates—emerges from the studies of the World Health Organization. In a comment on the annual report of 1989, an American spokesman for the agency declared: "It is at one level more a picture of poverty. A lot of these diseases are a function of poverty. People get sick because they are poor and they get even poorer as they get sicker and can't be that productive."[18]

No one has spoken more movingly of the human tragedies that these figures entail than Robert S. McNamara. When serving as president of the World Bank, he wrote a foreword to its "World Development Report, 1978" in which he stated that 800 million individuals—or one-fifth of humanity—"continue to be trapped in what I have termed absolute poverty: a condition of life so characterized by malnutrition, illiteracy, disease, squalid surroundings, high infant mortality, and low life expectancy as to be beneath any reasonable definition of human decency."[19] Two years later in his farewell speech after 13 years at the World Bank, he declared that such widespread poverty "is an open insult to the human dignity of us all . . . for we have collectively had it in our power to do more to fight poverty, and we have failed to do so." He concluded with these words: "What these countless millions of the poor need and want is what each of us needs and wants: the well-being of those they love; a better future for their children; an end to injustice; and a beginning of hope. We do not see their faces, we do not know their names, we cannot count their number. But they are there. And their lives have been touched by us. And ours by them."[20]

One could not paint in darker hues the immoral side of civilization in this century—particularly immoral because, despite some progress, we have the means, as McNamara so eloquently stated, to do far better.

Government in a Positive Role

As the contradictions in the social record of civilization during this century are connected with political factors, it is to these that I now turn. Not only is that connection very close, but equally significant are the differences in the manner of change in society and government, respectively. Social change is brought about by numberless actions of numberless individuals, responding severally to similar conditions in fairly similar ways. Examples of this are the long-term fluctuations in the birthrate, the succession of economic booms and slumps, the rise or decline of prices on the stock market, the behavior of drivers in city traffic, the methods of rearing children, and so on. In such phenomena trends arise that are statistically measurable. None of these is planned by those who have contributed to them, and the results are frequently unforeseen and unintended. Governments, however, operate differently from private persons. Their public acts—save when they are reacting to some unanticipated crisis—are normally planned with an objective in view. Although the outcome may often be at variance with what was expected, governmental programs can at least be said to contain an element of forethought, purpose, and direction. That is so because the political sphere requires a certain amount of organization and leadership, whereas society at large is leader-less and amorphous. Hence, in considering the political factors, one is focusing on those aspects of civilization where its values, whatever these may be, are consciously expressed. This introduces explicitly the basic question: What can be learned about ethics in contemporary civilization by observing its political record?

The two major political movements of this century, arrayed against each other in worldwide competition, have been democracy and communism. Each has had its ethical dimension, but the emphasis differed. Moreover, each developed in practice along lines that in certain particulars diverged from its founding philosophy.

The Democratic Achievement

In the case of democracy, we are witnessing a form of govern-ment that in the past was always a rare exception but that in this century has sought to translate itself to civilizations far removed from its point of origin. As was noted earlier,[21] democracy was created in the Western civilization, and nowadays may properly be viewed as one of its defining characteristics. In fact, it makes sense to say that democracy is the civilization of the Western peoples in its political mode. That, however, was not always so. European regimes of the past have traversed the entire gamut of types of government. There were monarchies, both absolute and limited, hereditary aristocracies, commercial oligarchies, theocracies, and military autocracies. But out of this unpromising background the democratic system—originally a flash in the pan of one Hellenic polis, Athens, in its finest hour—experienced a rebirth after the English, American, and French revolutions of the seventeenth and eighteenth centuries as the form of government most appropriate to the social and economic conditions of modernity.

Why did this happen? For two reasons. First, democracy is founded on respect for the worth and dignity of the individual. In the name of equality, that principle extends to every human being, irrespective of race, sex, language, religion, social class, economic status, or personal ability. Second, in a democracy the people at large possess the ultimate control over those in office by means of regular elections and competition among opposing parties. By these means, the public retains some measure of freedom. Freedom and equality, combined into one, are the basic political values of democracy, and it is in the Western civilization that they have flourished.

But these values are more than political. They are ethical in addition. The concept of equality is radical to the point of revolutionary. Most of the political record of civilization has been a sorry picture of privilege or inequality in one form or another, the masses of humanity being regarded and treated as inferiors. The single exception is democracy. The kind of political system that denies that any persons are superhuman or subhuman, and that instead affirms that all of us belong in the same category of a common humanity, is qualitatively different from all other forms of government. Also different is the concept that authority resides inherently in the citizen-body, whose members periodically decide by agreed constitutional methods to entrust limited powers to certain specified officials for fixed periods. No other system has installed effective machinery for making its officeholders responsible and holding them to account. This infusion of the virtues of equalized freedoms[22] into its public affairs is the supreme merit of democratic government. Where people govern themselves democratically, they do not fear the knock on the door of the secret police in the middle of the night or the disappearance of individuals without a trace. To rid humanity of the excesses of despotic power is no small achievement. This it is that justifies us in rating democracy as the highest ethically of the political systems yet devised.

In this century the democracies were successful in surviving the threats of two world wars. In the second of these, our values were directly challenged by the Nazis and Fascists who had seized control of Germany and Italy and by Japan's militarists and nationalists with their ambitions of empire over east Asia. The victory of the democratic regimes had the political results of stimulating further democratization internally and of encouraging its spread externally. Elsewhere in the world the democratic model was imported and imitated in many states, which adopted new constitutions and introduced the whole Western paraphernalia of periodic elections, opposing political parties, an uncensored press, and so forth. Most important of all, in the light of its size and the longevity of its civilization, was India's venture in democracy amid an unparalleled diversity of castes, cultures, languages, and religions.

But this positive picture has its negative side. All the gains
notwithstanding, nowhere does the perfect democracy yet exist.
The progress since 1945 is counterbalanced by several limitations
and imperfections and some downright failures. Because the subject of democracy is so vast a topic and because this is not the place
for a comprehensive evaluation,[23] I shall confine myself to those
aspects of the democratic experience that have ethical implications. Of these, one is of such central importance as to outweigh
the rest. It revolves around the basic issue of what we understand
by democracy and then how we apply that understanding to a
country's social realities. Democracy can be thought of in a restricted political sense, confining it to the institutions and processes of government—that is, to elections, parties, the rule of law,
and similar governmental matters. Or its meaning may be extended
to social factors, including therein the structure of the family,
opportunities for education, the beliefs of the prevailing religion,
the distribution of wealth and incomes, and so on. My own concept
of democracy is the latter, because my research into this subject
has convinced me that political factors are so intimately related to
the whole of society that they cannot be properly understood
unless those interconnections are included. Take one obvious example—the participation of citizens in elections. What does it
signify to say that a constitution or a law allows black persons to
vote if in practice they are effectively excluded by systematic
discrimination or outright intimidation? Or that the poor may vote
equally with the rich, when in fact many of the poor feel utterly
alienated from the system that relegates them to an underclass and
believe that their casting a vote makes no difference because the
system is still not going to change to their advantage?

The answers implied in these questions lead to this conclusion:
The principles of democracy cannot be fully applied in government
unless they also permeate the other institutions of which society
is composed. In other words, a democratic government cannot
fully function in an undemocratic society. A country whose social
order exhibits class distinctions, one where a disproportionate
amount of wealth is concentrated in the hands of a very few, or
where people are divided into first- and second-class citizens by
virtue of distinctions of language, religion, sex, or race—in such a
society the political parties will reflect the inequities of a house
divided against itself. For many citizens to conduct an election in
that context will be a bogus exercise. It is easy to think of countries
which fit that description, and a complete list of names would

unfortunately be long. Let us never be misled into thinking that the formal adoption of a constitutional text or putting into motion the machinery of an election is enough, by itself, to guarantee to the mass of citizens their equality and their freedom. Genuine political democracy cannot exist unless it is combined with economic and social democracy, and the latter are the harder to achieve because social and economic institutions are often the more resistant to change. Western democracy has accomplished wonders in the spheres of political, civil, and juridical rights. But as long as poverty and other forms of social and economic discrimination continue, there is still a long way to go before democracy becomes authentic.

The Record of Communism

That leads to an evaluation of the other major political innovation of this century: namely, communism. Its evolution is a classic case of the general tendency, which I stated earlier, for institutions to corrupt the ideals that create them. Let us consider communism therefore, as we did with democracy, from the ethical standpoint.

The *Communist Manifesto,* although caustic in phrasing and intentionally polemical in tone, had an electrifying effect because its central theme was a passionate plea for social justice. It justified revolutionary change by depicting the current possessors of wealth as immoral. Understandably, such a message was balm to the ears of the downtrodden, the poor, "the wretched of the earth." By the same token, it was a declaration of war—the *Klassenkampf,* as Marx named it—against the rich and powerful, who correctly discerned in his doctrines a deadly threat to their interests. When the monarchies of central and eastern Europe collapsed in 1917-1918, the Russian Communist party grabbed the first opportunity to seize power. With Lenin for its midwife, the Union of Soviet Socialist Republics was born.

A theory is always modified in practice by its social circumstances. So it was with Marxism. Marx had predicted that the inevitable revolution, which would end the class struggle once and for all, would be the climax to the later stages of industrial development and would be triggered by its internal contradictions. Instead of that, Lenin—the master strategist in whom the tactician triumphed over the theoretician—found himself adapting the Marxist formulae to a mainly rural society at an early stage of industrialization. His crucial decision was to concentrate all power in the Communist party and to restrict its membership to a disciplined band of dedicated revolutionaries, leading the masses for their own good. The inner logic of that fateful choice was carried to its ultimate conclusion by Stalin, who imposed his personal despotism on the party itself and dominated his country with a tyrannical concentration of power matched in modern times only by Adolf Hitler. For two whole generations the imprint stamped on the Russian Revolution by Lenin and Stalin together determined its subsequent evolution. What is more, it was exported to the other areas where Communist parties established their dominance after World War II.

The ethics of communism, as this evolved in practice, exhibited a paradox and a contradiction, which suggest an instructive contrast with the Western democratic experience. For communism was weak in those spheres where democracy is strong, but showed its strength where democracy is sometimes weak. The positive achievements of communism can be thus summarized. It opened the doors of opportunity for millions to whom they had been closed, principally by battling with illiteracy and expanding the facilities for education up to the university level. At the same time, it ensured to everybody the essential minima of social security, including employment and medical care. In comparison therefore with their condition under previous regimes, the quality of life improved for large segments of the population. But here is the attendant paradox. The political system that accomplished such gains remained unqualifiedly authoritarian. Intellectual freedom, experimentation in the arts, political dissent, were nowhere tolerated. The party "line"—whatever that happened to be at the moment—had to prevail. In all matters of fundamental doctrine, conformity was required. Deviants were suppressed with varying degrees of cruelty—from Stalin's "gulag" to Brezhnev's psychiatric hospitals; from Mao's "Cultural Revolution" to Deng's tanks in Tian-an-menh Square.

In this the reader of the literature of czarism or of the Ming or Ching dynasties will note some echoes of similarity. All authoritarian systems share much in common—principally in the relation of ruler to subject—and in this respect the commissars were brothers under the skin to the czars and to the "Sons of Heaven." What Dostoevski has the Grand Inquisitor say to Jesus in *The Brothers Karamazov* is the fundamental reasoning of every autocrat justifying his authority and is curiously akin to the rationale of the leaders of the Communist party in their relation to those whom they governed. The mass of human beings are considered childlike, as being far too weak to bear the burden of deciding for themselves. Security they desire more ardently than freedom. Thus willingly do they lay their freedom at the feet of any who assures them their daily bread and willingly they obey his orders. Yes, we shall give you your bread, said the party; but in return, you must obey us.[24]

Whatever its moral or intellectual content, the popular test of any doctrine is necessarily the pragmatic one: How does it work in practice? On this point, the events of 1989-90 lead to some definite conclusions. Communism, as it was tried, was a system that failed. It neither fulfilled the hopes that it aroused nor lived up to its own ideals. The evidence for that verdict is clear in the political sequence that unfolded in 1989 and 1990. During those years across eastern Europe and in the Soviet Union itself, the power of the Communist parties just withered away. When elections were held in which a plurality of parties presented themselves to the voters, the Communists were voted out of office almost everywhere and governments with a non-Communist majority were installed in their place. One by one, what had been the constituent Republics of the Soviet Union proclaimed their independence of Moscow and fell to quarreling over the distribution of its assets. Mikhail Gorbachev, who had unleashed the forces of change, was unable to control their direction. He was replaced by Boris Yeltsin, who then banned the Communist party. Thus was Moscow the scene of a second revolution within one century.

Why did communism come to this sorry dénouement? The reasons are partly political, partly organizational. To state the point succinctly: Communism failed because the Communist party hijacked the revolution. The fundamental flaw in the regime was the authoritarian character of the party and its dictatorial grip on society. The ideological requirement of conformity to the party "line," with the accompanying prohibitions on dissent and diversity, prevented the public expression of original thought. The planned economy was directed from the center in such excessive detail as to inhibit local initiative and individual experiment. What is more, in such sectors as agricultural production and the marketing of consumer goods, state ownership proved less successful than the inducement of personal profit for the individual entrepreneur. The Communist ethic, laudable as it was in guaranteeing economic security and raising the living standards of the lowest, failed in its efforts to stimulate productivity by means of social incentives. Patently, its psychological stimuli were inadequate.

China's experience under the Communist dynasty reinforces these conclusions. Maoism was both populist and egalitarian, so that the social order which it introduced was one of equals in poverty. After Mao's death, Deng sought to increase production by disbanding the rural communes and offering incentives to individuals, a policy that appealed strongly to the peasants and had the effect of speedily raising agricultural output. In industry and the urban areas, however, the same degree of innovation was not permitted except in some designated experimental regions along the coast. Political freedom, moreover, was not to be tolerated. When demands were increasingly voiced for the freer expression of diverse opinions and for a plurality of political structures, the reigning hierarchy of octogenarians—survivors of the Long March of the 1920s—discerned a threat to their power and privileges. In June 1989 Deng unleashed the army's tanks in the center of Beijing, literally crushing the youthful protestors in Tian-an-menh Square by an act of butchery that shocked the world.

"Power," Mao had declared, "grows out of the barrel of a gun." "How many divisions," asked Stalin, "has the Pope?" The Communist regimes, as was demonstrated time and time again, were ultimately based on their tanks and the secret police. The ethics of Marx succumbed to the power of the party. Such was how the "class struggle" evolved. The continuation of the authoritarian pattern of previous imperial dynasties, both Russian and Chinese, is depressingly obvious. What would Confucius be saying nowadays? Or Tolstoy?

Governing for Good or Evil

The remainder of the world's governments, that is, those that are neither democratic nor communist, are scattered across the spectrum of traditional types, with the proviso that many are so corrupt and chaotic as to preclude a rational classification. Augustine's pointed remark, that the state is a great robber band if it be lacking in justice, could be amply illustrated from contemporary cases. A large number of present-day regimes are controlled by military men who generally rule as despots and whose ethical standards seldom bear close inspection.[25] These crop up continually in Latin America, where the army *caudillo* has been an endemic disease, across the length of Asia, and in most parts of Africa. In western Europe, brutal soldiers tyrannized over Spain and Greece as late as the 1960s; and in eastern Europe in the 1980s the Communist party of Poland abdicated in favor of General Jaruzelski—the first step in that country's eventual transition to a non-Communist regime. In many a land, Rousseau's "general will" has degenerated into the will of a general. As we approach the end of the millennium, much of humanity is still ruled by regimes that abuse their power for the benefit of a few.

The potential of governments for either good or evil has seldom been illustrated in starker contrast than by the events of this century. A pair of individuals, and the fates of the two countries in which they attained the pinnacle of power, provide examples more dramatic than fiction could ever have invented. I am thinking of Franklin Delano Roosevelt and Adolf Hitler. Both came to power early in 1933—Hitler in January, Roosevelt in March; both died within two weeks of each other in April 1945. Both began governing in the depths of the most severe economic depression of modern times, and their lives were terminated shortly before the end of hostilities in the world war that Hitler's ambitions had launched. There the similarities end.

Roosevelt's domestic achievement was the social and economic reconstruction of a country that had lost its self-confidence when the economy collapsed. He restored confidence in the banks and regulated the stock market; stimulated employment by massive infusions of federal spending; encouraged leaders of industry and labor to work more cooperatively, while ensuring unions their right to bargain collectively; guaranteed the farmers an adequate income through subsidies and limits on production; fostered the conservation of the physical environment; and instituted a national system of social security. Meanwhile, he gave all possible encouragement to blacks, as well as to Catholics and Jews, to become more fully integrated within the mainstream of American life. Shortly before his death, he worked to found the United Nations. These liberal accomplishments had lasting effects. Indeed, they formed the context within which domestic politics was conducted in the United States for at least a generation after Roosevelt's death.

Contemporaneously in the heart of the European continent, Adolf Hitler proceeded with the plans that he had outlined earlier—in *Mein Kampf*—a book that many, when it first appeared, dismissed as the ravings of a madman. That he was mad is beyond doubt. For is one to characterize as sane a person who deliberately aimed at the military subjugation of Europe and Russia, in the course of which he started a world war and ordered the systematic extermination of more than 8 million captive Jews? That such an individual could seize complete control of the government of a major state and exercise a total domination over its people is a terrifying fact. Equally terrifying is the fact that he came so close to ultimate success. Hitler was a man obsessed with hatreds—hatreds for liberals, democrats, communists, Jews, Slavs, and colored peoples. No sooner was he in power than he mobilized the formidable talents and energies of the German people to preparing his war of aggression. After five years of feverish rearmament (1933-38), he was ready—and then he struck. For the first three years, everything went his way. After that, he became bogged down in Russia's heartland; and once the Japanese attack on Pearl Harbor had brought the United States into the war, the tide began to turn. Finally in 1945, in a bunker underneath the ruins of a Berlin about to be occupied by the Red Army, he ordered an aide to shoot him and burn his body. It was the *Götterdämmerung* of a monster.

The need of human society for government presents a dilemma that has never been wholly resolved, and probably never will be. We need the common services that only an organized institution such as the state can provide, and performance of these services requires power to carry them out. But with power comes the risk of abuse, and therewith the danger that the servant becomes the master. Some sensitive souls have so reacted to the cruelties that governments perpetrate in the furtherance of their power that they would sweep them away and rely on humanity's natural instincts, which they believe good, to manifest themselves through voluntary, spontaneous, cooperation. Such in the nineteenth century were the ideals of both an American, Henry David Thoreau, and a Russian, Leo Tolstoy—neither of whom would have been attracted to the spectacles of modern Washington or Moscow. But anarchism, though ethically enlightened because it eschews coercion, could not be made to function in large groups with complicated processes and interrelations. We are compelled therefore to live with government, trusting that we can maximize its benefits and construct effective safeguards against its abuses. For that, the least objectionable system yet devised is democracy because its operating values and institutions contain limitations on the arbitrary exercise of power. In those countries whose regime is not democratic, the system provides no protection; and if the person holding the reins happens to be a madman, a moron, or a militarist, as has frequently happened in this century, the techniques now available to any ruler make tyranny the more terrible.

The literature that has been written in various civilizations concerning the good and evil done by states and their functionaries extends for three millennia. Through it, two main themes emerge: those of the idealists and the realists. The former outline their hopes for society as it could be and of government as it should be. This note is struck continually down the ages. It was sounded by those classical Greeks who saw the polis, if well ordered, as the supreme agent for social and personal betterment. Aristotle encapsulated that vision in his terse observation: "The polis comes into being for the sake of life, then continues in existence for the sake of the good life."[26] The same litany is heard from Confucius, as he pleads for men of virtue, imbued with the right principles, to occupy the seats of power. Its optimism underlay the revolutions that ushered in the modern world and have marked the course of the current century.

The other main theme has been based on actuality (the "real world," so called) and has generalized therefrom. Or rather, it has extrapolated from those traits and happenings that confirm its pessimistic image of human nature. A connecting thread unites the cynical arguments of the Athenian envoy to the islanders of Melos with those of Thrasymachus in Plato's *Republic,* the maxims of the *Arthashastra* with the assumptions of the Chinese Legalists, the mordant generalizations of Machiavelli with the gnawing fears of Hobbes, along with all the power-obsessed analysts of contemporary political science. Those who assume that most human beings are basically selfish and bad will conclude that only the fear of a superior force can prevent us from doing evil. Thus envisioned, the state necessarily acts as policeman or "big brother." In this formulation there is nothing ethical. The state deploys its naked power because, if it does not, unscrupulous private persons will deploy theirs.

All governments are founded, in varying degrees, on a belief in one or another of these opposite images. Most civilizations have wrestled within themselves over which seemed the more appropriate; and as the philosophies have been opposed, so have the practices. No civilization is without its examples of the enlightened ruler and the despot, of Ashoka and Genghis, of Roosevelt and Hitler; but in no civilization has either of these ever been the norm. Indeed, most of the regimes known to history have acted on a mixed and muddy morality.

I am emphasizing the moral significance of the political system because in practice, if not in principle, which of a civilization's values will emerge into prominence depends to a considerable degree on the character of its governments. As instances of ethical betterment in which government has played a definitive role, consider the Scandinavian experience. Two centuries ago, both Sweden and Denmark were countries that had receded from earlier heights of military and political strength, and had settled into a placid stagnation under a dominant ruling class and a rigid Lutheran church. Judged ethically, the great flaw in their societies was the gulf separating elite from mass—a gulf that manifested itself not only in spheres of education and culture but in the distribution of wealth and levels of material comfort. How different is the spectacle of Danes and Swedes today! For these are now among the world's prime exemplars of social justice. They have created the welfare state, combining the politics of self-government with social egalitarianism in an economic mix of public and private enterprise. Both countries have eradicated poverty, hunger, and illiteracy. In both a culture has now matured that is secular and rationalist, humanistic and humane; and in both the democratic state has been the prime mover.

Government, which has the capacity to be beneficent, can also, by abuse of its power, be diabolical. When it is so, civilization degenerates swiftly into barbarism, of which there are recent tragic examples. Ugandans, according to the London *Times,* were "once noted for their charm and civility."[27] But in the 1970s under the despotism of Idi Amin, that country became a concentration camp, where butcheries and atrocities were the fate of its terrorized peoples. A transformation similarly horrendous befell Cambodia after the collapse of the French Empire in Indochina. The victory of Pol Pot and the Khmer Rouge brought the country under the control of a peculiarly primitive brand of communism, whose ruling ideas were a complex of hatreds. Primarily, they hated the West and all its works—not only its governmental apparatus but its schools and hospitals and urban life. Phnom Penh, the capital, became a ghost city. Hundreds of thousands of men, women, and children of all ages were forced to evacuate their homes and fend for themselves in the countryside, where large numbers died from hunger, exposure, and disease. I quote the words of a daughter of a Cambodian diplomat who survived these events within the walls of a foreign embassy:

> The war of 1970 and the subsequent fall of Cambodia to Communism five years later deprived us of everything—a home, a people, a civilization,

except for the will to survive and achieve. As a result of what happened in my life, my interest in politics becomes magnified mainly because I never cease to try to find an acceptable explanation for the events that almost eradicated Cambodia from the face of the map. I think the greatest tragedy lies not only in the long years of wartime plight for the Cambodian people which took on a distinctly macabre trait under Pol Pot, but in the fact that no one really has the answer as to how such a country, such a civilization, could digress from being once a vast empire to that of a twentieth-century charnel house.[28]

If one ventures an answer to so poignant a question, must it not be that such deeds were the deliberate actions of a government shaped by the perverted values of the men who controlled it? What happens at the political level is central to how a civilization evolves, because not only are governments animated by consciously formulated value goals, but the means at their disposal can be so very effective—deadly effective in the case just described.

The Warfare State

The state, which in so many ways is the giver of life, is also its destroyer. The self-same institution that can provide prenatal care and maternity hospitals may conscript the fully grown adult into its armed forces and dispatch him or her to war. War has been coeval with civilization, and war is waged by governments or by those who seek their overthrow. We like to imagine ourselves as more civilized than our predecessors. They, we think, were sunk in bigotry, in superstition, in irrational prejudices, from which we believe that we are exempt. If that be so, how can we explain not only the number of wars that have been fought in this century on every continent but their intensity, their long duration, and the slaughter they brought in their train? Whatever else we may be remembered for in the future, the generation that came to adulthood in the 1940s, 1950s, and 1960s has this unique accomplishment emblazoned on our record. It was we who first invented and used an atomic bomb on two populated cities; we then went on to fill our military arsenals with thousands of nuclear warheads. The labors of civilization in all past centuries attained their technological climax in a weapon that could bring civilization itself to an end. Ever since August 1945, humanity has lived with the dread of that knowledge. Need we be surprised that contemporary civilization contains in its midst so many disturbed persons of all ages whose actions become self-destructive or antisocial?

Let us review the record of warfare in the twentieth century. It will tell us something about what the human species has done to itself as a sequel to the Age of Progress, in particular about our values and our ethics.

The two major conflicts of the current century—the second erupting barely two short decades after the first had ended and involving the same belligerents—are the first to be called "world wars," a name they received because no continent or ocean was spared the hostilities. The imperial ambitions of the stronger nation-states, combining their political power with the technological instruments of twentieth-century science, had unified the planet into a single theater for military operations. Commensurate in scale was the destruction that resulted. "The cost of armament," wrote Emil Ludwig, "during the years from 1910 to 1914 amounted to 1.8 billions of dollars for Austria and Germany together and 2.4 billions for France and Russia. The total was more than four billion. Yet these were small sums compared with those piled up by the war. On land and sea or in the air, 12,990,570 soldiers were killed in the World War. The War cost the combined combatants . . . half their total national wealth."[29] More terrible still was the destruction caused by World War II. Because Japan's aggression against China started in 1931, this conflict lasted much longer; and the losses in Asia, added to those in Europe, brought the numbers of military personnel killed or missing to a total more than 15 million. But this figure was tragically augmented by the civilian dead. Their number in the Second World War vastly exceeded that in the earlier war because of the concentrated bombing from the air of heavily populated cities, a practice in which both sides engaged. The worst losses of all were sustained by the Soviet Union, which gave up more than 20 million lives (military and civilian) in the effort to resist the Nazi onslaught. The United States spent some $350 billion between 1939 and 1945 in arming its own forces and helping its friends and allies—and the dollar of that time was not the shrunken measure that it has since become. Great Britain, which entered the second war still leading the largest empire the world had ever known, emerged a "victor" with its empire shattered and was transformed from a great creditor nation into a debtor, a position that it had not known since the reign of the first Queen Elizabeth. Moreover, in terms of military technology, the ending of both wars contained ominous portents for the future. In the closing years of the first war, the tank and the airplane were introduced into combat. Both were put to deadly use two decades later. And in the final month of the second war, atomic bombs were unleashed on Hiroshima and Nagasaki. The decline since 1945 of what had been a dynamic and innovative civilization in western Europe is the direct result of the appalling self-destruction that the misguided leaders of its governments brought upon their unfortunate peoples. For four decades that region which for four centuries had reshaped the globe became the arena for decisive events initiated from outside— from the United States, the Soviet Union, or Japan. The one signifi- cant exception to that general indictment is the invention of the European Community—a truly creative idea—whose implications will be discussed in the next chapter.[30] Not until 1989 did the Europe- ans show signs of regaining the initiative—a fact made possible by the ending of the "cold war" between the United States and the Soviet Union.

The Insanity of the Arms Race

One would like to think that, after such a bloodletting as oc- curred in the first half of this century, the second half would have been pacific. Such, however, has not been the case. True, we have thus far avoided the eruption of World War III—which means that we are still here. But before congratulating ourselves on the fact that we have not yet committed collective suicide or terminated civilization on this planet, consider what we have been doing to ourselves during the second half of this century and contrast this with what we could have done.

In the sphere of war and peace, the record since 1945 should fill us with shame, not pride. Let us not forget these facts. After the defeat of Germany and Japan, the victorious coalition split into two hostile groups, the western led by the United States and the eastern by the Soviet Union. The governments of the two superpowers had an adversary relationship, their competition for hegemony being further expressed in the ideological opposition between the eco- nomic doctrines of capitalism and communism, and the political concepts of pluralist democracy and the autocratic monopoly of a single party. The result was an arms race that differed from any of the past in that the stakes were raised to a wholly new level of unacceptable risk. For decade after decade, both Washington and Moscow sought to outdo each other, periodically inventing new bombs of ever greater destructiveness along with ever more efficient means of delivering them to their targets. In August 1945, when Japan surrendered, only two atomic bombs existed in the world, both in the possession of the United States. Four decades later, there were more than 50,000 nuclear warheads, of which some two-fifths were of the so-called strategic kind, that is, those that could be dispatched from one continent to another with the capacity of exterminating millions in a matter of minutes. Although the great majority of nuclear weapons belong to the United States and four republics of the former Soviet Union, three other governments—China, France, and Great Britain—possess stocks of their own, and several other regimes have developed the components from which bombs could be speedily assembled. As soon as one state acquires such a weapon, any potential victim feels impelled to do the same.

A world in which mass extermination is a realistic possibility is a dangerous and unstable place. *Insanity* is the only word to characterize the mentality of leaders of governments who could knowingly and deliberately engineer the means to make such a result possible. Sane persons, acting rationally, do not seriously contemplate and plan for mass extermination as a viable policy. What has happened to human civilization? What perversion has corrupted our ethics? Why are we driving ourselves collectively mad?

Although the nuclear holocaust has not thus far occurred, innumerable wars of limited scale have been fought since 1945 with conventional weapons, which are nowadays far more destructive than their predecessors. The character of those wars has varied. Some were direct conflicts between states in the traditional manner, such as the hostilities between Iraq and Iran or between Britain and Argentina. Some have been civil wars, for instance, the ill-fated attempt of Biafra to secede from Nigeria. A great many have been conducted by political movements seeking more autonomy or outright independence, such as the campaign of the Basque nationalists against the Spanish government or that of the Palestine Liberation Organization against Israel. In these cases there is often a blurring of the dividing line between regular warfare (in the sense of combat between organized units of uniformed personnel) and terrorism (including indiscriminate attacks on innocent civilians by bands of conspirators operating in disguise).

When all the conflicts of the various types are totaled together, their sum is horrendous. For obvious reasons, the figures cited must be taken as estimates, not as exact numbers—as, for instance, when the hostilities consist of guerrilla action where reliable records are lacking. But the overall picture is not in doubt. Brian Urquhart, who served as undersecretary general of the United Nations in charge of peacekeeping, stated in 1986 that, from the birth of the United Nations in 1945 until 1979, there had been 135 regional conflicts involving 80 countries and resulting in 25 million casualties. Since 1979, he added, 15 more conflicts had occurred.[31] A report of the United Nations in 1985 affirmed that from 1945 to 1983 between 16 and 20 million had been killed in 150 armed conflicts.[32] In June 1988, James Reston wrote in *The New York Times* that 25 wars were still going on;[33] and in 1991 a war was waged against Iraq by an international coalition with the United States contributing the bulk of the armed forces. The *casus belli* in this instance was Iraq's seizure of Kuwait in August 1990 and its control over the supply of oil from that area. Self-evidently, the political system that humanity has constructed for itself—that of the so-called nation-state—is no guarantor of peace. Quite the contrary: Its divisions are an invitation to conflict.

This is further borne out by the conclusions that emerge from studying the expenditures of governments. When you see where it is that governments spend the money they collect, you learn their priorities. The facts are revealing; their implications, staggering. Consider these data: In 1988 the world was spending approximately $900 billion on military purposes, which works out at over $100 million an hour, or $1¾ million every single minute.[34] By contrast, the United Nations, the agency whose prime responsibility is peacekeeping, operated in that same year on a budget of $1 billion. This means that what the world was spending in 12 months for peace it spent in 10 hours for war. Given that militarization is the enemy of civilization, that comparison offers a measure, in financial terms, of how far we have advanced in civilization to this point.

Of the total amount that the world then devoted to military purposes, approximately three-fifths was the outlay of two governments, those of the United States and the Soviet Union. As a consequence of this tragically futile arms race, both economies, the U.S. and the Russian, slipped back in the international competition, and the consuming public suffered in both countries. For the peoples of the Third World, the situation is even worse, as the percentage of their pitifully small gross national product that goes to the military is often appallingly high. The annual report of UNICEF stated in December 1989 that "Third World governments are allocating half their total spending to armaments and debt servicing, at a cost of nearly $1 billion or $400 for every family." At the same time, the report emphasized, 40,000 children were dying every day for lack of basic medical care. The latter could have been provided at a cost of $2½ billion. That sum, as the executive director of the U.N.'s Children's Fund pointed out, "is a great deal of money. It is as much as the Soviet Union has been spending on vodka, as much as U.S. companies have been spending on advertising cigarettes, or 10 percent of the European Community's annual subsidy to its farmers."[35] Indira Gandhi encapsulated the folly of these misdirected priorities in a graphic statement. For the price of a single intercontinental missile, she stated, it would be possible "to plant 200 million trees, irrigate one million hectares, feed 50 million malnourished children in developing countries, buy a million tons of fertilizer, erect a million small biogas plants, build 65,000 health-care centers or 340,000 primary schools."[36]

If further evidence were needed to substantiate this point, it is vividly supplied by three articles side by side on the front page of *The New York Times* of February 7, 1991. One article described the damage inflicted on Iraq after 50,000 bombing missions by American warplanes. The adjacent article reported the remark of the secretary of state, Mr. James Baker, that international aid would be needed to rebuild Iraq when the war was over. The third article referred to proposals in the budget just submitted to the Congress by President Bush. Its intention was to combat infant mortality in ten cities. The money for this, $58,000,000, was to be taken from programs to finance community health centers and services for the health of mothers and children. In other words, first we spend billions on destroying another country's military installations and public infrastructure. Having done that, we would contribute more billions to repairing the damage. In the meantime, the needs of America's own poor are being neglected. More infants cannot be saved except at the expense of mothers and children. For comparison, the money that would be taken from the services for community health and for maternal and pediatric care amounted to only one-half of the price of an F117A fighter plane ($112 million).

Such were the values of our civilization in the year 1991. I cannot forbear from quoting the Latin saying: "Those whom the gods wish to destroy, they first drive mad."

Needed: The Priorities of Peace

Such a comparison necessitates the question: When will civilization begin changing its priorities? When will we reassert the fundamental needs of human ethics? Fortunately, there are some positive signs pointing nowadays in a more hopeful direction. As always in human affairs, when anything develops to an excessive degree, a reaction sets in. One may observe this happening in the mounting criticisms of military expenditures and in the revulsion evoked by the barbarities of war and terrorism. In numerous countries, movements have proliferated among ordinary private citizens animated by the stirrings of conscience and alarm. There is, in point of fact, a sizable public opinion that seeks to reverse the growth of military expenditures, to ban nuclear weapons, and to limit hostilities, or prevent them from erupting, wherever possible. The "Peace movement," as it is loosely described, is a fact of contemporary political life with which governments have had to reckon, and its influence extends beyond and across the national boundaries, which are themselves so often a source of the trouble. It can be felt and heard in places as far apart on the globe as India, Scandinavia, and the democracies of the South Pacific. Wherever expressed, it is a voice of decency, of rationality, and of universal humanity. Already it has had practical consequences in ways that are seldom dramatic and therefore do not arouse the attention of the sensation-oriented programmers of the television tube. The discreet and patient labors of Amnesty International have secured the release of numerous political prisoners, the victims of torture by brutal regimes. The quiet diplomacy of the United Nations has helped to bring an end to wars in Africa and the Middle East. Millions of individual donors have contributed to alleviating conditions of famine, as in Ethiopia, or have brought aid to regions that suffered natural disasters, as in Bangladesh or Armenia. Something has been manifesting itself that one may properly call the conscience of humanity, and this gives us genuine and reasonable grounds for hope. At the end of the 1980s, the governments of Washington and Moscow, after 40 years of mutual dislike and distrust, began to view one another in a less acrimonious light. The world situation at the time when I write remains perilous, but there are signs of healing.

The discussion in this chapter and the preceding one has been complex, because the contemporary scene exhibits so contradictory a character. Necessarily the topics under discussion had to be treated in the manner that proceeds from "on the one hand" to "on the other hand." This is frustrating if one seeks a clear-cut picture with firm outlines. But that would have distorted the delineation of a century whose data are so immense and where conflicting tendencies occur simultaneously. There is no one truth about our times; there are many truths. This is a multifaceted age. So too must be its analysis. Even when nine decades have been completed, it is impossible yet to say whether or not on balance the good outweighs the evil. The one certainty is that the choice between collective improvement and collective catastrophe remains open. The human species can still move either way. In that light the concluding chapter will estimate our prospects for the future.

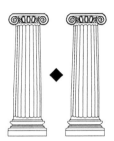

. . . a period [China's Mongol dynasty] when men, uncertain of the present, looked both backward and forward.

Michael Sullivan

10

Into a New Millennium

*W*hither humanity? Whither civilization? This review of past patterns and continuing contradictions leads to the inevitable inquiry: What do they tell us about the future? Can valid parallels be drawn between the human situation at this time and at any earlier period? If so, do these suggest what further development we might anticipate? Do they perhaps indicate what we could plan to do or avoid? And can past experience offer some guidance in our handling of those contemporary problems that have no precedent—our deadly nuclear stockpiles and our deadly pollution?

These questions acquire added significance at this moment in history, which in more than one sense marks a turning point in human affairs. In less than a decade from when I write this, we shall inaugurate the beginning not only of a new century but of a new millennium. Although that is not meaningful in itself—for such a calendar event is an arbitrary bench mark in the continuous flow of time—its arrival will nevertheless raise new hopes and expectations that something out of the ordinary could be about to happen, thereby endowing the occasion with heightened significance. The opening of another millennium may inspire a mood of acceptance for out-of-the-ordinary change, as the word *millennary* signifies. Doubtless, the advent of the year 2000 will be heralded both by the visionary prophets of a utopia about to be realized and by doom-saying pessimists, predicting that a "Day of Judgment" is at hand—exactly as their forebears did when the current millennium dawned. Such eccentrics we may leave to their fantasies. Our problem is to estimate what developments are the more probable among the numerous possibilities that lie between the not-to-be-attained extremes.

269

Shifts in World Politics

In addition to the change of a date on the calendar, however, a historic turn is now taking place that has been observable throughout this century and that will bear fruit in the century ahead. Plainly, we are at the end of the cycle that commenced five centuries ago when the peoples along the Atlantic coast of Europe spread around the world and transformed it under their dominance. The force generated by their radical innovations in science, technology, government, economics, and social values came to a self-destructive climax in this century's world wars. Spengler was correct, although for the wrong reasons, in discerning early in this century that the decline of the West had begun. Within 50 years of his writing, the United States, to which the hegemony of the West had passed from a burned-out Europe, was already experiencing the challenge to its economic supremacy from the harder-working, and highly efficient, Japanese. If that trend should continue, there would be a reenactment of the relations between East and West that had existed until the first half of the fifteenth century when an Asian civilization, that of China, not only stood in the forefront technologically but was dispatching huge armadas to the Indian Ocean and the Arabian Sea before the Portuguese or Dutch were ready to venture so far.

This geopolitical shift in the relative influence that civilizations, or their leading peoples, are able to exert on one another invites our speculation. What is it that accounts for the relative decline of the West and the contemporary prominence of Japan? What does this shift portend for the future of civilization in general? For answers to such questions, it is necessary to survey the major civilizations and note the trends within each as we near the end of this millennium. Our century is characterized by the novel fact that every civilization is in regular contact with most of the others. Nowadays therefore all must be comprehended as segments of a global unity, and not as if any existed independently.

The West and the Rest

Observing the relations between the several branches of humanity during this century, two salient facts stand out: the continuing impact of the Western civilization on the rest, and the latter's varied reactions. Even though the West has passed the peak of its supremacy, here is still the creative source for many of the initiatives that foreshadow the future. How the other civilizations develop results largely from the manner in which they absorb Western influence, or adapt to it, or modify it, or reject it. In this regard, their success or failure depends very much on the character of the value systems that receive the imports and on the internal balance of social forces that shapes their response. The Japanese are highly successful in the economic sphere, and their achievements have been emulated in Hong Kong and Taiwan, in South Korea and Singapore. But rapid economic growth always sets in motion a train of social readjustments where good and bad are intermingled. Keeping this in mind, let us review the major civilizations and look for any clues to indicate what the future may hold in store.

My first point is that the relation in this century between the Western civilization and the non-Western has been ambivalent. The latter simultaneously admire and resent us; they both imitate and repudiate what we have to offer. Or to speak more exactly, there are certain features of Western society that they eagerly welcome and willingly incorporate with their own. Other aspects of our culture, however, evoke their fears or even revulsion. As a consequence, many of the issues emerging in their political and social development revolve around the question of what to admit from abroad and on what terms.

What the West has exported to the world has been manifold in kind, and the reception has varied accordingly. Virtually everywhere, the most enthusiastic welcome is accorded to our technology because its practical uses are so immediate and obvious. The science, however, from which the technology derives, although generally well received, encounters in some quarters the opposition of an ideology, a theology, or a value system that perceives it as a threat and fears the challenge of adapting to the new thinking. The scientific method, after all, is rooted in rationalism and in the assumption of complete freedom for the inquiring intellect; and that is anathema both to religious dogmatists and to authoritarian social hierarchies, which object to anyone questioning their certitudes or doubting what they believe on faith.

When the innovations that flow from one civilization to another lie in the social domain, intense controversy is likely to be generated. Some individuals and groups discern opportunities to take the lead in fostering change and to profit handsomely therefrom. Those, however, whose influence and status are identified with the traditional order resist the novelties and attack them because they are foreign. Witness the reception accorded by different cultures to the industrial economy and its concomitants.

But the most controversial aspect of this whole process of inter-action among civilizations is the spread of ideas and the introduc-tion from outside of values that contrast sharply with what had hitherto prevailed. Whatever form these take—whether aesthetic tastes, or philosophical concepts, or political beliefs, or religious doctrines, or ethical principles—they constitute a direct threat to the central core around which a civilization is constituted. Because its values define a civilization and imbue it with meaning, when these are challenged and replaced, the character of the civilization will necessarily alter. It is on this terrain therefore that the tradi-tionalists conduct their most determined struggle for survival.

This general summary of the tensions and ambivalence in the relations between the Western civilization and the non-Western may offer some clues to the latter's future. What does their record in this century presage for the next?

What Future for India?

I begin with India, always a nightmare if one craves clarity and abhors confusion. As the Hindu god Shiva is depicted with numer-ous arms (to represent his supposedly manifold powers and attrib-utes), so might contemporary India be symbolized as a multi-headed body with many faces. One face displays the younger features of our day and age. This is the India of Bombay and Bangalore; of heavy industry and sophisticated finance; of scien-tific expertise and high technology; of television, movies, comput-ers, and nuclear energy; of urbanized millions and a new science-based agriculture resulting in the "green revolution." But next to it is the wrinkled, aged, face of immemorial India, surviving in a thousand villages. These are the people segregated into their castes and *jati*; observing the rituals of Vishnu, Shiva, Ganesh, and Kali; keeping their distance from Untouchables; selling their daughters into marriage; and ready on an instant's provocation to commit mayhem against Muslim or Sikh. We witness an India whose face for centuries lay under the heel of conquerors in its own land; but we see also the proud face that independent India has more re-cently displayed in the councils of the world. There is the face of affluent India, of its prosperous merchants and industrialists, culmi-nating at the extreme in the wealth of those latter-day Maharajahs and

Nabobs—the Birlas, the Tatas, and their ilk. But one is constantly reminded of that other face—emaciated, ravaged by disease, doomed to beg and sleep and die amid the neglect and degradation of the city streets. Which of these, one asks, will be the more prominent in the twenty-first century?

There are certain aspects of Indian life today that would justify a hopeful prediction. The famines from which so many used to die appear now to be of the past. Thanks to the agricultural revolution, India is able to feed itself. The country's technological prowess is evident in great feats of engineering, which result, for example, in the generation of energy or the storage and distribution of water. India has built on the foundations of the educational system that the British installed—a system of high quality in their day but inadequate in the numbers it served—and has been steadily reducing the high rate of illiteracy. And most remarkable of all, considering the subcontinent's size and diversity, the principles and procedures of democracy with which the republic was launched have on the whole been maintained—notwithstanding a temporary regression to autocracy under the personal rule of Indira Gandhi.

Those are some of the encouraging signs. Others, however, point in the opposite direction. In particular, three persistently negative factors form obstacles to a major breakthrough. In the first place, the cohesiveness of India is by no means assured, nor in consequence is its internal stability. The central government had to cope in the 1980s with a rebellion of Sikhs in the Punjab demanding their independence. The majority of the Kashmiris, if they could vote in a referendum, would almost certainly prefer to be united with their coreligionists in Pakistan. Likewise in the northeast, the tribes along the border are by no means loyal to Delhi, a troublesome strategic fact in view of their proximity to China. Correspondingly in the south, the Tamils have a culture and a language that differ from those of the north, and their kinship with their fellow Tamils in Sri Lanka places them frequently in opposition to central policies. After four decades of independence, the Republic of India looks more like a leaky sieve than a solid vessel.

This weakness is compounded by the decline in the quality and efficiency of governmental services. British imperial rule, while it lasted, was alien, elitist, and authoritarian. But where it acted, it was honest and incorruptible. Independent India has rightly extended the functions of government to foster needed social reforms (in education, for example, and in removing the stigma of untouchability). But at the same time the standards of administration have deteriorated. Neither in the various ministries of Delhi, nor in the police, nor even in the courts, are the same probity and efficiency manifested as of yore. Indians generally do not trust their officials—often with good reason; and because the country's development depends so heavily on governmental leadership, that does not augur well for the future.

This brings me to the third cause of concern: the rate of population growth. Since the British *raj* departed, India's population has more than doubled, already to a figure of more than 800 million. According to the projections, if current rates continue, at some time after 2020 not only will there be more than 1 billion Indians, but their total will eventually surpass the Chinese. In view of the appalling poverty of so many millions today and the wide gulf between rich and poor, such population trends are indeed tragic. Even though the middle class is expanding, and liberated women are less likely to bear so many children, what resources are available to raise the living standards of the poor, to transform the traditional village culture, and to make the distribution of wealth less glaringly unequal? Can one escape the conclusion that, at least in the first half of the twenty-first century, India will have to run very hard to stay in about the same place?

Such a conclusion is especially disappointing because India's awakening in the first half of this century was unique for these times in being led by a saintly man whose teaching was at the highest ethical level. Gandhi's philosophy was akin to those of Tolstoy and Thoreau, from both of whom he drew inspiration. He believed deeply in nonviolence, in living simply, in drastically curtailing one's material needs. His preference was for a preindustrial society. He behaved and spoke as a latter-day Don Quixote charging at the windmills of modernity. Against the political giants, his thrusts had deadly effect. The British police could block his movements and arrest him—for a while. Eventually, without ever firing a shot, he compelled them to surrender. Against Western machines, however, he had less success. Indian businessmen gladly supported him—and why not? If he drove out the British, they could replace the foreign imports with their own manufactures. For them, Gandhi's movement was a good bargain from whose victory they could only profit. When the imperial power was vanquished, the power of capital was not. That the merchants of Bombay had no patience for the values of Tolstoy or Thoreau need not surprise us. After all, it was not in India that the Buddha himself made his converts. Where today do Indians live by Gandhi's teachings, except in a few isolated *ashrams*?

Moreover, when finally the British had packed their bags and sailed for home, when India was once again ruled by Indians, the first leader of the independent regime was Jawaharlal Nehru, an intellectual, a socialist, and a statesman of enlightened ethical principles. Nehru believed sincerely in the literal meaning of a republic as the "public's possession" and in the duty of the state to serve the people by removing social injustices and by equalizing opportunities for all individuals. India was indeed changed by the combined achievements of Gandhi—the visionary, mystic, and saint—and of Nehru—the statesman, wielder of power, and socialist. Changed, yes; but not transformed. Many of the age-old inequities survive, overlaid nowadays by the tensions of industrialism. If two such individuals as Gandhi and Nehru could not together remake their civilization, who else could? The tragedy is that, after Nehru died, a dynasty of his family persisted as the inheritors of the *raj,* with first his daughter and then, after her assassination, her son occupying the imperial throne amid a rising tide of corruption. India came very close to an ethical rebirth, but it has let its moment slip away. The outlook for India in the coming century is not promising. Unless the subcontinent experiences an ethical revolution—for which a second Buddha or Gandhi would be needed—one may anticipate a chaos whose creaky machinery will be greased by opportunists and the corrupt.

Islam, in Search of Mecca

Turning from India to Islam, one encounters some striking similarities and no less striking differences. Although India is riven with diversities, the contrasts are even greater in an Islamic civilization extending from northwest Africa to southeast Asia. Here I shall focus on the core region consisting of the Arabs, Egypt, and Iran. How do Mohammed and modernity mix? What ethical synthesis is that mixture likely to produce?

Two events in particular have shaped the development of these peoples in the twentieth century. Like India, they became emancipated from the imperial rule of Turks, British, and French. Unlike India, however, several of these countries (notably Saudi Arabia, Iraq, and Iran) found themselves the possessors of vast subsurface lakes of oil whose extraction brought them not only wealth beyond all their prayers but also the technology, the engineering expertise, and the markets of the West. From riding a camel to a Cadillac, the change was revolutionary. What does that portend for the mentality of the rider?

When the twentieth century began, those who dwelled in the heartland of Islam were either the subjects of other peoples' empires or dependent thereon. The Arabs were governed by the Ottoman Turks; Egypt, by the British; and Persia, as Iran then was, maintained a precarious balance between the rival pressures of Britain and Russia. Turkey's defeat in the First World War had the effect of bringing Palestine and Iraq under British control, and Syria and Lebanon under that of the French, through the system of mandates supervised by the League of Nations. Not until the Second World War had ended did these countries become fully self-governing. Understandably, therefore, having for so long been ruled by outsiders, they have manifested their newly won independence with a nationalism that at best is ultrasensitive and at worst stridently self-asserting and aggressive. In the 1950s both Iran and Egypt gave expression to this—the former by expropriating what had been the Anglo-Persian Oil Company and the latter by seizing the Suez Canal.

Since then two further changes have influenced relations between Islam and the West. One is the establishment of the State of Israel as a result of the partition of Palestine by the United Nations. This injected a new political and cultural force into the center of the Arab core, one that is grounded in an ancient Semitic culture but that is also basically Western in its science and technology, its standard of living, and many of its social values. The second was the replacement of Britain and France by the United States as the leading power of the Western civilization. American influence, unlike that of the earlier Western empires, has not taken the form of direct governmental control. But it has been palpable nonetheless through economic aid, technological assistance, the supply of arms, and cultural penetration. Moreover, a special relationship has developed between the governments of Israel and the United States. Consequently, when Muslims have displayed hostility to the West in recent decades, it has frequently assumed the form of anti-Americanism. Two clear cases of this are the Iranian revolution, in which the Ayatollah Khomeini ousted the shah and branded the United States "the Great Satan," and the campaign by the Iraqi dictator, Saddam Hussein, who proclaimed "holy war" (*jihad*) on the United States and its allies in the conflict over Kuwait.

These latter events brought to a head in the most overt fashion some tendencies that had long been welling up within Islam. For centuries the region that forms the heartland of this civilization had been in a steady decline. The Arabs had never recovered from the Mongols' defeat of the Abbasids and their sack of Baghdad, nor had Egypt from the crushing of the Mamelukes by the Ottomans. Turkey itself had lapsed into decadence during the nineteenth century. At its core, Islam, which once had registered such glorious achievements in literature and the arts, in science, mathematics, and philosophy, lay culturally prostrate before the West. In what manner and to what ends would this civilization apply the political power acquired through independence and the wealth that flowed in from its oil? The answer has been a forking of the roads that lead from here to the twenty-first century. One way has been to assimilate the West's offerings with greedy enthusiasm; the other, to reject them with religious fervor.

The former mode confronts an Islamic society with a painful dilemma. Islam considers itself not only a religion but a whole way of life. If that is so, neither an individual Muslim nor a culture is free to select which traditions it will modify or abandon. Allah's supposed revelations in the Koran embrace all that is needed for this earthly existence; they do not have to be supplemented with the gifts of the infidel. But tell that to the sheikhs who own the oil beneath their vast expanse of rock and sand, or to the merchants who profit from economic development, or to the military who lust for tanks and aircraft, or to the literate who crave imported books. Once the theological curtain is pulled apart, anybody or anything may enter. A process that begins by accepting technology will next admit the social institutions that support it, and then embrace the values that impregnate the institutions. If modernizing means westernizing, where can anyone draw the line? Women will be educated, will drop the veil, and will work alongside of men; banks will charge the interest that the Koran forbids; and the legal system, especially its penal code, will deviate from the *shariya*.

To the devout, all this is a victory for Satan. Those who cling to the ancestral customs of their civilization prescribe an opposite formula. Their path is to reaffirm the fundamentals of the faith, insisting on conformity to what Allah enjoins in the Koran. Such fundamentalists act on the logic of the Arab conqueror who is said to have destroyed the library at Alexandria. If the books therein agreed with the Koran, he asserted, they were superfluous; if they disagreed, they were in error. In neither case were they needed. If taken literally, this would mean repudiating all that the West has to offer, exactly as Gandhi did in India when he extolled the values of the village culture and urged his countrymen to dress themselves in homespun cloth. Arab fundamentalists do not go to those lengths. On the contrary, they willingly employ the West's technology when it serves their goals. Their problem, after welcoming the equipment, is how to exclude the underlying ideas of the economy and the educational concepts that accompany its production and use.

Both Islam and India, as they face the future, must grapple with the difficulties for which the other-worldliness of their religions is responsible. If Hinduism avers that the soul can find peace and purity only by extinguishing desire for the objects of the senses, how can that be reconciled with the imperatives of an economic system that, to keep the wheels of production turning, must ever be stimulating new desires to acquire and consume material goods? Can Adam Smith's market coexist on the same plane with *nirvana*? And how are the banks of Islam to function in an economy now interdependent with the financial world, if charging interest on a loan is a sin? How can a society move forward under modern conditions if the female half of its population must remain veiled and socially handicapped? Outside of the Islamic heartland there are realistic possibilities of overcoming such obstacles. In Pakistan, for example, a woman was elected to head its government. Inside the heartland, however, the prospects are less promising. Neither Iran of the Shiites nor Saudi Arabia of the Sunnis looks like the wave of a promising future.

In fact, of all the major civilizations, the Islamic appears the least likely to undergo a successful revival in the century ahead. There are two factors which draw me to that conclusion. One is the prevalence of acute divisions within the Islamic societies, divisions that are accentuated by tribalism and the ferocity of religious sectarianism. Their disunity was indeed made evident to the entire world in 1991 when Saudi Arabia, Egypt, and Syria sided with the United States and Britain and France in the war against Iraq. Because unity is so much needed, but so hard to achieve, the Muslim reaction to discordant tendencies is to submit to authoritarian regimes where one segment of the population is occupied in policing the rest. That may be a formula for establishing order, at least temporarily; it is not a formula for progressive growth or social harmony.

This inherent weakness is connected with another defect that the spirit of the Islamic faith intensifies. Any monotheistic religion is prone to intolerance because it believes in only one deity whose truth was revealed through a chosen messenger—a Moses, Jesus, or Mohammed. As a consequence, rather than compromise, their true believers will fight fanatically. In the Islamic civilization, violence is peculiarly endemic by virtue of its martial propensities. In the contemporary world, that violence, as practiced by terrorist groups, results in the most shocking atrocities, many of whose victims are completely innocent persons. A civilization whose ethics tolerates such behavior, or fails to condemn it, cannot advance to higher levels. At some point the violence turns inward and destroys its own practitioners. When the oil reserves are eventually exhausted, there will be millions of desperate people throughout the Middle East.

Islam in the late twentieth century is a collection of peoples still in bondage to their religious inheritance and in crisis over their social and ethical values. One may anticipate that progressive elements will triumph in some countries of this geographically scattered civilization, while in others the forces of religious reaction will become dominant. In the former case, whatever emerges will achieve a new dynamic only by abandoning much that has been traditional to Islam. In the latter, where the Koran continues to hold sway, the price will be a society that remains stagnant. The dilemma for Muslims is painful. Could even an Ibn Khaldun chart an appropriate course to ride the tempestuous currents of the twenty-first century? Where in the coming millennium will the Muslims find their Mecca?

China's Yang and Yin

China possesses one characteristic that could ensure it an advantage over India and Islam. Its way to the future is unencumbered by the dogmas of an other-worldly faith and its revealed "truths." Because of its humanistic traditions and its philosophical focus on this world, China should be better equipped to apply rational criteria in choosing between the statics of tradition and the dynamics of innovation. At least, it could do so. Whether that will happen remains open to question. The problem for the Chinese is twofold. Their first dilemma is the choice of governance. Will they retain or abandon their age-old system that has been continuously authoritarian—the regime of the mandarin, the warlord, the landlord, or the party boss? Second, they must select among the various options that the twentieth century presents: democracy, capitalism, socialism, communism, fascism, or nationalism. This choice is complicated by the fact that all these, except for nationalism, are foreign imports—and Western ones.

The course actually followed by the Chinese Revolution thus far has traced a zigzag. The revolution's father, Sun Yat-sen, combined with his nationalism the Western notions of socialism and democracy. His successor, Chiang Kai-shek, reverted to the earlier tradition of the warlord, propped up by the bankers and the landlords. Mao Tse-tung looked outside for his ideas, both to Karl Marx and to the Soviet communism of Lenin and Stalin. But nationalism reasserted itself when, like Chiang before him, he sent his Russian advisers home, forcing China to rely on its own resources and be self-sufficient.

Under Mao, as well as his successors, communism in Chinese characters has displayed contradictory tendencies by attempting to reconcile the commands of an authoritarian centralism with the demands of grass-roots populism. Small wonder that the politics of the regime have fluctuated between movement and countermovement, action and reaction, thesis and antithesis. But never yet has a synthesis evolved. Not until the aging survivors of the Long March go to join their ancestors will the 1 billion Chinese be able to enter the new millennium with a new élan. The "sleeping giant," to use Napoleon's characterization, is once more awake and is stretching its limbs. In what direction its future rulers will choose to move is one of the biggest uncertainties facing the world in the near future. My own forecast is this: After a half-century of control by a dynasty of the Communist party, the Chinese people, when the opportunity presents itself, will grasp at an alternative. What no one can predict is how much of the party's works they will also reject.

It is an intriguing fact that, in the early 1990s, both variants of communism, the Soviet and the Sinic, were simultaneously in flux, if not in crisis. In 1936, when the British Fabian socialists Sidney and Beatrice Webb first published their two-volume work *Soviet Communism,* they added the subtitle *A New Civilisation?* In a later edition, they dropped the question mark, Stalin's trials, purges, and executions notwithstanding. Europeans at that time speculated widely about the possible emergence from the Russian Revolution of a people imbued with superior social values, and the Webbs apparently convinced themselves that they had seen this happening. Similarly, when China's Communist party marched into the "Forbidden City" and took power, the revolution's womb was expected to deliver a new ethic. Did not Mao decree that all would sup from the same iron rice bowl? Was it not understandable that a civilization molded into patterns of privilege and hierarchy should react in favor of an extreme egalitarianism? In the West many an idealistic observer and well-wisher of China anticipated the new utopia and watched for signs of its advent. The truth, as we can now see, is that neither in China nor in the Soviet Union did a new ethics take root. No new man or woman, Soviet or Sinic, has yet materialized. In these two countries many of the older customs have survived, albeit modified by recent policies and programs. An ethical new world still awaits the creating.

The "Secular Religions"

Various of the political Isms that have attracted a following in the twentieth century have been described as *secular religions,* a term applied to communism and fascism as well as to nationalism. Indeed, two points of similarity exist between these movements and the conventional faiths that rest on a belief in a deity. The so-called secular religions, like the traditional ones, are capable of generating a high degree of emotion, which can reach a fanatical intensity. From this, acts of violence frequently ensue. Second, the secular religions proclaim a dogmatic creed, certain of its truth and intolerant of other ways of thinking. The closed mind is the intellectual consequence of all irrational belief, whether theological or ideological. The burning of heretics and of libraries, the punishment of those who entertain "dangerous thoughts," the nightmarish society of Orwell's *1984* are readily justified by the true believer. If civilization is to advance in the direction of a higher ethic, it will require the tolerant attitude of the open mind. That brings us to consider the prospects for the West—the source and origin of the many doctrines that have made the twentieth century at once so stimulating and so turbulent, so hopeful and so dangerous.

Western Influence and America's Problems

What are the prospects for Western civilization as a new millennium approaches? Earlier, I referred to our decline, which is true in a relative sense. Until 1900 the worldwide hegemony of the West was unchallenged as well as unchallengeable. Such is far from being the case in the final decade of this century. Although the West continues to be the most influential of contemporary civilizations, its economic primacy is being successfully challenged by Asians. Even more seriously, the West is beset internally by contradictions and accompanying self-doubts in the sphere of values with serious effects on the general morale. What is happening, and why? And what could this portend for the future?

Until 1914 the hegemony of the West meant that of Europe. But once Europe had forfeited that leadership by its self-inflicted wounds, the states on the Atlantic seaboard could no longer control their colonies on other continents. Shrunk back from inflated empires to their original dimensions, they ceased to command the resources that were needed to play a major role on the world stage. The United States, which took their place after 1945, exercised the leadership for a bare quarter of a century (1945-1970). The turning point, after which the signs of decline became apparent, was the war in Vietnam— an utterly unnecessary conflict to engage in given that no vital American interest was at stake. The eventual military debacle, with the accompanying political fallout, had the same consequence for the United States as the Sicilian Expedition had for Athens during the Peloponnesian War. Each dealt a heavy blow to the self-confidence of a great power that learned the limits to its capacities.

But the problems that the United States has experienced since 1970 are related to a deeper underlying cause. Here let me restate the argument of Chapter 4, that a people emerges into prominence by utilizing some talent, or developing some trait, in which it excels; later, it declines when it pushes that same advantage to a harmful excess. The United States is a present-day case to illustrate that generalization. The outstanding American characteristic that made this country great has been the value placed on individualism. It was the emphasis on the enterprise and initiative of the individual which so unleashed the energies of immigrants that they developed the natural resources of a rich continent. But when overemphasized at the expense of countervailing values, this same quality produces negative results. It leads to excessive selfishness, to disregard for others, and to a lack of concern for the public good.

These tendencies have been much in evidence in the United States since the late 1960s, when people started reacting against the liberalism that had been dominant for four decades. That reaction reached its heights—or rather depths—during the 1980s. A chorus of well-orchestrated voices, with an actor-president for their cheerleader, intoned the litany that private activity is invariably superior to public, that government is the source of society's problems not the solution, that each individual should make and take whatever the opportunities allowed.

The effects on society at large of asserting such values were immediate, manifest, and devastating. The budgets of federal programs to help the needy and the underprivileged were drastically reduced. Military expenditures soared to levels unprecedented in peacetime—much of the money being dishonestly spent by the private contractors. The rich grew richer through tax cuts designed in their favor, and huge fortunes were rapidly amassed by financial speculators. The ranks of the poor increased. The homeless, living and sleeping in the streets, became a ubiquitous feature of the larger cities. Despite the conservatives' avowed fondness for "law and order," violent crime increased, at the same time as growing numbers of Americans, both in the affluent suburbs and in the city ghettoes, became addicted to drugs. A series of scandals was exposed in many sectors of society. Leading figures in the corporate and financial world, in politics and officialdom, in professional sports and organized religion, were found guilty of wrongdoing—much of it illegal, and all of it unethical. Dishonesty and deception are known to have been practiced at very high levels, including the White House itself. In short, America has been suffering an ethical meltdown. Among different sections of the population this has provoked cynicism, disgust, or alienation; while to the outside world the United States has not offered an inspiring enough model to persuade others to follow our example.

Add to all this the harm that we inflicted on ourselves by allowing the system of public education to deteriorate to such an extent that millions of Americans are now functionally illiterate and millions more are no better than semieducated. When the hearts and minds of so large a segment of the population are shaped by the commercial values that television and advertising repeat ad nauseam, how can we operate the complex processes of democracy, depending, as these do, on an enlightened public opinion? Can we provide to our civilization and to humanity at large a leadership with the wisdom to surmount the challenges?

The short answer to these questions is that it can be done, in the sense that the appropriate solutions lie within the bounds of human possibility. But major obstacles stand in the way of our succeeding. These take many forms. They are in part intellectual, in part institutional, in part ethical. To overcome them will require, first, a searching self-analysis, and then some boldly innovative departures from customary habits. I shall begin with the attempt at self-analysis, because, unless we comprehend why we are in our current situation, we shall be unable to consider the possible remedies that could bring regeneration.

Our Self-Inflicted Decline

Insight into our condition and our prospects must start from this irrefutable fact: If the West in this century has forfeited the hegemony that we once exercised around the world, this has not resulted from external challenges. What we are today is the direct consequence of our own choices, of our own actions. Western Europe predominated in most of the world until 1914. Then within three decades it slaughtered its youth, destroyed much of its treasure, and was engulfed in self-flagellation and despair. All of this was engendered from within; no external adversary was responsible. Europe's decline cannot be compared with that of the Arabs after the Mongols had sacked Baghdad, or that of the American Indian cultures when the Spaniards overran and occupied their lands, or that of Hinduism after Muslims and Europeans arrived. Europe weakened itself through the rivalries caused by its own divisions. Nationalism, the political factor that initially had made their regimes so strong, turned its weapons upon itself. Quite literally, in World Wars I and II, the Europeans cut their own throats. Then, after losing their empires, their weight in international relations was proportionately reduced.

The same has been true of the loss by the United States of the hegemony acquired on the production lines and battle lines of World War II. American preeminence was soon squandered by mistaken politics in the public sector and by errors of judgment in the private. It was the national obsession with the threat of communism both at home and abroad that led the federal government into the quagmire of Vietnam. Our economy suffered, as did that of the Soviet Union, from engaging in a prolonged arms race, which brought no benefit to either side. Thereby, we placed ourselves at a disadvantage in competing with the Japanese, who concentrated their skills and resources on designing and manufacturing the products that consumers wanted. Equally unwisely, we allowed the combined, but opposite, pressures from Left and Right to lower the standards of our public schools. The mistake of the Left was to encourage permissiveness to such an excess that adequate study of the basic subjects (English, history, and mathematics) was no longer required. The Right matched this with errors of its own—fostering the censorship of textbooks and insisting on such nonsense as giving "creationism" an equal place with evolution in the science curriculum. Once the schools start becoming inferior, as we have allowed to happen in the United States, we sacrifice the next generation. None of this, I emphasize, was done to us by adversaries or competitors beyond our borders. We did it to ourselves. Now, as a consequence, we must pay the price.

All is not necessarily lost, however; for the decline is reversible. In both of the main branches of Western civilization on each side of the Atlantic, there are some grounds for hope. Every argument of the determinists notwithstanding, no social tendency proceeds inexorably to a preordained conclusion. Nothing is inevitable about history except what some historians and social analysts can be regularly relied on to say about it. Whatever happens in human society is primarily the product of human will. By human will, therefore, it can be redirected. Both of the longest-enduring civilizations—the Chinese and the Western—have in their past record the experience of declines, and even of breakdowns. Yet both succeeded in recovering. China reverted to disunity and discord after the Han dynasty collapsed, but three and a half centuries later regained the heights with the T'ang. Western civilization lapsed into a seeming coma when Rome fell. But after the Dark Ages, it demonstrated a renewed vitality in a different form. With such reminders from the past, therefore, nobody has the right to predict in fatalistic terms that only doom awaits us. If a recovery was possible in the past, it is possible again in the present.

But—and this "but" is a big one—our civilization will be revitalized only if certain requirements are met. Two are fundamental. The first one is intellectual—a frank self-examination of what we are and why we are this way. The other is ethical—which signifies a radical leap (or revolution, if you will) in certain of our social relationships and practices. Let me discuss these points in turn.

Overcoming Our Split Personality

The central problem in Western civilization is the one described in Chapter 3: our inherent conflict of values. The contradiction between our two sources has never been resolved. It bedevils us to this day. Certain sectors of our society, some segments of our population, are influenced primarily by Greco-Roman this-worldliness, thus attaching priority to rationalism, secularism, and humanism. Some, however, aspire to the other-worldly goals of Judeo-Christian theology, which asserts that our species was created by a divine being and continues subordinate thereto. To the former frame of mind can be attributed our achievements in science and technology, our economic and political development, together with the philosophy that in general has animated our educational system. From the latter outlook are derived the beliefs that many persons accept uncritically concerning the nature of our species and of the universe, the origins of life, and the prospects of an existence after death. In addition, theology has preempted the formulation of the ethical values that shape our social relations. And therein lies the crux of the problem.

The two sides of the split personality of the West are in diametrical opposition. Frequently, this opposition is made manifest in overt fashion for all to see. Some examples are the conflict between groups, labeling themselves "pro-choice" or "pro-life," over the right of a pregnant woman to abort the fetus, or the controversy about how to teach biology in the schools and whether the presentation of the subject of evolution should be "balanced" by theological dogmas of a divine creation. As such disputes indicate, it is in the vital sphere of values—especially the ethical ones—that this split appears at its most glaring. The scientists, seeking to comprehend and explain the world of physical phenomena, conceptualize their data in materialistic terms. To ascertain the truth, and that alone, is their first principle. When they formulate hypotheses that extrapolate beyond what is currently known, these must always be credible to reason, their subsequent proof or disproof being settled by whether it conforms or not to the factual evidence. Likewise, when technology applies the discoveries of science to utilitarian ends, it too operates solely on physical assumptions. No miracle, nothing of a supernatural character, explains the success of human beings in voyaging to the moon or photographing a planet as far distant as Neptune. Such results were obtained by the strictest application of rational thought to physical forces and materials.

The same is true in much of our social conduct, particularly in that part of it which relates to government and the economy. Contemporary policymakers and the executives of large organizations are not in the habit of consulting astrologers or sacrificing live animals before they make their decisions. Nowadays in politics, as with industry, business, and finance, how people behave is influenced largely by judgments based on masses of statistical data and by calculations (or "guesstimates") of what seems psychologically most possible or probable. Whether the judgments turn out to be wise or not, all are wholly confined within the humanistic framework of this-worldly existence.

The Need for an Ethical Leap

As is clear, the values employed in what has just been described are essentially intellectual. They are concerned with such criteria as truth or falsity, success or failure in attaining one's intended goal, efficiency or incompetence. All of these are important; yet evidently, something even more important has not been included—and that is the whole ethical category. When technologists apply the knowledge acquired by science, are the results good for humanity? Is the power of a big business corporation or of a large department of government employed for socially beneficial purposes? When priorities are determined—that is, when something is approved and something else is rejected—was the option selected the better one in the sense that it will improve the lives of more human beings?

The exercise of reason in the quest for truth, or the demonstration of efficiency in attaining one's goals, can also be characterized as good; but our judgment should not stop there. It must be extended to the uses to which knowledge is applied and to the character of the goals that the means were designed to achieve. The managerial skills employed by the heads of a crime syndicate or a drug cartel, viewed purely as techniques, are in no way different than those displayed in running a department or a corporation or any other large organization. The same thought processes can design either a school or a bomb. In World War II some German and Japanese doctors conducted infamous experiments on helpless human beings at the behest of their evil regimes. Was their medical proficiency any different in its purely technical aspects than that which is normally applied to healing the sick? What all this tells us is patently clear: Ethics, not technique, is the essence of civilization.

What is the current situation, then, with our ethics in the West? The plain truth is that many of our ethical practices are seriously deficient. Much of our conduct—private as well as public—demonstrates that our priorities are often wrong and that the values we live by are in many instances the worse ones. Businessmen engaged in economic activity must make a profit. Because they operate in a competitive environment, the conditions of survival—let alone, of success—require them to be aggressive, sometimes ruthlessly so. Similarly in the realm of government; for as money is to the economy, so is power to politics. It serves as the indispensable tool, without which nothing can be accomplished. Many of those who enter politics do so because the exercise of power appeals to them, which is assuredly true of the great majority of those who climb to the top. To reach that height, they must often step over others. The desire for money or power is without doubt the dominant influence in those two crucial sectors of society—the political and the economic. Yet, as the historical record proves abundantly, both are likely to corrupt their possessors—especially when accumulated in excessive amounts.

What is there to serve as a brake, a restraint, on the lures of money and power? Only another value of higher ethical quality, and it is not difficult to suggest what this should be. Throughout this book, when referring to ethics, I have defined its content in terms of altruism. Selfish conduct can be, and often is, socially destructive; altruistic conduct is invariably beneficial. Clearly, the trouble with the unmitigated quest for money and power is that they are invitations to selfishness and aggressiveness. As such, their effects are antisocial. For a civilization to improve the quality of life for all its people, sentiments of altruism must animate those in positions of leadership. So our problem boils down to this: Why does contemporary civilization in the West exhibit so much more selfishness than altruism, so much more competition than cooperation?

The Values of Humanism

To this key question, my answer is this: The ethical values of Western civilization still emanate in the main from the organized religions that propound and preach them as the commandments of their faith prescribed by some supernatural being. Consequently, those individuals whose values are this-worldly are not persuaded to give credence to principles in whose alleged source and sanction they do not honestly believe. The reassertion of Greco-Roman values since the Renaissance was of course accompanied by ethical teaching grounded in humanistic principles, both during the Enlightenment and during the Age of Progress. But such ethical stimuli did not supersede or eradicate the influence of the other-worldly tradition in our culture.

There lies the basic explanation of the paradoxical truth that is so often enunciated about the problems of the twentieth century—

namely, that our advances in science and technology have not been matched by equal advances in ethical conduct. Precisely! Everybody says that; everybody agrees that such is the case. But no one, to my knowledge, has satisfactorily explained why this is so. The reason, in my view, is that, when we function in the political or economic sphere, or in science or technology or education, we are behaving in accordance with values that are humanist, rationalist, and this-worldly. In this sector of our civilization, the intellectual outlook of most leading figures toward religious beliefs is that of the skeptic, the agnostic, or the atheist. Their thinking and their practices are those of the French astronomer and mathematician Laplace, who stated of beliefs in the existence of a deity: "I have no need for that hypothesis." That is why their behavior can deviate from that of an ethics which invokes divine authority. Many are those who disregard or reject in their daily lives a morality whose theological underpinning was weakened in the Renaissance, destroyed by modern science, and buried in the economics of the Industrial Revolution. Altruism struggled hard to repair the damage thus caused; witness the work of the social reformers. But it was difficult to withstand the material lures of industrial capitalism. Greediness attracts more followers than goodness. Many are our contemporaries, from Wall Street to Main Street, who follow Faust and sign their contracts with the Devil.

Why Improvement Is Possible

What is the remedy for this state of affairs? It is easy to envisage, but exceedingly difficult to accomplish. Western civilization needs, as never before, an ethical revolution in accord with the concepts of humanism. We need radical changes in our social practices, and we must reconstruct inert institutions that have grown too stiff, static, and sclerotic. We must abandon the conceptual schizophrenia that has so long divided the West. We cannot form a clear vision of a better future if we have one eye focused on this-worldly concerns and the second fixated on another world with its never-yet-proven heaven or hell. A humanistic ethics is called for that will inspire us to behave altruistically without relying on the ethically inferior notions of rewards or punishments in an imaginary afterlife.

But even if this be desirable, you may be thinking, is it also possible? Yes, there are reasonable grounds for hope, and I will explain why. Hope is justified because we faced and surmounted earlier a crisis with some parallels to this one. Remember the conditions of western Europe during the sixteenth century and the first half of the seventeenth. The movements of the Renaissance and the Reformation had broken with the past, and great innovations were recorded in the arts and literature, in mathematics and the sciences. But upheaval was rampant in the social order and its politics. The same persons who, in one part of their lives, were using reason to tackle their problems, in another part turned irrationally to violence and to war. But consider what followed the breakdown and its barbarities. Gradually came a toleration of differences. Eventually, the Enlightenment arrived with new hopes and new visions.

Surely, what has happened before—and not so very long ago—could happen again. Western society broke down in the first half of this century, since when our civilization has teetered on a knife's edge. But is it not possible that, when the new millennium begins, a breakthrough could occur in a manner similar to that of the eighteenth and nineteenth centuries? We know for a fact that a previous breakdown in our civilization was followed by a breakthrough—as has also been the experience of other civilizations. Intellectually, we can affirm that this is possible; emotionally therefore we are justified in hoping that in this respect history may repeat itself. Formidable though our task may be, it is certainly not hopeless. To revitalize ourselves in a constructive fashion requires an act of will, the application of intelligent thought, and the deliberate pursuit of better values than we now habitually practice.

That last point in particular needs to be stressed. In expressing my preference for the Greco-Roman side of our civilization over the Judeo-Christian, I do not mean to imply that all the social practices that our this-worldly tradition has sanctioned are equally justifiable. Those scientists who claim to absolve themselves from the ethical consequences of their discoveries, those economists who maintain that production for profit is independent of morality, those students of politics who restrict themselves to the phenomenon of power, the types of technique, and the behavior of systems of government—all these condone what is socially pernicious by their vows of abstinence from the knowledge of good and evil. In the last two centuries the West has been so dazzled by the spectacle of its material accomplishments that it has allowed materialism, and the commercial priorities that accompany it, to become too dominant. The misgivings that Wordsworth voiced in the early phase of the Industrial Revolution[1] are even more relevant today.

Today's equivalent of the worship of the Golden Calf is the idolatry of the GNP. Economics remains what it has always been, a study of efficient means. The ends have to be sought elsewhere. They lie in our concepts of humanity, of the good citizen, and of the good society.

One World, Many States

From this review of the prospects awaiting the world's major civilizations, I return to the point stated earlier in this chapter. Our major problems nowadays have a global dimension. The once-separate, or separable, sections of humanity are impelled into closer contact. More than ever before, they influence one another and in turn are influenced. The One World, toward which human society is now in transition, will eventually generate a universal civilization.

Unlike any time in the past, every civilization nowadays confronts a group of problems that touch us all and basically affect us in the same way. Some of these are ancient issues, coeval with civilization itself. Others are the peculiar products of this century. In the first group belong the inequalities between individuals and peoples that have persisted throughout recorded history, the cruelties that we inflict on others who are different from ourselves, and the wars in which we regularly destroy our fellow creatures. From the annals of every civilization in every stage of its evolution, instances of those evils can be cited. In the twentieth century, however, we have introduced new evils, all of them due to our reckless methods of applying technology to practical uses: the existence of nuclear weapons, the pollution and destruction of our physical environment, and the increase of population in areas already suffering from desperately low standards of living. These are the problems that, if they are not rectified, will lead to one of two results. Either the quality of civilization will decline in all regions of the planet, including those that at present are the most affluent; or as a result of human action, the planet itself could become unlivable. The stakes are not small.

The question then arises: What is it that should be done to prevent such outcomes? In my judgment, the changes required of us are radical, in the literal sense that they reach to the roots of civilization as we know it. But that is inherent in the logic of humanity's present-day condition. Only a breakthrough that is truly radical in depth and dimension can rescue us from breakdown. For it to occur, this breakthrough has two prerequisites. One will involve a revolution in our institutions; the other, a revolution in our values. Both must go hand in hand, if civilization is to be preserved and then advance to new heights.

The institutions that need to be revolutionized, or made over, are those that currently shape much of the conduct of humanity everywhere on this planet. I refer to the political structures of the various states and the religious organizations of the several faiths. Both sets of structures, as managed by their respective governments and as fortified by doctrine and dogma, produce the same negative effect. They divide humanity into segments and infuse them with a consciousness of being separate and distinct. Then on this foundation of separate organizations, they erect a superstructure of parochial attitudes, provincial loyalties, and partisan emotions. These divisions foment the opposition between the familiar and the strange, the friendly and the hostile, the citizen and the foreigner, the faithful and the infidel. What has always followed from those dichotomies is rivalry, distrust, competition, aggression, and war. And these are caused—indeed, they are provoked—by the maintenance of the divisions that the institutions themselves created and perpetuate.

The governance of the present-day world is one of nation-states. By now this system has lasted for some four and a half centuries, and in the closing decade of this century 180 states, so-called, of this character, are functioning in one fashion or another. Some of these are mere specks of islands with exiguous populations. Others have been as huge as the Soviet Union, which for seven decades extended across one-sixth of the Earth's land surface, or China, housing one-fifth of the human race.

From Nation-States to Region-States

This system, a welcome innovation at the time when it replaced the feudal units and church-state dualism of medieval Europe, has now outlived its usefulness. In this day and age, it is manifestly obsolescent and rapidly becoming obsolete. That is so because the boundary lines within which the nation-states exercise their jurisdiction establish areas that are not coterminus with the territorial range of the problems that governments are supposed to resolve. The nation-state centralizes in the capital powers that may be needed in the localities, while externally asserting its independence of legal restraints, which it then justifies through the pretentious doctrine of "sovereignty." The usual consequence is that contemporary states are too small for some of the functions they should perform and, at the same time, are too large for others. Nowadays, their smallness renders them inadequate to cope with the problems of military defense and economic policy. National frontiers are utterly indefensible against nuclear bombs and the missiles that deliver them. In the same fashion, vital economic relationships fly over national boundaries and operate supranationally, as is evident in the cases of markets, capital flows, technology transfers, and manufacturing. An international economy has emerged in direct contradiction to the national confines of the political system.

When a unit of government is so structured that it can no longer cope successfully with the basic needs of economic well-being and military protection, it is doomed to disappear. This happened earlier in the history of the West, when the polis gave way to the *imperium,* and again when the latter was replaced by feudalism and church-state dualism, and once more when these were succeeded by the nation-state itself. Nowadays the time is due for this unit in turn to give way to a structure more appropriate to our social needs. Indeed, the embryos of the successor institutions are already taking form within the womb of today's emerging global community. These exist at two levels. On the world scene are the United Nations and its specialized agencies—the precursors to what could eventually become the government of a world state. For that ideal to become an effective reality, however, the combined labors of several generations will be required.

Neither politically nor administratively is humanity capable as yet of governing itself within a unified framework. Something more is wanted to pilot us through this period of transition from the existing chaos of nation-states. Already a new invention has appeared, a phenomenon for which I suggest the name of the *region-state.* The first example of this unit of government is now being created in western Europe, under the title of the European Community. If it continues to develop along its current course, it will evolve within the next two decades into a federal superstate. What a political revolution to contemplate in the light of the past history of rivalries and wars among its members! How significant that the same geographic and cultural region, which four centuries ago created the nation-state, should now when that unit is becoming obsolete be experimenting with its successor! How significant also that the same civilization which invented the democratic system should now be employing the democratic process of elicit-ing voluntary consent to create a union of previously separate states, instead of using the age-old method of force and conquest!

Along with the nation-state, what will one day become less potent than it was is its emotional counterpart: nationalism. The feelings that attach themselves to the nation-state are the subjective aspect of the institutions that form and frame our daily lives. One of their effects is to bind people together in a community larger than their locality or neighborhood; and to the extent that this happens, it is good. Our love of home and family, our bonds with friends and fellow citizens, are broadened by national feeling into pride and affection for that larger whole, our country. But the good has its negative accompaniment. The same feeling, which unites the citizens of the same state, ipso facto divides us from the members of other states. Nationalism heightens the consciousness of being distinct and therefore different—attitudes that can then slide into exclusiveness or superiority or outright hostility. The problems that our planet will face in the twenty-first century cannot be resolved by a human race whose members think, feel, and act primarily in national segments.

Divisive Effects
of the Organized Religions

The same argument holds true, *mutatis mutandis,* for those other major institutions that, like the state, divide human beings from one another. These are the organized religions. Their social impact, like that of states, is very mixed. They accomplish good by bringing people together within the embrace of a common faith; but they do commensurate harm by separating each group from the rest. Dogmatism and intolerance are the unavoidable outcomes of doctrines that claim to be divine truth. That is why some of history's bloodiest wars have been waged under the banner of religious belief. Even today, the tragic instances multiply of human beings destroying each other through enmities that in part have religion at their base. During the 1980s Protestants and Catholics slaughtered one another in Northern Ireland; as did Jews and Muslims in Israel and nearby areas; Sunnis and Shiites in Iraq and Iran; Hindus, Sikhs, and Muslims in India; Buddhists and Hindus in Sri Lanka; Muslims and Greek Orthodox in Cyprus; Christians and Muslims in the Sudan—the list is endless. In plain truth, organizations which arouse in their followers such a degree of fanaticism that they are ready to kill those who believe in other gods are a menace to civilization. Humanity cannot unite until the divisive influences of the organized religions are eradicated. To counteract the separatist influences of both the prevailing political system and the religious institutions will be a Herculean task. But unless it is accomplished, humanity will never reach the needed global consensus on issues of universal scope. Parochial minds cannot solve planetary problems.

The Unity of Humanity

So that my argument here may carry conviction and my meaning not be misunderstood, let me be as clear as possible about what I am affirming and what I am not. I speak in favor of the notion that humanity is one, and that our unity takes priority over the parts. I also believe that there will be a fundamental difference between the world of the coming centuries and those of the past. In the past, large areas of the world, large sections of humanity, existed in relative isolation from one another. Tomorrow's reality will be one of increasing contacts and interrelationships around the globe. The issues of civilization can only be handled by increased cooperation among all the civilizations. That is why the social institutions which divide human beings into separate structures and assert the first claim on their emotions have become obstructions in the way of finding global solutions to the problems that concern us all. Universal needs demand universal institutions. This is as true in politics as it is in economics and in religion.

But the unity, the universality, of which I speak, does not imply a world that is homogenized, uniform, or identical. Far from it—for such a world would be, both culturally and intellectually, a far duller, less stimulating, more sterile place. Diversities of thought and behavior add richness and color to the tapestry of the social fabric. Not only are they a welcome alternative to monotony, but they are needed as invitations to curiosity, comparison, and judgment. Indeed, their continuance is beneficial, provided that the differences are perceived to be complementary. Only when they are deemed antagonistic, and when they cannot peaceably coexist, do they become pernicious. The institutions at which I have directed my criticism have earned such condemnation by their record. The character of their structures reinforces divisions between human beings and contains the potential for hostilities. The wars of civilization have invariably been the work of its governments and of its religions. Unless their power is diminished, how else will warfare be eradicated?

The notion that the organized religions and the governments of existing nation-states are institutions that can no longer help, and can seriously hinder, humanity in coping with the conditions of the next century will strike some as radical, or even revolutionary. It should not be so. It appears thus only because such ideas, when explicitly stated, are in contradiction with prevailing thought and attitudes. But the ideas do not contradict contemporary practice. On the contrary: If one looks at how people actually behave, instead of attending to what they proclaim or profess, it is evident that the claims advanced by national governments and by organized religions are frequently disregarded or ignored. In the Western civilization, persons in business do not, for six days of the week, conduct themselves in accordance with the values to which ostensibly they subscribe if they happen to show up in synagogue or church on Saturday or Sunday morning. And what about those who set up their subsidiaries in Asian countries where sweatshop conditions are tolerated and a dictatorial regime represses the trade unions, thus placing Asian employees on their payroll and displacing their fellow citizens? Is such a practice consistent with protestations of concern for the national interest of the United States or with lamentations that the U.S. economy might be losing in the competition with Japan, Taiwan, South Korea, and Singapore? No matter what is said to the contrary, the facts disclose that Western civilization labors under a schizophrenia of values. We behave as Greco-Romans in most of our actions; but many of our words and attitudes are hypocritically Judeo-Christian. Would we not do ourselves a service if our deeds and our rhetoric were brought into conformity?

The same is true, of course, of other civilizations in the sense that their current practices are out of kilter with their traditional doctrines. There are Muslim bankers and financiers in the Middle East who express profoundest reverence for the teachings of the Koran but nevertheless charge interest on their loans because that is the prevailing custom in commercial transactions. Islam notwithstanding, they are bowing to the dictates, and grasping at the opportunities, of the international economy. In addition, the women of the Islamic civilization in country after country are increasingly asserting their rights to education, to financial independence, and to careers in commerce, in the professions, and in public life. Eventually they will win their rights against the fundamentalist clerics and other male bigots. The future does not belong to the Khomeinis—although for a short time in a particular area such fanatics are capable of gaining control and wreaking their havoc. The increasingly transnational or supranational character both of economic processes and of science and technology is a clear sign of the emerging realities of the twenty-first century. They are here to stay. In fact, their force will increase. What has to be superseded is the sectionalism of institutions that obstruct progress by their attachment to the legacies from the past.

The Priority of North-South Relations

In fact, the current shifts in the world's balance of power as exemplified by the reemergence of Germany and Japan, along with the collapse of communist regimes, suggests a new set of international priorities for the coming century. No longer will the adversary relationship between the philosophies and institutions of communism in the East and liberal democracy in the West be the principal axis of world politics. Instead of East-West relations, the North-South, or temperate-tropical, divide will occupy the forefront of global concerns.

In today's world material goods are distributed most unequally. The North has a minority of the world's population; but this minority possesses most of the wealth, and it both controls and consumes a disproportionate share of the planet's resources. The South, with a majority of the Earth's people, contains most of the poverty; and although many valuable resources lie in its territory, it lacks the means to develop them. A planet exhibiting so glaring a double standard is bound to be unstable. And here is where the affluent North has both an opportunity and an obligation. It should seize the initiative in reducing the inequalities between North and South, thereby accomplishing a fairer distribution than now exists. A prosperous minority (and, in relative terms, a diminishing one) cannot forever maintain its current privileges side by side with so much squalor. Nor is the necessary redistribution financially impossible. If the manufacture and sale of arms were drastically reduced by international agreements, the reallocation of resources from military to civilian needs could end the old vicious circle and inaugurate one that would be newer and more virtuous.

At this point, however, a proviso should be stated. Criticism of existing faults is always easy because they are obvious to the view. Recommendation of a superior alternative is also fairly easy—particularly if the alternative has never yet been tried and therefore has not been found wanting. But, there's the rub! The difficulty in suggesting solutions is that none is wholly ideal. Every proposed "remedy" has its potentially harmful side effects. Suppose enough of humanity were to reach a consensus that unity overrides differences, that global problems require global treatment, and that some redistribution of resources is required. Suppose even that this were followed one day by a world-state with its world government. Let no one imagine that this would constitute the infallible panacea, the guaranteed cure-all to break the harmful habits of the past and inaugurate a more peaceful world. In human affairs, no automatic safety devices exist. Certainly, universalism is required of us if we are to preserve our planet and live hereon in civilized fashion. But even in a world-state, war would not be totally impossible. Could not secession be attempted and civil war erupt within a world government? Moreover, the prospect of global governance for a unified world is enough to caution us that power would be concentrated there to a degree unparalleled in the past. Wherever there is power, there is always the possibility of its abuse. Some defense is needed therefore against tyranny by a world government if some evil person were ever to gain control of its powers. What kind of defense is possible?

A New Axial Age?

Such cautions are a salutary reminder that institutional changes, however radical and however necessary, will not suffice by themselves to guarantee that human civilization will survive on this planet—still less that it will improve. A still more basic change is required. For an insight into what that should be, I quote this luminous sentence from the charter of UNESCO: "Since wars begin in the minds of men, it is in the minds of men that the defenses of peace must be constructed." How true that is! And its truth can be extended beyond war to include injustice, persecution, intolerance, discrimination, and similar ills. By the same logic, all of the good for which civilization has been responsible issues from the same source—from human heads and hearts. In a word, I am reaffirming the point that has supplied a connecting thread throughout the argument of this book. Our lives are governed by the values we choose. It is the mixture of values, both the good and the bad, that gives civilization its character. What we are choosing today will shape the civilization of tomorrow. Everything depends therefore on the nature of our choices.

To bring about a change of values in the world's major civilizations amounts to saying that what humanity most needs in the twenty-first century is a new Axial Age. By that I mean a revolution in ethical consciousness as profound as those that occurred simultaneously in several civilizations during the period from the seventh to the fifth century B.C., and later in the Western civilization during the Enlightenment of the eighteenth century and the Age of Progress in the nineteenth. The earlier of those ethical revolutions was equally manifest in civilizations focused on this world (e.g., China and Greece) and in the other-worldly (e.g., India). The more recent revolution that originated in the West was the product of its Greco-Roman tradition because the governing philosophy was humanist, rationalist, and secular.

In the coming century such humanistic values would offer the fittest substitute for religious dogma. The organized religions attracted their followers with an image of humanity that transcended the limitations of the individual, picturing us all as parts of a universal whole. That image was appealing because it filled a human need to reach beyond our finiteness and grasp at some larger vision. This same vision, however, would be more constructively satisfied by the humanism that celebrates the unity and interdependence of our species but without importing a "Supreme Being" to keep us all moral with hopes of reward or fears of punishment. If the twenty-first century should be fortunate enough to generate a third Axial Age, its philosophy should be akin to that of the second—secular, rationalist, and humanist. Its intellectual foundations must be rooted in science, in the findings of research into humanity's past, in the exercise of critical intelligence, in the weighing of evidence and drawing of judgments from empirical data.

But the values of a new Axial Age, although grounded in reason, must enlist still another element in human nature. Even so thoroughgoing a rationalist as Aristotle declared that "thought by itself moves nothing."[2] For there lodges within us that glorious quality of fantasy and inventiveness which leaps beyond the facts, transcends the data that are known, and takes wing into the unknown. This is our imagination. Here is where we think about what might be, until our thinking makes it so. It is here that we dream and hope and aspire; here that we soar in free flight.

To engage people's imagination on the side of higher ethical values is the first task of the coming century. If you doubt that, just reflect for a moment on the problems that confront our species and demand solution. To close the horrendous gap that separates the majority from the minority in terms of standards of living and quality of life; to eradicate poverty, malnutrition, ignorance, and disease; to prevent wars; to foster a tolerance of diversity, both in matters of belief and in patterns of culture; to train our children as they grow up to be more altruistic and less self-serving; to treat every individual with equal consideration for his or her dignity as a human being; to feel that reverence for life which Schweitzer enunciated; to restrict the growth of population and to curb the despoliation of the Earth's resources; to create works of art that forever lift the spirit—these are the tasks that constitute the opportunity and the obligation of the generation now becoming adult.

Can such things be? Yes, they can, for efforts in these directions did happen before and hence could happen again. Nothing is impossible for human will to achieve in the redesign of our social fabric, once our minds are convinced and our imaginations are fired. Will such things be? That I do not know and cannot predict. Not being a determinist or a fatalist, either for good or for ill, and being aware only that our species treads a razor's edge and could end up on either side, I can speak with assurance only of the possibilities. None of these can be pronounced as certain, and even to indicate which possibility is the more probable lies beyond our knowing. But as a spur to the right choices, it should be enough to realize that achieving the greatest good for humanity is one of the genuine possibilities. No utopia, in the sense of an ultimate unchanging perfection, will ever be attained. What is attainable is a world far better than this very imperfect one that we now have. To bring that from hope to reality will be the supreme test for civilization.

Epilogue

When I had finished reading in preparation for this book, and before commencing to write, I traveled around the world, visiting ten countries en route. It was a mind-stretching experience to climb the Great Wall, to gaze at the Terracotta Army, to stand at the foot of the Pyramids, to walk in the tranquil beauty of Kyoto's gardens, to view the manuscripts in the library of the British Museum, and to be transported by the sublime aesthetics of the Parthenon and the Taj Mahal. While witnessing the monuments of past empires, their legacies of power and opulence and art and artifacts, I observed the contemporary efforts of struggling humanity—of the 800 million Indians and the 1 billion Chinese. It is both stimulating to see what the human spirit has achieved and saddening to contemplate where we have fallen short. But one cannot circumaviate the globe without renewed astonishment and admiration for the creativity, the resourcefulness, the imaginative and intellectual powers of our species expressed in the record of our several civilizations. That makes it reasonable to conclude that we shall yet surmount the current dangers by choosing better values with which to live. Without an ethical revolution, there will be no civilization; and without improvements in civilization, there will be no humanity.

A century ago, when France was torn apart by the impassioned controversies over the Dreyfus affair, the novelist Émile Zola rallied to the defense of the accused officer but died before his innocence was judicially established. At Zola's funeral, Anatole France eulogized his efforts in the cause of justice with these moving words: "He was a moment in the human conscience." Could not we of this generation make the start of a new millennium a moment in the conscience of humanity?

Notes

Chapter 1

1. Plato, *The Republic*, Bk. 9:592b.
2. "I see the good and approve it; but I pursue the bad" (Video meliora proboque/ Deteriora sequor). Ovid.
3. *British History in the Nineteenth Century* (New York: Longman's, Green, 1922), p. 292.
4. Described by Franz Fanon as "the wretched of the earth" in his book by that title (Paris: F. Maspero, 1961).
5. This was what happened in July 1988, causing an American cruiser in the Persian Gulf to shoot down an Iranian commercial airliner. Mistakenly, the crew informed the captain that the approaching airliner was hostile.
6. *"Si le rétablissement des sciences et des arts a contribué a épurer les moeurs."* Rousseau's essay on this theme was awarded the prize in 1750.
7. As Arnold Toynbee says in his essay "History" in *The Legacy of Greece*, ed. Gilbert Murray (Oxford: Clarendon, 1921), p. 295.
8. Hu Shih in *Whither Mankind: A Panorama of Modern Civilization*, ed. Charles A. Beard (New York: Longman's, Green, 1928), pp. 26-27.
9. Beard, ibid., p. 14.
10. Kenneth Clark, *Civilisation* (New York: Harper & Row, 1969), p. 79.
11. Lewis Mumford, *The Culture of Cities* (London: Secker and Warburg, 1938), p. 3.
12. Quoted by Kenneth Clark in *Civilisation*, p. 1.
13. Ignacio Silone has written: "On a group of theories one can found a school; but on a group of values one can found a culture, a civilization, a new way of living among men." Quoted by Herbert Muller in *The Uses of the Past* (New York: Oxford University Press, 1952), p. 322.
14. This view is developed in *Values and Humanity* by Elizabeth M. Drews and Leslie Lipson (New York: St. Martin's, 1971). "The ethical conception of civilization," wrote Albert Schweitzer, ". . . is the only one that can be justified." And in the same vein: "If the ethical foundation is lacking, then civilization collapses, even when in other directions creative and intellectual forces of the strongest nature are at work." *The Philosophy of Civilization,* trans. C. T. Campion (New York: Macmillan, 1964), pp. xii, 38. This volume combines Schweitzer's two related works, written at different times: *The Decay and the Restoration of Civilization* and *Civilisation and Ethics.*

15. Plato, *The Apology*, sec. 38a.
16. L. T. Hobhouse, *Morals in Evolution* (New York: H. Holt, 1906), vol. 1, p. 36.

Chapter 2

1. This phrase is used by A. D. Lindsay in *The Modern Democratic State* (London: Oxford University Press, 1943), where chap. 1 is titled "Political Theory and Operative Ideals."

2. From Goethe's *Conversations with Eckermann,* January 31, 1827. Quoted in Jacques Gernet, *A History of Chinese Civilization,* trans. J. R. Foster (Cambridge University Press, 1982), p. xxvii.

3. This point is made by Arthur Cotterell and David Morgan in *China's Civilization* (New York: Praeger, 1975), p. 32.

4. In this context, one may recall that the twentieth-century Danish physicist Niels Bohr took for his motto the phrase: *Contraria sunt complementaria* (contraries are complementary).

5. This cyclical theory was developed by Tsou Yen, a member of the Chi-hsia Academy, which was influential in the fourth century. See Benjamin I. Schwartz, *The World of Thought in Ancient China* (Cambridge, Mass.: Belknap Press, Harvard, 1985), pp. 354ff.

6. Gernet has written: "China does not know the transcendent truths, the idea of good in itself, the notion of property in the strict sense of the term. She does not like the exclusion of opposition, the idea of the absolute, the positive distinction between mind and matter; she prefers the notions of complementarity, or circulation, influx, of action at a distance, of a model, and the idea of order as an organic totality." *History of Chinese Civilization,* p. 29.

7. There is a good discussion of these in Werner Eichhorn's *Chinese Civilization,* trans. Janet Seligman (London: Faber and Faber, 1969), pp. 69ff.

8. On this point, Schwartz has written: "While it would be wrong to say that Confucianism simply conceives of the state as the family writ large, official Confucian rhetoric of later ages abounds in stock references to the king or emperor as the 'father-mother' of the people and to magistrates as 'father-mother officials.' " *Thought in Ancient China,* p. 415.

9. Wu Ti declared Confucius' teachings to be official doctrine 343 years after the sage had died. Constantine's conversion to Christianity occurred 279 years after Jesus was crucified. Islam, as will be seen later, took much less time to become the established religion.

10. For example, Hsün-tzu.

11. Arnold J. Toynbee, *Mankind and Mother Earth* (New York: Oxford University Press, 1976), p. 533.

12. C. K. Yang, in an essay, "The Functional Relationship Between Confucian Thought and Chinese Religion," in *Chinese Thought and Institutions,* ed. John K. Fairbank (University of Chicago Press, 1957), pp. 269-70.

13. Eichhorn observes: "We probably come closest to the core of Confucianism if we think of it as a rationally enlightened form of ancestor-worship." *Chinese Civilization,* p. 76.

14. *Analects,* Bk. 11, chap. 2. Yang argues this way, citing another of Confucius' well-known sayings: "While you are not able to serve men, how can you serve their spirits?" *Chinese Thought,* pp. 271-72.

15. Described by Gernet as "messianic revolutionaries" (*History of Chinese Civilization*, p. 155). Their movement erupted in 184 A.D.

16. Huston Smith, *The Religions of Man* (New York: Harper Colophon, 1958), p. 178.

17. Quoted by Yang, *Chinese Thought*, p. 270.

18. See Gernet, *History of Chinese Civilization*, pp. 221, 293.

19. The principal author of this was Chu Hsi (1130-1200), whose metaphysics was somewhat eclectic.

20. Lin Yutang, ed., *The Wisdom of China and India* (New York: Random House, 1942), p. 11. He went on to say: "The Hindu preoccupation with questions of the world soul and the individual soul is so intense that at times it must seem oppressive to a less spiritual people. I doubt there is a nation on earth that equals the Hindus in religious emotional intensity except the Jews." Incidentally, the Jewish philosopher, Spinoza, has been described as *"ein Gott-betrunkener Mensch"* (a person intoxicated with God). Lin's characterization of India sounds like an echo of that phrase.

21. Romila Thapar has written thus of the social structure that evolved with the Aryans: "The unit of society was the family, which was patriarchal. . . . The family unit was a large one, generally extending over three generations and with the male offspring living together." *A History of India* (Harmondsworth, England: Penguin, 1966), vol. 1, p. 40.

22. Percival Spear observes: "The outstanding Hindu institution is caste. Hindu society is divided into a great number of these, which amount to some three thousand today." *India* (Ann Arbor: University of Michigan Press, 1972), p. 41.

23. *Chinese Thought*, p. 279. Yang goes on to state: "In Chinese culture a striking difference lies in the dominance of Confucianism over the ethical values."

24. *"Dharma* . . . can perhaps be best described as the natural law. The natural law of society was the maintaining of the social order, in fact the caste laws." Thapar, *History of India*, p. 46.

25. Rig-Veda 10:90. The *brahmins* were said to have grown from the mouth; the *kshatriyas,* from the arms; the *vaishyas,* from the thighs; the *shudras,* from the feet.

26. Bhagavad-Gita, chap. 1:37, trans. Swami Paramananda, reprinted in Lin, *Wisdom of China*, p. 60.

27. Ibid., chap. 2, p. 37.

28. See Chapter 7, pp. 168-169.

29. Stanley Wolpert refers to "the Buddha's heterodox rationalism." *A New History of India* (New York: Oxford University Press, 1977), p. 49. Spear says of him: "About ultimates, he was agnostic. There was no personal God in the original system." *India*, p. 63. Thapar states: "Buddhism was also atheistic, in as much as God was not essential to the Universe, there being a natural cosmic rise and decline." *History of India*, p. 66.

30. Spear, *India*, p. 68.

31. Muller, *Uses of the Past*, pp. 332-37.

32. Wolpert, *New History of India*, p. 82.

Chapter 3

1. *History*, Bk. 1:4, 8.

2. Grahame Clark has made the same point: "A spirit of liveliness and freedom blows through their art, whether this took the form of frescoes or was applied to

pottery or metal-work." *World Prehistory* (Cambridge University Press, 3rd ed., 1977), p. 167. Carroll Quigley's appraisal of the Minoans is strikingly similar. *The Evolution of Civilizations* (Indianapolis: Liberty Press, 1979), pp. 239, 255, 261. A French archaeologist, one of the earliest to see the excavations, gazed at a group of women with elegant coiffures and low-cut gowns and exclaimed approvingly: "*Ce sont des Parisiennes!*"

3. See the discussion of these concepts in A. W. H. Adkins, *Moral Values and Political Behavior in Ancient Greece* (London: Chatto and Windus, 1972), pp. 60ff., and Bruno Snell, *The Discovery of the Mind,* trans. T. G. Rosenmeyer (Oxford: Blackwell, 1953), pp. 158-59.

4. Quoted in the article on Xenophanes by A. C. Lloyd in the *Encyclopaedia Britannica,* vol. 23 (1969), p. 843.

5. Protagoras, a sophist of the fifth century B.C., opened a treatise on *Truth* with the words: "Man is the measure of everything."

6. What we know about Socrates is contained in the writings of Plato and Xenophon, both of whom admired him, and of Aristophanes, who ridicules him in *The Clouds*. A negative portrayal of Socrates, representing him as basically critical of Athenian democracy, has been written by I. F. Stone in *The Trial of Socrates* (Boston: Little, Brown, 1988).

7. An example occurs in the *Republic,* Bk. 1:338c-339a.

8. In *The Legacy of Greece,* ed. R. W. Livingstone (Oxford: Clarendon, 1921), p. 15. Murray wrote the introductory essay, "The Value of Greece to the Future of the World."

9. For maintaining the status quo, their policies included periodic expulsions of aliens and the maintenance of a secret police (*he krupteia*), which on one occasion was known to have rounded up numerous Helots and to have executed them summarily.

10. The epitaph that Simonides composed for the handful of Spartans who held back the entire Persian army at Thermopylae for three days, and were killed to a man, was as follows: "Stranger, tell the Spartans that we lie here, obeying their orders."

11. Summarized from Pericles' Funeral Oration, in Thucydides' *History,* Bk. 2:35-46. The passage I have translated is in sec. 40.

12. *History,* Bk. 3:82-83 (on *stasis*); Bk. 5:85-116 (the Melian dialogue).

13. Sophocles, *Antigone,* 11:449-60.

14. See Chapter 10, pp. 292-294.

15. Horace, *Epistles,* Bk. 2:1, 11.156-57 (my translation).

16. Aeneas personifies the theme of Cicero's philosophical discourse, *De Officiis* (Concerning the Performance of Duties). He behaved correctly on every occasion, except in Carthage, where he had an affair with Dido and then deserted her. Virgil was writing this only a few years after the disastrous ending of Antony's liaison with Cleopatra. Was he reminding his audience of the risks for Romans of being involved with a North African queen?

17. I have discussed the significance of these in *The Great Issues of Politics* (Englewood Cliffs, N.J.: Prentice-Hall, 9th ed., 1993), chaps. 5, 12.

18. Ibid.

19. Belloc wrote of the British that they were less concerned about the equality of Man than about the inequality of racehorses.

20. Pastoral societies tended to think that the forces controlling the world were located in the sky, and the supreme force was personified in masculine terms as a

god. Agricultural peoples believed that the Earth was the life-giver, given that their food grew out of its soil. This notion was personified in the feminine as a goddess. The earliest Hebrews, be it remembered, were pastoralists.

21. Deuteronomy 6:4.

22. The relations in Judaism between religion, law, and ethics are explained thus by Israel Mattuck: "Judaism in its formative period, and in its historical development, has been a religion of the Law, which contains injunctions for every aspect of human life. Ethics belongs to it. Neither Biblical nor Rabbinic Hebrew has a word for ethics. . . . Ethics is not conceived apart from religion, so that it is included in whatever expression, or expressions, Bible and Talmud use for religion." *Jewish Ethics* (London: Hutchinson's University Library, 1953), p. 19.

23. James H. Breasted, *The Dawn of Conscience* (New York: Scribner's, 1933, reprinted 1961). See especially chap. 17, "The Sources of Our Moral Heritage."

24. For example, in Deuteronomy 20:11-17.

25. Leviticus 19:34.

26. Isaiah 2:4.

27. According to the account in the New Testament, he started precociously, questioning the authorities in the Temple itself when he was only 12 years old. Luke 2:42-49.

28. Matthew 5:44. Also Luke 6:27-28. Jesus expressed quite contradictory values, however, in this statement: "Think not that I am come to send peace on earth: I came not to send peace, but a sword. For I am come to set a man at variance against his father, and the daughter against her mother." Matthew 10:34-35. Also Luke 12:49-53.

29. From *De Carne Christi*, 5. The Latin is *Certum est, quia impossible est.* It has been wrongly quoted as *credo quia impossible* (I believe it because it is impossible) and has been attributed to Augustine with the wording: *credo quia absurdum* (I believe it because it is absurd).

30. In his *De Civitate Dei*, written after the fall of Rome in 410 to defend the Christians against the charge that their values were the cause of Rome's weakening and defeat.

31. "In seventh-century Rome, the members of the clerical oligarchy of the city still proceeded to their churches as the consuls had processed in the early sixth century—greeted by candles, scattering largesse to the populace, wearing the silken slippers of a senator. The Lateran Palace was so called, it was thought because 'good Latin' was still spoken there. In their great basilicas, the popes continued to pray for the *Romana libertas.* The idea that western society had to recognize the predominance of a sharply defined, clerical elite, as the emperors had once recognized the special status of members of the Roman Senate, was the basic assumption behind the rhetoric and ceremonial of the medieval papacy." Peter Brown, *The World of Late Antiquity* (London: Thames and Hudson, 1971; reprinted by Harcourt Brace Jovanovich, 1980), p. 135.

32. Thomas Hobbes, *Leviathan*, Pt. 4, chap. 47 (italics in the original).

33. Muller, *Uses of the Past*, p. 95.

34. The intolerance of the Roman church in contrast with the Byzantine Empire was already evident in the reign of Anastasius (491-518). Peter Brown writes: "In 517, Anastasius received a delegation of priests from Rome that showed how far apart the western and the eastern halves of Christendom had already drifted. The Catholic Church in the West had become a closed elite—like a colonizing power in underdeveloped territories, it regarded itself as obliged to impose its views, by force if need be, on the unregenerate 'world.' . . . The Roman legates told Anastasius that

he should impose the Catholic faith on his provincials with the firmness of a crusader. To the east Roman emperor, such advice came from another, more barbarous world." *World of Late Antiquity,* p. 148.

35. "During the whole period from the seventh to thirteenth centuries the two great civilizations of Eurasia were those of Islam and China." Gernet, *History of Chinese Civilization,* p. 287.

36. Consult *History of Mankind,* vol. 3, *The Great Medieval Civilizations* by Gaston Wiet, Vadime Elisseeff, Philippe Wolff, and Jean Naudou (UNESCO, published by Harper & Row, 1975), Pt. 2, chap. 7, pp. 443-58. Also see "Muslim Cordoba" by A. J. Arberry in *Cities of Destiny,* ed. Arnold J. Toynbee (London: Thames and Hudson, 1967), p. 175.

37. See Chapter 5, p. 120.

38. This phrase is the subtitle of her brilliant book, *A Distant Mirror* (New York: Knopf, 1978).

39. There is a good discussion of this by David Douglas in "The Paris of Abelard and St. Louis" in *Cities of Destiny,* ed. Toynbee.

40. To judge from what Stephen Hawking relates, the contemporary church has not yet learned its lesson. The British physicist writes that in 1981 he "attended a conference on cosmology organized by the Jesuits in the Vatican. The Catholic Church," he says, "had made a big mistake with Galileo when it tried to lay down the law on a question of science, declaring that the sun went round the earth. Now, centuries later, it had decided to invite a number of experts to advise it on cosmology. At the end of the conference the participants were granted an audience with the pope. He told us that it was all right to study the evolution of the universe after the big bang, but we should not inquire into the big bang itself because that was the moment of Creation and therefore the work of God." *A Brief History of Time* (New York: Bantam, 1988), p. 116.

41. Bertolt Brecht in his play *Galileo* superbly dramatizes the contrast between the scientist who forms his conclusions on the basis of observed data and those who refuse to look through his telescope.

42. The title of a book by E. L. Jones (Cambridge University Press, 1981).

43. Quoted by J. H. Plumb in *The Renaissance* (New York: Harper & Row, 1965), p. 199.

44. See Chapter 7, passim.

Chapter 4

1. The several volumes of *The Decline and Fall of the Roman Empire* were published at different dates: vol. 1 in 1776, vols. 2-3 in 1781, and vols. 4-6 in 1788. It is significant that Benjamin Franklin, when American minister in Paris, wrote to Gibbon while he was on a visit there, suggesting that they meet. Gibbon declined on the ground that he could not properly consort with a British subject in rebellion against the king. Franklin had the last word, responding that, had they met, he could have provided the historian with material on the decline and fall of the British Empire!

2. These phrases are the titles of parts of his *Study of History* or of chapters within the parts.

3. For critiques of Spengler, see Lewis Mumford's *The Transformations of Man* (New York: Collier, 1962), pp. 93-94, and Toynbee, *A Study of History,* Pt. 4, chap. 20 (Oxford University Press, one-volume ed., 1972), pp. 154-55.

4. The *locus classicus* for this hypothesis is in Hesiod's poem *Works and Days.*

5. The phrase is Milton's, from his poem *Lycidas.* There, he applies it to the desire for fame.

6. I have developed this argument about the nature of human society in *The Great Issues of Politics,* chap. 2, p. 37.

7. *Study of History,* one-volume ed., p. 72.

8. *The Evolution of Civilizations,* pp. 78-84.

9. Chapter 2, pp. 21-22.

10. Chapter 3, p. 64.

11. Chapter 5, pp. 108-110.

12. Cited in Chapter 2, p. 23.

13. For a discussion of European voyages to North America before Columbus, see Carl O. Sauer, *Northern Mists* (Berkeley: University of California Press, 1968).

14. George Berkeley, "On the Prospect of Planting Arts and Learning in America." Stanza 6.

15. Ibn Khaldun, *The Muqaddimah* (An Introduction to History), trans. Franz Rosenthal (Princeton University Press, 2nd ed., 1967), vol. 1, pp. 64-65.

16. Ibid., p. 56.

17. Ibid., p. 83.

18. *Study of History,* p. 489.

19. This key concept is continually reiterated throughout *The Muqaddimah.*

20. "Superiority results from group feeling. Only by God's help in establishing His religion do individual desires come together in agreement to press their claims, and hearts become united." "When people [who have a religious coloring] come to have the [right] insight into their affairs, nothing can withstand them, because their outlook is one and their object one of common accord. They are willing to die for [their objectives]." Khaldun, *The Muqaddimah,* pp. 319, 320.

21. Giambattista Vico, *The New Science,* trans. Thomas Goddard Bergin and Max Harold Fisch (Ithaca, N.Y.: Cornell University Press, 1968), Bk. 1, sec. 3:331, p. 96.

22. Ibid., sec. 4:342-43, p. 102.

23. Ibid., Conclusion, 1110, p. 426.

24. Ibid., Bk. 5:1047, p. 397.

25. Ibid., Bk. 1, sec. 4:349, p. 104.

26. This point is made by R. G. Collingwood in *The Idea of History* (New York: Oxford University Press, 1956), pp. 67-68.

27. See his Introduction to *New Science,* Bk. 4:915, p. 335. I have referred to two phases because of my contention that the West has known one continuous civilization. Toynbee, who maintains that there have been two successive civilizations in the West, attributes this view to Vico. He states that "Vico, working at Naples in the early eighteenth century, had only two civilizations within his historical horizon, namely his own Western Civilization and its Hellenic predecessor" (*Study of History,* p. 491). It seems to me that Toynbee is reading into Vico more than he actually says. In the first place, although Vico uses such terms as *civilized* and *civilization,* he does so sparingly as the antithesis to "barbarian" or "barbarism." For his thought, the primary category is not civilization, but nation. What he writes about in the later sections of his work is titled "the course the nations run" and "the recourse of human institutions which the nations take when they rise again." Vico was struck by the parallelism he detected between the ancient barbarian periods and the return of a similar period lasting

through what we call the Dark and Middle Ages. He is saying that nations go through cycles—which can repeat themselves. He is not saying, as Toynbee does, that the West has experienced two separate civilizations.

28. *The Decline of the West,* trans. C. F. Atkinson (New York: Knopf, 1928), vol. 1, Introduction, p. 46.

29. Mumford, *Transformations of Man,* p. 94.

30. "The philosophy of this book I owe to the philosophy of Goethe, which is practically unknown today, and also (but in a far less degree) to that of Nietzsche." *Decline of the West,* vol. 1, p. 49, n. 1.

31. His attempt at an explanation is contained in this sentence, which I find meaningless: "A culture is born in the moment when a great soul awakens out of the proto-spirituality of ever-childish humanity, and detaches itself, a form from the formless, a bounded and mortal thing from the boundless and enduring." Ibid., p. 106.

32. Ibid., p. 31 (italics in the original).

33. "Decline" is a weak rendering of the German *Untergang.* "Drowning" would be the better translation.

34. Foreword to the one-volume *Study of History,* p. 11.

35. See p. 71 of this chapter and note 2 above.

36. This phrase is the title of chap. 13 in Pt. 2 of the one-volume *Study of History.*

37. William H. McNeill, who worked with Toynbee in London for two years, 1950-52, writes as follows: "He had abandoned his classical frame of mind. Serious personal stresses, climaxing in a powerful mystical experience that occurred in 1939, convinced him of the existence of a supernatural reality which he soon felt able to refer to familiarly as God. History indeed became the record of God's self-revelation to humanity; and civilizations became instruments whose recurrent breakdown sensitized men to the supernatural." *New York Times,* Book Reviews, December 29, 1985, p. 25.

38. The "schism in the soul" is a phrase that Toynbee employs in discussing "The Disintegration of Civilizations." It is the title of chap. 30 in Pt. 5 of the one-volume *Study of History.*

39. C. M. Bowra generalizes thus in his discussion of Athens: "Most great civilizations fail in the end from the defects of their virtues." From his essay "Athens in the Age of Pericles" in *Cities of Destiny,* ed. Toynbee, p. 47. See also note 43 below.

40. Plato, *The Republic,* Bk. 8:563e.

41. *Distant Mirror,* pp. 563, 577.

42. Philip Van Ness Myers has stressed that the Islamic culture was superior to the Christian in the eighth century but subsequently stagnated. He explains this by "the requirement of unswerving obedience to an unchangeable law." *History as Past Ethics* (Boston: Ginn, 1913), p. 298.

43. Bowra writes: "Athens failed mainly from the superabundance of that energy which had made her great, but also from placing too great a trust in the intelligence, which turned from the clarifying of great issues to undermining their assumptions." "Athens" in *Cities of Destiny,* ed. Toynbee, p. 47. See note 39 above.

44. This term is used by William James, who refers to "the bitch-goddess, success."

Chapter 5

1. Abraham H. Maslow, *Toward a Psychology of Being* (Princeton, N.J.: Van Nostrand, 1962), chaps. 6, 7. See also the related discussion in Elizabeth M. Drews,

The Higher Levels of Human Growth (New York: Philosophical Library, 1979), and Gardner Murphy, *Human Potentialities* (New York: Basic Books, 1958).

2. "The art of the Sung Dynasty which we admire today was produced by, and for, a social and intellectual elite more cultivated than at any other period in Chinese history." Michael Sullivan, *A Short History of Chinese Art* (Berkeley: University of California Press, 1970), p. 195.

3. In his article on the caliphate, H. A. R. Gibb refers to "the brilliant Islamic civilization of the [ninth] century." *Encyclopaedia Britannica*, vol. 4 (1960), p. 649.

4. *Configurations of Culture Growth* (Berkeley: University of California Press, 1944), p. 761. The words quoted are the beginning of chap. 11, titled "Review and Conclusions."

5. Xerxes asked Demaratus, a renegade Spartan, what compelled a handful of Spartans to stay at their posts and hold the pass at Thermopylae against hopeless odds. Being free men, why did they not run from certain death? To this, Demaratus replied: "Free though they are, they are not free in everything. For over them is set a master—the Law—which they fear much more than your subjects fear you." Herodotus' *Histories*, Bk. 7:103-4 (my translation).

6. See Chapter 3, note 11, and the discussion of Sparta and Athens on p. 48.

7. I have based my account of these events on Hans Baron, *The Crisis of the Early Italian Renaissance* (Princeton University Press, 1955), pp. 3-46.

8. Here is the list: Brunelleschi (1377-1446), Ghiberti (1378-1455), Donatello (1386-1466), Uccello (1397-1475), Masaccio (1401-28), Alberti (1404-72), Lippi (1406-69), Verrocchio (1435-88), Botticelli (1444/5-1510), Leonardo (1452-1519), Machiavelli (1469-1527), Michelangelo (1475-1564), Guicciardini (1483-1540). Galileo lived a century later (1564-1642).

9. For these comparisons, see Baron, *Early Italian Renaissance*.

10. On Bruni, see Nicholai Rubenstein, "The Beginnings of Humanism in Florence" in *The Age of the Renaissance*, ed. Denys Hay (London: Thames and Hudson, 1967), pp. 29-33.

11. Quoted by Rubenstein, ibid., pp. 12, 33.

12. Ibid., p. 29.

13. Quoted by Kenneth Clark in *Civilisation*, p. 101.

14. An earlier parallel is the case of the Netherlands, after fighting for independence from Spain. Consider the names of Huygens (1629-95), Spinoza (1632-77), and Leeuwenhoek (1632-1723). Along with Rembrandt (1606-69), the Dutch school of painting includes Hals (c. 1580-1666), Ruysdael (c. 1602-70), Ter Borch (1617-81), Steen (1626-79), de Hooch (1629-c. 1683), Vermeer (1632-75), and Hobbema (1638-1709).

15. Sullivan, *History of Chinese Art*, p. 146.

16. See Chapter 9, pp. 251-254.

17. See Chapter 1, p. 8.

18. For example, in *The Culture of Cities* (New York: Harcourt, Brace, 1938).

19. *Politics*, Bk. 3:3(5), 1276a.

20. In the New Comedy, which succeeded the Old, Menander excelled. But not enough of his work has survived for him to be fairly judged in relation to Aristophanes.

21. See note 14 above.

22. He is quoted by Kroeber, *Configurations*, pp. 17-18.

23. Another literary expression of this idea is in G. K. Chesterton's *The Napoleon of Notting Hill*—the story of a man who had studied intensively the strategy of all

past wars and had analyzed the tactics of all their battles but who lived in a country at peace (tragically for him) with no opportunity to turn his knowledge to practical use!

24. My translation from the original line, which reads: *Sint Maecenates, non deerunt, Flacce, Marones.* Martial, 8:58.5.

25. See Toynbee, *Mankind and Mother Earth,* pp. 512, 558-59, and Gernet, *History of Chinese Civilization,* p. 509.

26. This point is emphasized by Kroeber, *Configurations,* p. 269.

27. *History of Chinese Civilization,* pp. 297ff.

28. Sullivan, *History of Chinese Art,* p. 195.

29. In his essay titled "Of the Rise and Progress of the Arts and Sciences," David Hume makes this point: "That nothing is more favorable to the rise of politeness and learning than a number of neighboring and independent states connected together by commerce and policy. The emulation which naturally arises among those neighboring states is an obvious source of improvement." Reprinted in *David Hume's Political Essays,* ed. Charles W. Hendel (New York: Liberal Arts Press, 1953), p. 116.

One may discover examples of this phenomenon almost anywhere in the world. When visiting Nepal, I traveled by car from the capital, Kathmandu, to the nearby city of Patan, which contains some quite remarkable architecture and sculptures. My guide explained why they happened to be located there. Five centuries ago, the Kathmandu valley with its three principal cities—Kathmandu, Patan, and Bhadgaon—was ruled as a unit. The king, however, on his death gave each of the cities to one of his three sons. A rivalry then ensued, and it was the ruler of Patan who adorned his city with especially notable structures to outdo his brothers.

30. See Kenneth Clark, *Leonardo da Vinci* (Harmondsworth, England: Penguin, rev. ed., 1967), pp. 45-46.

31. Toynbee, *Mankind and Mother Earth,* p. 448.

32. Yehudi Menuhin and Curtis W. Davis, *The Music of Man* (Toronto: Methuen, 1979), p. 298.

33. Gernet, *History of Chinese Civilization,* pp. 25, 27.

34. Ibid., p. 72.

35. Ernest Renan, *Apôtres,* p. 364 (my translation). Quoted in Burckhardt, *Force and Freedom* (New York: Pantheon, 1943), p. 232, n. 1.

36. Ibid.

37. *Dynamics of World History* (New York: Sheed and Ward, 1956), p. 61.

38. Ibid., p. 62.

39. J. L. Myres, *The Dawn of History* (New York: Holt, 1911) pp. 216, 220-221.

40. William H. McNeill, *World History* (New York: Oxford University Press, 1979), pp. 68-69.

41. See Gernet, *History of Chinese Civilization,* pp. 231-32.

42. Ibid., p. 288.

43. Ibid., pp. 311-12.

44. The chief architect, Ustad Isa, is said to have been of Turkish or Persian extraction.

45. E. L. Jones, *The European Miracle,* p. 73.

46. From F. Whyte, *China and Foreign Powers* (London: Oxford University Press, 1927), appendix. Quoted in Toynbee, *Civilization on Trial* (New York: Oxford University Press, 1948), p. 72.

Chapter 6

1. Thucydides, *History,* Bk. 3, chap. 82:2 (my translation). He is writing here about the effects of stasis (internal conflict) at Corcyra and elsewhere.

2. Machiavelli, *Discorsi,* Bk. 2, chap. 43. In Bk. 1, chap. 34, he says: "Whoever considers the past and the present will readily observe that all cities and all peoples are and ever have been animated by the same desires and the same passions; so that it is easy, by diligent study of the past, to foresee what is likely to happen in any republic."

3. Montaigne, *Essays,* Bk. 2, chap. 12.

4. *Force and Freedom,* pp. 81-82 (italics in the original).

5. *Christianity and History* (New York: Scribner's, 1949), pp. 31, 33.

6. *Force and Freedom,* p. 355.

7. *Leviathan,* Pt. I, chaps. 9, 13.

8. Boris Pasternak, *Doctor Zhivago,* trans. Max Hayward and Manya Harari (New York: Pantheon, 1958), p. 378.

9. John Calvin, *Institutes of the Christian Religion,* Bk. 2.

10. Schopenhauer wrote this in *Parerga und Paralipomena,* published in 1851, under the heading of "Parables."

11. Sigmund Freud, *Civilization and Its Discontents,* trans. Joan Riviere (London: Hogarth, 1957), pp. 85-89.

12. Ibid., p. 89.

13. Edward A. Westermarck, *Origin and Development of the Moral Ideas* (London: Macmillan, 1906-8), vol. 1, p. 373.

14. For instance, L. T. Hobhouse, *Morals in Evolution,* and the writings of Morris Ginsberg, *On the Diversity of Morals,* vol. 1, *Essays in Sociology and Social Philosophy* (London: Heinemann, 1956) and "Comparative Ethics" (in *Encyclopedia Britannica,* 1969).

15. Thomas Henry Buckle, *History of Civilization in England,* quoted in P. M. Martin, *Is Mankind Advancing?* (New York: Baker and Taylor, 1910), p. 163, n. 1.

16. Crane Brinton, *History of Western Morals* (New York: Harcourt, Brace, 1959), p. 417.

17. *Daedalus* 104, no. 2 (Spring 1975), titled "Wisdom, Revelation, and Doubt: Perspectives on the First Millennium, B.C."

18. *Daedalus,* "Wisdom, Revelation, and Doubt," p. 3.

19. Ibid.

20. Ibid., p. 26.

21. Ibid., p. 4 (quotation marks are in the original).

22. Thapar, *History of India,* p. 119.

23. The traditional sources state that Zoroaster lived "258 years before Alexander," which is taken to refer to the latter's conquest of Persia in 330 B.C. Presumably the meaning is that the major event of Zoroaster's life occurred 258 years earlier, and this could be his first vision, or the start of his preaching, or his success in converting Hystaspes. Tradition also records that he died when he was 77, therefore, his possible dates are 630-553, 628-551, or 618-541.

24. Plato, *The Laws* (trans. Benjamin Jowett), 10:896.

25. Thapar's essay is titled "Ethics, Religion, and Social Protest in the First Millennium, B.C. in Northern India."

26. See Chapter 2, p. 34ff.

27. *Thought in Ancient China,* p. 4.

28. Amos 3:6. Similarly in Isaiah 45:7, Yahweh says: "I form the light, and create darkness: I make peace, and create evil."

29. See Chapter 5, p. 121.

30. See Chapter 2, p. 36.

31. Chapter 2, p. 27.

32. This is discussed in Chapter 8, p. 225ff.

33. L. T. Hobhouse has written: "All that we can hope to do in comparing different stages of growth is to deal with recognized customs, accepted maxims, and ideas expressed in mythology, in literature, or in art. In other words, we could only hope to give the history of those ethical conceptions which are recognized as rules of conduct, and we must give up as wholly beyond our power the investigation of the degree in which conduct itself conforms to those rules. . . . A rule of conduct may be a genuine expression of what people actually feel and think, or it may be an ideal bearing as little relation to common practice as the Sermon on the Mount to the code of the Stock Exchange." *Morals in Evolution,* vol. 1, p. 26.

34. *"Wie es wirklich war."*

35. See Chapter 3, p. 52.

36. Edward Gibbon, *The Decline and Fall of the Roman Empire,* vol. 1. He offers this judgment in chap. 3.

37. Peter Brown, *World of Late Antiquity,* p. 57.

38. The quotations are from Marcus Aurelius' *Meditations* (trans. George Long), 4:17, 48; 7:3.

39. Mumford, *The Condition of Man* (New York: Harcourt Brace, 1944), p. 42.

40. See Chapter 3, pp. 58-59.

41. From *The Prince,* chap. 6.

Chapter 7

1. Blaise Pascal, *Pensées,* no. 894, trans. W. F. Trotter (New York: Random House, Modern Library, 1941), p. 314.

2. Among his works were the *Letters on Toleration,* 1689.

3. So central to the Enlightenment was its elevation of reason that the eighteenth century is generally called the Age of Reason. Alan Bullock disputes this, however, in a recent work, *The Humanist Tradition in the West* (New York: Norton, 1985). "The common identification of the eighteenth century with the Age of Reason is misleading," he writes. "In this context it could be better applied to the seventeenth than the eighteenth" (p. 63). The Enlightenment, in his judgment, stressed feeling (the passions) no less than reason, and sometimes more so. He quotes Descartes as saying: "There is no soul so weak that it cannot, if well directed, acquire absolute power over its passions." (In *Les passions de l'âme,* 1649, Art. 50, ed. G. Rodis Lewis, Paris, 1955). Hume, on the other hand, made the well-known statement: "Reason is, and ought only to be, the slave of the passions, and can never pretend to any other office than to serve and obey them."

That the Enlightenment had its precursors in the seventeenth century, and that such movements of thought are not confined to the precise divisions of our calendar, no one will deny. What is central, it seems to me, was the objective of the Enlightenment that individuals should seek knowledge by using their own faculties. This involved a repudiation of external authority (whether secular or ecclesiastical) and a rejection of revelation accepted on faith—hence the reliance on reason. Beyond that, there was disagreement about the source of our ideas (whether some are innate or whether all are derived from experience after birth) and about the relative influence of reason and feelings in impelling us to act.

I would concur with Berlin, who lists "the central principles of the Enlightenment" as "universality, objectivity, rationality, and the capacity to provide permanent solutions to all genuine problems of life or thought, and (not less important) accessibility of rational methods to any thinker armed with adequate powers of observation and logical thinking." *Against the Current* (New York: Penguin, 1982), pp. 19-20. Voltaire, whom Berlin characterizes as "the central figure of the Enlightenment" (ibid., p. 88), concluded his work *The Ignorant Philosopher* by saying "this age . . . is the dawn of reason." In any case, Bullock contradicts his own argument because he himself refers to "the rationalism of the Enlightenment" (*Humanist Tradition*, p. 74).

4. It is evident that this line of reasoning (however attractive the conclusions) contains a logical flaw because of the ambiguity in the concept of law. Law in the scientific sense is not identical in meaning with law in the moral sense. The former states how physical phenomena must necessarily behave because of their inherent characteristics; the latter, how human beings ought to behave in their relations with one another.

5. From his chapter, "Free Inquiry and the World of Ideas," in *The Eighteenth Century: Europe in the Age of Enlightenment,* ed. Alfred Cobban (London: Thames and Hudson, 1969), p. 275.

6. See Gernet, *History of Chinese Civilization,* pp. 521, 524.

7. Muller, *Uses of the Past,* p. 323.

8. Jean-Antoine-Nicolas Caritat, Marquis de Condorcet, *Esquisse d'un Tableau Historique des progrès de l'esprit humain* (1794). The quotation is from the Introduction (my translation).

9. Muller, *Uses of the Past,* p. 284.

10. Quoted by Robert Shackleton, to introduce his chapter, "The Enlightenment," in *The Eighteenth Century,* ed. Cobban, p. 260.

11. For a discussion of this ambiguity, see my *Democratic Civilization* (New York: Oxford University Press, 1964), pp. 54-56.

12. Brinton, *History of Western Morals,* p. 324.

13. Muller, *Uses of the Past,* p. 358.

14. Quoted by Barbara Tuchman, *Distant Mirror,* p. 31, from J. J. Jusserand, *English Wayfaring Life in the Middle Ages* (London, 1950), p. 166.

15. "After [Innocent III] . . . the Church stood as a triumphant, ruthless reaction against the true spirit of the age. It was a police force, habituated to the most extreme methods, which artificially re-established the Middle Ages. . . . The Church presented the supreme example of a religion overwhelmed by its institutions and representatives." Burckhardt, *Force and Freedom,* pp. 205-6.

16. Quoted by P. M. Martin, *Is Mankind Advancing?,* p. 113.

17. The exceptions to this generalization are only apparent. John Howard was a sheriff, in which capacity he became familiar with prison conditions. But his office was one of strictly local jurisdiction. Anthony Ashley Cooper, the seventh Earl of Shaftesbury, was a religious man who belonged to an aristocratic Whig family. He served briefly in one British ministry but carried through most of his legislation from his seat in the House of Lords when he was not holding ministerial office. Chadwick wrote reports based on his investigations into social conditions. He was appointed to administrative posts that enabled him to enforce the legislation inspired by his recommendations.

18. Immanuel Kant, *Fundamental Principles of the Metaphysic of Morals*, trans. T. K. Abbott (London: Longman's, Green, 10th ed., 1929), p. 56.

19. E. J. Hobsbawm has written: "The Industrial Revolution marks the most fundamental transformation of human life in the history of the world recorded in written documents." *Industry and Empire* (Harmondsworth, England: Penguin, 1969), p. 13.

20. See his work *The Subjection of Women*, published in 1869 (reprinted in 1974, Oxford: World's Classics).

21. L. T. Hobhouse, *Morals in Evolution*, vol. 1, p. 229.

22. Ibid., vol. 1, p. 114.

23. On this point, see G. M. Trevelyan, *British History in the Nineteenth Century* (London: Longman's, 1922), p. 31, where these examples are cited.

24. Hobhouse, *Morals in Evolution*, vol. 1, p. 115.

25. Kenneth Clark, *Civilisation*, pp. 329-30.

26. This is based on Myers, *History as Past Ethics*, p. 373.

27. Quoted by A. P. Thornton in "The Century of European World Power" in *The Nineteenth Century*, ed. Asa Briggs (London: Thames and Hudson, 1970), p. 231.

28. F. Bedarida, "Population and the Urban Explosion" in *The Nineteenth Century*, ibid., p. 122.

29. C. E. A. Winslow, "Health" in *Whither Mankind*, ed. Beard, p. 188.

30. The date 1870 is significant. The Prussians had just crushed the French, and the British attributed their victory to two factors: their efficient railroads and the education the soldiers had received from their schoolmasters.

31. Gladstone is quoted in Roger Fulford's chapter, "Victorian and Edwardian London," in *Cities of Destiny*, ed. Toynbee, p. 294.

32. For the quotation from Wallace, see Asa Briggs's "The Shape of the Century" in *The Nineteenth Century*, ed. Briggs, p. 25.

33. Benjamin Disraeli, *Sybil* (London: Longman's, 1871), p. 198.

34. Roger Fulford, "Victorian and Edwardian London" in *Cities of Destiny*, ed. Toynbee, pp. 276, 290-91.

35. Myers, *History as Past Ethics*, p. 205.

36. Edmund Burke, *Reflections on the Revolution in France* (New York: Dutton, Everyman's Library, 1910), p. 73.

37. From his sonnets "The World" and "England, 1802."

38. Ralph Waldo Emerson, *English Traits*. These are the opening sentences of chap. 10, "Wealth."

39. These two quotations may be found in Tuchman, *Distant Mirror*, p. 37, who takes St. Augustine from G. G. Coulton, *Medieval Panorama* (Cambridge University Press, 1938), p. 369, and St. Jerome from Henri Pirenne, *A History of Europe* (New York: Norton, 1958), vol. 2, p. 229.

40. Toynbee, *Mankind and Mother Earth*, p. 20.

41. Henry Willets, "The Slav Nations" in *The Age of Expansion* (London: Thames and Hudson, 1968), p. 268.

42. See Olwyn Hufton, "The Rise of the People: Life and Death Among the Very Poor" in *The Eighteenth Century*, ed. Cobban, p. 280.

43. Ibid., p. 309.

44. Hobhouse, *Morals in Evolution*, vol. 2, p. 255.

45. Mill wrote this in midcentury, in that epochal year 1848. Asa Briggs quotes him in his introductory chapter, "Man at the Crossroads of History" in *The Nineteenth Century*, ed. Briggs, p. 30.

46. These quotations are from Burckhardt, *Force and Freedom*, pp. 149, 73.

Chapter 8

1. John Stuart Mill, *The Subjection of Women*, p. 451.

2. For example, when the world economy suffered a recession in the 1970s, women were affected more adversely than men. In 1980, a document prepared for the Copenhagen conference midway in the United Nations' "Decade for Women" described their situation since 1975 as one of "stagnation and deterioration."

3. The figure for the United States is cited by the economist Lester C. Thurow in an article titled "Why Women Earn Less than Men," reprinted in *The San Francisco Chronicle*, This World sec., March 22, 1981. By the late 1980s, however, American women's earnings, on the average, were 70 percent of what men earned (*The New York Times*, August 21, 1989). The European figures are derived from Britain's Equal Opportunities Commission and from the Organization for Economic Cooperation and Development and were quoted by Gary Yerkey in *The Christian Science Monitor*, June 18, 1981.

4. "Women in Political Office," *The Christian Science Monitor*, June 17, 1983; "Elections Change Face of Lawmaking Bodies," *The New York Times*, November 5, 1992.

5. "Fair Shares for Women," *The Christian Science Monitor*, October 5, 1986.

6. "Women's Brave New World Is Far Away," *Economist*, July 19, 1980.

7. See the series of five articles by Kristin Helmore in *The Christian Science Monitor*, December 17-20 and 23, 1985.

8. "Female Circumcision Is Debated in Third World," Sheila Rule in *The New York Times*, July 29, 1985.

9. This abominable practice was outlawed by the British in 1829 and is banned by law in present-day India. But it still occasionally happens in some of the villages—a case being reported from Rajasthan in 1987.

10. *The San Francisco Chronicle*, June 21, 1983, from the United Press.

11. A report on this subject was prepared in 1955 by Hans Engen, Norwegian Ambassador to the United Nations. When Ethiopia was admitted to the League of Nations in the 1920s, the League attached the condition that slavery must be abolished within a definite period—this being the enslavement of Africans by Africans.

12. On this point, the opinion written by Chief Justice Earl Warren in the landmark case of *Brown v. Board of Education* (1954) stated: "Segregation of white and colored children in public schools has a detrimental effect upon the colored children. The impact is greater when it has the sanction of the law; for the policy of separating the races is usually interpreted as denoting the inferiority of the Negro group. . . . Separate educational facilities are inherently unequal." 349 U.S. 294.

13. Contemporary Brazil also has a minority of Japanese immigrants and their descendants who belong to a fourth race.

14. This is the subject of a classic work, *Casa Grande e Senzala* by the Brazilian sociologist, Gilberto Freyre.

15. Brazilians recognize this in the saying: *Rico negro e branco, e pobre branco e negro:* "A rich black is white, and a poor white is black."

16. See articles in *The New York Times*, May 14, 1988, and *The Christian Science Monitor*, May 3, 1988.

17. Wolpert, *New History of India*, p. 32.

18. On this, see the discussion later in this chapter, pp. 218-219.

19. The projects in the South Bronx were discussed in *Manas* magazine, September 2, 1981.

20. This was reported in *The New York Times,* August 24, 1987.

21. From *The Christian Science Monitor,* March 30, 1982.

22. The World Bank Development Report for 1982 offered these figures for the literacy rate in the less developed countries: 33 percent in 1950 and 56 percent in 1970. *The Christian Science Monitor,* May 12, 1983, "Literacy–The Third World's Beacon of Hope" by David Winder.

23. Shakespeare, *Merchant of Venice,* Act II, sc. 7, 1. 65.

24. The estimate of one adult in five as "functionally illiterate" was generally used in public discussion of this topic in the early 1980s. But many gave much higher figures–ranging between 30 and 60 million–as being unable to participate adequately in the economy or in social or political activities because of their educational deficiencies. See, for example, Jonathan Kozol in a book titled *Illiterate America* (New York: Doubleday, 1985).

25. The Nielsen ratings estimated the average daily hours of viewing television in American households at 4½ in 1950, 5 in 1960, 6 in 1970, and more than 7 in 1984. See *The San Francisco Chronicle,* April 27, 1985, p. 1.

26. To his great credit, no less an ecclesiastical dignitary than the Archbishop of Canterbury, Dr. Robert Runcie, in 1989 denounced the fundamentalism of all faiths for their intolerance. "All over the world," he said, "–in most religions and cultures there are those who believe they should not tolerate others, should avoid completely those whose beliefs they consider in error. It is not merely individuals who practise ecclesiastical apartheid. Whole communities of fierce conviction remain vigorous. Where there is strife in the world, you do not have to look far to see the hand of various brands of fundamentalism–Islamic fundamentalism in the Middle East, Christian fundamentalism in Ulster, or Jewish fundamentalism in Israel. The hands of such communities are stained with blood. Where toleration is in peril, persecution stalks not far behind." Reported in the *Manchester Guardian Weekly,* July 16, 1989.

27. This was the judgment expressed to me in conversation by Dean Milton Stern, my colleague at the University of California, Berkeley. It is one with which I heartily concur.

28. In an article she wrote in *The Christian Science Monitor,* October 7, 1986.

Chapter 9

1. Letter of Michelangelo to Domenico Buoninsegni, from Carrara, May 2, 1517. Printed in a collection of his letters edited by Irving Stone, titled *I, Michelangelo, Sculptor* (New York: Doubleday, Signet, 1962), p. 85. Incidentally, despite his regular complaints about his health, Michelangelo was almost 89 when he died–a great exception to the norm for that period, as he was in every other respect.

2. The system of medical care in the United States is exceedingly complex. Much of it is privately financed or consists of insurance schemes designed for different sections of the population. Through Medicare, as it is called, the elderly now receive some measure of protection under a program that the federal government has instituted. In general, such is the strength in American public opinion of the values of individual initiative and of what is quaintly described as "free" enterprise that the distribution of health is largely correlated with the distribution of wealth.

3. Tuchman, *Distant Mirror,* pp. 102-3.

4. From the article titled "According to the U.N., 1 Billion Are Unhealthy" by Warren E. Leary. *The New York Times,* September 26, 1989.

5. These data are from an article by Malcolm Dean in the *Manchester Guardian Weekly,* December 20, 1981. Dean was reporting on a conference in Karachi to discuss primary health care.

6. For details, consult the informative series of annual reports by Ruth Leger Sivard, *World Military and Social Expenditures,* published in Leesburg, Virginia, by World Priorities.

7. For a discussion of these problems, see *Our Common Future,* the report of the World Commission on Environment and Development, presented to the United Nations' General Assembly in 1987 (Oxford University Press, 1987).

8. Machiavelli, *The Prince,* chap. 9, "Of the Civic Principality."

9. John 12:8.

10. "The food of the needy is the purchase-money of the kingdom of heaven," said Leo the Great, pope from 440 to 461. Similarly, St. John Chrysostom affirmed: "As long as the market lasts, let us buy alms, or rather let us purchase salvation through alms." Both quotations are from Westermarck, *Moral Ideas,* vol. 1, p. 555.

11. Quoted by Sidney and Beatrice Webb in *Whither Mankind,* ed. Beard, p. 116.

12. See the article by Anthony Lewis, "The Two Nations," in *The New York Times,* April 4, 1985. Nationally in 1988, one American child in five was living in poverty. For black and Hispanic children, the rate is twice as high. See Spencer Rich, "One in Five American Children Living in Poverty," in *The Washington Post,* reprinted in the *Manchester Guardian Weekly,* December 3, 1989. For a full analysis of how the Reagan policies helped the rich become even richer, and the poor still poorer, see Kevin Phillips, *The Politics of Rich and Poor* (New York: Random House, 1990).

13. *The New York Times,* July 31 and October 27, 1987.

14. Cited in *The Christian Science Monitor,* June 28, 1978, in the article "Spaceship Earth: Riders vs. Food" by Richard L. Strout.

15. From *Living Conditions in Developing Countries in the Mid-1980's,* Supplement to the 1985 *Report on the World Social Situation* (New York: United Nations, 1986), p. 5.

16. *The New York Times,* December 19, 1988.

17. *The New York Times,* December 20, 1988.

18. Statement by Dr. Barry Bloom of the Albert Einstein Medical School, New York. Quoted in *The New York Times,* see note 4 above.

19. *The Christian Science Monitor,* August 16, 1978, in the article "World Bank: 800 Million People with Too Little to Eat" by Richard L. Strout.

20. As reported by the Associated Press in the newspapers of October 1 and 2, 1980.

21. See Chapter 3, p. 48, and Chapter 7, p. 180ff.

22. I have argued that freedom and equality are really one concept, not two, in an article titled "The Philosophy of Democracy—Can Its Contradictions Be Reconciled?" *Journal of International Affairs* 38, no. 2 (Winter 1985), pp. 151-60.

23. Elsewhere I have contributed to the literature on democracy in my work *The Democratic Civilization.*

24. *The New York Times* quoted a Soviet journalist, Artyom Borovik, as saying: "If you ask people now whether they want bread and order or freedom and democracy, they will say we want bread and order." From an article by Bill Keller, February 3, 1991.

25. There have been exceptions, of course, such as Kemal Ataturk, the founder of the modern, secularist Turkish state. In some of the democracies, professional

soldiers have held civilian office honorably—for instance, the Duke of Wellington, George Washington, Dwight D. Eisenhower, and Charles de Gaulle.

26. Aristotle, *Politics,* Bk. 1:ii, 8, 1252b (my translation).

27. *The Times* of London, October 6, 1982, in one of a series of articles reviewing Uganda's experience on the twentieth anniversary of its independence.

28. Statement written in an application to do graduate work at the University of California, Berkeley, 1982.

29. Emil Ludwig, in chap. 7, "War and Peace," in *Whither Mankind,* ed. Beard.

30. See Chapter 10, p. 292ff.

31. Cited by Philip Geyelin in the article "The Will for Peace Is Lacking," in *The Washington Post,* reprinted in *Manchester Guardian Weekly,* May 11, 1986.

32. *Report on the World Social Situation* (New York: United Nations, 1985), p. 14.

33. James Reston in *The New York Times,* June 3, 1988.

34. For information on this subject, see the yearbooks of the Stockholm International Peace Research Institute.

35. Quotations from an article titled "Children Dying as Money Goes on Debt and Arms," *Manchester Guardian Weekly,* December 31, 1989.

36. Quoted in *The Washington Spectator,* November 1, 1985, pp. 1-2.

Chapter 10

1. For the quotations from Wordsworth, see Chapter 7, pp. 189-190.

2. *Nichomachean Ethics,* 6.2:1139a.

Bibliography

In the case of classics and older works that have been reprinted many times, I have not always specified a particular edition.

Adams, Brooks, *The Law of Civilization and Decay* (New York: Macmillan, 1910).

Adkins, A. W. H., *Moral Values and Political Behavior in Ancient Greece* (London: Chatto and Windus, 1972).

Andrewes, Antony, *Greek Society* (Harmondsworth, England: Penguin, 1967).

Arberry, A. J., in *Cities of Destiny,* ed. Arnold J. Toynbee.

Aristophanes, *The Clouds.*

Aristotle, *Nichomachean Ethics.*

———, *The Politics.*

Arrian, *Historia Indica.*

Augustine, *Concerning the City of God,* trans. John Healey (1610).

Aurelius, Marcus, *Meditations.*

Baron, Hans, *The Crisis of the Early Italian Renaissance* (Princeton University Press, 1955).

Beard, Charles A., *Whither Mankind* (New York: Longman's, Green, 1928).

Bedarida, F., in *The Nineteenth Century* (London: Thames and Hudson, 1970).

Berkeley, George, *Poems.*

Berlin, Isaiah, *Historical Inevitability* (London: Oxford University Press, 1954).

———, *Against the Current* (New York: Penguin, 1982).

The Bhagavad-Gita, trans. Swami Paramananda.

The Bible, Old and New Testaments.

Bloom, Allan, and Jaffa, Harry V., *Shakespeare's Politics* (University of Chicago Press, 1964).

Boardman, John, Griffin, Jasper, and Murray, Oswyn, eds., *The Oxford History of the Classical World* (Oxford University Press, 1986).

Bowra, C. M., in *Cities of Destiny,* ed. Arnold J. Toynbee.

Breasted, James H., *The Dawn of Conscience* (New York: Scribner's, 1933).

Brecht, Bertolt, *Galileo.*

Briggs, Asa, ed., *The Nineteenth Century* (London: Thames and Hudson, 1970).

Brinton, Crane, *History of Western Morals* (New York: Harcourt Brace).

Brooks, Van Wyck, *The Flowering of New England* (New York: Modern Library, 1936).

Brown, Peter, *The World of Late Antiquity* (New York: Harcourt Brace Jovanovich, 1980).

Buckle, T. H., *History of Civilization in England* (New York: Appleton, 1958-61).

Bullock, Alan, *The Humanist Tradition in the West* (New York: Norton, 1985).

Burckhardt, Jacob, *Force and Freedom* (New York: Pantheon, 1943).

———, *The Civilization of the Renaissance in Italy* (New York: Oxford University Press, 1945).

Burke, Edmund, *Reflections on the Revolution in France* (1790).

Bury, J. B., *A History of Freedom of Thought* (London: Thornton Butterworth, 1913).

———, *The Idea of Progress* (New York: Dover, 1960).

Butterfield, Herbert, *Christianity and History* (New York: Scribner's, 1949).

Calvin, John, *Institutes of the Christian Religion.*

Chesterton, G. K., *The Napoleon of Notting Hill.*

Childe, V. Gordon, *What Happened in History* (Harmondsworth: Penguin, rev. ed., 1954).

———, *Man Makes Himself* (London: Watts, 1965).

Clark, Grahame, *World Prehistory* (Cambridge University Press, 3rd ed., 1977).

Clark, Kenneth, *Leonardo da Vinci* (Harmondsworth, England: Penguin, 1967).

———, *Civilisation* (New York: Harper & Row, 1969).

Cobban, Alfred, *In Search of Humanity* (New York: Braziller, 1960).

Cohen, Morris R., *The Meaning of Human History* (La Salle, Ill.: Open Court, 1947).

Collingwood, R. G., *The Idea of History* (New York: Oxford University Press, 1956).

———, *Essays in the Philosophy of History,* ed. William Debbins (New York: McGraw-Hill, 1965).

Condorcet, Marquis de, *Esquisse d'un Tableau Historique des progrès de l'esprit humain* (1794).

Confucius, *The Analects.*

Cotterell, Arthur, and Morgan, David, *China's Civilization* (New York: Praeger, 1975).

Coulton, G. G., *Medieval Panorama* (Cambridge University Press, 1938).

Crossman, R. H. S., ed., *The God That Failed* (New York: Harper, 1949).

Dawson, Christopher, *Dynamics of World History* (New York: Sheed and Ward, 1956).

Dean, Malcolm, in *The Manchester Guardian Weekly,* December 20, 1981.

Disraeli, Benjamin, *Sybil* (London: Longman's, 1871).

Douglas, David, in *Cities of Destiny,* ed. Arnold J. Toynbee.

Drews, Elizabeth Monroe, *Learning Together* (Englewood Cliffs, N.J.: Prentice-Hall, 1972).

———, *The Higher Levels of Human Growth* (New York: Philosophical Library, 1979).

———, and Lipson, Leslie, *Values and Humanity* (New York: St. Martin's, 1971).

Eichhorn, Werner, *Chinese Civilization,* trans. Janet Seligman (London: Faber and Faber, 1969).

Emerson, Ralph Waldo, "Brahma" in his *Poems.*

———, *English Traits* (1856).

Ettlinger, L. D., in *The Eighteenth Century,* ed. Alfred Cobban (London: Thames and Hudson, 1969).

Fairbank, John K., ed., *Chinese Thought and Institutions* (Chicago: University of Chicago Press, 1959).

Fanon, Franz, *The Wretched of the Earth* (Paris: F. Maspero, 1961).

Fitzgerald, C. P., *China: A Short Cultural History* (New York: Praeger, 1954).

Freud, Sigmund, *Civilization and Its Discontents,* trans. Joan Riviere (London: Hogarth, 1957).

Freyre, Gilberto, *Casa Grande e Senzala.*

Fulford, Roger, in *Cities of Destiny,* ed. Arnold J. Toynbee.

Fuller, Peter, *Theoria: Art and the Absence of Grace* (London: Chatto, 1988).

Gernet, Jacques, *A History of Chinese Civilization,* trans. J. R. Foster (Cambridge University Press, 1982).

Gibb, H. A. R., "The Caliphate," in *Encyclopaedia Britannica* (1969).

Gibbon, Edward, *The Decline and Fall of the Roman Empire in the West.*

Gimpel, Jean, *The Medieval Machine* (New York: Holt, Rinehart & Winston, 1976).

Ginsberg, Morris, *Essays in Sociology and Social Philosophy* (Harmondsworth, England: Penguin, 1968).

Goethe, Johann Wolfgang von, *Conversations with Eckermann.*

Hawkes, Jacquetta, *The First Great Civilizations* (New York: Knopf, 1973).

Hawking, Stephen W., *A Brief History of Time* (New York: Bantam, 1988).

Hegel, G. W. F., *The Philosophy of Right,* trans. S. W. Dyde (London: George Bell, 1896).

———, *Reason in History,* trans. Robert S. Hartman (New York: Liberal Arts Press, 1953).

Heilbroner, Robert L., *An Inquiry into the Human Prospect* (New York: Norton, 1974).

Helmore, Kristin, in *The Christian Science Monitor,* December 17-20 and 23, 1985.

Herodotus, *History of the Persian Wars.*

Herskovits, Melville J., *Man and His Works* (New York: Knopf, 1948).

Hesiod, *Works and Days.*

Hingley, R. F., "N. Y. Danilevsky," in *Encyclopaedia Britannica* (1969).

Hobbes, Thomas, *Leviathan.*

Hobhouse, L. T., *Morals in Evolution* (New York: Holt, 1906).

Hobsbawm, E. J., *Industry and Empire* (Harmondsworth, England: Penguin, 1969).

Horace, *The Epistles.*

Hu Shih, in *Whither Mankind,* ed. Charles A. Beard (New York: Longman's, Green, 1928).

Hufton, Olwyn, in *The Eighteenth Century,* ed. Alfred Cobban (London: Thames and Hudson, 1969).

Hume, David, "Of the Rise and Progress of the Arts and Sciences," in *Hume's Political Essays* (New York: Liberal Arts Press, 1953).

Jefferson, Thomas, *The Papers of Thomas Jefferson,* ed. Julian P. Boyd (Princeton University Press: 1950-58).

Jones, E. L., *The European Miracle* (Cambridge University Press, 1981).

Jusserand, J. J., *English Wayfaring Life in the Middle Ages,* trans. Lucy Toulmin Smith (London: Unwin, 1889).

Kamen, Henry, in *The Age of Expansion,* ed. Hugh Trevor-Roper (New York: McGraw-Hill, 1968).

Kant, Immanuel, *Fundamental Principles of the Metaphysic of Morals,* trans. T. K. Abbott (London: Longman's, 1929).

Keats, John, "Ode to a Grecian Urn" from his *Poems.*

Kennedy, Paul, *Rise and Fall of the Great Powers* (New York: Random House, 1987).

Khaldun, Ibn, *The Muqaddimah,* trans. Franz Rosenthal (Princeton University Press, 1967).

Kitto, H. D. F., *The Greeks* (Harmondsworth: Penguin, 1951).

Koch, Adrienne, and Peden, William, eds., *The Life and Selected Writings of Jefferson* (New York: Modern Library, 1944).

Kozol, Jonathan, *Illiterate America* (New York: Doubleday, 1985).

Kristeller, Paul Oskar, *Renaissance Thought* (New York: Harper, 1961).

Kroeber, A. L., *Configurations of Culture Growth* (Berkeley: University of California Press, 1944).

Lawrence, T. E., *Seven Pillars of Wisdom* (Garden City, N.Y.: Doubleday, 1938).

Leary, Warren E., in *The New York Times,* September 26, 1989.

Lewis, Anthony, in *The New York Times,* April 4, 1985.

Lewis, Bernard, ed., *Islam and the Arab World* (New York: Knopf, 1976).

Lin Yutang, ed., *The Wisdom of China and India* (New York: Random House, 1942).

Lindsay, A. D., *The Modern Democratic State* (London: Oxford University Press, 1943).

Lipson, Leslie, *The Politics of Equality* (University of Chicago Press, 1948).

————, *The Democratic Civilization* (New York: Oxford University Press, 1964).

————, "The Philosophy of Democracy," *Journal of International Affairs,* 38, no. 2 (Winter 1985).

————, *The Great Issues of Politics* (Englewood Cliffs, N.J.: Prentice-Hall, 9th ed., 1993).

————, and Drews, Elizabeth Monroe, *Values and Humanity* (New York: St. Martin's, 1971).

Lloyd, A. C., "Xenophanes," in *Encyclopaedia Britannica* (1969).

Locke, John, *Letters on Toleration.*

————, (second) *Treatise of Civil Government.*

Ludwig, Emil, in *Whither Mankind,* ed. Charles A. Beard.

Mabbett, Ian W., *A Short History of India* (North Melbourne: Cassell, 1968).

Machiavelli, Niccolò, *The Prince* and *The Discourses.*

Malinowski, Bronislaw, *Freedom and Civilization* (Bloomington: Indiana University Press, 1944).

Martial, *Epigrams.*

Martin, P. M., *Is Mankind Advancing?* (New York: Baker and Taylor, 1910).

Marx, Karl, *The Communist Manifesto.*

Maslow, Abraham H., *Toward a Psychology of Being* (Princeton, N.J.: Nostrand, 1962).

Maspero, Gaston, C. C., *The Dawn of Civilization* (London: Society for Promoting Christian Knowledge, 1910).

Mattuck, Israel, *Jewish Ethics* (London: Hutchinson's University Library, 1953).

McNeill, William H., *A World History* (New York: Oxford University Press, 1979).

Meadows, Donella H., and Dennis L., et al., *The Limits to Growth* (New York: Universe, 1972).

Menuhin, Yehudi, and Davis, Curtis W., *The Music of Man* (Toronto: Methuen, 1979).

Michelangelo, Letters in *I, Michelangelo, Sculptor,* ed. Irving Stone (New York: Doubleday, 1962).

Mill, John Stuart, *On Liberty.*

————, *The Subjection of Women.*

Milton, John, *Lycidas.*

Montaigne, Michel de, *Essays.*

Muller, Herbert J., *The Uses of the Past* (New York: Oxford University Press, 1952).

Mumford, Lewis, *The Culture of Cities* (London: Secker and Warburg, 1938).
———, *The Condition of Man* (New York: Harcourt Brace, 1944).
———, *The Transformations of Man* (New York: Collier, 1962).
Murphy, Gardner, *Human Potentialities* (New York: Basic Books, 1958).
Murray, Gilbert, in *The Legacy of Greece*, ed. R. W. Livingstone (Oxford: Clarendon, 1921).
Myers, Philip Van Ness, *History as Past Ethics* (Boston: Ginn, 1913).
Myres, J. L., *The Dawn of History* (New York: Holt, 1911).
Northrop, F. S. C., *The Meeting of East and West* (New York: Macmillan, 1946).
Pascal, Blaise, *Pensées*, trans. W. F. Trotter (New York: Modern Library, 1941).
Pasternak, Boris, *Doctor Zhivago*, trans. Max Hayward and Manya Harari (New York: Pantheon, 1958).
Peccei, Aurelio, *One Hundred Pages for the Future* (New York: Pergamon, 1981).
Peters, F. E., *The Children of Abraham* (Princeton University Press, 1981).
Phillips, Kevin, *The Politics of Rich and Poor* (New York: Random House, 1990).
Piggott, Stuart, ed., *The Dawn of Civilization* (London: Thames and Hudson, 1962).
Pirenne, Henri, *A History of Europe* (New York: Norton, 1939, 1958).
Plato, *The Apology, The Republic, The Laws,* and *Protagoras.*
Plumb, J. H., *The Renaissance* (New York: Harper & Row, 1965).
Plutarch, *Lives.*
Pollitt, J. J., *Art and Experience in Classical Greece* (Cambridge University Press, 1972).
Quigley, Carroll, *The Evolution of Civilizations* (Indianapolis: Liberty, 1979).
Rich, Spencer, in *Manchester Guardian Weekly,* December 3, 1989.
Roszak, Theodore, *Unfinished Animal* (New York: Harper & Row, 1975).
Rousseau, Jean Jacques, *Discourse on the Origin and Foundation of Inequality Among Human Beings,* trans. G. D. H. Cole (New York: E. P. Dutton, Everyman's Library, 1913).
———, *Has the Restoration of the Arts and Sciences Had A Purifying Effect upon Morals?*
Rubenstein, Nicholai, in *The Age of the Renaissance,* ed. Denys Hay (London: Thames and Hudson, 1967).
Rule, Sheila, in *The New York Times,* July 29, 1985.
Russell, Bertrand, *Power: A New Social Analysis* (London: Unwin, 1938).
Sakharov, Andrei, *Memoirs* (New York: Knopf, 1990).
Sauer, Carol O., *Northern Mists* (Berkeley: University of California Press, 1968).
Schopenhauer, Arthur, *Parerga und Paralipomena.*
Schwartz, Benjamin I., ed., *Daedalus* 104, no. 2 (Spring 1975).
———, *The World of Thought in Ancient China* (Cambridge, Mass.: Belknap, 1985).
Schweitzer, Albert, *The Philosophy of Civilization* (New York: Macmillan, 1964).
Shackleton, Robert, in *The Eighteenth Century,* ed. Alfred Cobban (London: Thames and Hudson, 1969).
Shakespeare, William, *Hamlet, Henry the Fourth, Henry the Sixth, Romeo and Juliet, Julius Caesar, The Merchant of Venice.*
Silone, Ignacio, *The God That Failed,* ed. R. H. S. Crossman.
Sirard, Ruth Leger, *World Military and Social Expenditures* (Leesburg, Va.: World Priorities, annually).
Smith, Huston, *The Religions of Man* (New York: Harper Colophon, 1958).
Snell, Bruno, *The Discovery of the Mind,* trans. T. G. Rosenmeyer (Oxford: Basil Blackwell, 1953).
Sophocles, *Antigone.*
Spear, Percival, *India* (Ann Arbor: University of Michigan Press, 1972).

Spengler, Oswald, *The Decline of the West*, trans. C. F. Atkinson (New York: Knopf, 1928).

Springborg, Patricia, *Royal Persons* (London: Unwin Hyman, 1990).

Starr, Chester G., *The Economic and Social Growth of Early Greece* (New York: Oxford University Press, 1977).

Stone, I. F., *The Trial of Socrates* (Boston: Little, Brown, 1988).

Storer, Morris B., ed., *Humanist Ethics* (Buffalo, N.Y.: Prometheus, 1980).

Strout, Richard L., in *The Christian Science Monitor*, June 28, 1978.

Sullivan, Michael, *A Short History of Chinese Art* (Berkeley: University of California Press, 1970).

Tawney, R. H., *Religion and the Rise of Capitalism* (Harmondsworth, England: Penguin, 1926).

Teggart, Frederick J., *Rome and China* (Berkeley: University of California Press, 1939).

Tertullian, *De Carne Christi*.

Thapar, Romila, *A History of India* (Harmondsworth, England: Penguin, 1966).

———, in *Daedalus*, ed. Benjamin I. Schwartz (Spring 1975).

Thoreau, Henry David, *Walden*.

Thornton, A. P., in *The Nineteenth Century*, ed. Asa Briggs (London: Thames and Hudson, 1970).

Thucydides, *History of the Peloponnesian War*.

Thurow, Lester C., in *The San Francisco Chronicle*, March 22, 1981.

Toynbee, Arnold J., *History*, essay in *The Legacy of Greece*, ed. R. W. Livingstone (Oxford: Clarendon, 1921).

———, *A Study of History*, abridged by D. C. Somervell (New York and London: Oxford University Press, 1947); new edition, revised and abridged, with Jane Caplan (New York: Weathervane, 1972).

———, *Civilization on Trial* (New York: Oxford University Press, 1948).

———, ed., *Cities of Destiny* (London: Thames and Hudson, 1967).

———, *Mankind and Mother Earth* (New York: Oxford University Press, 1976).

Trevelyan, G. M., *British History in the Nineteenth Century* (New York: Longman's, 1922).

Trotsky, Leon, *Their Morals and Ours* (New York: Pioneer, 1942).

———, *The Revolution Betrayed*, trans. Max Eastman (London: Faber and Faber, 1937).

Troyat, Henry, *Tolstoy* (New York: Doubleday, 1967).

Tuchman, Barbara, *A Distant Mirror: The Calamitous Fourteenth Century* (New York: Knopf, 1978).

United Nations, *Report on the World Social Situation* (New York, 1985).

———, *Report on Our Common Future* (Oxford University Press, 1987).

Vico, Giambattista, *The New Science*, trans. T. G. Bergin and M. H. Fisch (Ithaca, N.Y.: Cornell University Press, 1968).

Warren, Earl, opinion in *Brown v. Board of Education*, 349 U.S. 294 (1954).

Webb, Sidney and Beatrice, in *Whither Mankind*, ed. Charles A. Beard.

———, *Soviet Communism: A New Civilisation?* (New York: Scribner's, 1936).

Weber, Max, *The Protestant Ethic and the Spirit of Capitalism*, trans. Talcott Parsons (New York: Scribner's, 1958).

———, *On Capitalism, Bureaucracy, and Religion*, ed. Stanislav Andreski (London: Allen & Unwin, 1983).

Westermarck, Edward A., *Origin and Development of the Moral Ideas* (London: Macmillan, 1906-8).

Whyte, F., *China and Foreign Powers* (London: Oxford University Press, 1927).

Wiet, Gaston, et al., eds. (UNESCO), *History of Mankind*, Vol. 3, *The Great Medieval Civilizations* (New York: Harper & Row, 1975).

Willets, Henry, in *The Age of Expansion* (London: Thames and Hudson, 1968).

Winder, David, in *The Christian Science Monitor.*

Winslow, C. E. A., in *Whither Mankind*, ed. Charles A. Beard (New York: Longman's, 1928).

Wolpert, Stanley, *A New History of India* (New York: Oxford University Press, 1977).

Wordsworth, William, *Poems.*

Wright, Arthur F., in *Cities of Destiny*, ed. Arnold J. Toynbee.

Yang, C. K., in *Chinese Thought and Institutions*, ed. John K. Fairbank (University of Chicago Press, 1957).

Yerkey, Gary, in *The Christian Science Monitor*, June 18, 1981.

Newspapers and Journals

The Christian Science Monitor
The Daily Telegraph (London)
The Economist (London)
Manas
The Manchester Guardian Weekly, together with *Le Monde* and *The Washington Post*
The New York Times
The Times (London)
The Washington Spectator

Index

Abbas, Shah, 121, 124
Abbasids, 81, 106, 112, 155, 277
Abbott, T. K., 315 n. 18
Abd al-Rahman III, 60, 80
Abdera, 122
Abelard, 62
Achaemenids, 148
Adams, John, 111
Adkins, A.W.H., 305 n. 3
Aeschylus, 46, 108, 115, 151
Aesthetics, 9, 43, 48, 113, 119, 301. *See also* Arts
Afghanistan, 128, 186
Africa, 5, 79-80, 82, 97, 122, 129, 197, 199, 203, 205, 207, 210, 221, 235, 254, 265, 275, 316 n. 11
Agincourt, 94
Agnosticism, 23, 53, 289
Agra, 81
Agriculture, 29, 50, 51, 80, 123, 145, 187, 253, 272
AIDS, 5, 196, 234
Ajanta, 120
Akbar, 106, 124, 142
Alaric, 58, 74
Alaska, 240
Alberti, Leon Battista, 310 n. 8
Albert the Great, 62-63
Albigenses, 60
Alcotts, the, 114, 178
Alexander of Macedon, 50, 312 n. 23
Alexandria, 60, 277
Alhambra, 106
Al-Ma'mun, Caliph, 106
Altruism, 140, 153, 184, 214-215, 288-289, 300-301

Amin, Idi, 196, 258
Amnesty International, 265
Amos, 151, 313 n. 28
Amsterdam, 115, 117-118, 119, 123, 190
Anarchism, 256
Anarchy, 91
Anastasius, 306 n. 34
Anatolia, 81
Anthropology, 7, 116
Antonines, 142, 160, 170. *See also* Aurelius, Marcus
Antony, Mark, 305 n. 16
Aquinas, Thomas, 168
Arabs, 62, 80 ff., 97, 106, 112, 127-128, 142, 163, 207, 213, 275, 277-279, 284
Arberry, A. J., 307 n. 36
Argentina, 262
Aristocracy, 94-95, 117-118, 120, 170, 184, 189, 248. *See also* Elite
Aristophanes, 46, 115, 151, 173, 305 n. 6, 310 n. 20
Aristotle, 37, 50, 59, 62, 114, 224, 243, 257, 299, 319 n. 26, 319 n. 2
Arkwright, Richard, 191
Armenians, 186, 265
Arts, 8, 46, 99, 105-106, 109, 113, 115, 117, 119, 122, 124, 128, 176, 227-228, 277, 290, 300-301, 310 n. 2, 310 n. 14, 311 n. 29
Aryans, 29, 211, 213, 304 n. 21
Ashoka, 35, 97, 105, 142, 160, 179, 257
Asia, 5, 8, 26, 34, 37, 80, 97, 112, 122, 127, 129, 142, 157, 165, 172, 197, 199, 203, 207, 235, 246, 249, 254, 260, 275, 296. *See also* China; India; Japan

327

About the Author

Leslie Lipson's abiding intellectual interest has been interpreting the course of human history and using the past as a guide to the present and the future. In addition to his 33 years of service as Professor of Political Science at the University of California, Berkeley, he is known in the United States and abroad as an author, visiting lecturer, and consultant to international agencies. He has worked for the United Nations in Brazil and for the Atlantic Institute in Paris; he founded the academic discipline of political science in New Zealand; and he has lectured under the auspices of the USIA at numerous universities in Europe and Asia.

His best-known book, *The Great Issues of Politics,* in print since 1954 and now in its ninth edition, has been translated into eight languages and is studied in universities worldwide. His other major work, *The Democratic Civilization,* has also been widely translated and is considered by many a classic in its field. Of his many articles, some have been published in the *Encyclopedia Britannica* (1969 edition) and UNESCO's *Dictionary of the Social Sciences.* Others have appeared in professional journals of several countries and in the media.

He came to the United States as a Commonwealth Fund Fellow from Balliol College, Oxford University, where he was senior scholar, and took his doctorate in political science at the University of Chicago. The University of California has honored him with the award of the "Berkeley Citation."

In addition to his academic pursuits, he is known nationally for his 13 years of participation in the Public Broadcasting System's weekly televised program *World Press,* on which he reported on the press of Great Britain.